Soviet Decisionmaking for National Security

Published under the auspices of the
Center for International and Strategic Affairs (CISA),
University of California, Los Angeles
and of the Program of Soviet and East European Studies
(PSES), Department of National Security Affairs, Naval
Postgraduate School, Monterey.

*A list of other PSES and CISA publications appears
at the back of this book.*

Soviet Decisionmaking for National Security

Edited by
Jiri Valenta
Naval Postgraduate School

William C. Potter
*Center for International and Strategic Affairs,
University of California, Los Angeles*

London
GEORGE ALLEN & UNWIN
Boston   Sydney

George Allen & Unwin (Publishers) Ltd,
40 Museum Street, London WC1A 1LU, UK

George Allen & Unwin (Publishers) Ltd,
Park Lane, Hemel Hempstead, Herts HP2 4TE, UK

Allen & Unwin Inc.,
9 Winchester Terrace, Winchester, Mass. 01890, USA

George Allen & Unwin Australia Pty Ltd,
8 Napier Street, North Sydney, NSW 2060, Australia

First published in 1984
Second impression 1985

British Library Cataloguing in Publication Data

   Soviet decisionmaking for national security.
1. Soviet Union—Military policy
I. Valenta, Jiri
II. Potter, William C.
355′.0335′47   UA770
ISBN 0-04-351063-9
ISBN 0-04-351065-5 Pbk

Library of Congress Cataloging in Publication Data

Main entry under title:
   Soviet decisionmaking for national security.
Includes bibliographical references and index.
1. Soviet Union—National security—Decision making.
2. Soviet Union—Defenses—Decision making.   I. Valenta,
Jiri.   II. Potter, William C.
UA770.S658 1984   354.470089   83-21357
ISBN 0-04-351063-9
ISBN 0-04-351065-5 (pbk.)

Set in 10 on 11 point Times by
D. P. Media Limited, Hitchin, Hertfordshire
and printed in Great Britain by
Butler & Tanner Ltd,
Frome and London

On behalf of Jiri Valenta this book is dedicated to the students of the Naval Postgraduate School

On behalf of William Potter, to Anya

Contents

Preface

The 1980s promise to be a period of considerable flux in Soviet-American relations. In a sense, an era ended with the Soviet invasion of Afghanistan, followed by the political demise of the second SALT agreement and the change in American leaders. Nevertheless, many observers see the present as a period for Soviet strategic opportunities, an optimal period for advances before certain internal complications set in. Do the Soviet leaders share this view? If so, what decisions follow?

The death of Leonid Brezhnev on 10 November 1982 marked the end of an era in Soviet politics, an era marked by unprecedented political continuity. Now, many of the major figures of the late sixties and seventies have passed from the scene: Brezhnev, Kosygin, Suslov and Podgorny are dead; Kirilenko's political career is in evident eclipse. The question now arises of how long will the new leadership, initially under the stewardship of Secretary-General Andropov, continue the policies of the Brezhnev era, and if and when will they initiate a redirection of policy? All indications are that Andropov may become one of the Soviet Union's most clever and intelligent leaders, one who will diligently strive to maximize and preserve Soviet power. The impetus for new policy directions may come from younger members of the leadership. The younger generation, which had been shut out of the top leadership for years as the Brezhnev collegium tenaciously held on to power, may push to accelerate the implementation of new policy initiatives. Certainly, understanding the processes of Soviet decisionmaking, the object of the chapters in this volume, is complicated by the volatile nature of Soviet politics during a succession crisis.

For many years Western Sovietology was preoccupied with the 'sources of Soviet conduct', to borrow Kennan's phrase. But to a large extent its preoccupation turned into either a highly abstract debate about the precise blend of Russian tradition and Soviet communism, or a political contest over the policy to be employed against the USSR. The art of understanding how the Soviet system worked tended to be overshadowed by the politics of the system's ambitions. When confronted with an unexpected event – the Berlin Wall or the Soviet invasion of Afghanistan – it was comforting to seek refuge in the idea that, after all, Russia was still a riddle wrapped in an enigma.

The Soviet system is itself to blame, for the obsessive secrecy in which policy is practiced and put into operation leaves a great deal to the popular imagination. The brief accounts of weekly Politburo meetings that have begun to appear in *Pravda* during the Andropov era hardly shed any more light on the subject. The difficulties in interpreting the Soviet system inevitably permit a proliferation of various theories. For example, one theory has it that Soviet and Western societies are 'converging' and thus conflict should diminish. Another theory, popular for a time after the removal of Khrushchev, was that the Soviet system was degenerating and that a new pluralism would gradually emerge. More operationally, trade was seen as a key to policy; others saw a leveling off of the strategic arms race as creating a mutual interest in stability and deterrence. Finally, others saw China as the dominant element, moving the Soviets toward a settlement in the West.

Obviously no single theory is satisfactory, so in recent years analysts have begun to abandon the ethereal for the more practical realm of politics and to examine Soviet decisionmaking at an operational or functional level. Surprisingly, a great deal of information, albeit in many cases inferential, is in fact available and the various studies in this volume illuminate Soviet reality.

Of course, we still cannot reproduce the discussion or debates in the Politburo itself. But we can begin to reconstruct the process by which the decisions are made. And this may well be the beginning of wisdom. It is already obvious that the Soviet decisionmaking process is a complicated one, reflecting all of the factors one might assume are present in the deliberations of a Great Power and a Great Bureaucracy.

Some personal observations might be in order as the reader begins the productive survey of Soviet decisionmaking represented in this volume. First, despite a quantum leap in knowledge and understanding, we should not be overconfident that we understand the system and the process of reaching critical decisions. A number of key variables are shielded from view, making any detailed analysis difficult. And whatever the Marxists may claim, the human dimension still looms large in politics, whether in the USSR or the USA.

Secondly, we should not underestimate the power of continuity and momentum in the Soviet system. It is rather amazing how persistent the Soviets have been on certain foreign policy issues. In the early 1950s Molotov began to agitate for a European Security Conference, which was finally convened two decades later. The ghosts of the past, whether Russian or Soviet, still exert an influence over whoever occupies the Kremlin. Initially, at least, the new leadership will strive to implement the agenda set during Brezhnev's last years.

Finally, it is necessary to remember that there is a long-term perspective at work in daily affairs, which is often not consciously expressed or understood. Only in retrospect do we understand history's turning-points, whether Sarajevo, Munich, or Stalingrad. The wise analyst tries to recreate the historical framework and recognizes that decisions do not spring fully grown, but are usually the product of a long maturation. Thus, as we enter what is a new, post-Brezhnev era, we should bear in mind that though circumstances differ, and new personalities will appear, certain geographic and strategic realities will continue to operate in the Soviet system. Sovietologists cannot guarantee that there will be no surprises, or occasional Soviet mysteries, but perhaps they can reduce the serious shocks. Nor can Sovietologists guarantee good policies but their work, as represented here, can shed considerable light on an inherently dark subject.

William G. Hyland

Acknowledgments

The editors are pleased to acknowledge their gratitude to the Department of National Security Affairs of the Naval Postgraduate School, and the Center for International and Strategic Affairs of the University of California, Los Angeles, whose encouragement and assistance made it possible to hold the August 1980 Conference on Soviet Decisionmaking for National Security. Most of the contributions to this book were originally presented at that conference. The assistance of the Council on Foreign Relations is gratefully acknowledged, as is the assistance of the Rockefeller Foundation and Woodrow Wilson Center, with the preparation of the manuscript.

The conference participants were a mix of experts in Soviet security and foreign policy, and in the theory of international relations and international security. They came from both the United States and the United Kingdom, from academia (University of California, Berkeley, California State University, Columbia University, Duke University, MIT, Occidental College, Pennsylvania State University, the Royal Military Academy, Stanford University, the University of Southampton, UCLA, and Johns Hopkins University) and various research institutes (RAND, the Carnegie Endowment, the Brookings Institution), and from different branches of the government (Department of the Navy, Office of the Airforce Chief-of-Staff, the Defense Department of Net Assessment, the Defense Intelligence Agency, the Central Intelligence Agency, National Security Council, International Communication Agency and the Permanent Select Committee on Intelligence, US House of Representatives). William Hyland, former Deputy Assistant National Security Advisor, delivered a principal address at the conference and wrote a short preface for this book.

In addition to the authors of the chapters of this book, others who served as panelists at the conference were Richard Anderson, Lawrence Caldwell, Alexander Dallin, Karen Dawisha, Donald Daniel, Sergei Freidzon, Lt Commander Mac Henderson, USN, Charles Gati, Alexander George, William Spahr, Philip Stewart, Peter Vigor and Edward Warner. Other conference participants to whom we are indebted for their comments and suggestions are Norman Abrams, Richard Ackley, George Breslauer, Robert Dean, Thane Gustafson, Arnold Horelick, Michael Intriligator, Andrzej Korbonski, Gail Lapidus, Stephen Larrabee, Edward Laurance and Steven Rosefielde.

Students in the Soviet and East European Studies Program coordinated by Jiri Valenta, of the Department of National Security Affairs of the Naval Postgraduate School, helped to organize and run the conference. They have taken seminars and written research papers or theses on topics discussed at the conference. This was a new research and pedagogical experience for all of them. Among those whose assistance was essential were Lt Commander Roy Chapple, USN (a winner of the Naval Institute Award and distinguished graduate of the Naval Postgraduate School in 1981), Captain Thomas F. Boudreau, USA, Captain Robert E. Bush II, USAF, Captain

Douglas A. Fraze, USA, Captain Neil F. Hasson, USA, Captain Steven D. Swegle, USAF, Captain Lynette Tatsch, USAF and Lieutenant William A. Weronko, USN.

We also wish to thank Rear-Admiral J. J. Ekelund and Provost David Schrady of the Naval Postgraduate School, Sherman Blandin, Chairman of the Department of National Security Affairs, Roman Kolkowicz of the CISA, UCLA and their staffs for assistance with the manuscript. The students of NSA 3450 (Winter Quarter, 1983) at the Naval Postgraduate School made numerous valuable suggestions concerning the final shape of the book. Lieutenant Robert Williams, USN, and Lieutenant Guy Holliday, USN, were especially helpful in this regard. We would also like to thank Robert English of Princeton University for his editorial assistance.

We must also mention the contribution of Captain Charles Duch, USAF, who helped in many ways to prepare the manuscript just prior to publication. His knowledge of Soviet domestic politics in the period of the Brezhnev succession was helpful in keeping the manuscript current as the book went to press. Appreciation is also due to my editor Carol Evans and to my research assistant Elizabeth Sandberg who meticulously and diligently coordinated and proofed the book for final publication.

Finally, we are especially grateful to Virginia Lyda Valenta for the magnificent banquet she prepared for our colleagues.

March 1983

Jiri Valenta
William C. Potter
New York
Los Angeles

Introduction

JIRI VALENTA and WILLIAM C. POTTER

Since becoming General Secretary of the Communist Party of the Soviet Union in November 1982, Yuri Andropov has raised, ever so slightly, the veil of secrecy surrounding Soviet decisionmaking. As one Western diplomat observed, 'Before, they wouldn't even admit they held Politburo meetings on Thursdays. Now *Pravda* is reporting what they discussed.'* That the Western press should be fascinated by such minor revelations highlights the paucity of data on Soviet policymaking. The lack of information is especially acute concerning national security policy, that is, defense-oriented problems, particularly weapons acquisition, arms control and the military deployment of the use of force and military aid to client countries. The decision to go to war, as Vernon Aspaturian notes in this volume, is the ultimate national security decision. Although vitally important to Western policymakers, this subject has received surprisingly little attention from Western scholars. This book was conceived with the intention of helping remedy this deficiency by dealing specifically with the process and product of Soviet policymaking for national security.

To be sure, the book does not fill all the gaps in the literature on Soviet decisionmaking. Many of the old questions remain unanswered while other new questions come to the fore. This is particularly apparent in the initiation of the decisionmaking process, involving intelligence gathering and evaluation and agenda setting, and in its implementation. The lack of success in solving the mysteries inherent in the shrouded Soviet decisionmaking process, however, highlights the strength of the book, which is its attempt to clarify the nature and extent of the information void. While the book does not of itself provide the solution to the puzzle, it gives considerable insight into its nature. As it constitutes a 'beginning of wisdom' on the subject it is a book designed not only for students of Soviet politics but also for policymakers and analysts both within and outside the US government as well as in other English-speaking countries. It appeals to an intelligent general readership which is interested in learning about a subject of vital concern to themselves.

The book is divided into four sections. To promote more rigorous study of Soviet decisionmaking, the conceptual analysis is combined with a number of case studies and contemporary decisionmaking actors and institutions are linked to their historical antecedents. Part 1 suggests means to conceptualize Soviet decisionmaking for national security and examines how Soviet

* Cited in Robert Gillette, 'Kremlin places new men in top security posts', *Los Angeles Times*, 19 December 1982.

policymaking has evolved since the Stalin era. This is followed in Part 2 by sections on the role of the military in Soviet decisionmaking, weapons development, defense R&D, and the SALT negotiations. Part 3 is a series of case studies of Soviet decisionmaking during the 1968 crisis in Czecho-slovakia, the 1973 Yom Kippur War, and the intervention in Afghanistan in 1979. The chapters comprising these three sections are a representative sampling of the current state of the art of scholarship on Soviet national security decisionmaking in the United States. The contributors, though often disagreeing among themselves, at least implicitly, have tried to develop ingenious and sometimes innovative research techniques. Part 4 contains two essays that critique the previous approaches, as well as others not represented in the book. They suggest techniques for integrating the disparate elements of the state of the art of scholarship on Soviet decision-making into a cohesive and rigorous methodology. Such an approach poten-tially can improve the analytical and ultimately predictive capabilities of the effort to understand Soviet decisionmaking under the new leadership.

The first chapter by Arthur Alexander outlines a model of Soviet national security decisionmaking that 'follows the flow of the decision process'. A major distinction made by Alexander in this model is between high- and low-level actors. The former category, comprised of the Politburo, Central Committee Secretariat and Presidium of the Council of Ministers, has authority to make decisions. The second group, Alexander argues, is made up of the production ministries, Defense Ministry and regional party organ-izations and exerts influence on the decisionmaking process by virtue of its monopoly of expertise and information and its position to implement policy. A significant contribution of Alexander's essay is the hypothesis, drawing on his own work and the work of other analysts in the book (Valenta), that at various levels of decisionmaking different processes are at work.

Vernon Aspaturian, in Chapter 2, examines the evolution of national security decisionmaking under Stalin. Understanding the norms and struc-tures of the Soviet decisionmaking process as they evolved during Stalin's almost thirty years of leadership is an essential base for understanding Soviet security policy. While acknowledging the limits of the sometimes conflicting memoirs he draws upon as sources, Aspaturian reveals the operation of a largely idiosyncratic, inconsistent and often irrational process in which one of the few constants was complete subordination to Stalin. Although the most onerous characteristics of the policymaking process (for example, the reliance on terror and arbitrariness) were tempered during World War II, the system remained a 'complicated mosaic of shifting and interlocking, but relatively simple institutions, resting on a formula of one-man dictatorship'.

The wartime regeneration of decisionmaking institutions, such as the creation of the State Defense Committee some months after the Nazi invasion, paralleled the decline of party forums as important decisionmak-ing groups. A postwar shakeup of party and state institutions destroyed much of the order that was created during the war, and Stalin's last years were especially chaotic. In his article, Aspaturian portrays the often arbit-rary, sometimes bizarre, but always pragmatic nature of Stalin's rule. Aspaturian notes that while the growing complexity of the Soviet Union demands more effective decisionmaking, the basic institutions of today are largely the same as those created by Stalin, in spite of the great potential for development that exists in the Soviet system.

In Chapter 3, Dimitri Simes analyzes the contemporary national security policymaking process in terms of 'controlled pluralism', that is, a political system in which debate among elites takes place within carefully defined limits. Simes notes that a growing number of groups participate in the 'debate', such as foreign policy thinktanks, scientists and the bureaucracy itself, but cautions that 'controlled pluralism' in Soviet decisionmaking should not obscure the fact that Lenin's concept of democratic centralism was still very much alive under Brezhnev. It will hardly change significantly under Andropov. Most important, Simes notes, national security requirements in the USSR usually are given greater priority than in the West.

The role of the military in Soviet weapons development is the focus of Chapter 4 by Jerry Hough. Taking some exception to Aspaturian's thesis that Stalin monopolized important defense decisions, Hough maintains that, in fact, Stalin created an elaborate committee structure in which a range of individuals participated in defense policymaking. Especially important was the Committee of Defense, with responsibilities for defense issues which cut across military and civilian institutions, and the self-sustaining military and civilian R&D bureaucracy.

Drawing extensively on the Soviet memoir and biographical literature, Hough concludes that the basic relationships between the military and other actors in Soviet weapons development have changed little over the past forty years. The same problems involving tradeoffs between innovation and ease of production and quality control versus plan fulfillment also remain much the same, as does the basic clash of organizational interests.

Ellen Jones, disagreeing at least implicitly with some of Hough's conclusions, seeks to demonstrate in Chapter 5 that the policy goals of the top Soviet leadership, more than organizational momentum or bureaucratic inertia, determine direction and pace of military research and development. According to Jones, military development is largely free from the majority of problems that mar other sectors of the Soviet administered economy. Highly centralized institutional arrangements, with strict monitoring by the party and military at a level far above that of civilian industries, maximize the leadership's ability to translate overall defense priorities into specific programs.

The focus of Chapter 6 by Raymond Garthoff is the Soviet military's posture toward SALT and the effects of SALT on Soviet political-military relations. The Soviet military, Garthoff maintains, played an active and major role in SALT decisionmaking, and one most likely involving a conservative but not obstructive influence. Since the mid-1970s, moreover, the military, Garthoff believes, has moderated its aversion to SALT and increasingly has accepted its strategic premises (for instance, mutual deterrence). Garthoff suggests that SALT has also affected Soviet political-military relations by broadening the perspectives on strategic matters of both political and military leaders and regularizing contacts between Foreign and Defense Ministry officials. SALT also has had the effect, Garthoff believes, of reducing, at least marginally, the monopoly of expertise on strategic issues of the military and has drawn members of the research institutions (for instance, the Institute of World Economy and International Relations and the USA Institute) into the strategic affairs community.

In Chapter 7 Jiri Valenta examines the 1968 Soviet invasion of Czechoslovakia from a bureaucratic politics perspective. This approach, in contrast to the more traditional rational actor model, sees Soviet decisionmaking as the result of bureaucratic 'pulling and hauling' among Politburo members, bureaucratic elites and other actors, depending on the issue.* Valenta suggests that the stands adopted, at least by some Soviet leaders on various issues, may be conditioned by their specialized functions or previous bureaucratic experience. Though little is known about Andropov's position on the Czech or any other issue, it would seem that he must be conditioned by his KGB experience and this itself may have some impact on Soviet national security decisionmaking under his leadership. According to Valenta, the failure of most Western analysts to understand the unpredictable and bureaucratic nature of Soviet decisionmaking probably contributed to their inability to anticipate the invasion of Czechoslovakia. This underscores the need for the West to consider bureaucratic factors in analyses of Soviet national security decisionmaking.

Galia Golan, in Chapter 8, examines the case of Soviet decisionmaking during the 1973 Yom Kippur War. Considering a number of key decisions/ events throughout the war, Golan focuses on Soviet priorities (global, regional and local interests) in these decisions, and uses Kremlinological techniques to analyze the differing approaches toward crisis resolution within the Soviet leadership. She discerns that Soviet global interests centered on the preservation of US-Soviet détente, while regional and local interests lay in expanding Soviet influence in the Middle East as a whole, and with individual countries such as Egypt and Syria in particular. According to Golan, the Yom Kippur War highlights the central dilemma facing Soviet policymakers today, the reconciliation of these conflicting interests. In this case, the Soviets miscalculated and the results were a blow to détente and to Moscow's position in the Arab World.

Valenta's examination of the Soviet decision to invade Afghanistan in December 1979, in Chapter 9, reveals some common features between the 1979 case and the 1968 Czechoslovak invasion. In both instances, Soviet decisionmakers feared the existence of an unfriendly or unstable regime or one unable to control revolutionary changes (a situation that potentially could threaten bordering Soviet, non-Russian republics, this being more serious in the Czechoslovak case), and, in both cases, signals from the United States convinced Soviet leaders (wrongly, in the case of Afghanistan) that the risks of actual military deployment would be minimal. One major difference between the two invasion decisions, judging from the available evidence as noted by Valenta, was a more consensus-oriented and less bureaucratic-infighting style of decisionmaking in the Afghan case. Another one was the offensive implications of the latter invasion.

Dennis Ross, in Chapter 10, sympathetic to Valenta's conclusions on

---

* For a good discussion of the bureaucratic politics paradigm and other approaches toward Soviet decisionmaking, see Robert M. Cutler, 'The formation of Soviet foreign policy: organizational and cognitive perspectives, *World Politics*, vol. XXXIV, no. 3 (April 1982), pp. 418–36.

Czechoslovakia and Afghanistan, argues that the underlying characteristic of the Soviet regime in foreign policy decisionmaking is risk aversion. According to Ross, both the oligarchic nature of Soviet elites and the relevant experiences and sociology of these leaders have made a fear of failure a more important motivating factor than the desire for major successes. As oligarchical rule developed in the Soviet Union, Ross maintains, the Soviet decisionmaking process necessarily acquired the traits of coalition maintenance. This has meant, he argues, a kind of 'muddling-through' approach to policymaking in which precipitous decisions and policy innovation are eschewed in favor of incrementalism. Soviet military interventions abroad, according to this interpretation, derive primarily from the perceived high costs of inaction. However, Ross cautions that the next generation of Soviet leaders, likely to be more self-assured about its own position and that of the Soviet Union in world affairs, may be less cautious, 'less concerned about failure, and more convinced of the need to act decisively'. It is too early in 1983 to see if Ross's prediction may become true under the new leadership of Andropov.

The purpose of Stephen Meyer's contribution in Chapter 11 is to use various models, or as he frankly admits 'hunches', from the vast body of literature on Soviet decisionmaking for defense to identify what we should be able to learn given data constraints. Meyer notes that most prior research on Soviet weapons acquisition and force structuring relies heavily on the case-study approach, lacks a comparative perspective and underutilizes the available database. He discerns a similar situation in analyses of Soviet decisionmaking regarding military deployment and the use of force. The *ad hoc* approach that characterizes most studies in both decisionmaking realms, he observes, makes it difficult to draw the research results together to form a single body of knowledge. Meyer concludes with suggestions on how to begin construction of more coherent but complex models of Soviet defense decisionmaking.

In the concluding Chapter 12, William Potter suggests the utility of viewing Soviet national security decisionmaking as a sequential process, involving four analytically distinct phases: policy initiation, policy controversy, the formal decision and policy implementation. Most research to date, he argues, has concentrated on the second and third phases with the result that we know very little about how problems make their way onto the foreign and defense policy agenda and how decisions, once taken, are actually implemented. Models of Soviet decisionmaking, Potter argues, may well vary not only in their applicability to different policy issues (for instance, high politics and low politics, as Alexander suggests), but also in their applicability to different stages of the policymaking process for the same issue. Sympathetic to Meyer's perspective, Potter suggests that the lack of progress in understanding Soviet national security decisionmaking may be due as much to a failure to employ explicit decisionmaking models and to test hypotheses against available data as it is to a lack of data. He concludes that the prudent combination of alternative methods of analysis, such as those represented in this volume, may enable us to exploit the strengths and avoid the more serious costs of the respective approaches.

Jiri Valenta and William C. Potter

Part One

Conceptualizing Soviet National Security Decisionmaking

1 Modeling Soviet Defense Decisionmaking

ARTHUR J. ALEXANDER

INTRODUCTION: SETTING THE PROBLEM AND THE SOLUTION

My goal in this chapter is to set out a simple model of decisionmaking in Soviet defense. A structured, abstracted description may help to clarify the subject, draw out disagreements, and perhaps resolve misunderstandings. In order to do this, I purposely keep things simple, restricting the number of variables and interactions in order to focus on the chief effects. Sparseness may help illuminate better than detail at this stage of our knowledge.

This effort was stimulated by analytical problems in the literature on Soviet defense decisionmaking. The presence of such problems is demonstrated by a score of theories and models, each distinctively named and painstakingly laid out, but with little integration among them or testing of their validity with additional, independent data. One common analytical deficiency in this literature is the incorrect imputation of influences, effects and relationships. Political decisions on strategic policy, for example, are attributed to the military. Activities engaged in by ministries or plant managers are ascribed to the ruling circles in the party. The state bureaucracies' actions in solving complex, technical problems or in implementing policies are interpreted as interest group politics.

Some of these problems emanate from an approach that ignores the flow of the decision process – a flow where different parties do different things at different times for different reasons – and on a lack of care in ascribing processes to actors. The fact that this flow is different in the Soviet Union from other countries, particularly the United States, and that it is also different in defense from other Soviet sectors further complicates the issue.

I begin by picturing the decisionmaking system as comprised of relatively stable and long-lived fundamental elements of decisionmaking that derive from Russian history, Bolshevik principles and learned behavior (see Figure 1.1). These inputs help fashion the shape of the decisionmaking process *per se*, which is the main subject of this chapter.

Constraints imposed by 'nature' place bounds on behavior; these constraints include resources, technology, and the individual and social reactions of people within and outside the Soviet Union. The decisionmaking process, as shaped by inputs and constrained by the natural environment, generates the outputs with which we are concerned: budgets, resource allocations, weapons, policies and decisions.

I divide the decisionmakers into two groups: high level and low level. Politics color behavior among the high-level participants. Lower-level

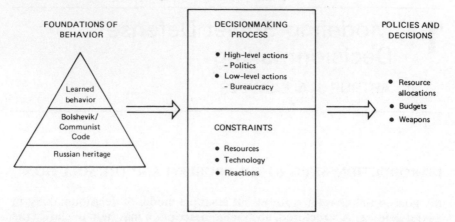

Figure 1.1   A conceptual view of decisionmaking, including the foundations of behavior, process and constraints.

behavior is characterized by bureaucratic processes. The linkages between the two levels are critical to understanding outcomes. The things that each of the levels do and don't do define decisionmaking practices. Explanation of these practices requires our being able to separate those aspects of behavior arising from politics, bureaucratic activities, Soviet and Russian culture, and the peculiar organizational structure of the political-military-industrial complex.

Before proceeding, it will be useful to clarify my use of the term 'decisionmaking'. It is broader than the dictionary definition: 'the process of arriving at a solution that ends uncertainty or dispute, or that makes a choice of judgement.' I enlarge this to include all the processes that generate outcomes. This recognizes the possibility of 'decisions' or outcomes without decisionmakers, of decisions without results and of results that may deviate considerably from the goals intended by decisionmakers. In this sense the passive voice, so often blue-penciled by my editors, is appropriate. The use of the active voice would mistakenly suggest, in many instances, the existence of high-level, purposeful agents who decide. 'Decisionmaking' therefore involves the whole panoply of actors and activities: high and low levels; systematic incentives and constraints; formation of policy and doctrine; information flows; organizational processes; bureaucratic politics; and – even – unitary, rational behavior.

THE ECLECTIC VIEW: NECESSARY BUT NOT SUFFICIENT

Theories of Soviet defense decisionmaking are typically asked to account for a wide variety of phenomena and to answer a broad range of questions. How do we explain a twenty-year, steady, high-rate accumulation of arms? Is this likely to change? Under what conditions? What explains the basic style of Soviet weapons design? How can new and exotic technological thrusts be integrated into the more conservative approach? What determines the allocation of budgets: to the defense sector, to missions, to services? How and why does the Soviet Union decide to march or not to march into Czechoslovakia, Afghanistan, or Poland?

In order to address these questions, we require theories of how things happen in the USSR. We need abstracted and generalized models of decisionmaking and behavior. I say 'models' because no single explanation can adequately cover the many different kinds of behavior suggested in the earlier questions. Indeed, the literature supplies our theoretical needs in overabundance. Unfortunately, the authors rarely put boundaries around the behavior and events they purport to explain, nor do they describe the conditions that make it necessary to switch from one theory or model or explanation to another. In order to make the eclectic view, which I believe to be appropriate, more productive, we also require coverage specifications and switching algorithms.

To illustrate the coverage problem, consider a representative list of behavioral models (shown in Table 1.1) put forward in the literature.[1] I have grouped these roughly according to the actors and the behavior implied by the models. By placing similar models on the same footing, addressing similar actors and classes of behavior, we can become more precise in testing them, in setting them against each other and in confronting them with independent data. For example, we can ask whether the Soviet Union acts mainly according to high-level goals. If so, what are they: paranoid, top leaders, strategic, rational? These models may generate different predictions about specified actors and behaviour. They may be wrong.

Table 1.1   *Alternative Models of Soviet Decisionmaking Behavior*

Model	*Type of behavior and action to which model applies*
Operational code	
Historical-cultural dominance	
Strategic actor	
Strategic actor with master plan	Top-level
Strategic actor, opportunistic	motivations and
Paranoid national behavior	behavior
Top leader behavior: Lenin, Stalin, Khrushchev, Brezhnev	
Top leadership politics	
Interest groups	
Pluralistic models	
Consensus models	Procedures
Organizational routine	
Mission approaches	
Technological push	
Action–reaction	Constraints

HIGH-LEVEL/LOW-LEVEL: PATTERNS OF BEHAVIOR

For analytical purposes, I divide the actors in the Soviet defense decision-making process into two levels: high and low. The high-level actors comprise the Politburo, Central Committee and its Secretariat, and Presidium of the Council of Ministers. The lower-level actors include the production ministries, Defense Ministry and party organizations below the Central Committee. A few organizations bridge the gap between these levels and coordinate lower-level activities: the Military Industrial Commission being one of these. At the top the Defense Council may consolidate the high-level views.[2]

These two classes of actors play different roles and respond to diverse classes of forces and influences. The high levels have *authority* to make decisions. They hold power. They can decide, intervene, review, accept, decline. They often face problems of conflicting goals that require political action to resolve. The lower levels *act*, implement, generate information (from their activities and from analyses); they face problems that require high-level solution; they put forward proposals, initiatives, alternatives; they generate conflict among themselves that often must be resolved by political decisions.

The high levels produce policies, but in most cases do not have the tools or capabilities to carry them out. Theirs is the role to decide – but to decide *what*, and *why*? The subjects, the information and the arguments usually come up from below. The totalitarian model recognizes and highlights the power and authority, but often ignores the power inherent in implementation and in the generation of alternatives.

The fundamental bases of behavior of the high-level actors can be pictured as layers or strata, with those at the bottom being more enduring and those at the top more amenable to change. At the lowest level I would put such goals as 'national security' and defense of the homeland. These derive from and must be understood in terms of Russian history and culture. Directly above this layer comes the Bolshevik influence, emphasizing preservation of socialism at home and in the Soviet Commonwealth. Associated with these views is what Leites thirty years ago called the operational code of the Politburo.[3] It lays out not a detailed master plan, but a consistent world view and guidelines for dealing with that world. Based on the writings and utterances of Lenin and Stalin, it continues to have relevance to present-day behavior.[4] The code is centered on the expectation of lasting struggle with the main antagonist. It provides a stable framework from which to assign priorities as decisions and events emerge (Gelman, 1981, p. 5).

The top layer is built on learned behavior – experience. It is generated by the accretion of events. For example, over the past ten to fifteen years, it includes the growing confidence of the Politburo in the political rewards to be obtained through the military instrument. According to Gelman's convincing argument,

> the total political environment, inside and outside the Soviet Union, *gradually* impelled the leadership toward a consensus view that this line of policy was in the net Soviet interest. Each individual was increasingly

inclined to assume that it was in his personal political interest to lean in the direction favored by military endorsement. (Gelman, 1981, p. 23)

Since this behavior is learned and based on experience, it can also be unlearned by contrary events, and therefore can be influenced by the actions of others.

In addition to the shared motivations, goals and objectives just discussed, the higher-level organs are dominated by politics, personalities and strongly held individual goals arising from the specialized functions of high-level actors. As shown in Figure 1.2, for example, all of the individuals are concerned with ideology, international affairs and economic progress; but individual A (the Prime Minister, perhaps) is focused primarily on economics; the responsibility of individual B (possibly the Foreign Minister) is international affairs; and C is the spokesman for ideology. Sometimes the specific responsibilities of individuals conflict with each other – but not always. Not every problem generates tradeoffs and conflicts requiring political resolution. Sometimes specific goals conflict with general goals – but not always. Issues coming to the top may just concern the responsibilities of one or two senior individuals. For some issues, one of the subgoals may assume such overriding importance that all would accept a resultant policy, though it harmed particular goals. In the hypothetical illustration of Figure 1.2 economic problems dominate the concerns of the different leaders, despite their diverse functional responsibilities. On other occasions the higher-order shared values of the leadership may elevate an issue (defense of the homeland, for example) to such central national importance that the ruling elite could act as one. Ordinarily, though, bureaucratic politics is the norm at this level of authority as the conflicting functional responsibilities of different individuals generate a requirement for political solutions.

To make the above argument more concrete, consider Valenta's (1979) analysis of the Czechoslovak intervention. (For details see Chapter 7.)

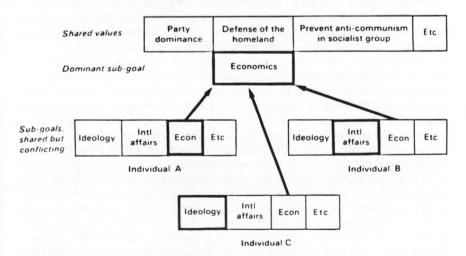

Figure 1.2   Goal conflict and dominance.

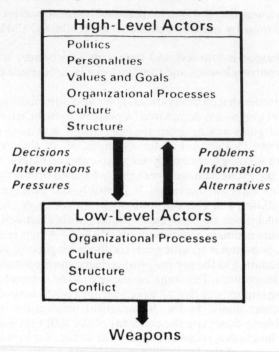

Figure 1.3 High- and low-level actions and interactions.

In the early stages of the crisis specific goals held by functional specialists came into conflict with each other. Those pushing for intervention were concerned with imported ideological infections, or the spread of political ferment across the border into the Ukraine, or the internal security problems created by Czech dismemberment of KGB activities in Czechoslovakia. The noninterventionists were worried about the effects of armed intervention on relations with other communist parties, or future trade negotiations, or international relations with the noncommunist world. Each of the members of the ruling elite probably shared all of these concerns to some degree, but their individual responsibilities or personalities led them to emphasize specific goals in the earlier phases of debate over the emerging crisis. These individuals probably shared, also, a set of higher goals – 'images of national security' (Valenta, 1979, p. 5). According to Valenta, one such image was: 'The Soviet Union should prevent the spread of anticommunism in the socialist commonwealth. Thus, the restoration of a multiparty system within any of the Warsaw Pact countries would jeopardize the responsibility and control of the Communist Party and must not be allowed.' In the later phase of the crisis this goal appeared about to be violated, and the high-level actors responded in a unified way to prevent it. Only when the general, shared goals dominated the specific goals did the noninterventionists agree to intervene. It was not that the interventionists prevailed politically in a demonstration of power against the others' conflicting goals, but rather the shared goals came into play and dominated the rest.

The decision process in the invasion of Czechoslovakia was, at first, describable by a bureaucratic politics model. It was then transformed into one involving the unified action of the state. In this case the models are not *alternative* descriptions or explanations, but rather describe *different* phenomena. To extend this line of reasoning, we turn now to the linkages between the higher and lower levels.

Most decisions (that is, outcomes) in Soviet military decisionmaking originate in the bureaucracies; they are consequently routine and bureaucratic. Some of these decisions, however, are settled at higher levels; they may be forced up to the top by the nature of the system; or are drawn upward by routine methods; or are wrenched up by purposeful interventions (see Figure 1.3).

The strong tendencies toward conservatism and inflexibility impel the high-level leadership into assuming the leading role as initiator of change. This is typically accomplished by way of interventions in the decision process. It is worthwhile here to consider several kinds of intervention or involvement by high-level leaders in operations. First, there are the routine, often trivial interventions that keep the system moving: for example, to relieve difficulties caused by problems crossing organizational boundaries; or to handle situations not covered by explicit delegation of authority. Many of these problems involve conflict between organizations that do not have the *authority* to resolve the issues at the lower levels. These organizations often possess the technical capabilities to accomplish their tasks, but the operation of the system throws problems upward for high-level resolution. An example is Stalin's sending Khrushchev in 1939 to clear up production problems in the rubber tire factories (Khrushchev, 1970, pp. 119–25).

A second kind of intervention is the review and approval of programs. These interventions are passive when all projects of a given type, meeting certain criteria, are reviewed by higher bodies; guidelines, for example, may be established that would direct investments larger than a certain size to be reviewed by the ministry collegium, or the Council of Ministers, or the Politburo. Such reviews *could* take place at a lower level; the review levels, established by custom or regulation, are therefore decision variables that can be changed according to the desire for intervention and control.

Active interventions reach down into the operating organizations to review programs because of some special consideration: perhaps because of strategic sensitivity, or because a political figure is somehow entwined in the situation.

Another kind of intervention comes about from routine information gathering by high-level individuals: from visits to factories and institutes, newspaper reports, party channels, KGB informants, or from suggestions and information sent to the Central Committee by citizens. Any good manager makes sure that he is not dependent only on the formal, hierarchical channels, but makes forays into the field to check things out for himself. Often a manager is not looking for specific problems or malfeasance, but uses such informal methods to get the feel of the situation that formal reports do not often convey. Information derived in this way can lead to intervention in specific cases, but it also plays a role in keeping the official channels more honest and forthcoming.

Major decisions to move in new directions are the types of intervention usually analyzed by outside observers. They are important and visible. The Politburo's 1965 acceptance of a new political-military doctrine and its weapons procurement implications is an example of this type of decision.

The political character of the act varies among the different types of interventions. Major interventions are clearly political: they involve major reallocations and change. The other types of intervention will also be political when there are gainers and losers. Change itself can generate politics: new directions imply that old directions were wrong – and someone is to blame. New projects that improve efficiency imply that inefficiencies prevailed, and again, someone can be blamed. In an era of collective leadership and cautious politics pervasive forces, therefore, work against change, especially when they are likely to introduce politics into decisionmaking.

Despite the vast number of decisions reaching the Politburo, Council of Ministers, Central Committee Secretariat, or Military Industrial Commission, demanding attention, an even larger number of routine decisions never leave the technical levels where they originate. Long-time participants in Soviet weapons procurement claim that although the important, exceptional and nonroutine issues are forced or are drawn to the top, the larger class of unexceptional projects remain in the hands of the managers. They point out, for example, that strategic systems may fall on the Politburo agenda, but that support systems, navigational systems, infantry weapons, and so on, are handled by lower-level technical organizations. It is, therefore, useful to know what is likely to go upward for decision and what will happen to it there; and what will be held at the lower levels, and the consequences arising therefrom.

The decisions, interventions, policies, or new directions that come out of the higher levels go forward for implementation, stimulating and initiating the organizational processes. Although the lower levels have the power to subvert, ignore and otherwise modify the moves from on high, this power is quite asymmetrical. In any single case the rulers can apply the necessary resources to accomplish their purpose. Their problem is that they have neither the resources, nor the predilection, to pay attention to every activity not moving the way they prefer. The lower levels, for their part, have the ability and often the incentive to send up advice, initiatives and information, but these are received only at the pleasure of the potential audiences. The people at the top have the power to turn off the channel if they do not like, or are not interested in, what is being transmitted. The leadership can limit policy debate, define the issues to be considered and set the range of activities contemplated for policy consideration. They can open discussions and call forth ideas, and just as certainly cut off the flow when they have heard enough. However, they cannot receive alternatives that the bureaucracies are not prepared to deliver, unless there are such diverse sources of expertise that competition of ideas can take place. This is less likely to occur in military-industrial matters than in civilian, and even less likely in purely military issues where the General Staff prevails. A byproduct of this process, as Gustafson notes, is that if new policy ideas flow only when the leadership is receptive, 'then, when the official window is opened, they come in a flood, unrefined, unintegrated, and untested' (Gustafson, 1981, ch. 10). When this happens, there is little independent argument from other sources, 'so as to ask, How much is enough?' (ibid.). One wonders whether this process could explain some of the presumed anomalies in Soviet weapons development: directed energy, for example.

Our analytical separation of actors forces us to ask questions about the frequency of key decisions from the top levels and their ability to implement them. It further raises the possibility of whether, indeed, most of the high-level activity is not simply caught up in the low-level routines – solving problems, resolving conflicts, approving or disapproving plans, or reviewing activities that the lower levels could do for themselves, but won't or are not allowed to.

Most outcomes are produced by small decisions, or even nondecisions. Nevertheless, in my own review of Soviet weapons procurement decisionmaking, I am struck by the substantial redirection of resources under new regimes, and sometimes also at key points in existing regimes. There was a sharp demobilization of military production capability at the end of World War II, and a turnaround in 1949 – both under Stalin. Khrushchev and his fellow-politicians turned this phase off in 1954–5 when, for example, fighter aircraft production plummeted from more than 5,000 per year to less than 500. In a still-unexplained turnaround conventional weapons production resumed an upward trend around 1960, which was reinforced by key Brezhnev decisions in 1965–6. Out of eleven types of conventional weapons, at least seven showed declining production rates in 1957, while only two showed rising trends. By the early 1960s five were rising and only one was falling. These key decisions could only have been made at the top levels, and were most probably political decisions in that they involved conflicting goals. Between the decision points, however, the organizations took over. By and large the specific types of weapons, their characteristics, technologies, unit costs and capabilities were determined by individuals and thousands of suborganizations operating in their own environment of constraints and incentives.

Doctrine, in the broad Soviet sense, is important in this context because it ties political and military views into a unified policy. It brings together both levels, enabling the lower-level actors to proceed under the umbrella of agreed principles. But what if doctrine is contested or imposed, as under Khrushchev? Then the lower levels will fight the doctrine and resist it unless the leadership can push it forcefully, consistently, and with agreement among themselves. It would also be necessary to couple the doctrine to a vigorous cadres policy and perhaps with some organizational restructuring. Without the forceful follow-through on contested doctrine, the cumulative impact of small bureaucratic decisions could deflect the high-level policy from its course.

Even when the lower levels basically accept a policy requiring considerable and complex interactions among the suborganizations, local discretion operating under local incentives and routines is likely to lead events into unforeseen directions, requiring constant monitoring and continual high-level adjustments and fine-tuning through numerous interventions and decrees. Among groups, such as the military, whose functions and outlooks are very close to those of the political leadership – as they seemed to be under Brezhnev – with little disagreement on basic doctrinal concepts, an approximation to autonomy is gained by the lower levels. However, under these conditions, there are likely to be inconsistencies between doctrine and outcomes as policy is implemented in unaccountable small actions (Gustafson, 1981, ch. 10).

The role of different actors at different times is well illustrated by the production trends of armored personnel carriers and infantry fighting vehicles over the past thirty-five years. For several years after World War II, production of these systems was essentially nil. In the early 1950s Soviet factories began to turn out the first postwar models. Production rates grew gradually and one model replaced another until the 1970s when annual quantities of 3,000–4,000 were reached (US Department of Defense, 1978). In the early years of this growth armored personnel carriers were mainly of narrow military-technical concern. A major debate then took place in the early 1960s, within the military, on the use and tactics of these vehicles. This discussion was embedded in the doctrinal debate on the likelihood of a nuclear battlefield and the Soviet response to the possibility of such an eventuality. The requirements for the BMP (armored personnel carrier) were laid out at that time. I suspect that as the BMP entered volume production, its future was raised as a political decision, mainly because of the resources called for but also because of the implications for doctrine. In the years since the mid-1960s production would have become routine and decisions over annual quantities and resources would also be routine. Continuing debates on the tactics of these systems would once again fall within the competence of the military. In this example we can observe a shift in the focus and style of decisionmaking according to the scale of resources and doctrinal changes implied by the programs.

CONDITIONS FOR CHANGE

What, then, is the likelihood of major change in the political-military sphere, of new doctrine or sharply altered policy? The view put forward above of the interactions and behavior of the high and low levels can help us speculate on the conditions that would be necessary to enforce change, and on the consequences if the conditions were not forthcoming. Suppose, for example, that those who follow the Brezhnev generation wished to reallocate resources away from the military. I have already mentioned that the leadership would have to push such a policy forcefully, consistently and with internal agreement. This last requirement could take several years to achieve, as it did in the major redistribution seen in Soviet agriculture policy since 1965.[5] Even with such agreement, we should expect to find old habits dying rather slowly. Decades of experience under the old policy produced routines, norms, goals, values and processes that enabled the old policies to be effected. Gosplan, for example, would routinely reallocate resources during the planning year to meet shortfalls in military production. Plans would be redrawn with only marginal changes from the preceding planning period, so that for a considerable period, considerable resources would continue to flow to old users. Managers who had grown up under the old system would continue to operate in much the same way as they had.

Capable new managers attuned to the new goals would be difficult to find, despite the experience of the purges when a new generation was installed virtually overnight – today's technologies and management complexities would be less tolerant of such change than they were in the 1930s. Even if there were a policy shift, the military and military industry would still be an important sector, reflecting the no doubt continued value of military force. Therefore, the sector could not be alienated and downgraded. A shift in priorities away from defense would perhaps be more difficult to accomplish than a new emphasis applied to a hitherto low-priority area. Soviet leaders have made the mobilization of political effort and economic resources in new programs into almost a routine method for reform. There has been less experience in the other – negative – direction, although the Stalin and Khrushchev phases of arms reduction did indeed achieve those ends. Could a collective leadership in the future repeat that experience?

I have already noted in passing that Khrushchev had attempted many un-Russian and un-Bolshevik policies. He cut the size of the ground forces, concentrated on nuclear strategic weapons, reduced total defense expenditures, substituted bluster for capabilities and disagreed with his military leadership on doctrinal issues. In order to consider the future, it is necessary to ask whether Khrushchev was a mere dogleg in the path of history, or whether he demonstrated the possibility of a future Soviet leader disregarding his peculiar heritage. One could convincingly argue that his appearance was idiosyncratic, that the reaction to his policies and style made future repetition impossible and that the system has congealed around present practices. Yet the many sharp turns of Soviet policy in the past sixty years should also induce some caution in predicting a future of little change. Though the forces for continuity are strong and pervasive, the central importance of a few people at the top makes prediction difficult. It is also necessary to recognize that continuity is likely to lead to growing divergence between what is possible and what is achieved, and that some important actors in the system might become thoroughly dissatisfied with the operation of the system. It is to such actors that we should look for hints of change.

SOME QUESTIONS FOR RESEARCH

Organizational practices, cultural forces acting on individuals and the way in which organizations are structured and relate functionally to one another strongly influence decisionmaking at both high and low levels – more so, of course, at the lower levels. The very phrase 'Soviet defense decisionmaking', however, throws these three sets of forces into an analytical mélange. Key questions, therefore, include: how much of what we observe is Soviet and Russian, how much organizational and bureaucratic, and how much defense?

The general flow of decisionmaking as portrayed in Figures 1.1 and 1.2 is generally applicable to a broad range of behavior spanning both subject-matter and nations. What is peculiarly Soviet in this description? It is evident from Figure 1.1 that the foundations of behavior, particularly Russian history – but also the Bolshevik reactions to this history and to Russian culture – shape Soviet decisionmaking in basic ways. One example is the Russian view of national security and defense. This view does not accept the notion of overinsurance. One can never have enough security to protect oneself from the always-present possibility of annihilation. Indeed, the belief that implacable foes are continually seeking the annihilation of the Russian state and the Bolshevik-communist system is not inconsistent with history. It must also be recognized, however, that Soviet behavior flowing from this belief has the propensity to generate in other countries the very actions feared most by the Soviet leadership. Such views – and their consequences – also have their counterparts in domestic matters and color the decisionmaking practices of the Soviet bureaucracies.

To what degree, then, is Soviet defense decisionmaking characteristic of bureaucracies in general? Indeed, much of the preceding discussion in this chapter could be applied with few amendments to United States government decisionmaking. Interviews with Soviet bureaucrats reveal little that people with experience in the Pentagon or elsewhere in the American military establishment have not seen. Yet one can also discern nuances of behavior that are quite unlike the United States analogue. An example is the apparent unwillingness to compromise, emanating from the *kto-kogo* principle: that is, *who* dominates *whom*; *who* is victorious over *whom*. With such a view, there can be only winners and losers. Is it possible, though, to disentangle the effects of bureaucracy, *per se*, from such forces, or to identify those common aspects of bureaucratic behavior that may be intensified or diminished in the Soviet environment?

Many studies have had an obligatory section on bureaucratic processes, and have often gone on to analyze the specific features of their cases in revealing detail. For example, Warner (1977), Spielmann (1978) and Valenta (1979) include sections on bureaucratic politics and behavior. The behavior that is described, however, is not compared to that found elsewhere in a manner that extends understanding of the particular case or of the general subject. There has been little surprise at what has been found, and therefore little advance in the refinement of theories. In the field of Soviet defense decisionmaking the comparative viewpoint has not been addressed.

Cultural effects on Soviet bureaucratic processes, in most cases, have been alluded to only in passing. Crozier (1964, pp. 213–36), however, attempted a multicultural comparison of France, the United States and the Soviet Union, but his focus was on bureaucratic behavior in general and not on the defense sector. Alexander's (1978–9, pp. 28–9) explorations in this area were no more than an initial foray to test the ground. This area appears to be both overdue for analysis and rewarding in its potential. For example, the likelihood of an individual or agency raising a new alternative in the face of expected opposition appears, generally, to be associated with deep-rooted views on personal conflict. The Soviet disinclination to generate new policies from below, and the consequent necessity of intervention from above may depend to a large degree on peculiar Russian cultural forces. Comparison with Eastern European practices may be a fruitful area for analysis because much of the Soviet organizational structure has been duplicated there, whereas the cultural effects would certainly be different. One study on Polish armaments decisionmaking (Checinski, 1980) was explicitly designed to use the Polish experience as a 'window' on Soviet activities. This study, however, excluded the possibility of comparison because it deliberately assumed analogous behavior between Poland and the Soviet Union.

Organizational structure is one of the distinguishing characteristics of the Soviet defense sector that influences decisionmaking there and sets it apart from other areas of Soviet decisionmaking. We know a good deal about structure. The identity of the bureaucratic actors, their organizational affiliations, their missions and their interrelationships have been fairly well delineated. Nevertheless, a group as seemingly important as the Defense Council is still shrouded in considerable uncertainty as to its day-to-day role, and even its membership. Despite these gaps (and they may be important), the sources of behavior arising from organizational structure should be amenable to analysis, and comparisons between Soviet defense and other Soviet sectors, or between Soviet and United States defense are feasible. For example, the information flows in sectors such as energy or agriculture are much broader and varied than in defense, where the military holds a strong monopoly over information. Policy formulation and decisionmaking in those other sectors should therefore include a larger number and greater variety of participants, with more vigorous debate, than in defense. In addition to structure, other features of defense set it apart from other sectors, but we are less able to ascertain the importance of these features. Technology, priority, secrecy, immediacy of threats and historical values seem to influence behavior. However, it is difficult, analytically, to 'hold other things constant' in order to measure the effects of these possible influences. Ofer (1980) makes a convincing argument that priority granted to defense industry significantly contributes to its capabilities and, by the same token, detracts from the technological level of civilian industry. Moreover, he argues that priority can be granted and taken away; that it is not a natural feature of the defense sector. However, one could ask whether priority will maintain its previous role. Will defense technology in the future become so complex, and draw on so many sectors of Soviet science and industry that the customary management techniques and organizational structures would no longer be able to cope? Will anti-aircraft defense or anti-submarine warfare, for example, require the subtle integration of electronics, armaments, weapons platforms, and command and control – all of advanced technological levels that push against the frontiers of knowledge? Or will the Soviet military be able to make do as they have in the past by careful design and constrained use of technology? Can the vertically organized system of ministries and the central allocation of planned resources, even with priority and coordination, continue to function successfully? Comparative studies of the effects of structure can help answer these questions.

We have made much progress in understanding Soviet defense decisionmaking. Indeed, it is because of this progress that we are now at the stage where greater care is needed in the choice of alternative models to structure the available facts and to promote the search for new information. We must do more to test alternative theories, taking care that they are really alternatives. Additionally, it is necessary to specify the conditions under which a theory is to be applied. If we are also able to identify the relative effects of organizational behavior, culture and organizational structure, we will have advanced our understanding not only of Soviet defense decisionmaking, but of decisionmaking more generally.

NOTES: CHAPTER 1

1   These models are covered in detail by Steve Meyer, below. Meyer's analytical framework and the one presented here are similar to each other, but not identical. Review of the same literature has led us to see the subject in roughly comparable terms; however, we have not attempted to present a single, agreed-upon view.
2   Some writers, Checinski (1980), for example, suggest that the Defense Council may be *superior* to the Politburo, at least for those questions dealing with defense matters.
3   Leites (1951) provides the most succinct description of this code; the subject is spun out in fascinating detail in a longer work on Bolshevik writings; see Leites (1953).
4   In a recent study of Soviet behavior on the international scene the author states that he 'was impressed by the frequency with which certain patterns and reactions postulated by Leites did appear to emerge from the maneuvers of the Brezhnev leadership', Gelman (1981, p. iii).
5   Much of this discussion is derived from Thane Gustafson's (1981) review of agricultural reform.

REFERENCES: CHAPTER 1

Alexander, Arthur, J. (1978–9), *Decisionmaking in Soviet Weapons Procurement*, Adelphi Paper No. 147/148 (London: International Institute for Strategic Studies).
Checinski, Michael (1980), *A Comparison of the Polish and Soviet Armaments Decision-Making Systems* (Santa Monica, Calif.: Rand).
Crozier, Michel (1964), *The Bureaucratic Phenomenon* (Chicago: Chicago University Press).
Gelman, Harry (1981), *The Politburo's Management of Its American Problem*, R-2707-NA (Santa Monica, Calif.: Rand), April.
Gustafson, Thane (1981, forthcoming), *Reform and Power in Soviet Politics: Lessons of Recent Policies on Land and Water* (Cambridge: Cambridge University Press).
Khrushchev, Nikita (1970), *Khrushchev Remembers*, trans. and ed., Strobe Talbott (Boston, Mass.: Little, Brown).
Leites, Nathan (1951), *The Operational Code of the Politburo* (New York: Rand/McGraw-Hill).
Leites, Nathan (1953), *A Study of Bolshevism* (Glencoe, Ill.: The Free Press).
Ofer, Gur (1980), *The Relative Efficiency of Military Research and Development in the Soviet Union: A Systems Approach*, R-2522-AF (Santa Monica, Calif.: Rand).
Spielmann, Karl F. (1978), *Analyzing Soviet Strategic Arms Decisions* (Boulder, Colo: Westview Press).
United States, Department of Defense (1977), *US Defense Perspectives, Fiscal Year, 1978*, Donald Rumsfeld, Secretary of Defense, January.
Valenta, Jiri (1979), *Soviet Intervention in Czechoslovakia, 1968: Anatomy of a Decision* (Baltimore, Md: Johns Hopkins University Press).
Warner, Edward L. (1977), *The Military in Contemporary Soviet Politics: An Institutional Analysis* (New York: Praeger).

2 The Stalinist Legacy in Soviet National Security Decisionmaking

VERNON V. ASPATURIAN

INTRODUCTION

The Soviet decisionmaking process under Stalin in 1934–53, at any given stage in its evolution, was the product of dynamic interaction between institutions and personalities, both of which are much easier to identify and chart than the interactive processes between them. In their formal and outward dimensions the institutions of the party and state have remained remarkably uniform over the past six decades of Soviet history in spite of the fact that they have survived four constitutional changes and several adoptions of party statutes. The relationships among these institutions, the interactive patterns and networks of personalities, the processes that were generated, and the changing contextual domestic and external environments within which they functioned, however, have undergone vast alterations.

The availability of data and information covering this period varies greatly with respect to both time periods and policy/issue areas. Needless to say, information and data with respect to decisionmaking processes involving foreign policy and national security continue to be the most difficult to acquire, largely because so few people were involved in these decisions at the highest levels, so little information filtered down to proximate non-participants and even executors and administrators of these decisions, and finally because revelations concerning decisions of this character would have serious reverberations involving other countries which could still damage the interests of the leadership and the state.

In Soviet policymaking the tremendous asymmetry which has always existed between knowledge concerning how, why and by whom decisions were made or rejected involving national security matters, that is, the inputs into the process, and knowledge concerning the output of the process, remains intact even for events of the past. Even relatively high-level Soviet administrators and executors of decisions and policies often were ignorant of how, why and by whom they were appointed, promoted, or demoted in the first place, to say nothing of how decisions they were commanded to carry out were arrived at, except that ultimate authority, sanction and approval rested with Stalin.[1] Often orders and commands would come directly from Stalin, at other times they were relayed through Politburo members, but even the extent and character of other Politburo members' participation in the process remains obscure, since they often appeared to have been manipulated and implicated in the process rather than drawn in as active participants.

The highly idiosyncratic character of the Soviet decisionmaking process during this two-decade period creates severe if not impossible barriers to conceptualizing the system, since personal rule would seem to negate the very concept 'process' itself. We are, of course, at this point making a distinction between the process of arriving at decisions and the process of carrying them out. Even during the Stalinist period, the latter was more vulnerable to analysis than the former. Decisionmaking under Stalin involved 'procedures' which were nonrational or even irrational in character. Elements of Stalin's personal style and personality, as recounted by many eyewitness observers, including pre-eminently Khrushchev, included personal hate, vengeance, distrust, suspicion, paranoia, personal taste, whim and caprice. Decisions involving personnel, whether to be appointed, promoted, removed, arrested, or executed, often were the consequences of chance or Stalin's whim or caprice, which by their very nature are immune to conceptualization beyond enumeration and acknowledgement.[2]

Institutions and bureaucracies existed; elaborate legal procedures and regulations were enacted and published. But the formal legal procedures and regulations were flagrantly violated, whereas alongside the published laws and regulations, there existed an enormous body of secret or unpublished circulars, regulations, decrees, orders, resolutions, and so on, which superseded the published norms. Although various party and state institutions were invested with certain well-defined formal functions and powers, identifiable lines of legal responsibility, and specified procedures, the actual process was far different. Before 6 May 1941, Stalin held no formal position of legal responsibility, yet he would dictate the texts of party resolutions and decisions, laws of the Supreme Soviet, decrees of the Presidium, orders of the Sovnarkom, regulations of various ministries and administrative agencies, speeches of subordinates and even the proposed texts of treaties and agreements with foreign powers. All were issued under the authority of responsible institutions or over the signature of responsible authorities. Furthermore, Stalin would frequently issue oral and verbal orders and instructions face-to-face, over the telephone, or in various meetings; he would decide appointments, promotions and removals; he would decide whom to arrest, how interrogations should be conducted, specify the crimes to which victims would confess, and whether they should live or die. Invariably he would implicate others, particularly Politburo members, in his decisions, circulating them for signature and assent. Thus, Stalin's personality and character were inextricably intertwined with the decisionmaking process and constituted one of its main conditioning factors.

The Soviet political superstructure prior to 1953 was a complicated mosaic of shifting and interlocking, but relatively simple institutions, resting upon an entrenched foundation of one-man dictatorship, solidified by the war, in which all powers were delegated from Stalin. The institutions of both party and state, in terms of both their relationships to one another and the relationships of various organs within the party and state structures to each other, were essentially creations of Stalin and were designed not to limit his own power, but to limit that of his subordinates and potential rivals and to facilitate the solidification or consolidation of his own authority. Conflicting lines of authority between party and state provided an *ad hoc* system of crosschecks and balances. What clearly comes through in all the available Soviet memoir literature, especially that of Khrushchev, is that Stalin considered himself to be above the law and above the party statutes, and freely violated both whenever he determined that the occasion warranted it.

Theoretically, the division of labor or functions between party and state assigns policy formulation to the party and policy execution and administration to the state. But since the party was also invested with the function and responsibility of checking and verifying the execution of policy, the lines of demarcation were not always clear, and presumably this was Stalin's intention. Furthermore, the investiture of personalities with both state and party positions further complicated the situation, and after Stalin assumed the headship of the government in 1941, the redundancy of two duplicative parallel structures became obvious and Stalin allowed the party decision-making organs to atrophy. Still, from the available literature, it is not always clear whether Stalin and his colleagues were meeting in their capacity as state or party officials when making decisions, since, with few exceptions, the personalities at the apexes of the party and state during and after the war were virtually identical.

The exceptions, while few, were important, because one of our most important sources on the decisionmaking process during the Stalin era was one of the exceptions, namely, Khrushchev. During the entire Stalin period, even when he described himself as one of Stalin's confidants and a member of Stalin's small inner circle, Khrushchev never held a central state office. Khrushchev served exclusively as a party official and hence was not entitled to attend the meetings of state organs, unless specifically invited. During the war a new super or inner war cabinet, the State Defense Committee, was established by Stalin, which virtually superseded both the Politburo and the Presidium of the Council of People's Commissars as the principal decision-making institution during the war. Although an official organ of the state, its composition served further to blend and intermingle state and party functions. Its membership was exclusively made up of full, candidate, or future members of the Politburo most of whom also held other state appointments. Of the nine full members of the Politburo, Khrushchev, Andreev and Zhdanov were deliberately excluded from this body. Kalinin was not a member, because as chairman of the Presidium of the Supreme Soviet, his membership on a state administrative organ (Council of People's Commissars or its derivative organs) was constitutionally prohibited.

Although Marshal Zhukov reports that 'In all, the State Committee for Defense adopted some 10,000 resolutions on military and economic matters during the war',[3] Khrushchev's memoirs and even his Secret Speech of 1956 make virtually no references to the State Defense Committee or various state organs as decisionmaking bodies during the Stalin era. Indeed, the State Defense Committee is not even listed in the index of either volume of Khrushchev's reminiscences.

In fact, Khrushchev is curiously derelict in identifying the institutional setting of most of the meetings of the leadership which he describes, just as his account is sorely deficient in recounting decisions involving foreign policy and security-related matters. Khrushchev's writings thus may reflect his restricted membership on central decisionmaking institutions (Politburo and Secretariat) and his peripheral involvement in foreign policy and defense-related policies and decisions during the Stalin period. His restricted participation certainly accounts in large measure for Khrushchev's compartmentalized and fragmentary knowledge about the decisionmaking process under Stalin, and his constant lament about not being consulted, of which the following is typical:

> When I say, 'our government', I mean Stalin. He believed he *was* the government . . . Even though I was a member of the Politburo, I wasn't let in on all matters which came up between Stalin and the Chinese. I knew only what I was supposed to know. Stalin made countless decisions with respect to China – usually, I think, in consultation with Molotov.[4]

On the other hand, when recounting the events of the post-Stalin period, decisions and matters relating to foreign policy and defense occupy center-stage in his memoirs, just as he occupied center-stage in making those decisions.

This long period of flagrant illegality and erratic procedures at the top contributed in no small measure to the relative lack of legitimacy which has always appeared to characterize the Soviet political system. Since the major state decisionmaking institutions at the macrolevel under the Brezhnev Constitution (1977) are essentially those created by Stalin and carried over from the 1936 Constitution, and the current central organs of the party are also those of the pre-1952 Stalinist era, some reference to the status of these institutions during the Brezhnev period is necessary in order to place the Stalinist period in proper evolutionary perspective and historical context.

Whether or not the long period of stability since 1964 (almost as long as the Stalinist era) and the new Brezhnev Constitution will finally dispel the aura of illegitimacy and impermanence which has hovered over Soviet party and state institutions, the continued separation of power from institutional responsibility will always create its own singular political pathology, procedural confusion and personality disorientation. Both Khrushchev and Brezhnev were obviously uneasy functioning from only party positions, and although Brezhnev resurrected the old Stalinist title of secretary-general to give enhanced status to his party position, like Khrushchev before him, he ultimately sought to bridge the gap between informal power and formal responsibility.[5]

Although the 1977 Constitution can scarcely be described as a daring and innovative document, and leaves the major institutions of the Soviet state relatively intact, it is a much longer instrument and recognizes that preservation of the duality between party and state, with the party outside and above the law and the state inside and subordinate to the law, would perpetuate a serious source of considerable misunderstanding and anxiety as to where real power was legally lodged. When the draft Constitution was circulated for examination and discussion, apparently proposals were made to resolve the confusion and apprehension engendered by the party's anomalous status by vesting party bodies with legislative and other state functions, that is, to bring legality into congruence with political reality. This proposal, however, was rejected by Brezhnev in his speech on the draft Constitution.[6]

The new Constitution instead resolved the juridical hiatus by neither investing the party with state functions nor subordinating the party to state law, but by subordinating both party and state to the new Constitution, which Soviet juridical commentaries emphasize is more than a simple state Constitution. Chapter 1 of the Constitution introduces an entirely new juridical concept, 'the political system', which is superior to both party and state and of which the two are discrete, separate and approximately coequal components, each with its own institutional structures and procedures. The new Constitution embraces the totality of Soviet society and by implication imparts new legal reinforcement to the concepts 'total law' and 'plenary authority'. Until the adoption of this document, Soviet constitutional doctrine subscribed to the notion that the Soviet Constitution was a product of the party and that the party's authority and legitimacy derived ultimately from the working class and history. The Brezhnev Constitution, while affirming in article 6 that the party is 'the leading and guiding force of Soviet society and the nucleus of its political system', now goes onto emphasize unambiguously that 'all Party organizations shall function within the framework of the Constitution of the USSR'.[7] The proposals to invest state power in party organs reflected continuing widespread confusion and disorientation concerning the ambiguity of the Soviet political system and the shadow of illegitimacy it continued to cast. Brezhnev's progressive assertion of center-stage in Soviet foreign policy in his capacity as Secretary-General also became increasingly awkward and created similar confusion and disorientation, since he was functioning as *de facto* chief of state or head of government, although his title was not invested with state authority. He created protocol problems and caused confusion abroad concerning lines of responsibility and authority between him and the formal, legal heads of government (Kosygin) and state (Podgorny). As Brezhnev himself noted in his speech to the Supreme Soviet upon his election as chairman of the Presidium, his new appointment resolved his anomalous position:

> I, as General Secretary of the Central Committee have repeatedly, as you know, had to represent our country on some occasions . . . in inter-state relations and in talks on significant topics concerning the strengthening of our peace and insuring the security of our people. Now this practice will be given its logical form.[8]

Brezhnev's assumption of the chairmanship of the Presidium only resolved Brezhnev's personal ambiguous status but did little to resolve the institutional ambiguities and confusion between party and state. Proposals to amend the draft Constitution that in effect would have subordinated the state to the party were rejected not in favor of subordinating party to state, but rather in favor of subordinating both to the Constitution as approximate coequals in the Soviet political system. By holding both positions simultaneously Brezhnev, in effect, became head of the entire Soviet political system and was invested with what Soviet jurists call plenary authority, that is, authority to represent and speak for the entire political system, not simply the state or party.

Under the new Constitution when a single person is head of both party and state the question of plenary power appears resolved and Brezhnev's continued use of his party title in international diplomacy assumed a new appropriateness. Nevertheless, given the institutional ambiguities and procedural uncertainties that have characterized the Soviet political system, Brezhnev's use of both party and state titles in signing international agreements, including the SALT II treaty, with his party title listed first, engendered confusion as to whether the *institutional* source of his authority was the party or state. And if the two positions are separated, as they were in the early post-Brezhnev era, where will plenary power reside?

Among other matters which remain unresolved is the question of who assumes the position of commander-in-chief of the Armed Forces, which seems intimately connected with plenary power. And while the concept of plenary power is hypothetically compatible with collective leadership, the concept of commander-in-chief is not. This creates a serious complication. As long as no single post or institution exists which can symbolize the entire political system, only a single person can perform that function or role and to do so unambiguously would require him to assume leadership of both party and state, which simultaneously invests him with plenary authority and automatically resolves the question of who becomes commander-in-chief. It should be emphasized that under the Soviet system there is no predesignated commander-in-chief. Neither the general secretary of the party, nor the chairman of the Presidium of the Supreme Soviet, nor the chairman of the Council of Ministers, nor the Minister of Defense, nor the chairman of any defense committee, council, or commission is *ipso facto* or *ex officio* commander-in-chief. The High Command and commander-in-chief of the Armed Forces are separate and distinct appointments to be made by the Presidium of the Supreme Soviet and anyone holding one or more of the above institutional positions can be – and has been – appointed in the past as commander-in-chief.[9]

Until the mid-1920s the position was viewed as essentially military in character and was thus occupied by a professional military officer, but his authority did not extend to the entire armed forces of the USSR. The absence of a High Command or commander-in-chief during the first weeks of the war, by all accounts, enormously contributed to the initial military disasters suffered by the Soviet armed forces. Stalin finally assumed the post, with some reluctance, on 8 August 1941, but his appointment was kept secret and not made public until after the Battle of Stalingrad. The unseemly details of this period are discussed more fully below.

Stalin retained the title, augmented with other military appointments and ranks, until his death, but the problem surfaced once again after his death and the position remained unfilled until 1955. Again the appointment apparently involved some contention and was improvised rather than regularized or institutionalized. Khrushchev writes that, after the war, Stalin's successors were faced with the possibility of nuclear war but had little or no knowledge of the armed forces or experience as to how to manage the country's defenses:

> Toward the end of his life, he [Stalin] did everything in his own name. He refused to discuss military matters with us; he gave us no training in the

management of the army. Defense was his exclusive concern and he guarded it fiercely. If someone else expressed the slightest interest or curiosity about this or that new weapon, Stalin immediately became jealous and suspicious.[10]

It is true that Bulganin had served as deputy minister and then minister of defense for about a decade and had been invested with the rank of marshal of the Soviet Union, but Khrushchev had nothing but contempt for his abilities and considered him to be incompetent.[11] Thus, when Bulganin replaced Malenkov as premier in 1955 under Khrushchev's sponsorship, Khrushchev relates that Bulganin suggested that Khrushchev be appointed commander-in-chief. Since Khrushchev held no formal post of constitutional authority, his appointment even as described by Khrushchev can only be characterized as curiously convolutive and osmotic, reminiscent of an earlier Stalinist *modus operandi*:

> He suggested that since I'd had considerable experience in military affairs, I, as First Secretary of the Party Central Committee, take on the job of Commander in Chief of the armed forces as well. The other Comrades in the leadership had no objection, and my appointment as Commander in Chief was approved. This was a strictly internal decision. We decided not to publicize the decision and made no mention of it in the press. If we had been at war, we would certainly have announced my military appointment to the Soviet people. As for top officers of our armed forces, they certainly knew who their Commander in Chief was without having to read an announcement in the newspaper.[12]

The appointment remained secret even after Khrushchev assumed the post of premier in 1958, but he was mentioned almost in passing, on a few occasions by various military figures as commander-in-chief. With his ouster from power in 1964, Brezhnev assumed his party post and Kosygin took over as premier. No mention was made of commander-in-chief and the position was once again temporarily vacated. Just as no decision was published appointing Khrushchev to this position, no announcement was made concerning his resignation or deposition as commander-in-chief. It is almost a certainty that at some point Brezhnev, while still only secretary-general, was also designated as commander-in-chief by secret decree. After he became chairman of the Presidium in 1977, he assumed the military rank of marshal of the Soviet Union, chairmanship of the constitutionally established Council of Defense of the USSR and was formally and publicly appointed commander-in-chief of the Armed Forces. As chairman of the Presidium of the Supreme Soviet, he literally appointed himself, that is, signed the decree formally investing him with all three military positions.

Thus, on the surface, it would appear that the new Constitution establishes the basis for the legal subordination of the party to the state, but in fact makes them both subordinate to a new abstract entity called the 'political system' of which they are the two principal components, each with its own institutions, procedures and sphere of authority. Even the Constitution is no longer a Constitution simply defining *state* power, but is a plenary

Constitution defining political power and superimposed upon both party and state. Thus, whereas the party is subordinate to the Constitution, it is not necessarily subordinate to the state. As one authoritative commentary on the new Constitution notes:

> The new Constitution of the USSR has extended the limits of constitutional regulation. All previous Soviet constitutions, as Fundamental Laws of State, not only contained a definition of its structure . . . but also regulated other important social relations . . . The 1977 Constitution of the USSR makes another step forward in this direction. *The first chapter deals with questions relating not only to the State, but also the entire political system of society. In particular it defines the position of the CPSU . . . within this system.* [13]

Thus, while the new Constitution subordinates both party and state to its authority, it does little to clarify the institutional relationship between the two in the decisionmaking process. It is likely that now Brezhnev has passed from the scene, both the issues of plenary power and who should become commander-in-chief have again become contentious. The full legalization of the party without its simultaneous subordination to state authority simply continues the old ambiguities but within a new framework. The fate and role of institutions will continue to be determined more by personalities than *vice versa*. Yet it must be emphasized that since Stalin's death, the role and importance of institutions in the Soviet decisionmaking process have been enhanced and will probably continue to be expanded. What makes the Soviet scene so disorienting, however, is the vast remaining gulf between the limited *de facto* role of Soviet institutions in the decisionmaking process and their enormous *potential* capacity as described in Soviet constitutional and party documents.

Some definition of the term 'decisionmaking' is in order at this point. To describe the Soviet political system under Stalin as a one-man dictatorship does not, of course, imply that Stalin made every decision in the Soviet system or approved every decision, or was even aware of every decision. Obviously thousands, perhaps millions, of decisions were made and no one person could make all decisions. What is meant by decisions and decisionmaking are ultimate decisive authority and final judgement, whether it was exercised directly by Stalin or indirectly through delegation of authority, implicitly or explicitly, or whether it was understood authority by inference or more tangible communication. [14] In any large political system authority must be delegated, and thousands of 'decisionmakers' exist at various levels. Furthermore, aside from the sheer number of decisions and their qualitative distinctions, one must also take into account the entire character of the decision as well. Since one man, no matter how powerful and how omnipresent he may wish to be, must concern himself with priorities in terms of decisions, there is little question, but that Stalin – in spite of the fact that he may have wanted to decide everything, including trivial matters, as Khrushchev repeatedly asserts – had to delegate some authority to others. The character of the issue and its level of importance would determine Stalin's range of consultation and degree of delegation. There is strong reason to believe that on foreign policy and security-related matters Stalin's range of consultation was relatively restricted and that the degree of delegation was severely circumscribed. According to Khrushchev:

> [Stalin] jealously guarded foreign policy in general and our policy toward other socialist countries in particular as his own special province. He has never gone out of his way to take other people's advice into account, and this was especially true after the war. The rest of us were just errand boys. Stalin would snarl threateningly at anyone who overstepped the mark.[15]

Of course, Khrushchev's account may merely reflect the fact that he, Khrushchev, was rarely, if ever, consulted on foreign policy and defense matters, but the general validity of Khrushchev's description of the decisionmaking process under Stalin will be dealt with in more detail below.

CONDITIONING FACTORS AND PERIODIZATION

Among the factors which conditioned and often defined the decisionmaking process was Stalin's personality and character. Decisionmaking during the Stalin era was highly idiosyncratic and intensely personal. Social, personal and official relationships were often intermingled. The institutional setting of decisionmaking was often ambiguous, ill-defined, or nonexistent. State and party institutions were juggled and rejuggled in bewildering fashion, and many participants and observers of the Soviet decisionmaking process were themselves uncertain concerning the formal institutional setting of discussions, conversations, or decisions during this period. Stalin would often arrive at a decision before, during, after, or without consultation and then arbitrarily decide whether it would be a decision of this or that party or state organ. Although foreign diplomats and statesmen often described Stalin as charming and courteous, knowledgeable and highly intelligent, other accounts, notably those of Khrushchev and Djilas[16] give an entirely different picture. Svetlana's[17] account is a mixture of the two extremes. Stalin has been described by Khrushchev and others as coarse, crude and rude in personal relations; primitive in speech and behavior; capricious, arbitrary and treacherous with relatives, friends, strangers and enemies; one who practiced false modesty and was extremely susceptible to flattery and praise from among his retainers. He was a practitioner of peasant cunning in testing and tormenting his subordinates, frequently using vile, obscene and violent language. Meetings of the Politburo would often degenerate in scenes of violent argumentation, smashing of fists and crockery on the table, and ominous accusations. Khrushchev and others have also charged him with incompetence, fear and negligence, especially during the early days of the war.

Stalin could be extraordinarily cruel and perverse. Thus, Khrushchev relates that at various times Stalin accused Voroshilov of being a British spy and Molotov and Mikoian of being unspecified 'Western agents'. He arrested and exiled Molotov's wife and Kaganovich's brother, obscenely accused prominent Soviet Jews of being Nazi spies and agents and directed the torture of the arrested Kremlin doctors. In the words of Khrushchev, 'Stalin was crazy with rage, yelling at Ignatiev [the Minister of State Security] and threatening him, demanding that he throw the doctors in chains, beat them to a pulp, and grind them into powder'.[18]

Decisionmaking under Stalin took place in an atmosphere of suffocative fear and constant anxiety within a complicated network of changing personal alignments, enveloped in a web of intrigue and treachery. Stalin's capriciousness apparently knew no bounds, since subordinates who were in favor with Stalin one day might be slated for execution the next and members of the Politburo feared for their lives as they obeyed Stalin's often sudden and unexpected summons at unreasonable hours, never knowing whether they would be attending a banquet or facing arrest and execution.

It should be emphasized that descriptions of Stalin at work and assessments of his character and abilities are often bewildering and contradictory. In general the views and assessments of 'bourgeois' diplomats and statesmen are uniformly favorable, those of 'insiders' both favorable and unfavorable, while contemporary official views were always intolerably obsequious. The Soviet and communist memoir literature is mixed, often contradictory, inconsistent and not susceptible to easy resolution. In some measure these differences reflect time and place of publication, which in turn reflects the attitude of the post-Stalin leadership toward Stalin at any given time. This is particularly true of material published in the Soviet Union, where it is subject to examination and censorship. Even Khrushchev's memoirs are full of contradictions and inconsistencies which cannot be easily reconciled. While constantly condemning Stalin for not consulting anyone before making decisions, his account is replete with Stalin in consultation with various members of the Soviet leadership, including Khrushchev, who described himself several times as a member of Stalin's select inner circle. Khrushchev's account must, therefore, be approached with great care and discretion. It is highly biased, full of inaccuracies and faulty recollections, and extremely contentious. Yet it coincides remarkably well with the accounts by Djilas and Svetlana. It should be pointed out that the memoirs of Ilya Ehrenbourg,[19] Ivan Maisky[20] and others confirm many of Khrushchev's characterizations, but with greater prudence and circumspection as one would suspect. Roy Medvedev's accounts also square with those of Khrushchev in most particulars.[21] The most difficult memoirs to contend with are those of the wartime generals and marshals, whose views are contradictory and inconsistent and often totally at variance with Khrushchev's description of Stalin in wartime.

Marshal Zhukov, in particular, although he was victimized by Stalin, gives an unusually favorable picture of Stalin as a wartime commander totally at variance with Khrushchev's characterization and more in accordance with those of Western observers.[22] Of course, Stalin was probably a man of many sides and characters, and his behavior may have varied depending upon time, personality, circumstance, or location.

Not only was the boundary between Stalin as a person and the Soviet state difficult to distinguish, but boundaries between state and society, public and private life, formal and informal rules, governmental structures and private associations were equally unclear. Similarly, the conceptual boundaries that distinguish other factors and environments which condition the decision-making process are not always separable from the process itself and are imprecise, inchoate, and unchartable. The most important of these, after Stalin's personality itself, were the following:

(1) The amorphous and elastic character of the sociopolitical system at the macrolevel characterized by well-defined institutions and ill-defined jurisdictional authority, overlapping functions, interchangeable personnel combined with the relative absence of subunits and structures at the intermediate and microlevels of the political system.
(2) The system of ideological infallibility and cognitive omniscience invested in Stalin's person.
(3) The value system in which loyalty to Stalin as a person superseded all other values and loyalties, and the system of rewards and punishments based upon this value system.
(4) The system of individual and mass terror, which functioned simultaneously as an incentive system and an enforcement mechanism.
(5) The system of mass mobilization and concentration of human effort and energy directed toward the achievement of goals and objectives commanded by the central authorities.

The intensity and precise nature of Stalin's style varied over time and from issue to issue with respect to the various personality characteristics that animated or incited him. Similarly, these conditioning factors operated with uneven force from one time period to another, with various conditioning factors relatively predominant at different times.

The more closely the entire Stalinist era is examined, the more apparent it becomes that beneath the immobility and rigidity of the system an evolution of both institutions and processes was taking place. The term 'evolution', however, should not be interpreted to necessarily indicate a 'progressive' evolution, that is, evolution from less desirable to more desirable forms, but rather in the sense of gradual, but definite change in a different direction. In the case of the Stalinist era the evolution of institutions and processes was less linear than cyclical in character, in the sense that they first degenerated, were regenerated and then entered a renewed phase of sustained disintegration until Stalin's death, when a new period of regeneration and renovation was set into motion.

The Stalinist era can be broken down into five distinct subperiods, each with its own discrete and distinctive characteristics. Any periodization is analytically arbitrary and this one is no exception. The periodization proposed is both chronological and analytical in character, since each subperiod is bounded by time periods and identifiably distinguishing analytical characteristics. Much of the contradictory and confusing descriptions of the Stalinist era stem at least in part from the fact that various observers refer to different subperiods conditioned and influenced by different contextual situations as well as by the role and character of the observer himself in his relationship and contact with Stalin. Various facets of Stalin's complex personality were orchestrated and modulated by Stalin himself. He would vary his behavior and style to suit the occasion, and thus project images of his personality that were deliberately and carefully calculated in advance. Even in his meeting with Ribbentrop in 1939, he adjusted to the occasion by proposing a toast to Hitler because he was so loved by the German people.[23] Thus, depending upon whether he was dealing with domestic rivals or subordinates or with foreigners, and if they were foreigners, whether they were communists or noncommunists, statesmen, representatives of small states or large, journalists, and so on, Stalin's projected personality could change accordingly.

The five subperiods are as follows:

(1) from the 17th Party Congress (1934) to the 18th Party Congress (March 1939);
(2) from the 18th Party Congress to the Nazi invasion of the Soviet Union (June 1941);
(3) the war period (1941–6);
(4) the postwar period (1947–52);
(5) the post-19th Party Congress period (October 1952–March 1953).

FROM THE 17th PARTY CONGRESS TO THE 18th PARTY CONGRESS: SHATTERING THE RESIDUAL LENINIST PROCESS

By the time the 17th Party Congress met in 1934 Stalin had already made enormous progress in substantially altering the decisionmaking process established by Lenin and in fastening his grip on the party. Aside from Trotsky who had been exiled, most of Stalin's peers, 'old Bolsheviks' who were part of Lenin's entourage and whose stature, prestige and standing were equal or near-equal to Stalin's, had been forced out of leadership positions by 1934. They were still alive and in the country, but their places were taken by a combination of 'Stalinists' who owed their highest loyalty and fidelity to Stalin as a person and 'Stalinists' who supported Stalin's position against the left and right opposition out of conviction and agreement on policies, but with no particular loyalty to Stalin as a person. This distinction between the various kinds of 'Stalinists' was to be a crucial factor in the purges that were to ensue almost immediately after the Congress.

Leading figures like Zinoviev and Kamenev had not only been expelled from the leadership but from the party as well, whereas the leaders of the right opposition, crushed at the 16th Party Congress (1930) were humiliatingly placed on probation. Bukharin, Rykov and Tomsky, for example, were even re-elected as candidate members of the Central Committee at the 17th Congress. Thousands of their followers, however, remained active in the party and still occupied state and party positions. Many of them had recanted their former views but the sincerity of their recantation was also suspect. Hence as long as the former leaders remained alive and their adherents in place, they constituted a potential alternative to the Stalin regime should it falter or fail to deliver, and thus in Stalin's mind posed a threat to his position.

Stalin's overwhelming dominance was thus not yet decisively established until after the purges and the convocation of the 18th Communist Party

Congress in March 1939, which also assembled the definitive Stalinist-dominated oligarchy which was made up almost exclusively of obsequious subordinates, clearly junior to Stalin in stature and prestige and completely beholden to him for their positions. This Stalinist core was to remain largely intact throughout the war and to even survive Stalin's death in 1953.

Although the right opposition, the last of the substantial oppositionist groups in the leadership, had been crushed and forced to publicly recant at the 16th Party Congress, Stalin's position remained precarious because of the stormy and bloody events that took place between the 16th and 17th congresses. It would be an understatement to say that it is now generally accepted that all was not well at the 'Congress of Victors' held in early 1934, where Stalin reassuringly announced that all internal opposition to the party line had ceased and that consequently since no dissent to his report and that of others had been registered, there was no need for a reply or a defense.[24]

The unreality of Stalin's boast was to be tragically confirmed within the next five years. Of the ten full members and five candidate members of the Politburo elected by the Congress of Victors, only six full members and one candidate survived to be reelected at the 18th Party Congress convened only five years later. Furthermore, 1,108 (56·4 percent) of the 1,966 delegates to the 17th Congress and 98 (70·5 percent) out of the 139 full and candidate members were arrested, most of them executed.[25] So much for the 'Congress of Victors'.

Although confirmed information in precise, accurate and unimpeachable detail is still far from complete, it appears that Stalin was actually challenged at the congress itself by a core of his own supporters who had become disillusioned and even frightened by his leadership and tried to prevail upon Sergei Kirov, the leader of the Leningrad organization and second man in the Secretariat, to allow his name to be placed in nomination against Stalin for the post of secretary-general.[26] Stalin quickly learned of the incipient rebellion and took measures to ensure that Kirov would not be given a second opportunity to replace him. According to some reports, Stalin actually set into motion events that were to result in the fatal shooting of S. M. Kirov on 1 December 1934, which in turn unleashed the terror of the 1930s.[27] In rapid-order fire another full member of the Politburo V. V. Kuibyshev died under mysterious circumstances in 1935;[28] G. K. Ordzhonikidze, also a full member, was murdered or driven to suicide in 1937;[29] and I. V. Kossior, still another full member, was arrested and shot on the eve of the 18th Party Congress.[30] The fate of other members of the 1934 Politburo and those co-opted in the years after is charted in Table 2.1.

Other party and state institutions suffered accordingly. Nearly 80 percent of the membership of the Council of People's Commissars and an even-larger proportion of regional party secretaries suffered a similar fate, as did party and government officials of the union republics and other national units.[31] The armed forces and the diplomatic service were similarly decimated. Over 30,000 professional military officers were consumed by the purges.[32]

Virtually the entire senior membership of the diplomatic service, including most of Litvinov's deputy commissars, perished, as did hundreds of lesser foreign commissariat officials. Little more than half-a-dozen senior

Table 2.1 Evolution of the Politburo under Stalin, 1934–52

Member	Date of Birth	Candidate member	Full member	Party member	Fate (year)
1934 Politburo					
J. V. Stalin	1879		1919	1898	Died (1953)
M. I. Kalinin	1875	1921	1926	1898	Died (1946)
V. M. Molotov	1890	1921	1926	1906	
K. E. Voroshilov	1881		1926	1903	
V. V. Kuibyshev	1888	1922	1927	1904	Died (1935)
Ya. E. Rudzutak*	1887	1926	1926	1905	Shot (1938)
S. M. Kirov	1886	1926	1930	1904	Assassinated (1934)
G. K. Ordzhonikidze	1886	1926	1930	1903	Suicide (1937)
L. M. Kaganovich	1893	1926	1930	1911	
A. A. Andreev	1895	1926	1932	1914	
I. V. Kossior	1889	1927	1930	1907	Removed Shot (1938)
A. I. Mikoyan	1895	1926	1935	1915	
V. Ya. Chubar	1891	1926	1935	1907	Removed Shot (1939)
P. P. Postyshev	1887	1926	1934	1904	Removed Shot (1938)
G. I. Petrovsky	1878	1926		1897	Removed (1938)
R. I. Eikhe	1890	1935		1907	Removed Shot (1938)
A. A. Zhdanov	1896	1935	1939	1915	Died (1948)
N. I. Yezhov	1895	1937		1907	Removed, shot? (1939)
N. S. Khrushchev	1894	1938	1939	1918	
L. P. Beria	1899	1939	1946	1917	Arrested, executed (1953)
N. M. Shvernik	1888	1939		1905	
G. M. Malenkov	1901	1941	1946	1920	
N. A. Voznesensky	1903	1941	1947	1919	Arrested, shot (1949)
A. S. Shcherbakov	1901	1941		1918	Died (1945)
A. N. Kosygin	1904	1946	1948	1927	
N. A. Bulganin	1895	1946	1948	1917	

* Removed from Politburo and restored in 1932 as candidate member.

——— full member;

- - - - - candidate member.

career diplomats, including Maxim Litvinov, miraculously were spared to recruit and train the new Stalinist diplomatic service.[33]

Not a single bureaucracy or apparat connected with national security issues escaped the ravages of the purge. The price Stalin paid to secure his dominance was enormous, but it did assure his control over every aspect of Soviet life. The destruction of thousands of experienced party military, political and administrative officials could not but shatter the existing decisionmaking process. From that point on the decisionmaking process was wrenched from institutions and relocated in Stalin's person. Nevertheless, the apparatus and bureaucratic structures had to be rebuilt to function as instruments of Stalin's will. All of Stalin's peers and equals had perished; even those of second rank, that is, those who entered the leadership after Lenin's death, were also eliminated. As will be shown below, Stalin was now surrounded by junior, third-rank officials, who had little or no personal link with Lenin, and with but few exceptions were about ten years or more junior to Stalin.

The memoir literature is full of accounts of the young, bewildered and inexperienced, but evidently promising, replacements that were being recruited for the highest positions in the military, diplomatic service, economic bureaucracy and party apparatus. Young men in their twenties and thirties were catapulted in a few years to the apex of their structures. Many, like Gromyko, recruited at age 33 to be ambassador to the United States, were still there in the early eighties. Gromyko's own personal account of his interview with Stalin is typical of the times:

One day I received a summons from Stalin. Until then I had only seen him at a distance, in Red Square . . . Of course, within minutes of receiving the summons I was in the waiting room of Stalin's office in the Kremlin . . . I soon found myself in Stalin's office . . . With him was Molotov . . . with whom I had often discussed questions concerning relations with the USA. I was courteously greeted by Stalin and Molotov. Stalin spoke first. He said that they proposed to post me to the Soviet Embassy in the USA as the number 2, as counsellor. Frankly, this took me somewhat by surprise . . . Sparing of words, as was his custom, he named the areas of priority in Soviet-American relations . . . Molotov put in a few remarks in support of what Stalin was saying . . . Umansky, who evidently did not impress Stalin or Molotov very much, had been recalled to Moscow . . . He was replaced by Maxim Litvinov, who likewise held the post of Ambassador for a short time . . . Thus the author of this book soon replaced Litvinov as Ambassador in the USA.[34]

During the period between the 17th and 18th congresses, of course, Stalin still made decisions from his position as secretary-general of the party. Even when the new Constitution was promulgated, and in his name, Stalin still did not assume a post of legal responsibility. V. M. Molotov acted as head of the Soviet government and functioned as Stalin's front man over whose signature the principal decisions were executed. Stalin's closest approximation to holding a position of responsibility was his election as a deputy to the Supreme Soviet and ordinary member of its Presidium, of which Mikhail

Kalinin was the chairman. Stalin belonged to many committees, commissions and institutional collectives, but in accordance with the false image of communist modesty that was widely propagated, that is, a wise but simple and taciturn man, Stalin rarely presided as chairman of the various bodies on which he served, except the party Secretariat of which he was the formal head. Other observers, most notably Khrushchev, have since confirmed Alexander Barmine's account that Stalin did not always even preside over meetings of the Politburo which then as now did not have a formal chairman or presiding officer, although the secretary-general (or first secretary in 1953–66) normally would have precedence. In this way the Politburo preserves its virginal character as the sole remaining immaculate collective of 'equals' in the Soviet political system.

Khrushchev's account of Stalin's decisionmaking procedures during this period is quite favorable, but this may reflect the fact that Khrushchev was on the periphery of power rather than near its center, and most importantly that he was one of the principal beneficiaries of Stalin's methods of this period, having been appointed to the Politburo as a young man to replace those who were being shot. Politburo meetings during this period were described by Khrushchev as being informal and comradely. He writes that he 'was spellbound by the patience and sympathy for others that he [Stalin] showed at Politburo meetings in the mid-thirties'.[35] Even members of the Central Committee who were in Moscow were invited to attend Politburo meetings as observers. Furthermore, according to Khrushchev:

> Actually in those days Stalin never chaired the Politburo sessions himself. He always left the job to Molotov. Molotov was Stalin's oldest friend . . . I often went by Stalin's office and Molotov was almost always with Stalin when I got there. They regularly went on vacations together, too.[36]

The highly personal and favorable character of Khrushchev's account serves to highlight the fact that Khrushchev could describe Stalin as being sympathetic and comradely in settings where he was present, at a time when Stalin was arresting and executing Stalinist members of the Politburo, Central Committee, Council of People's Commissars and the High Command, which Khrushchev earlier described with such outrage and graphic quality at the 20th Party Congress. Nevertheless, Khrushchev's account of a relatively reasonable and comradely Stalin is not incompatible with other accounts. According to Alexander Barmine, who was an eyewitness to some Politburo meetings in 1933:

> A thin appearance of collective work is still kept up at Politburo meetings. Stalin does not 'command.' He merely 'suggests' or 'proposes.' The fiction of voting is retained. But the voter never fails to uphold his 'suggestions.' The decision is signed by all ten members of the Politburo, with Stalin's signature among the rest . . . The other members of the Politburo mumble their approval of Stalin's 'proposal' . . . Stalin is not only in general called 'the Boss' by the whole bureaucracy, but *is* the one and only boss.[37]

Furthermore, no matter what the organ or committee might be, whether at the highest levels or at the lowest, dealing with trivial issues or major crises, if Stalin were a member or sat in attendance, his presence dominated the proceedings. This emerges as the virtually unanimous observation of all eyewitnesses, foreign and domestic.[38]

In spite of the purge, with its massive arrests, executions and repeated turnover of personnel during a relatively short period of time, essential governmental, social and economic functions were carried on in the midst of the terror. A small core of dedicated and terrorized Stalinist loyalists survived in the Politburo and Central Committee and a minimal number of competent experienced professionals also survived sufficient to maintain essential continuity, recruit and train replacements and administer the necessary functions of government. No matter how often government and party bureaucracies, economic enterprises, military units, academies, research institutes and various other agencies were depleted of their personnel, ever-younger and inexperienced but promising recruits could be found to replace them.

The disorientation of the decisionmaking process which characterized the apex of the system filtered down to whatever feeble and rudimentary intermediate and microlevel institutions existed. Committees, commissions and other subinstitutional units were constantly rearranged and reorganized, with the composition unpredictable at any given time, as members were arrested while in attendance or on the way or after leaving such meetings. One never knew whether he would be arrested or not when summoned to such a meeting and membership on these bodies could be extremely and excruciatingly brief, as Stalin would cruelly move individuals slated for extinction from one body to another.

During this period important substantive domestic, foreign policy and national security issues had to be resolved. War clouds were gathering on the horizons of East and West as Hitler came to power in Germany and Japan embarked upon a program of conquest in East Asia. Italy invaded Ethiopia, the Spanish Civil War broke out, Japan attacked China and Hitler embarked upon the militarization and territorial aggrandizement of Germany. These external events played no small role in the paranoia that gripped Stalin. Stalin had nightmarish visions of conspiracies between his various internal opponents, real and imagined, and the Japanese and Germans designed to overthrow his leadership.

Stalin, in formulating his policies and making decisions, seemingly trusted none of his associates, including the survivors, whose close and dear relatives were often arrested, threatened with arrest, or exiled in order to ensure their fidelity. Stalin's paranoia obviously infected the behavior and character of his subordinates, their relationships with their own subordinates and the functioning of the organizations of which they were in charge or members.

Nevertheless, it should be noted that Stalin, as secretary-general of the party, invariably delivered the main political report at party congresses and the principal reports before plenums of the Central Committee. These were the closest approximations of public displays of his personal leadership and authority, and even these were relatively rare. In contrast, his contemporaries, Adolph Hitler and Benito Mussolini, adopted highly flamboyant, charismatic and emotive exercises of leadership on repeated and conspicuous public occasions.

The new macro-institutions introduced by the 1936 Constitution streamlined the government considerably, but they were untested and since Stalin occupied no responsible post within it, they were not taken seriously. Instead the ravaged but institutionally unchanged party organs (Politburo, Secretariat, Orgburo and Central Committee) assumed almost direct control of administration and served as the institutional vehicles of Stalin's personalized decisions. A one-man dictatorship was thus enveloped by two thick bands of institutions which served to disorient Stalin's subordinates without effectively concealing this dictatorship which they were designed, in part, to do.

In spite of the elaborate institutional framework at the macrolevel, considerable organizational, administrative and procedural improvisation was the result as the composition, functions and interrelationships of organs and agencies were constantly subjected to restructuring and reorganization. Institutional and procedural chaos appeared to characterize this period as even the highest officials were unable or unwilling to distinguish between party and state institutions or their division of labor. Everything was simply relayed upwards until it landed on Stalin's desk for final resolution. As will be noted below, some systematic order was restored only when Stalin assumed the formal position of chairman of the Council of People's Commissars on 6 May 1941, when everything was then routed through state agencies.

At the highest administrative levels national security matters were executed through the people's commissariats of Defense, Internal Affairs, Foreign Affairs and to a peripheral degree Foreign Trade. No attempt will be made here to keep track of the numerous reorganizations and renaming of these commissariats which took place during this period. Marshal Voroshilov was Commissar for Defense, Litvinov (under Molotov's supervision) was in charge of foreign affairs, whereas internal affairs (the secret police) were directed successively by Menzhinsky, Yagoda, Yezhov and Beria.

Coordinating and supervisory agencies existed for all of the commissariats, but those dealing with defense matters were the most important. Stalin was a member of some and read the minutes of the meetings of others. Until 1934, two committees were in charge of coordinating defense matters. The first and broadest in scope was the Defense Commission, formed within the Council of People's Commissars (Sovnarkom), both of which were chaired by Molotov. The second was the Revolutionary Military Council (RVS), which was a subordinate unit of the Commissariat for Military and Naval Affairs (as it was then called). Marshal Voroshilov served as both defense commissar and chairman of this committee.[39] In June 1934 the RVS was disbanded as redundant and Voroshilov's commissariat was renamed Commissariat for Defense.

In April 1937 the Defense Commission was reconstituted and elevated into a higher organ called the Committee of Defense, with Molotov remaining as chairman, but now with both Voroshilov and Stalin as members.[40] And in March 1938 a further reorganization revived the RVS as the Main

Military Council with Voroshilov as chairman and Stalin as one of its members along with high-ranking military officials and officers.[41] When the navy was separated out from Voroshilov's jurisdiction as a separate commissariat, a smaller Main or Supreme Council for Naval Affairs was also established but Stalin was not a member. A. A. Zhdanov, the Leningrad party leader, was the Politburo and party secretariat member in charge of naval affairs, although the naval commissar was its formal chairman. Other members of this body included I. V. Tevosyan, Commissar for Shipbuilding, and high-ranking navy officers and officials. The new and fragile Navy Commissariat was initially headed by Smirnov and then Frinovsky, both of whom were purged, and then by Admiral Kuznetsov, who was first appointed first deputy commissar and elected at the 18th Party Congress to the Central Committee. He was both bewildered and surprised by his sudden eminence. As first deputy, Kuznetsov sought advice and direction from Zhdanov, who told him, 'You decide and call me on the more important or doubtful questions . . . We'll get it done'.[42] Zhdanov, in turn, would take all important questions to Stalin for resolution.

After Kuznetsov was promoted to commissar, in his political naïveté, he reported to Molotov, his formal superior as chairman of the Sovnarkom and its Committee of Defense. Molotov would promptly refer him to Stalin, an ordinary member of the committee, who, according to Kuznetsov, meticulously paid attention to the smallest detail and no one would dare act without his approval.[43]

Increasingly, as Commissar for the Navy, he would report directly to Stalin or be called in by him, although he continued to consult with Zhdanov as well. The important point was that Stalin in his capacity as the *de facto* ultimate political authority could deal directly with government ministers and high-ranking military officials, or through his representatives on the various defense committees and commissions, that is, Molotov, Voroshilov, or Zhdanov.

The Main or Supreme Military Council under Voroshilov functioned in much the same manner, except that Voroshilov's personal relationship and political standing were substantially different from that of either Kuznetsov or Zhdanov. Voroshilov was not only a senior member of the Politburo, member of the Committee of Defense, Commissar of Defense and chairman of its Main or Supreme Military Council, but also a close personal confidant of Stalin's.

Nevertheless, since the Main Military Council was much more important than the Naval Council, Stalin's presence was more conspicuous and he assumed an active and dominant role in its proceedings, even though it was formally an administrative-military rather than a political-military body. Marshal K. A. Meretskov, who upon his appointment as deputy chief of the General Staff simultaneously functioned as secretary of the Higher Military Council, gives us a rare and vivid glimpse of its procedures and relationship to other national-security decisionmaking organs, and Stalin's role within them:

The Higher Military Council assembled two or three times a week, usually to hear the reports by commanders of military districts on various arms of the service. The Council, whose Chairman was the People's Commissar for Defense, consisted of eight leading officials of the Commissariat. A decision would be adopted on each question discussed by the Council. After that it had to be endorsed by the People's Commissar and then forwarded to Stalin. This meant that virtually every military or military-economic issue was settled with the direct participation of the General Secretary of the Central Committee of the CPSU. From him the draft Party and Government decision would be submitted to the Soviet Government where it would be adopted, sometimes with certain amendments, and then handed down to the General Staff in the form of a directive. Stalin often attended the meetings of the Higher Military Council and in the evenings he would invite its members and Commanders and Chiefs of Staff of military districts to supper. The conversation would continue, sometimes, late into the night. Stalin asked the commanders for details about the situation in their military districts, their needs, wishes and shortcomings and in this way was always well-informed about army life as a whole.[44]

Thus, in following the trail of the council's decisions, it should be noted that Stalin was involved at various points along its entire labyrinthine route (Figure 2.1). First, the decisions of the council, with or without Stalin's participation, would be endorsed by Voroshilov in his capacity as Defense Commissar and chairman of the council. They would then be forwarded to Stalin in his capacity as secretary-general of the Central Committee of the party, where he would then draft a policy decision, which would be submitted to the appropriate Politburo commission and/or Politburo for examination and discussion. From the Politburo or its commission the draft would be transmitted to the Committee of Defense, with Molotov as chairman and Stalin as a member. It then would be issued as a Government Directive to the General Staff for execution and administration by operational military units and commanders.

The formal procedure was exceedingly cumbersome and was rarely used in its entirety. Given Stalin's strategic location in various bodies along its course, he could and frequently did shortcircuit the formal process at various points and often issued directives and commands to military units and commanders by phone or in face-to-face oral instructions and orders. Stalin's personal staff, headed by Poskrebyshev, would handle formal drafting of documents and transmitting functions for Stalin, whether in accordance with formal processes or *post facto* paperwork, whereby Stalin would often fabricate the necessary documentation and affix the signatures of various responsible functionaries, if necessary. It was this peculiar combination of cumbersome formal procedures and frequent *ad hoc* illicit circumvention of the procedures which caused so much confusion and anxiety among subordinate decisionmakers and executors.

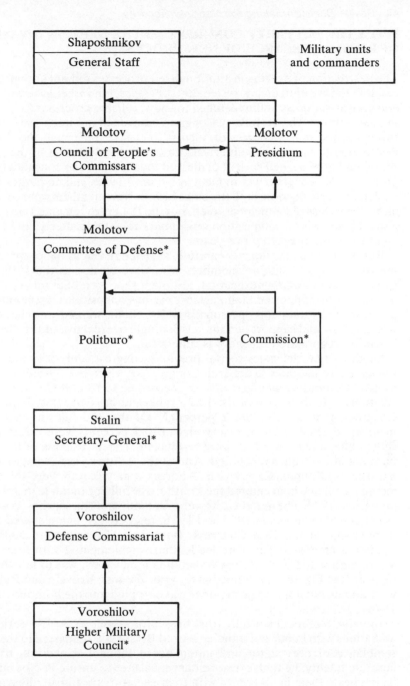

* Stalin included as member

Figure 2.1 National security: decisionmaking procedures before World War II.

FROM THE 18th PARTY CONGRESS TO THE GERMAN INVASION OF RUSSIA: IN SEARCH OF NEW PROCESSES

The destruction of existing institutionalized processes did not automatically result in the creation of new systematic processes, but rather gave way to *ad hoc* improvisation as Stalin searched for new, reliable processes for governing the country. The 18th Party Congress, convened in March 1939, was in this sense the real 'Congress of Victors', because it signaled the decisive destruction of his enemies and rivals, the institutionalization of the terror, the assembly of a small core of dedicated loyalists and the consolidation of his power. No congress was to meet again until 1952, and no purges of the leadership were to ensue until the end of 1949. New members were co-opted along the way as older members died, but the Politburo remained essentially a small body, whose composition was remarkably stable after 1939 in sharp contrast to the preceding five years.

But the new leadership was carefully selected. Even as the congress was meeting, several Politburo members who were elected at the 17th Party Congress were awaiting execution, although they were 'Stalinists', that is, members who supported Stalin against various oppositions, apparently out of conviction rather than personal loyalty. Stalin wanted associates who would follow and support him unquestioningly irrespective of the direction he chose to go and in this he was successful.

Of the 1,966 delegates to the previous congress, only fifty-nine were re-elected as delegates to the 18th Congress, of which twenty-four were old Central Committee members, leaving according to Robert Conquest's calculations only thirty-five of the 1,827 rank-and-file delegates to the 1934 Congress, that is, less than 2 percent.[45] Of the 139 full and candidate members elected in 1934, ninety-eight (70·5 percent) were arrested and shot, while only twenty-four were re-elected. The destruction of the Politburo has already been recounted. And of the Politburo survivors, Molotov, Voroshilov, Kalinin, Kaganovich, Andreev and Mikoyan were the senior members, all of whom entered the Politburo as full or candidate members as far back as 1926. The new recruits were Zhdanov and Khrushchev, co-opted as candidate members in 1935 and 1938, respectively, and elevated to full membership at the 18th Congress. Beria and Shvernik were appointed candidate members. This core leadership, supplemented with Malenkov, Voznesensky and Shcherbakov as candidate members, was to last through the war (see Figure 2.1). Immediately after the war, Kosygin and Bulganin were added, but not a single member was co-opted into the Politburo during 1946–52.

Initially, Stalin did not fully trust his senior associates, whose peripheral affiliations with Lenin and standing as 'old Bolsheviks' imparted to them the semblance of peer status and independent thought. Uncertain of their absolute fidelity, he took extraordinary measures to ensure it. Not only did he implicate them in his crimes with their signatures but in an idiosyncratic yet characteristic exhibition of conspicuous and sadistic brutality, Stalin ordered the arrest of Kalinin's wife in 1937 (released only a few days before the Soviet ceremonial president's death in 1946, only to be exiled again), arrested Mikoyan's two sons, Kaganovich's brother and, after the war,

Molotov's wife. None of these arrests appeared to cripple their efficiency or undermine their loyalty to Stalin.[46]

The 18th Party Congress may have succeeded in stabilizing the leadership and arresting the debilitating and massive turnover of personnel, but it did not succeed in establishing a rational, systematic and predictable decision-making process. Until just prior to the Nazi attack, the Politburo was still the most important decisionmaking organ of the political system, or more properly, was the principal institutional setting in which Stalin made his decisions.

As secretary-general of the party, Stalin had a wide array of institutions and organs to select as the formal vehicles of consultation and communication. He juggled and rejuggled party and state institutions and instituted confusing joint meetings, resolutions and decisions. Although the institutions were often duplicating and overlapping in authority and interlocked in terms of membership, some associates were inevitably not members of this or that organ. By judicious selection Stalin could thus conveniently exclude certain colleagues from the decisionmaking process by his selection of institutions to conduct a meeting. Stalin still did not occupy an official executive or administrative position. Nevertheless, all decisions of the Politburo, Secretariat, or various governmental bodies on questions of foreign policy or national security policy were his in one form or another, no matter how they were processed, whether through a commission, at Politburo meetings, or in consultation with select members of the Politburo and others whom he might choose. Rival and dissident views were quashed and their adherents eliminated. In his relations with the Politburo Stalin could either announce his decisions and expect unanimous approval; submit them for examination and ask for discussion, with or without a vote; simply act without consulting his colleagues and have it formally implemented through an appropriate organ; or simply consult with various members on certain questions to the exclusion of others.[47]

Stalin devised various strategies to consolidate and maintain his authority and to weed out recalcitrants and potential opponents. An intensely suspicious person, bordering on paranoia, even before the war, Stalin avoided excessive reliance and dependence upon single subordinates or institutions for support or information. He encouraged rivalry and intrigue among them, rotating his favoritism and arousing jealousy and fear; no single subordinate ever emerged as a clearcut designated successor and Stalin took care to prevent the undue accumulation of power by any one associate. Thus, Khrushchev writes:

> After taking up my job in Moscow . . . I even began to suspect that one of the reasons Stalin had called me back to Moscow was to influence the balance of power in the collective and to put a check on Beria and Malenkov. It seemed sometimes that Stalin was afraid of Beria and would have been glad to get rid of him but didn't know how to do it.[48]

Stalin also resorted to the creation of alternate channels of information as additional crosschecks on the reliability, competence and trustworthiness of his Politburo associates. Thus, Khrushchev again reports that apparently

'Stalin had useful channels of information which by-passed me and which he trusted more than my own report'.[49] Khrushchev himself often served as an alternative channel for Stalin; as his own account betrays. A particularly unnerving way of checking on his subordinates was to intrigue with their immediate deputies and to arouse their ambitions. This was especially true with the secret police, where Stalin successfully employed Menzhinsky against Derzhinsky, Yagoda against Menzhinsky, Yezhov against Yagoda and Beria against Yezhov.

Another check was to assemble a personal staff or chancellery separate and distinct from the established organs of the party and state. Consisting of particularly brutal and servile types they would cater to Stalin's penchant for unusual whims, feed his suspicions and orchestrate the dark side of his personality, which was ample. Beholden only to Stalin, with neither superiors nor subordinates, they constituted an inner check on other Politburo members. Khrushchev and others mention as particularly odious people like Mekhlis, Shkiryatov, Shcherbakov, Sergienko and Poskrebyshev.

This was, of course, part of his pattern in segmenting and compartmentalizing issues and personalities. He convened full regular sessions episodically and haphazardly, preferring instead to establish various 'commissions' on different topics or issues, consisting of from three to nine members, the so-called triplets, quartets, quintets, septets and novenaries.[50] The latter could have been devised to exclude a single person, given the size of the Politburo at that time. According to Khrushchev, this device served to disorient the other members of the Politburo. It is apparent from Khrushchev's account that he was not consulted regularly or very often during the prewar and early war period. From this he mistakenly assumed that Stalin rarely consulted anyone. Yet Khrushchev's own account suggests that Stalin was simply consulting with others more regularly than with Khrushchev.[51] Khrushchev was particularly bitter about being excluded from decisions on foreign policy and defense. He asserts that he learned about foreign policy decisions usually by accident or happenstance and that Stalin discussed military matters only once with him and just because he happened to be around.[52] Khrushchev writes elsewhere that Stalin took particular pains to isolate other Politburo members from the professional military to forestall the possible cultivation of personal relationships with them that could pose a threat to Stalin's authority.[53]

Institutionally, decisionmaking procedures concerning national security should have posed no particular difficulty. The Sovnarkom's Committee of Defense, presided over by the head of the Soviet government and including high party and state officials, could have functioned effectively as an inner defense cabinet or national security council, coordinating matters at the highest levels, resolving issues and problems and transmitting decisions to the Defense and Naval commissariats through their respective Supreme Councils, which in turn could transmit them to operational agencies. This did not happen because Stalin not only did not fully trust the loyalty of his subordinates, but considered himself more competent than they in the exercise of political, military and even technological judgement.

Surrounded by subordinates, who were clearly junior in both age and experience, carrying imposing titles and ranks which Stalin had bestowed upon them, but who were fearful of acting independently, Stalin had created a situation in which only he could function as coordinator. Almost all observers argue undeviatingly that Stalin considered himself the foremost authority on higher military and strategic affairs. He involved himself in virtually all military and defense-related decisions whether as trivial as the design of a rifle bullet, or as important as going to war. Stalin would not hesitate to reach deep down into the bowels of the ministries and to call without warning deputy commissars, heads of design bureaus and military commanders to consult with them on various matters or to issue direct orders and instructions to them without bothering to inform their formal superiors.

Estimates of Stalin's military competence vary considerably ranging from those, including many foreign statesmen, who were impressed with both his grasp of high strategy and mastery of detail, to those, like Khrushchev, who considered him meddlesome, incompetent and inept.[54] Irrespective of his military competence, Stalin was essentially untutored and self-taught in military matters and his inordinate self-appreciation of his brilliance and contempt for his closest military advisors like Voroshilov made him particularly susceptible to charlatans and quacks. In fact, Stalin had himself anointed as the 'Coryphaeous of all science', not simply in military affairs, and was victimized by the pseudoscientific claims of quacks like Lysenko in biology and Dr Bogomolets in medicine, who convinced Stalin that his antirecticular cytotoxic serum would prolong his life. Various charlatans claiming the invention or discovery of miracle weapons and materials frequently found an audience with Stalin.

The decision to go to war, whether initiated or in response to an attack, is the ultimate national security decision. And the Soviet Union soon after the 18th Party Congress was confronted with the issue of impending war, as Hitler marched into Prague and threatened Poland with destruction. Moscow had to choose between the risks of aligning itself with the Western powers against Hitler or seeking an arrangement with Germany. Hitler was determined to attack Poland and Stalin was confronted with a grave problem of national security for a state that was seriously weakened by the purges.

Although independent documentation, particularly on the German side, conclusively demonstrates that the events leading to the Nazi-Soviet pact in 1939 involved careful, calculated and secret negotiations and involved many Soviet officials in various meetings and contacts, Khrushchev maintains that the Nazi-Soviet pact came as a complete surprise to him and other members of the Politburo, who were kept in the dark about the negotiations. He further claims that this was typical of the way he and other members of the Politburo learned about important foreign policy and national security decisions. According to Khrushchev, the entire matter was handled by Stalin and Molotov, whom he described several times as being the associate who 'stood closest to Stalin in decisionmaking' during this period.[55] One day when he arrived in Moscow on his way to a duck-hunt at Voroshilov's preserve, he was informed by Stalin that Ribbentrop was about to arrive with a proposal and that he would discuss it with the leadership that evening. To Khrushchev's surprise, he found Voroshilov, the defense commissar, at the duck-hunt with Malenkov and Bulganin. Voroshilov at the time was the chief Soviet negotiator with the British and French. Other marshals and generals were also at the duck-hunt. They were then briefed about the pact that evening. What is remarkable about this account is that apparently Voroshilov was also kept uninformed of Ribbentrop's impending arrival.

According to Khrushchev, Stalin fully expected Hitler to violate the treaty and attack the Soviet Union once the opportunity presented itself. Under the stresses and strains of an impending confrontation, particularly after the Nazi victories in the West, Stalin, according to Khrushchev's account, isolated himself even more in the decisionmaking process and engaged in continuous violation of party and constitutional norms. The system of compartmentalization was intensified:

> We had long since become accustomed to the practice that if you weren't told anything, you didn't ask . . . Information was carefully selected, limited and weighed by Stalin before it was passed on to the Politbureau. He had no right to do this, according to the Party statutes. The fact that he did it anyway was another manifestation of the arbitrary rule which acquired the aspect of law under Stalin.[56]

Among other things, the Nazi-Soviet pact and its various secret annexes and protocols amounted to a contingent decision to go to war against Poland, and in accordance with these agreements, the Red Army invaded Poland from the east and the country was partitioned. The Soviet military occupation of eastern Poland was characterized by gross ineptitude, which did not go unnoticed by the Germans, and the lack of military preparation and coordination at the top was to become even more evident during the war with Finland, which was initiated by Moscow on 30 November 1939. Khrushchev maintained that it was Stalin's idea and decision to send an ultimatum to Finland in 1939 and to start the war, and he accused Stalin of both political misjudgment and military incompetence in dealing with Finland.[57] His charge of military incompetence and lack of direction from the top is supported by others. Thus, Admiral Kuznetsov writes that in the midst of the war with Finland, 'there was no organ to coordinate the operations of the army and navy'.[58] Presumably this was the function of the Committee of Defense, but this body was composed only of high political officials and, except for Voroshilov, included no military professionals. Hence, according to Kuznetsov:

> Major decisions were still made in Stalin's office, where the People's Commissar of Defense and the Chief of the General Staff were usually present. Some executives were also summoned. Apparently this system dated back to the time when the People's Commissariat of Defense was in charge of all the armed forces including the navy. Now that the People's Commissariat of the Navy was independent, the navy men found themselves in an awkward position. Very often decisions concerning our fleet were adopted without them.[59]

It should again be emphasized that Stalin, at this time, still held no formal position of legal responsibility in the state. Nevertheless, he was *de facto* head of the government and Commander-in-Chief of the Armed Forces, although there was warrant for this neither in the constitution nor party statutes. It was as if the Soviet system was designed only to function at the macrolevel, and even at the apex, the process was murky.

Admiral Kuznetsov was particularly sensitive to the lack of coordination at the top and vulnerable to the disorientations of institutional and procedural ambiguities and uncertainties:

> Before the War, neither military institutions nor high defense officials had clearly defined rights and obligations. Experience has shown that in questions of supreme importance, the smallest ambiguity is intolerable. Each official should know his place and the limit of his responsibility.[60]

Kuznetsov, furthermore, did not perceive any great improvement in the situation after Stalin became head of government:

> In the late 1930s, although the People's Commissariat of Defense was considered subordinate to the Council of People's Commissars and its Chairman, military questions were, in reality, decided by Stalin. When I was appointed People's Commissar of the Navy, in my ignorance I at first attempted to bring all questions to V. M. Molotov, Chairman of the Council of People's Commissars. But it was very difficult. Minor, daily affairs still moved but important ones got stuck. Whenever I was persistent, it was suggested that I turn to Stalin. And this was not easy at all. At first he treated me indulgently, since I was a new People's Commissar, but soon he became stern, official and rarely accessible. He often left our written reports unanswered . . . In 1941, when Stalin assumed the post of Chairman of the Council of People's Commissars, the system of leadership did not, in effect, change. In any event, I cannot say that it became better. Stalin himself supervised the People's Commissariat of Defense, without delegating any of his authority. The People's Commissar of the Navy found himself in a still more complicated situation. Molotov, as Stalin's deputy, and A. A. Zhdanov, as Secretary of the Central Committee, handled naval affairs. But naval affairs were connected, as a rule, with general military questions, which these men were in no position to decide.[61]

The precise role of the Secretariat, the Orgburo and the Central Committee in decisionmaking on foreign policy and defense policy during this period is not entirely clear. The Orgburo concerned itself primarily with party organizational matters, while the Secretariat was invested with the responsibility of monitoring the execution of party policies and decisions through government organs. The Central Committee served largely as a soundingboard for reports and addresses by Stalin and other leaders on various matters, including defense and foreign policy. Reports to the Central Committee would often be published, but not the stenographic proceedings themselves. Andrei Zhdanov, the Leningrad leader, was the party secretary overseeing foreign policy and on at least one occasion he criticized Molotov on Soviet foreign policy before the Supreme Soviet, to which Molotov responded deferentially, a dead giveaway that Stalin was behind the criticism.[62] In a more restricted sense the Central Committee served more as a vehicle for communicating current and intended policy to important second-echelon Soviet leaders rather than as a forum for debate and policy formulation. The Supreme Soviet served much the same purpose for broader Soviet and foreign audiences.

The coordination of the foreign and defense commissariats also posed special problems, especially the role of the Foreign Commissariat, before it was headed by Molotov. The Defense Commissariat was headed by Marshal Voroshilov, a full member of the Politburo, who was an old crony of Stalin's and part of the core leadership. The Foreign Commissariat, however, was headed by a lower-ranking party member, Maxim Litvinov, who did not always enjoy Stalin's confidence. The relationship between the Foreign Commissariat and Politburo was unique. Although Litvinov normally dealt with Molotov, his formal and immediate superior, who would make decisions himself or take it to Stalin for a decision or for further discussion in whatever forum Stalin chose, Stalin would frequently deal directly with Litvinov and his chief advisors and on a few occasions Litvinov would report directly to the Politburo. The principal function of the Foreign Commissariat, aside from conducting routine diplomacy, would be to coordinate the work of various departments dealing with foreign affairs, assemble and evaluate intelligence information flowing from different channels, devise strategy and policy, examine analyses, projects and reports drawn up by foreign policy specialists, study reports of diplomats abroad and then make a comprehensive report either to Stalin, or the Politburo as a whole.

Once decisions were made, channels would be reversed: decisions would be transmitted orally or in writing by Molotov to Litvinov for execution. These bureaucratic channels were often ignored in extremely important or urgent matters and Stalin would act directly with Molotov or his Politburo Commission. Then they would personally give instructions to Litvinov.

When Molotov replaced Litvinov as Foreign Commissar in May 1939, this cumbersome procedure was simplified. The Nazi-Soviet pact, as noted earlier, was worked out principally by Stalin and Molotov, with Zhdanov and Mikoyan the only other members of the Politburo apparently appraised of the crucial decisions contemplated. The Politburo commission on foreign affairs gradually increased in size until by 1945 it was large enough to be converted by Stalin from a 'sextet' to a 'septet'.[63] As it grew in size, so its importance diminished. During the war, as will be detailed below, Stalin appeared to consult only Molotov on questions of foreign policy and frequently made decisions on the spot at Big Three conferences.

Khrushchev claims that 'Stalin depended upon the *Cheka* for intelligence', and there is little question but that Stalin relied upon the secret police not only to provide him with intelligence data and information, but also to keep watch on Soviet diplomats abroad and to keep an eye on the military. Both were riddled with Chekists. But Stalin relied on more informal methods of verifying information from his administrative channels. In foreign affairs, for example, Stalin employed personal emissaries like Boris Steiger as informal liaison with the foreign press and diplomatic community who often served as conduits for information and communication in both directions.

Coordination at the top was lacking largely because Stalin preferred compartmentalization and fractionalization of authority and functions in order to minimize the possibilities of intrigue and conspiracy. This became increasingly counterproductive and so on 6 May 1941, on the eve of the German attack, Stalin cut the procedural Gordian knot and replaced Molotov as chairman of the Council of People's Commissars. But the consequences of the institutional and procedural confusion at the top were to wreak their vengeance during the period just prior to the war and in the immediate weeks thereafter. By 8 August 1941, a bare three months after having held no formal office of legal responsibility for nearly two decades, Stalin collected all of the loose institutional strands of the decisionmaking process and was invested with the following titles and positions:

(1)   secretary-general of the party;
(2)   head of the Politburo;
(3)   head of the Secretariat;
(4)   chairman of the Orgburo;
(5)   head of the Central Committee;
(6)   chairman, Council of People's Commissars;
(7)   chairman, State Defense Committee;
(8)   Commissar of Defense;
(9)   head of the General Headquarters of the Supreme High Command;
(10) Commander-in-Chief of the Armed Forces.

DECISIONMAKING DURING THE WAR: THE STALINIST PROCESS INSTITUTIONALIZED

Decisionmaking institutions and processes were subject to serious modifications during the war. The prewar setup contributed in no small measure to the lack of military preparation and the initial military disasters. The chief scapegoat in retrospect was Stalin, but by most accounts he is also judged the principal architect of victory and emerged as a gifted commander. Considerable controversy continues to rage around both issues inside and outside the Soviet Union. Stalin was principally responsible for the lack of preparation and the initial military reverses because all decisions had to be made in Stalin's office and this became logistically impossible. According to most Soviet eyewitness accounts and military historians, Stalin refused to believe that Hitler would violate the pact with Moscow and attack without provocation in spite of mounting evidence coming from all directions that Germany was preparing for war. In the days before the invasion reliable intelligence and espionage reports of an impending German attack were also waved away by Stalin as possible provocations designed to stampede the Soviet Union into some imprudent action.[64] Conversely, Stalin may have thought the Soviet Union woefully unfit to fight a war and judged that the risks of provoking the Germans to attack by taking military preparations were higher than the risks of an attack if Moscow continued to appease Hitler and thus avert war. By ignoring German military preparations, Stalin in this way could signal his *bona fides* to Hitler. Even after the German planes had attacked Soviet cities and tanks had lumbered across the frontier, Stalin was reluctant to order resistance, considering these attacks to be provocations by German generals bent on inciting war between Moscow and Berlin. Apparently, no clear plans existed concerning the operational organization and function of a Soviet High Command. The situation was so chaotic on the day of the German attack that no provisions had even been made to house a High Command headquarters.[65]

Only after Molotov reported to Stalin that the German ambassador had delivered a formal declaration of war did Stalin finally accept the reality of war. Much valuable and critical time had already been wasted during these early hours, and the institutional channels of national security decision-making that were still chaotic at the top were now to be further pathologized by Stalin's erratic behavior. All power had been concentrated, *de facto*, in Stalin's person; he was now also saddled with legal responsibility because of his formal position as head of government, but lines of authority were still confused. Marshal Timoshenko had replaced Voroshilov as Commissar of Defense in May 1940 after the Finnish war, and Voroshilov was kicked upstairs to serve as deputy chairman of the Committee of Defense, now chaired by Stalin. The Soviet Constitution, then as now, did not stipulate a commander-in-chief in advance, and the post, which was held by a professional military officer, was abolished in the 1920s as too dangerous. Neither the Commissar of Defense nor the Defense Committee, nor the Main Military Council could function as a surrogate. The *de facto* commander was, of course, Stalin, who at the beginning of the war was still loathe to accept formal responsibility for the powers vested in his person. Marshal Timoshenko, who was likely to be saddled with the *de facto* responsibility for military reverses, sought to eliminate the confusion and prepared a draft decree for Stalin's signature naming Stalin as commander-in-chief. Stalin waved it aside for Politburo discussion and the next day, 23 June, had issued over the names of the Central Committee and the Sovnarkom a decree establishing a general headquarters of the High Command (*Stavka Glav-novo Komandovaniya*), with Timoshenko as chairman and Stalin, Molotov, Voroshilov, Budenny, Zhukov and Kuznetsov as members. No commander-in-chief or supreme commander was named, although Timoshenko was clearly saddled with legal responsibility.[66]

According to Zhukov, who participated in the meetings, 'the Commissar of Defense was not consulted about these alterations, whereas it would have been better to have adopted our draft in which Stalin was named Commander-in-Chief'. Zhukov then graphically describes the channels of confusion:

> After all with the present scheme of things, Commissar for Defense Timoshenko could not take any fundamental decision without Stalin anyway. So there were actually two Commanders-in-Chief: Commissar for Defense Timoshenko, *de jure*, in accordance with the decree, and Stalin, *de facto*. This gravely complicated troop control and unavoidably led to a waste of time in decision-making and in issuing instructions.[67]

Thus, Timoshenko was Commissar of Defense and chairman of the High Command, but he did not make the actual decisions, for Stalin continued to dictate the texts of his directives. Stalin at the beginning of the war even issued a directive calling for an absurd military action to which he affixed Marshal Zhukov's name, although the marshal was 600 miles away at the time and unaware of its contents. Naturally, Zhukov had to bear full responsibility for the débâcle that resulted.[68]

Controversy still rages over Stalin's behavior during the first weeks of the war, from 24 June to 2 July 1941. According to Khrushchev, Stalin became so depressed and withdrawn that he disappeared from view and abandoned his party and state posts in panic. Other eyewitness and participant accounts about Stalin's behavior during this period are mixed; many are self-serving and some participants have given contradictory versions.[69] Among the most confusing are the memoirs of Marshal Zhukov.[70] In any event Stalin's name was back in circulation on 30 June when the definitive top wartime decisionmaking body was created, the State Defense Committee (*Gosudarstvennyi Komitet Oborony*), with Stalin as chairman. This body was established by a joint decree of the Central Committee of the party, the Presidium of the Supreme Soviet and the Council of People's Commissars, thus touching all institutional sources of authority. This new body had sweeping and extraordinary powers. 'A State Defense Committee has been formed to deal with the rapid mobilization of all the country's resources; all power and authority of the State are vested in it.'[71] With the establishment of this body, order was gradually extricated from chaos. Informal and formal lines of power and responsibility were finally merging in Stalin's person, where real decisionmaking authority was located. The unsatisfactory and confusing state of affairs created by the existence of the two commanders-in-chief was soon rectified. On 10 July the State Defense Committee reorganized the General Headquarters of the High Command into the General Headquarters of the Supreme High Command (*Stavka Verkhovnovo Glavnokomandovaniya*), with Stalin now as chairman and Molotov, Voroshilov, Timoshenko, Budenny, Zhukov and Shaposhnikov as members. With the inclusion of Molotov, this body was transformed from a purely military body into a politico-military organ. Admiral Kuznetsov and the navy were left out. On 19 July Stalin was appointed Commissar of Defense, and on 8 August he assumed the post of Supreme Commander-in-Chief (*Verkhovnyi Glavnokomanduyushshii*). Two days later the jurisdiction of the General Staff was extended to cover the entire armed forces with its reconstitution as the General Staff of the Armed Forces.[72] All of the loose political and military strands were now tied at the top. Henceforth the supreme body of strategic leadership would be known as General Headquarters of the Supreme High Command (*Stavka*). Directly below *Stavka* in the chain of command was the General Staff:

The General Staff was the General Headquarters' sole executive apparatus. The General Headquarters' orders and instructions were normally issued through the General Staff. Stalin's study in the Kremlin was, in fact, a place where General Headquarters' decisions were taken and directives for the Fronts adopted.[73]

Changes in decisionmaking processes followed in the wake of the creation of these new intermediate institutional structures. First of all, the major institutional settings of decisionmaking shifted from party organs, that is, Politburo and Secretariat, to state organs, that is, the Council of Ministers, the State Defense Committee and the General Headquarters of the Supreme High Command.

Stalin retained his position in the Secretariat, but his title of general secretary fell into disuse. The Politburo and the Secretariat atrophied as decisionmaking organs, when virtually the entire Politburo membership found itself serving on various state institutions. Only six plenums of the Central Committee, for example, met from 1938 until Stalin's death, and only two party congresses were convened during 1934–52. In contrast, after the war, elections to the Supreme Soviet and meetings of the Supreme Soviet were resumed on schedule.

Stalin now held the following five positions and titles, affiliated with the state: (1) chairman of the Council of Ministers and its Presidium, that is, head of government; (2) chairman of the State Defense Committee; (3) Commissar of Defense; (4) chairman of General Headquarters of the Supreme High Command; and (5) Supreme Commander-in-Chief of the Armed Forces. He was subsequently appointed to the rank of Marshal of the Soviet Union and Generalissimo of the Armed Forces.[74]

This array of state, party and military positions and titles served to tie every possible gap or crack in the decisionmaking network. Stalin now covered all of his institutional bases, and this accounts for much of the confusion concerning which institution was meeting at any particular time, since the membership was overlapping. It has been stated that the Politburo, Orgburo and Secretariat met over 200 times during the war, and that 'the chief questions of the war were decided' at these meetings.[75] But since many Politburo sessions were held jointly with the State Defense Committee, the real viability of party organs as decisionmaking institutions during the war remains in doubt. The most important decisionmaking institution during the war was the State Defense Committee. Initially, it consisted only of Stalin (chairman), Molotov (deputy chairman), Voroshilov (Defense Commissar), Beria (secret police) and Malenkov. It was later expanded to include Kaganovich (Commissar of Railroads), Mikoyan (Trade Commissar), Bulganin (Deputy Commissar of Defense) and Voznesensky (Chairman of Gosplan). All members but Malenkov held positions in the state apparatus and not all were Politburo members. As noted earlier, Zhdanov, Khrushchev, Andreev and Kalinin were excluded from this body. This serves to explain the paucity of information in Khrushchev's memoirs on decisionmaking during wartime and the work of central state agencies and the State Defense Committee.

Curiously enough, it is Marshal Zhukov who gives us a rare glimpse of the State Defense Committee at work under Stalin's direction:

> The State Committee for Defense, whose sittings took place at any time of day or night in the Kremlin or at Stalin's country house, discussed and decided upon the crucial issues. Together with the Party Central Committee, and the People's Commissars whose rights had been considerably

broadened, the Committee examined the plans for the biggest military operations . . . Often sharp arguments arose at the Committee sittings. Views were expressed in definite and sharp terms. Stalin would usually walk up and down the room past the table, carefully listening to those who argued. He himself was short-spoken and would often stop others with remarks like 'come to the point', 'make yourself clear'. He opened the sittings without any preliminaries and spoke in a quiet voice and freely, and only on the main points. He was laconic and precise.

If no agreement was reached at the sitting, a commission would be immediately formed of representatives of the two extreme sides which had to reach agreement and report on the proposals it would work out. Such incidents happened only when Stalin himself had not arrived at a definite decision. But should he come to the sitting with a ready resolution there would be no argument at all, or it would die down soon, if he supported one of the parties.[76]

It should also be noted that during the war and afterward Stalin's private secretariat or staff, autonomous, distinct and separate from the regular bureaucracies, grew and functioned as Stalin's personal staff. The body was neither a party nor state organ and scheduled agendas and meetings for state and party bodies, gathered information, functioned as an extension of Stalin's control and coordination authority, and drafted Stalin's speeches and various state and party documents. It grew into a relatively large body and was headed by Poskrebyshev, Stalin's 'shieldbearer' as Khrushchev called him, who was elected a candidate member of the Central Committee in 1934 and was one of the few to survive to be re-elected a full member in 1939 and again in 1952.

All decisions of the State Defense Committee were binding on all party and state institutions. On purely military matters the general headquarters of the Supreme High Command was the principal decisionmaking organ and consisted of Stalin and his principal military commanders. Stalin's role as a wartime commander and decisionmaker has been subject to considerable controversy, but mainly among Soviet observers. The accounts are contradictory and inconsistent and the reliability, accuracy and honesty of some material is highly questionable. In particular, Khrushchev's image of a frightened, bumbling, incompetent wartime leader is to be seriously questioned. It is at variance with most Soviet military memoir literature and with those of outside observers. It is probably true that Stalin may have panicked to some degree in the early days of the war, but Marshal Zhukov's memoirs challenge Khrushchev's account. He gives the following description of Stalin at work as commander-in-chief:

> There was a big table on which members of the General Staff and General Headquarters spread out maps and reported on the situation at the fronts. They stood while they reported; sometimes they used notes. As Stalin listened to a report, he paced the room in big strides, waddling somewhat. From time to time he would come up to the table and, bending over, scrutinize a map. Or he would go to his desk, take up a pack of tobacco, tear it up and slowly fill his pipe . . .

Conferences to project strategic policies were normally held in the presence of the Members of the State Committee for Defense. Also summoned were top officers of the General Staff, Chief of the Air Force, Chief of Ordinance, Chief of Armour and Automotive Service, Chief of Rear Services, heads of some of the Defense Commissariat departments. Front Commanders were summoned whenever matters within their province came up for discussion . . . As a rule, the General Headquarters worked in an orderly, business-like manner. Everyone had a chance to state his opinion. Stalin was equally stern to everybody and rather formal. He listened attentively to anybody speaking to the point.

Incidentally, I know from my war experiences that one could safely bring up matters unlikely to please Stalin, argue them out and firmly carry the point. Those who assert it was not so are wrong . . .

It was impossible to go to Stalin without being perfectly familiar with the situation plotted on the map and to report tentative or (which was worse) exaggerated information. Stalin would not tolerate hit-or-miss answers, he demanded utmost accuracy and clarity . . . He had a tenacious memory, perfectly remembered whatever was said and would not miss a chance to give a severe dressing-down. That is why we drafted staff documents as best we possibly could under the circumstances.[77]

Zhukov describes Stalin at work not only in the State Defense Committee and *Stavka*, but also in decisionmaking sessions convened informally outside institutional settings:

Many political, military and other issues of nation-wide importance were debated and decided upon not at official meetings of the Central Committee Politbureau or its Secretariat, but at night, over dinner at Stalin's apartment or his summer cottage, usually attended by those members of the Politbureau who were most closely associated with Stalin. And it was there, during those customarily very modest dinners, that Stalin would parcel out instructions to members of the Politbureau or to People's Commissars who were invited whenever something within their jurisdiction was discussed. The Chief of Staff was sometimes invited to participate in these functions together with the Defense Commissar.[78]

Marshal Zhukov's rival, Ivan Konev, gives a similar appraisal of Stalin as did Marshals Malinovsky and Vasilievsky. In fact, with few exceptions, Stalin won high praise from his former military subordinates, who viewed him as a harsh, difficult and often brutal man, but one who nevertheless was highly effective, competent and intelligent as a wartime leader.[79]

It is probably true, as Khrushchev writes, that Stalin involved himself in all kinds of decisions, large and small, important and trivial, and relied excessively upon his self-perceived superior qualities of judgement and intelligence to compensate for his lack of technical knowledge and competence. 'Stalin', Khrushchev writes, 'valued his own abilities and views much more than those of anyone else', which was probably true.[80] He complains that

Stalin insisted on making decisions or being consulted on the nature, design and production of military weapons, which Khrushchev maintains was partly responsible for Soviet unpreparedness at the time of the German attack: 'Part of the problem was that Stalin tried to supervise our manufacturing of munitions and mechanized equipment all by himself, with the result that nobody knew what state our arsenal was in.'[81] Marshal Zhukov confirms Khrushchev's observation that Stalin concerned himself somewhat excessively about the design of military equipment, but provides both a different characterization and judgement about the consequences:

Before the war . . . I can only repeat that Stalin devoted a good deal of attention to problems of armament and *materiel*. He frequently met with chief aircraft, artillery and tank designers whom he would question in great detail about the progress achieved in designing various types of equipment in our country and abroad. To give him his due, it must be said that he was fairly well versed in the characteristics of the basic types of armament. Stalin urged the chief designers and managers of munitions plants . . . to produce new models of aircraft, tanks, guns, and other major *materiel* within established time-limits and to make sure their quality should not only be on a par with foreign-made models but even superior to them. Without Stalin's approval not a single item of armament or *materiel* was either adopted or discarded – and this certainly curtailed the initiative of the Commissar for Defense and his deputies responsible for armaments of the Red Army.[82]

It is not always easy to discern the fine line which distinguishes quackery from brilliance, the charlatan from the authentic genius. It should be noted that perhaps the identical vulnerability which rendered Stalin susceptible to the importuning of charlatans and quacks made him also receptive to the urgent letter of a young Soviet physicist in the armed forces that he authorize the mobilization of resources and effort for the development of an atomic bomb.[83] Stalin was also probably persuaded in part by intelligence information concerning both the American and German efforts in the same direction. And so Stalin on the eve of the Battle of Stalingrad, when the fortunes of the Soviet Union appeared to be at their nadir, had the State Defense Committee issue a directive establishing an atomic program, with I. V. Kurchatov in charge. It was Stalin also who quickly grasped the political and strategic implications of the American achievement, when it was casually revealed by Truman at the Potsdam Conference. According to Marshal Zhukov, Stalin and Molotov immediately understood the ominous signal and interpreted it as what one might call the first exercise in attempted atomic blackmail:

In actual fact, on returning to his quarters after this meeting, Stalin, in my presence, informed Molotov about his conversation with Truman. 'They are raising the price,' Molotov told Stalin. The latter reacted immediately with a laugh. 'Let them. We'll have to talk it over with Kurchatov and get him to speed things up.' I realized they were talking about research on the atomic bomb.[84]

Upon his return to Moscow and after the destruction of Hiroshima, Stalin summoned Kurchatov and other specialists and high officials to the Kremlin and told them:

> 'A single demand of you,' said Stalin. 'Provide us with atomic weapons in the shortest possible time. You know that Hiroshima has shaken the whole world. The equilibrium has been destroyed. Provide the bomb – it will remove a great danger from us.'[85]

Even Khrushchev grudgingly concedes that 'Stalin drew the correct conclusion' about the strategic and political implications of the atomic bomb, but captiously contends that Stalin was animated more by fear than political insight:

> Stalin was frightened to the point of cowardice. He ordered that all our technological efforts be directed toward developing atomic weapons of our own. I remember that Beria was in full charge of the project.[86]

As David Holloway points out, 'the Soviet decision to build the atomic bomb was one of the most important weapons decisions of this century, leading ultimately to the formation of Soviet strategic forces, which are such a major factor in international policies today', and suggests that the decision was largely the product of Stalin's intuitive political judgement and his penchant for intervening in scientific and technological developments:

> The military rationale for the atomic bomb was simple . . . The military appear to have played absolutely no part in the decision. This was not surprising since Stalin was Supreme Commander-in-Chief during the war and the final authority on all military matters, whether doctrinal or technological . . . The political rationale for the atomic bomb was more important: in order to safeguard its own political gains and to restrain the United States from offensive military or political moves, the Soviet Union would have to have the atomic bomb.[87]

That Stalin inordinately intervened in decisions concerning the design, development and production of weapons and armaments is rather universally conceded, but whether, on balance, the net effect of his interference was positive or negative remains a subject of substantial controversy.

There appears to be little question, in spite of the avalanche of postwar Soviet accounts emphasizing the importance of party organs in organizing the country during wartime, that the organs and institutions of the state, including the State Defense Committee, superseded in importance and virtually eclipsed those of the party. After all, it was the Soviet state, not the party, that was engaged in war, dealt with allies and other states, and provided the source of patriotism that was so essential in mobilizing the population. The party, Marxism–Leninism and party institutions were deliberately played down; Russian history, glories, victories, heroes and patriotic symbols were played up; even the Orthodox Church was partly rehabilitated, much to the consternation of some party purists. The Comintern was dissolved as an obstacle to victory; the war was defined in patriotic not ideological terms. It was thus called the Second Great Patriotic War (the first being the war against Napoleon), not the Great Anti-Fascist War. Motherland and Fatherland were resurrected as symbols, and the word 'proletariat' virtually disappeared from the Soviet lexicon. Former imperial-type titles, ranks and uniforms were introduced into the military, the diplomatic service and other bureaucracies. Stalin, himself, emphasized his formal state and military positions rather than his party titles. The ideological foundation for the resurrection of the state as a positive, permanent institution was laid down by Stalin in his report to the 18th Party Congress, where he castigated those who were impatiently waiting for the Soviet state to 'wither away' and declared that it would be around for some time to come.

After the war, the new status of the state was emphasized with an important change in nomenclature. The designations People's Commissariats and Council of People's Commissars, which were cherished by Lenin because they smacked of 'revolution' and emphasized the temporary character of the state, were replaced with minister and Council of Ministers, the same designations used by the Imperial regime. The state and its institutions emerged as the most important structural base for power challenging the hitherto declared legitimate monopoly of the party and its institutions.

Khrushchev in his memoirs and in his Secret Speech repeatedly moans about the virtual withering away of party decisionmaking organs. No party congress to legitimize the party leadership was convened for a dozen years, in patent violation of party rules, but the Supreme Soviet met on schedule to legalize the leadership of the state; the Central Committee literally vanished, and the same fate appeared to be overtaking the Politburo. Thus, in his Secret Speech at the 20th Party Congress, Khrushchev maintained:

> Even after the end of the war . . . Central Committee plenums were hardly ever called. It should be sufficient to mention that during the years of the Patriotic War, not a single Central Committee plenum took place . . . Stalin did not even want to meet and talk with Central Committee members.[88]

And with respect to the Politburo:

> After the war, Stalin became even more capricious, irritable, and brutal; in particular his suspicion grew. His persecution mania reached unbelievable dimensions. Everything was decided by him alone without any consideration for anyone or anything. . . . Sessions of the Political Bureau occurred only occasionally . . . many decisions were taken by one person or in a roundabout way, without collective discussion. . . . The importance of the Political Bureau was reduced and its work disorganized by the creation within the Political Bureau of various commissions. . . . *The result of this was that some members of the Political Bureau were in this way kept away from participation in the decisions of the most important state matters*.[89]

Decisions were being made, meetings were held, consultations took place, but mainly in state organs with Stalin and the principal figures in his entourage installed in the commanding heights of the state apparatus. Party organs for Stalin apparently appeared as redundant and unnecessary as decision-making institutions, forums, or settings. During this period Soviet decision-making was concentrated in a core of relatively permanent personalities, especially Stalin, rather than in institutions and they moved from institution to institution to make their decisions, which were made by people and not abstractions.

DECISIONMAKING IN THE POSTWAR PERIOD: THE DISINTEGRATION OF PROCESS

Whereas before the war Stalin separated process from institutions and relocated both process and power in his person, during the war his behavior was somewhat institutionalized and orderly and relatively predictable processes emerged. Subordinates gradually developed a sense of what Stalin wanted, anticipated his decisions, and even were able to distinguish between those decisions they could risk making on their own and those that had to be referred to Stalin. This varied, of course, from one person to another, but it was a decisionmaking process. After the war, the process once again began to disintegrate not because of purges and destruction of institutions, but because institutions were allowed to atrophy. Stalin's behavior became increasingly erratic, unpredictable and even irrational. The distinction between social gatherings and official meetings of the leadership became increasingly blurred as Stalin conducted much of his work at banquets, at the Kremlin cinema, or at his dacha on the outskirts of Moscow.

The proliferation of state institutions during the war, the military victory over the Germans, the occupation of Eastern Europe and territorial acquisitions, and the USSR's emergence as the second most powerful state in the international community all served to enhance the importance, status and prestige of state institutions to the detriment of the party. The state assumed greater and greater functions and responsibilities: its bureaucratic structures grew and proliferated; many new potential institutional bases of power were developing, all outside the party structure; Stalin was aging and personal rivalries for Stalin's favor were gradually converted into personal rivalries to succeed Stalin. And while institutional power structures were not necessary in the competition to gain favor, which was highly personal, competition to gain power and to succeed or survive the demise of Stalin made institutional bases critical and important. It was during the postwar period that the foundations were laid for the emergence not only of cliques and personal networks among members of the Politburo or leadership, but of nascent competing bureaucratic structures and other quasi-interest aggregates. This meant that Stalin's subordinates, if they were to survive or succeed Stalin, would have to cultivate, develop and consolidate a reliable and loyal network of supporters, and to do this would in turn have to represent their interests as well. Thus Khrushchev inadvertently reveals in his memoirs that he was, indeed, assimilating into his outlook the interests of the Ukraine and its population, as he was criticized for doing. In another connection he mentions the 'bureaucratic resistance of the Moscow apparatus'.[90] As Khrushchev was consolidating his base in the Ukraine, and Zhdanov his in Leningrad, Beria was consolidating his in the secret police and the Caucasus and Malenkov his in the central party apparatus. At this point, no one dared to establish a base in the armed forces, since this could be viewed as not only a base against rivals, but against Stalin as well. Indeed, he did come to recognize that Beria's grip on the police constituted almost as much a threat to him as to Beria's peer rivals, and he tried to separate him from the police apparatus.

Stalin's physical infirmities and mental debilities increasingly manifested themselves – as he became more suspicious, paranoid, irascible, vicious and brutal. Important changes were taking place in the outside world which he could not control; international crises occupied front and center-stage as the Cold War developed. The sense of isolation and encirclement returned, as Stalin saw himself increasingly surrounded by internal and external enemies, imagined or real. Zhdanov died under mysterious circumstances and his Leningrad organization was pulverized. Molotov was married to a Jew and the establishment of the state of Israel unleashed Stalin's anti-Semitic tendencies against Soviet Jews as possible instruments of American manipulation via American Jewry and Israeli dependence upon its goodwill. Madame Molotov, who was indiscreet enough to describe herself as a 'daughter of Israel' to the new Israeli envoy to Moscow, Golda Meir, soon found herself stripped of her positions and exiled to Siberia.[91] Voroshilov's wife was also Jewish and this may have accounted for Stalin's accusations against him.

All this was to have a debilitating impact on the decisionmaking process. Sometime in 1949 Stalin apparently decided to revamp the Soviet leadership and to somehow separate his associates from their nascent power bases. The major beneficiaries of these moves were Malenkov and Khrushchev, since Stalin moved first to nullify or neutralize state structures as possible impediments to his power or choice of successor.

In 1950 Stalin with characteristic suddenness separated all of his ministerial associates from their ministries. They remained as deputy chairmen of the Council of Ministers and on the Politburo, but Molotov was removed as Foreign Minister, Beria as Police Minister and Mikoyan as Foreign Trade Minister. It was during this period that Voroshilov, Molotov and Mikoyan came under suspicion, and that Politburo member and chief of Gosplan, Voznesensky, was ordered executed by Stalin along with other surviving members of Zhdanov's organization, all apparently on Stalin's orders. According to Khrushchev:

> It is a characteristic thing that the decision to remove him [Voznesensky] from the Political Bureau was never discussed but was reached in a devious fashion. In the same way the decision concerning the removal of Kuznetsov and Rodionov from their posts. . . . Stalin also separated one other man from the Political Bureau – Andrei Andreyevich Andreev. This was one of the most unbridled acts of willfulness.[92]

Khrushchev implicates both Beria and Malenkov as coconspirators in the so-called 'Leningrad affair', but Stalin's maneuvers seemed aimed at Beria no less than Voroshilov, Molotov and Mikoyan, and hardly at all at Malenkov and Khrushchev. The old guard was being replaced with new people and they might be just as technically competent or even more so than their predecessors. They were also less dangerous and less likely to intrigue against Stalin or his planned successor.

Nevertheless, during this period of seeming chaos in the Moscow decisionmaking process, decisions continued to be made between 1950 and Stalin's death, including many important decisions dealing with foreign affairs and national security. For example, it was during this period of preparation for a new purge that Stalin was involved in the decision of North Korea to attack South Korea.

In this connection Khrushchev's memoirs throw some interesting light upon Stalin's decisionmaking involving the heads of foreign communist states, that is, Stalin's role in the initiation of the Korean War. According to Khrushchev, Kim Il Sung came to Moscow in late 1949 to consult with Stalin on his intention to incite a rebellion in South Korea that would enable North Korea to intervene and unite the nation. Stalin cautioned prudence and 'persuaded Kim Il Sung that he should think it over, make some calculations, and then come back with a concrete plan'.[93] Stalin expressed doubts about the idea, but Kim returned from North Korea with a plan and told Stalin that he was certain of its success. Stalin was still doubtful and thought the Americans would intervene. Khrushchev writes: 'He was worried that the Americans would jump in, but we [who?] were inclined to think that if the war were fought swiftly – and Kim Il Sung was sure that it could be won swiftly – then intervention by the USA could be avoided.' Stalin decided to consult Mao Tse-tung about Kim's plan. Mao approved and argued that the United States would not intervene because the war would be an internal Korean matter. Khrushchev notes, however:

> I must stress that the war was not Stalin's idea . . . Kim was the initiator. Stalin, of course, didn't try to dissuade him . . . I would have made the same decision myself if I had been in his place.[94]

It was also during this period that Stalin increasingly called midnight 'sessons' of the 'leadership' at his Kremlin study, the Kremlin movie theater or at his dacha, which often lasted until dawn. Stalin systematically attempted to exclude first Voroshilov and then Molotov and Mikoyan from these sessions. Khrushchev does not make clear what institutions the 'sessions' represented informally or otherwise before the 19th Party Congress. He refers to 'us', 'we', the 'leadership', but whether it is meeting as Politburo, Politburo Commission, or anything else, is never made clear. It had to be a party organ, since Khrushchev claimed to be one of Stalin's trusted confidantes during this period at least. As for the others, 'Stalin', who 'himself decided whom to execute and whom to spare', apparently had designs for executing some of the older members of the Politburo. According to Khrushchev:

> Stalin evidently had plans to finish off the old members of the Political Bureau. He often stated that Political Bureau members should be

replaced by new ones. His proposal, after the 19th Party Congress . . . was aimed at the removal of old Political Bureau members and the bringing in of less experienced persons so that these would extol him in all sorts of ways. We can assume that this was also a design to the future annihilation of the old Political Bureau members and, in this way, a cover for all shameful acts of Stalin, acts which we are now considering.[95]

DECISIONMAKING UNDER STALIN AFTER THE 19th PARTY CONGRESS: LAYING THE FOUNDATIONS FOR A NEW PROCESS

Stalin introduced major structural changes in the party decisionmaking organs at the 19th Party Congress that could have resulted in far-reaching changes in the Soviet decisionmaking process, with profound social and political implications. It appears that Stalin once again, in his own idiosyncratic, cruel and treacherous manner, intended to renew the Soviet leadership with young people, to shake up the system, and to pass on not an ossified sociopolitical order governed by a one-man dictatorship that may have served his purposes but would be inadequate to serve those of posterity, but one that would allow upward social mobility and rotation of leadership and ensure stability after his demise. He correctly surmised that Beria, because of his control of the police, and Voroshilov, Molotov and Mikoyan, because of their experience and prestige as 'old Bolsheviks', would persist in holding onto power. In his 'Economic problems of socialism', issued on the eve of the 19th Party Congress, he had accused unspecified 'mistaken comrades' of holding dangerous and incorrect views concerning internal economic development and Soviet foreign policy. Although it appears in retrospect that Molotov and Mikoyan were at opposite ends of 'erroneous' views, they both constituted an impediment to Stalin's plans.

In spite of what Khrushchev has said and written about Stalin and Malenkov, it appears that he and Malenkov were major intended beneficiaries of Stalin's prospective purge, but that he resented his intended role as secondfiddle to Malenkov. This comes through rather clearly in his memoirs, where he reiterates over and over that he, along with Malenkov, constituted part of Stalin's new select inner circle. Khrushchev's account of how the 19th Party Congress was convened clearly illustrates Stalin's decisionmaking procedures in his declining years:

Stalin called us [who?] together and suggested that we should convene a Party Congress. He didn't need to persuade us. We all considered it incredible that there hadn't been a Party Congress for thirteen years. Nor had there even been a Central Committee plenum for some time. The Central Committee hadn't met in either its policy-making or its consultative capacity for years. In short, the Party at large and the Central Committee in particular had been taking no part whatever in the collective leadership. Stalin did everything himself, by-passing the Central Committee and using the Politbureau as little more than a rubber stamp. Stalin rarely bothered to ask the opinion of Politbureau members about a given measure. He would just make a decision and issue a decree.[96]

Stalin also, according to Khrushchev, alone decided the agenda for the Congress and,

> announced that we would assign the General Report to Malenkov . . . As Stalin told us our assignments, they were recorded forthwith. We listened and received our instructions in silence. That's how the agenda for the Nineteenth Party Congress came to be determined and accepted.[97]

Khrushchev was assigned to give a report on the party statutes, probably the second most important report, and drafts of various reports were circulated to other members of the Politburo. Khrushchev's report was, predictably, he writes, criticized and shortened by Malenkov and Beria.

More surprises, however, were in store for Khrushchev and other Polit-buro members at the 1st Plenum of the Central Committee elected after the party congress. Significantly, Khrushchev says nothing about how Central Committee members were selected, but he has some harsh words about other selection procedures. He claims that no one on the Politburo knew in advance of Stalin's plan to enlarge and rename the Politburo as the Pres-idium, except perhaps for Kaganovich, who helped him select the new members. Stalin, he writes, hardly knew some of the new members and therefore needed assistance. But they were all drawn from the full member-ship of the Central Committee, and Khrushchev provides us with no clue as to how they were selected. It could hardly be accidental that the new enlarged Presidium of twenty-five full members and eleven candidate mem-bers represented a calculated balance between Malenkov's supporters and those of Khrushchev.

Stalin's most startling surprise was his proposal for an inner bureau of the new Presidium, which was not provided for in the party statutes. Everybody seemed to agree that the size of the new Presidium was too large to be an effective decisionmaking organ. Stalin said the bureau would meet more often than the full Presidium, 'and would make decisions on all operational questions that might come up'.[98] Stalin then revealed a membership list for the new bureau. It excluded Molotov and Mikoyan, but surprisingly included Voroshilov, along with Malenkov, Khrushchev, Beria, Kaganovich, Saburov, Pervukhin, Bulganin and, of course, Stalin. It was obvious that one intent of the maneuver was to isolate Molotov and Mikoyan. Stalin charged at the plenum that Molotov and Mikoyan were 'Western agents' and for that reason were excluded, but then, everyone wondered, why were they still on the Presidium?

In spite of Stalin's elaborate organizational changes, the same pattern of decisionmaking was resumed: calls or summons from Stalin in the middle of the night, whether in Moscow or on vacation in the Caucasus, long intermin-able dinner sessions, boisterous and often coarse language, dancing, wine, vodka, but no women. Stalin, writes Khrushchev, hated to be alone and these sessions were often more a device to keep Stalin company rather than to transact business.

Apparently, even nine members was too large for Stalin, and from the nine members, Stalin would select an inner core of five, with changing membership. The usual five were: Stalin, Malenkov, Khrushchev, Beria and

Bulganin. Kaganovich and Voroshilov were rarely invited, although both, and Molotov and Mikoyan, as well, would periodically 'crash' these sessions and join against Stalin's will. Stalin tried to put an end to this by telling his staff not to give out information on his sessions to Molotov and Mikoyan, who were then informed by other members, and therefore continued to attend until Stalin warned them also and they were finally excluded.

The 'sessions' which Khrushchev described, presumably, could now be called Bureau sessions, although they were obviously both social and business sessions. In actual fact, Khrushchev reports, the new full Presidium was never convened; the Bureau decided or rather discussed all questions and the Bureau usually meant the inner core of five. 'All decisions', Khrushchev writes, 'were made by the same methods which Stalin had put into practice after 1939'.[99]

In addition, Stalin created among the new Presidium members various commissions, but according to Khrushchev, they turned out to be ineffectual. Since Stalin died about six months after the 19th Party Congress, the new institutions did not have much time to function and they were scrapped after Stalin's death. Stalin apparently established a similar smaller Bureau of the Presidium of the Council of Ministers to exclude his old associates from that body as well, since they were still formally members of the larger Council Presidium. But since Khrushchev was not a member of this body, we know little of its operations.

Decisionmaking in Stalin's final years was chaotic. 'The last years with Stalin', writes Khrushchev, 'were hard times. The government virtually ceased to function'.[100] In the final months of Stalin's life institutional decisionmaking resembled a theater of the absurd:

> When we got to the dacha, 'the session,' continued, if you call it a session. This system of work, if you can call it work, continued from after the war until Stalin's death. Neither the Central Committee, nor the Politbureau, nor the Presidium Bureau worked regularly. But Stalin's regular sessions with his inner circle went along like clockwork. If he didn't summon us for two or three days, we would think something had happened to him, that he'd gotten sick.[101]

And that is precisely what happened one day in March 1953; he got sick and died.

CONTINUITY AND CHANGE IN THE SOVIET DECISIONMAKING PROCESS: THE STALINIST LEGACY

The basic Soviet decisionmaking institutions in both party and state today at the macrolevel are essentially indistinguishable from those created and fashioned by Stalin in the 1920s (party) and the mid-1930s (state). Even the semantic emendations of the 19th Party Congress were renounced in 1966 in favor of resurrecting the old Stalinist names for central party institutions. These institutions reflected Stalin's personality, style, tastes, experiences and requirements. There is a curious asymmetry between the evolution of state institutions and those of the party. Party institutions are remarkably uniform with those of the 1920s. Only the Orgburo of those days has passed into oblivion, its functions having been assimilated by the Secretariat. The infrastructure of the central party apparatus, however, has grown enormously, but this correlates with the growth and evolution of state institutions which have been expansive.

It should come as no surprise that as Soviet power and influence in the world community have grown, they have been accompanied by an expansion in the complexity and differentiation of the Soviet decisionmaking process. This expansion reflects itself both in the expansion of the universe of personalities and institutions, in the proliferation of channels, access points and information flows, in the quantity and quality of variables and inputs, and in the number and diversity of possible outputs, outcomes, decisions and policies. Soviet options are greater and so are the products and character of Soviet decisions.

Although the Political Bureau (Politburo) of the Central Committee of the CPSU remains a relatively small body of men and continues to function as the ultimate institutional repository of Soviet decisions, judgments and policies, in its superficial dimensions and formal relationships with other party and stage organs it appears to have changed remarkably little since 1939. Its role and functioning have undergone tremendous, even perhaps fundamental, transformations over the past four decades. This has come about not so much because of changes in the Politburo as an institution, or because new personalities have filled old chairs, but principally because of the vast transformations in the political, social, economic, technological and military landscapes, including both foreign and domestic, within which the Politburo now functions.

In 1939 the Politburo was the decisionmaking organ of an internally unstable and semideveloped pariah state isolated from the mainstream of international politics. It was reckoned as the weakest and most vulnerable of the major powers, 'a colossus with feet of clay', to employ the favorite metaphor of the day, without allies, friends, or client states and surrounded on all sides by both weak and powerful enemies.

Both the domestic and foreign settings in which the Politburo operated were relatively simple and uncomplicated, but extremely unfavorable and dangerous for the Soviet state. The Soviet Union itself was still a relatively simple society and its external relationships were also relatively unencumbered. Domestic information processing and decisionmaking institutions were still new, largely untested and seriously weakened and under severe strain because of the socioeconomic convulsions and purges of the preceding decade.

In sharp contrast today the Politburo makes decisions for a mighty global power, second only to the United States in military, economic-industrial and scientific-technological capabilities. No longer isolated, but surrounded by an inner retinue of subordinate communist allied states and an outer ring of other communist states and assorted client states, the Soviet Union has assumed far-flung international commitments and obligations. Its leadership has been stable, its decisionmaking institutions have become more rooted and its decisionmaking processes less arbitrary but more routine.

As Soviet power and influence in the world have grown and as Soviet society has continued to develop and modernize, this has been accompanied by an expansion in the complexity and differentiation of Soviet decision-making processes and institutions. This has manifested itself at several different institutional levels, both party and state, and in changes in the information-data conditioning environment. Changes have been most conspicuous and extensive not at the center of the decisionmaking process, but at its margins, in the administrative realm and in the information-data conditioning environment.

Before the war, for example, three commissariats were largely responsible for the administration of national security and foreign policy decisions: foreign affairs (under various names), and internal security (under various names). Foreign trade played a peripheral role. Today these three ministries have expanded massively in the scope and range of their responsibilities and the number and diversity of their personnel. They have spawned hundreds of subinstitutional agencies to correspond with the myriad of discrete and differentiated functions and responsibilities they have been called upon to perform. Furthermore, they now function within an extensive and growing environment of consulting, advisory and information-processing institutions that have spun out of the Academy of Sciences. New ministries and state committees with foreign policy and security-related functions have sprung up, including an impressive array of interrelated military, scientific and industrial ministries and state committees that have assumed the characteristics of a military-industrial complex.

Even at higher levels of the state structure, closer to the center of Soviet decisionmaking, important substructural and intrastructural changes have taken place that affect national security and foreign policy decisionmaking. Both the Supreme Soviet and its Presidium have become more involved in the formal, juridical execution of decisions, and increasingly provide a legitimizing cover for party functionaries masquerading as legislators. The Foreign Affairs Commissions of the two houses of the Supreme Soviet, for example, have been reorganized, expanded and given greater responsibility in recent years. Their membership is generously sprinkled with high party officials and their two chairmen are party Politburo and Secretariat members, K. V. Chernenko, elected to replace Suslov in November 1982, and B. N. Ponomarev.

The election of Secretary-General Brezhnev as chairman of the Presidium of the Supreme Soviet was an entirely new way of legitimizing this party office with *de jure* authority and correspondingly investing the chairman of the Presidium with *de facto* power. As secretary-general of the party and chairman of the Presidium, Brezhnev presided at the apex of both party and state structures, becoming the authentic president of the USSR. In many ways Brezhnev's investiture as chairman converted the Soviet political system from a Soviet variant of a parliamentary system into a Soviet variant of a presidential one, much in the same way that de Gaulle transformed the French Republic. However, his successor Andropov failed initially to be elected chairman of the Presidium, suggesting that the role of 'president' has yet to become institutionally transferable.

The role of the Council of Ministers, its chairman and its Presidium, has been downgraded in the decisionmaking process relating to foreign policy and national security, as that of the Presidium and its chairman have increased. It is noteworthy that under Brezhnev the most important ministers dealing with foreign affairs and national security, foreign affairs and defense, were neither first deputy, nor deputy chairmen, of the Council of Ministers, and hence not members of the Presidium of the Council of Ministers, but were full members of the Politburo. This suggests that they may be subordinate to the Council of Ministers only in their capacity as ministerial administrators, but not in their capacity as policymakers. In the latter capacity they probably report directly to the Politburo. Until relatively recently the Presidium of the Council of Ministers usually included several powerful Politburo members serving as first deputy or deputy chairmen of the Council of Ministers. It is highly unusual for ministers with full Politburo status not to be members of this Presidium. However, only Tikhonov and Aliyev are members of the Presidium of the Council of Ministers and of the Politburo.[102]

In the party structure similar expansion and proliferation of subinstitutions has taken place, but on a lesser scale. The formal and overt role of the secretary-general, in the past decade, has grown enormously in both foreign affairs and national security. As secretary-general, Brezhnev assembled a private secretariat, made up of highly qualified and energetic specialists on foreign policy and national security matters, resembling very much the nucleus of a 'Kremlin staff', separate and distinct from both traditional party and state institutional channels. And within the party Secretariat and its Central Staff foreign policy and defense-related responsibilities have also increased. Five departments of the Central Secretariat Staff, aside from the Main Political Administration, which is simultaneously within the Ministry of Defense, have international and defense responsibilities: (1) international; (2) cadres abroad; (3) defense industry; (4) liaison with communist and workers' parties of socialist countries; and (5) international information. Aside from Andropov, at least four other members of the Secretariat have foreign affairs and national security responsibilities: Chernenko, Ponomarev, Rusakov and Zimyanin. Thus, while the Soviet political system institutionally is still the house that Stalin built, much of the potential that existed in these institutions has been developed through the generation of new processes and procedures. And even greater potential for development still exists.

NOTES: CHAPTER 2

1   Compare accounts of the purges by Ilya Ehrenbourg, *Memoirs: 1921–1941* (New York: World, 1964); Roy Medvedev, *Let History Judge* (New York: Knopf, 1971), and *On Stalin and Stalinism* (New York: Oxford University Press, 1979); Robert Conquest, *The Great Terror* (New York: Macmillan, 1968); and N. S. Khrushchev's two volumes of reminiscences, *Khrushchev Remembers* (Boston, Mass.: Little, Brown, 1970, 1974), among others.

2   Maxim Litvinov's survival is a case in point. His friend Ilya Ehrenbourg writes: 'Why, having put to death almost all of Litvinov's assistants, did he [Stalin] not have the obstreperous Maxim himself shot? It is extremely puzzling. Certainly Litvinov expected a different ending. From 1937 till his last illness he kept a revolver on his bedside table because, if there were to be a ring at the door in the night, he was not going to wait for

what came after', Ilya Ehrenbourg, *Post-War Years: 1945–54* (New York: World, 1967), p. 277.

3   G. K. Zhukov, *The Memoirs of Marshal Zhukov* (New York: Delacorte, 1971), p. 268.
4   Khrushchev, op. cit., Vol. 2, p. 238.
5   In the second volume of his memoirs Khrushchev explains why he occupied both posts as follows: 'I've often criticized Stalin for allowing a single person to have two posts, one in the government and one in the Party. Therefore my acceptance [of the premiership] represented a certain weakness on my part – a bug of some sort which was gnawing away at me and undermining my power of resistance', Khrushchev, op. cit., Vol. 2, p. 17. What was gnawing at Khrushchev was this very ambiguity and anxiety concerning the legitimacy of his authority.
6   L. I. Brezhnev, *On the Draft Constitution* (Moscow: Novosti, 1977), p. 16.
7   Boris Topornin, *The New Constitution of the USSR* (Moscow: Progress, 1980), p. 238.
8   *Izvestiia*, 17 June 1977.
9   The new Constitution includes two new chapters on foreign policy and defense and provides for a Council of Defense for the USSR, to be created by the Presidium of the Supreme Soviet, which is also empowered to determine its composition. Up to this point counterpart organs of this character were established by state or administrative organs. The Council of Defense is now a constitutional body which is not necessarily subordinate to the Council of Ministers.
10 Khrushchev, op. cit., Vol. 1, p. 11.
11 ibid., p. 12. It should be noted that Bulganin at one time was a close associate of Khrushchev's but double-crossed him at the time of the Antiparty Group crisis, for which Khrushchev never forgave him.
12 ibid.
13 Topornin, op. cit., p. 18; emphasis added. For his extended commentary on the legal status of the party under the new Constitution, see pp. 54–66. For other authoritative commentaries on the relationship between 'state power' and 'political power', 'state' and 'political system', cf. B. M. Lazarev, 'Power and administration', *Sovety Narodnykh Deputatov*, no. 2 (1978); F. M. Burlatsky, 'Political system of developed socialism', *Voprosy Filosofii*, no. 8 (1977); and V. S. Shevtsov, 'On the notion of "Political power" under conditions of socialism', *Sotsiolofcheskie Issledovaniya*, no. 2 (1980).
14 On this point I agree very strongly with the views of Seweryn Bialer, in *Stalin's Successors* (New York: Cambridge University Press, 1980), pp. 29 ff.
15 Khrushchev, op. cit., Vol. 2. pp. 256–7.
16 Milovan Djilas, *Conversations with Stalin* (New York: Harcourt, Brace, 1962).
17 Svetlana Alliluyeva, *Twenty Letters to a Friend* (New York: Harper & Row, 1967), and *Only One Year* (New York: Harper, 1969).
18 Khrushchev, op. cit., Vol. 1, pp. 286–7.
19 cf. especially n. 1 above.
20 Ivan Maisky, *Memoirs of a Soviet Ambassador* (New York: Scribner's, 1967).
21 cf. Medvedev, *On Stalin and Stalinism*, op. cit., and *Let History Judge*, op. cit., ch. 14.
22 Zhukov, op. cit. Both Khrushchev and Roy Medvedev take strong exception to Zhukov's characterization of Stalin as wartime commander and both in circumspect manner suspect Zhukov's sincerity on this issue. Medvedev charges that Zhukov's original manuscript gave a harsher appraisal of Stalin. Both cast aspersions on the sincerity of other favorable views by Soviet military commanders: cf. Khrushchev, op. cit., Vol. 2, pp. 4–5; and Medvedev, *Let History Judge*, op. cit., pp. 437–79.
23 *Nazi-Soviet Relations, 1939–1941* (Washington, DC: US Department of State, 1948), p. 75. According to the German records of the meetings, Stalin's exact words were: 'I know how much the German Nation loves its Führer: I should therefore like to drink to his health.'
24 Joseph Stalin, *Leninism: Selected Writings* (New York: International, 1942), p. 360.
25 These figures were first revealed by Khrushchev in his Secret Speech to the 20th Party Congress in 1956.
26 cf. Medvedev, *Let History Judge*, op. cit., pp. 155–6.
27 The most lurid account of this incident and Stalin's complicity in Kirov's murder is also the most recent, see Anton Antonov-Ovseyenko, *The Time of Stalin* (New York: Harper & Row, 1981), pp. 77–84.
28 cf. Medvedev, *Let History Judge*, op. cit., pp. 177–8; and Conquest, op. cit., pp. 83–4.

29   cf. Conquest, op. cit., pp. 185–91; and Medvedev, *Let History Judge*, op. cit., pp. 193–7.

30   Conquest, op. cit., pp. 467 ff.

31   Medvedev, *Let History Judge*, op. cit., pp. 192 ff.

32   ibid., p. 485; Conquest gives a low figure of 33,000 and a high figure of 40,000, which accounted for about one-half of the entire officer corps. According to Roy Medvedev and other authorities, three of five marshals, three of four first-rank commanders, all twelve of the second-rank commanders, 60 of 67 corps commanders, 126 of 199 division commanders, 221 of 397 brigade commanders, the head of the Main Political Administration and eleven deputy commanders of defense were arrested, incarcerated, or executed. A similar fate blighted the leadership of the small navy, including its commissar and first deputy commissar; cf. Medvedev, *On Stalin and Stalinism*, op. cit., pp. 192 ff. As a result of the purges, according to now-exiled Soviet historian A. M. Nekrich, at the outbreak of the war, young, inexperienced and ill-trained replacements were in responsible military commands: only 7 percent of the officers had higher military education, 37 percent had not completed their intermediate military education and, by the summer of 1941, about 75 percent of the commanders and 70 percent of the political commissars had been at their jobs only a year or less; see A. M. Nekrich, 1941 *22 Iyunya* (Moscow: Nauka, 1965).

33   For details of the purge in the Foreign Commissariat and Soviet diplomatic service, cf. 'The evolution and organization of the Soviet diplomatic service', in V. V. Aspaturian, *Process and Power in Soviet Foreign Policy* (Boston: Little, Brown, 1971), ch. 18, pp. 610–65.

34   A. A. Gromyko, *Only For Peace* (New York: Pergamon, 1979), pp. 6–7.

35   Khrushchev, op. cit., Vol. 1, p. 50.

36   ibid., p. 58.

37   Alexander Barmine, *One who Survived* (New York: Putnam, 1946), p. 213. Barmine also noted that 'thousands of relatively unimportant, as well as all-important problems must pass through Stalin's hand for final decision . . . Weeks are spent in waiting; Commissars wait in Stalin's office', ibid.

38   A long passage from the eyewitness testimony of E. G. Feldman concerning Stalin's purge of Yezhov from the Central Committee in 1939 illustrates graphically Stalin's style and paranoia and their impact upon decisionmaking processes: 'As the Congress was drawing to a close, the *Senioren Konvent* [Committee of Elders] gathered in one of the halls of the Kremlin. Sitting in front at a long table, as if on stage, were Andreyev, Molotov, and Malenkov. Behind them, far to the back in a corner on the left . . . Stalin took a seat, puffing away at his pipe. Andreyev spoke. He said that as the Congress was finishing up its work, it was time to propose candidates for election to the Central Committee . . . Then it was Yezhov's turn.
'   "Any opinions?" asked Andreyev. After a brief silence, someone remarked that Yezhov was a good Stalinist commissar, known to them all, and should be kept.
'   "Any objections?" There was silence. Then Stalin asked for the floor. He got up, walked to the table, and, still puffing at his pipe, called out:
'   "Yezhov! Where are you? Come on up here!" Yezhov appeared from a row at the back and came to the table.
'   "Well, what do you think of yourself?" Stalin asked. "Are you fit to be a member of the Central Committee?"
'Yezhov turned pale and in a cracked voice replied that he didn't understand the question, that his whole life had been devoted to the Party and to Stalin, that he loved Stalin more than his own life and had no idea what could have prompted such a question.
'   "Really?" asked Stalin ironically. "And who was Frinovsky? Did you know him?
'   "Yes, of course I did," answered Yezhov. "Frinovsky was my deputy. He . . ."
'Stalin interrupted Yezhov and began to ask about others: who was Shapiro? did he know Ryzhov [Yezhov's secretary]? and what about Fedorov, and so on . . . [all these people had been arrested].
'   "Iosif Vissarionovich! But you know that it was I – I myself – who exposed their plot. I came to you and reported that . . ."
'Stalin didn't let him continue. "Yes, of course! When you felt the game was up you came in a hurry. And what about before that? There was a plot, a plot to kill Stalin. Do you mean to tell me that top people in the NKVD were organizing a plot and you weren't in on it? Do you think I'm blind?" Stalin went on: "Well, come on! Think about it! Who

did you send to guard Stalin? With revolvers! Why revolvers near Stalin? Why? was it to kill Stalin? And if I hadn't noticed? Then what?"

'Stalin accused Yezhov of running the NKVD at a feverish pitch, arresting innocent people while covering up for others.

'"Well? Clear off! I don't know, comrades, can this man be a member of the Central Committee? I have my doubts. Of course, think it over . . . it's up to you . . . but I have my doubts."

'Yezhov of course was crossed off the list by unanimous vote; he did not return to the hall after the break and was not seen again at the Congress', as reported in Medvedev, *On Stalin and Stalinism*, op. cit., pp. 109–10.

39   John Erickson, *The Road to Stalingrad* (New York: Harper & Row, 1975), pp. 52 ff.; and Albert Seaton, *Stalin as Military Commander* (New York: Praeger, 1976), pp. 84–5.
40   Seaton, op. cit., p. 84.
41   ibid., p. 85.
42   N. G. Kuznetsov, 'Pered Voinoĭ', *Oktiabr*, no. 9 (1965), as reprinted in Seweryn Bialer (ed.), *Stalin and His Generals* (New York: Pegasus, 1969), p. 95.
43   N. G. Kuznetsov, in *Oktiabr*, no. 9 (1963), p. 174; cf. also Kuznetsov as reprinted in Bialer, *Stalin and His Generals*, op. cit., pp. 347–8.
44   K. A. Meretskov, *Serving the People* (Moscow: Progress, 1971), p. 95.
45   Conquest, op. cit., p. 471.
46   Medvedev, *Let History Judge*, op. cit., pp. 309–10.
47   Thus, Khruschev writes: 'I've never really known for sure why Stalin decided as he did. As I've already said, he was the sort of man who kept his opinions to himself. If he talked over some problems with the rest of us, it was only to fish from one of us the information he needed', Khrushchev, op. cit., Vol. 1, p. 20.
48   ibid., Vol. 1, p. 250.
49   ibid., p. 234.
50   cf. Khrushchev's Secret Speech to the 20th Party Congress, 1956, reprinted widely.
51   Khrushchev, op. cit., Vol. 1, p. 151.
52   Concerning an episode of this period Khrushchev relates: 'When I got there Stalin was lying on his couch reading . . . Then he started to talk about military matters. This was possibly the only time he ever talked about military matters when we were alone . . . [U]sually, he felt no urge to exchange opinions with others. He valued his own abilities and views much more than those of anyone else', Khrushchev, op. cit., Vol. 1, p. 21.
53   'Stalin', Khrushchev writes, 'never gave us a chance to get to know military people unless we had specific business with them'.
54   cf. Seaton, op. cit.; Medvedev, *Let History Judge*, op. cit., pp. 454–69; and *On Stalin and Stalinism*, op. cit., pp. 120–41.
55   Khrushchev, op. cit., Vol. 1, p. 160.
56   ibid., pp. 132–3.
57   ibid., p. 153. According to Marshal Meretskov, who played a prominent role in the war with Finland, Stalin was already concerned with the possibility of war with Finland as early as 1938 and ordered an intensification of local and military preparedness and the construction of military fortifications. Nevertheless, the Soviet military once again displayed astonishing ineptitude and Meretskov reports that Stalin was concerned, because 'the whole world had its eyes on us . . . [and] if we should get stuck for long against such a weak adversary . . . we would be encouraging the imperialists to further their anti-Soviet efforts': Meretskov, op. cit., pp. 97–112.
58   Kuznetsov, as reprinted in Bialer, *Stalin and His Generals*, op. cit., p. 135.
59   ibid.
60   ibid., p. 348.
61   ibid.
62   *Zasedanii Verkhovnogo Soveta SSSR* (Moscow, 1938–9), p. 135.
63   The Politburo Commission on Foreign Affairs, that is, the sextet probably consisted of Stalin, Molotov, Zhdanov, Mikoyan, Beria and Voroshilov. Malenkov or Bulganin was perhaps the addition that raised it to a septet.
64   cf. Bialer, *Stalin and His Generals*, op. cit., pp. 179–262.
65   As reprinted in ibid., p. 203.
66   cf. Erickson, op. cit., p. 136; and Seaton, op. cit., p. 100.
67   Zhukov, op. cit., p. 238.

68   ibid., p. 239.

69   cf. Medvedev, *Let History Judge*, op. cit., pp. 454–69.

70   According to Medvedev, Zhukov's original manuscript was critical of Stalin but his revised version gives a more favorable but misleading picture. Medvedev, himself, considers Stalin to have been a mediocre military commander, and he generally agreed with Khrushchev's negative assessment, ibid., p. 455.

71   Stalin in his speech of 3 July 1941, *Izvestiia*, 4 July 1941. For a text of the Decree establishing the committee, cf. *Vedomosti Verkhovnogo Soveta CCCP*, no. 31 (1941).

72   cf. Zhukov, op. cit., pp. 279–80, and N. G. Kuznetsov, *Voennoistoricheskii Zhurnal*, no. 9 (1966), p. 65.

73   Zhukov, op. cit., p. 280.

74   In spite of all these titles and posts Stalin continued to avoid assuming personal responsibility for directing the war until victory was assured. Thus, Khrushchev writes: 'During the first part of the war, when things were going badly for us, I hadn't failed to notice that Stalin's signature never appeared on a single document or order. "High Command", "General Staff", or some other term was used but never his name. This practice didn't change even after we repulsed the Germans outside of Moscow and Stalin began to regain his confidence. Directives continued to be issued from him without his signature. Sometimes they appeared over his title "Commander in Chief", but never over his name. And this was no accident. Nothing Stalin ever did was an accident. His every move was deliberate and calculated. Every step he ever took, good or bad, was measured carefully', Khrushchev, op. cit., Vol. 1, pp. 170–1. Khrushchev makes it quite clear that this was an 'example of Stalin's refusal to accept direct responsibility for what was happening at the Front': ibid. Khrushchev's view is consistent with Admiral Kuznetsov's snide observation that Stalin's appointment as supreme commander-in-chief was kept secret from the public and 'it was only after victory at the front that Stalin began to be called supreme commander-in-chief in the communiques published in the press': Kuznetsov, op. cit., p.66. A brief comment on Stalin's assumption of titles, which manifested itself as more than a penchant but less than an obsession. Stalin's 'modesty' may have initially dissuaded him from accepting appointment as a mere commander-in-chief, but once he decided to assume formal responsibility 'it was no accident', as Khrushchev might say, that he upgraded the title to supreme commander-in-chief and assumed the military rank of not only Marshal of the Soviet Union, but Generalissimo (held previously in Russia only by Suvorov), a title whose eminence was so rarefied that only three other contemporary luminaries dared be graced by it: Francisco Franco, Chiang Kai-shek and Rafael Trujillo.

75   J. F. Hough and M. Fainsod, *How the Soviet Union Is Governed* (Cambridge, Mass.: Harvard University Press, 1979), p. 178.

76   Zhukov, op. cit., pp. 267–8.

77   Zhukov characterized Stalin as 'certainly a worthy Supreme Commander', and an 'outstanding organizer' of material and human resources during the war: ibid., p. 285.

78   ibid., p. 284.

79   cf. Medvedev, *Let History Judge*, op. cit., pp. 454 ff.; and Bialer, *Stalin and His Generals*, op. cit., pp. 351–439.

80   Khrushchev, op. cit., Vol. 1, p. 133.

81   ibid., Vol. 1, p. 159. Elsewhere Khrushchev complains that 'Politbureau mail' dealing only with Ukrainian affairs or matters dealing with him personally were forwarded to him in Kiev.

82   Zhukov, op. cit., p. 284.

83   Senior Soviet physicists and scientists had earlier suggested the establishment of a research program on an atomic weapon, but were concerned about diverting scarce resources and effort to an uncertain project and so they had relented. Stalin, however, was nevertheless outraged that it was a junior officer at the front and not the academicians who forced the issue; cf. David Holloway, 'Entering the nuclear arms race: the Soviet decision to build the atomic bomb, 1939–45', in *Social Studies of Science* (Beverly Hills, Calif.: Sage, 1981), Vol. 2, pp. 159–97, for a detailed examination of the Soviet decision to build the atomic bomb; cf. also Herbert York, *The Advisors* (San Francisco, Calif.: Freeman & Col, 1976), pp. 29–40; Arnold Kramish, *Atomic Energy in the Soviet Union* (Stanford, Calif.: Stanford University Press, 1959); and I. N. Golovin, *I. V. Kurchatov*, 2nd edn (Moscow: Atomizdat, 1973).

84   G. K. Zhukov, *Vospominaniya i Razmyshleniya*, 2nd edn (Moscow: 1974), Vol. 2, p. 418.

85 As cited by Holloway, op. cit., p. 183.
86 Khrushchev, op. cit., Vol. 2, p. 58.
87 Holloway, op. cit., p. 189.
88 From Khrushchev's Secret Speech, 1956.
89 ibid; emphasis added.
90 Thus, Khrushchev complains: 'Some people were spreading the rumor that I was giving in to local Ukrainian influences. . . . People were saying that I didn't deserve full confidence anymore, and Stalin started to regard my reports with a certain familiar cautiousness . . . Some of this information filtered up to Stalin himself. Usually people were afraid to give Stalin information because they knew that discouraging reports would displease him and jeopardize themselves. Stalin liked to think the country was thriving', Khrushchev, op. cit., Vol. 1, p. 233.
91 Golda Meir, 'Mrs Meir's Moscow memory', *New York Times*, 30 December 1970, p. 25.
92 From Khrushchev's Secret Speech, 1956.
93 Khrushchev, op. cit., Vol. 1, p. 368.
94 ibid., p. 260.
95 From Khrushchev's Secret Speech, 1956.
96 Khrushchev, op. cit., Vol. 1, pp. 276–7.
97 ibid., p. 277.
98 ibid., p. 281.
99 ibid., pp. 281–2.
100 ibid., p. 297.
101 ibid., p. 299.
102 The situation in regard to the Presidium of the Supreme Soviet is somewhat different. Aside from Andropov (who was elected in November 1982), no less than four full members of the Politburo (Romanov, Kunayev, Shcherbitsky and Grishin) and two candidate members (Kuznetsov and Rashidov) are members of the Presidium of the Supreme Soviet. Since this was written, Gromyko has been appointed a first deputy chairman of the Council of Ministers.

3 The Politics of Defense in the Soviet Union: Brezhnev's Era

DIMITRI K. SIMES

During the eighteen years of Leonid Brezhnev's leadership (1964–82) the Soviet Union was gradually transformed from a continental empire into a truly global military power. The USSR has considerably improved its military position *vis-à-vis* its principal rival – the United States. Simultaneously, Soviet forces stationed in the Far East have been strengthened to a degree which further shifts the balance with China in Moscow's favor. In Europe traditional Soviet conventional superiority is being increasingly complemented by a preponderance on higher levels of escalation. The Kremlin's new ability – and indeed willingness – to project force to remote regions never before in its sphere of influence or even interest is on the record.

It is equally on the record that this impressive military buildup was not without political and economic costs for the Soviet regime. The apparent determination with which the Soviet leadership sought to improve its military standing, while adding in some respects to the USSR's security, seriously complicated the search for accommodation with the West. Eventually the United States, Western Europe, Japan, China and a growing number of important Third World nations became so concerned with Moscow's accumulation of military power and its perceived geopolitical advances that they began to feel compelled to pull closer together and respond with a defense effort of their own.[1]

Domestically, declining economic growth rates associated with the end of an era of cheap and easily available labor and natural resources have made continual increases in defense spending a greater burden. After avoiding a painful choice between guns and butter for many years, the Soviet Union has probably arrived at a point when the luxury of presiding over a consumer revolution at home and dramatically expanding military power will begin to look like a beautiful dream of the past to the Politburo.[2]

But if the costs of the Soviet military buildup and international assertiveness are so high and in many respects so obvious, why does the Soviet regime pursue it with such dogged and inflexible determination? How do the Soviets reach fundamental decisions regarding how much is enough for the security of their country and their political system? What considerations influence their thinking and what political and bureaucratic actors contribute to them?

Answers to these questions on Soviet policy formulation and mindset are not easy to come by on the basis of evidence available to outsiders. Frustration with second-guessing and especially with trying to influence the Soviet political process is inevitable and understandable. This is especially the case when attempts are made to understand the inner workings of the Soviet system determining actions that encroach on American interests. Intentions are ambiguous and impossible to document as a rule. Soviet missiles and tanks, on the other hand, are something tangible, easy to count and threatening.

Notwithstanding the inevitable difficulties, there is no choice but to try to learn as much as possible about the Soviet decisionmaking process in areas of such crucial interest to the United States as Moscow's military effort. Commonsense requires us to attempt to find out what is behind the endless Soviet accumulation of military power: an aggressive grand design, an irresistible but not particularly thought-out urge to expand influence, historical tradition and political culture, a sense of insecurity, the search for domestic legitimacy through foreign policy exploits, bureaucratic bargaining and inertia, or a combination of some or all of the above?

There are three basic alternative models of the Soviet political process developed by Western scholarship. The first suggests that the Soviet Union is a totalitarian state approaching international issues of critical importance as a single rational actor. Adherents of this school of thought argue that the highly centralized and disciplined Soviet party–government machine is totally responsive to commands of the top political leadership, which makes decisions on the basis of perceived national needs.

Few analysts accept the *totalitarian model* in its more extreme simplistic form dating back to the Stalin period, when Soviet society and policies were far less complex and political terror made any form of disagreement, including those through institutional channels, a particularly risky business. Nevertheless, those who believe in the single rational actor model tend to argue that the differences between Stalin and his successors in terms of rules and methods of policy formulation are primarily cosmetic. Representatives of this school also tend to dismiss the seriousness of disagreements between various functional and institutional participants in the Soviet decision-making process. Such disagreements are perceived either as deliberate misinformation, or as petty squabbling not really relevant for understanding important Soviet national security choices.[3]

A very different point of view is expressed by supporters of the *pluralistic model* of Soviet policy formulation. Emphasis is put not on a sense of strategic purpose among Soviet leaders, but rather on the interplay of interest groups competing for resources in ways not unfamiliar to industrial democracies. No serious scholar would go so far as to dismiss completely obvious differences between political processes in the West and the USSR. However, when advocates of this school talk about 'participatory bureaucracy'[4] or 'institutional pluralism',[5] they clearly imply that official bureaucratic-functional complexes have a great deal of independence which allows them impressive freedom to present their cases to the top leadership and to a great degree to have their way without much interference or control from the top. The choices the Politburo makes in the national security area, consequently, are viewed as a product of political and bureaucratic bargaining rather than as the outcome of a careful search for optimal solutions.

Both the totalitarian and pluralistic models of Soviet national security policy formulation have their utility in focusing on important elements of the phenomenon. Nevertheless, in both cases there seem to be considerable parts of the overall picture which they fail to take into account. The basic handicap of the totalitarian model is that it does not appreciate sufficiently what one perceptive observer described as 'the increasingly bureaucratized nature of Soviet institutions'.[6] During Brezhnev's political dominance a consensus style of leadership was clearly prevalent in the USSR. The Politburo was gradually transformed from a group of personal associates and aides to the dictator, as it was under Stalin and to a lesser extent under Khrushchev, into a kind of supreme legislative-executive committee of the Soviet elite, representing all principal power groups – the central party apparatus, local party cadres, economic management, the military, the KGB, the foreign policy establishment and the military-industrial complex.

Spokesmen for these bureaucratic-functional powerhouses were in many cases associated with their respective constituencies for decades, and it would be inhuman indeed if they managed to escape at least some sense of identity with special interests of which they were a part during their whole careers.[7] In the absence of political terror and furthermore, in a time of unprecedented security and stability for senior officeholders, members of the Soviet leadership are less constrained than in the past in presenting their policy requests.[8] Even under Stalin – as a number of memoirs testify – there were occasional fierce debates on defense issues till the tyrant himself made it explicitly clear that he had reached a conclusion and there was nothing more to talk about.[9] Khrushchev admits in his memoirs that some military decisions were not dictated by a rational analysis, but rather were made in order not to alienate the military. 'There were some men in our navy who couldn't get over being completely deprived of cruisers, so we made a few concessions', he tells, explaining that the decision was against the Politburo's better judgement but was necessary as a concession to the admirals.[10]

As far as the pluralistic model is concerned, its principal problem, according to Tom Wolfe's wise reminder, is 'what is popularly called "mirror imaging" – the tendency to project American institutional habits, interests and values onto the Soviet scene'.[11] Scholars who develop this model are the first to point out that 'Soviet "interest groups" are not the kind of independent private pressure groups of a pluralistic society'.[12] But despite such helpful cautionary notes, there is a tendency among many pluralistic model supporters to emphasize similarities rather than differences between Soviet and Western political processes. Undoubtedly, it reflects some polemical overreaction to the also simplistic totalitarian model. Still, a realistic appreciation of the complexities of Soviet decisionmaking on military issues should come to grips both with the multidimensional and pluralistic nature of Soviet policy formulation and with the severe systemic limits imposed on it by the regime.

What exists in the USSR today is a *controlled pluralism* within carefully defined totalitarian limits – pluralism confined to official institutions, pluralism only for and among the elite, without much input from other political constituencies and, finally, pluralism which implicitly accepts several key unifying themes and rules of the game which should remain unchallenged.[13] The fact that Soviet bureaucratic-functional complexes frequently pursue their own special interests rather than some kind of an abstract 'good of the nation' is hard to dispute. But it is even more difficult to ignore the narrow margins within which this institutional interplay is allowed to operate in the Soviet Union. Quite naturally, a Minister of Defense and a Foreign Minister, spokesmen for defense and consumer industries have different perspectives and on occasion may sharply disagree about national priorities. However, such debates among senior Soviet officials may reflect not so much bureaucratic predominance, but rather the highly diversified functions of a modern state inevitably leading to differences in views among those officially responsible for carrying them out.

Going beyond generalizations, three fundamental questions are usually asked about Soviet national security policy formulation – who reaches decisions in Moscow, how they are made, and why these choices are selected. The first question is by far the easiest one. A number of recent studies provide a reasonably comprehensive and detailed anatomy of the Soviet decisionmaking structure in defense and foreign policy areas.[14] The top policymaking body is the Politburo. Officially the supreme party organ, the Politburo is in fact composed of leading representatives of all major power groups and not just the party apparatus. On the party apparatus side the principal authority just below Politburo level is in the hands of the Central Committee Secretariat. The government bureaucracy is directed by the Council of Ministers and particularly its Presidium – a rough state equivalent of the Party Secretariat. Leading members of both the Secretariat and the Council of Ministers serve on the Politburo. During the last years of the Brezhnev era, Secretary-General Leonid Brezhnev was simultaneously *de facto* chairman of the Politburo and of the Defense Council – a body with clearly important but not well-identified functions. According to some informed sources, in addition to Brezhnev, its members included: Prime Minister Nikolai Tikhonov, Foreign Minister Andrei Gromyko, Minister of Defense Dimitri Ustinov, former KGB chairman and currently Central Committee secretary Yuriy Andropov and Central Committee secretaries Andrei Kirilenko and Mikhail Suslov (now possibly Constantin Chernenko).[15] Officially the Defense Council is appointed by and is responsible to the Supreme Soviet Presidium.[16] But the latter, according to the consensus among analysts, has little more than a rubber-stamp role on matters of national significance. Consequently, in reality, the Defense Council is likely to derive its authority directly from the Politburo.

The responsibilities of the Defense Council were never discussed in any detail in Soviet literature. Brezhnev himself gave a boost to the Defense Council's image when during the SALT discussions he mentioned to his American counterparts that he would need to consult this body.[17] Coordination of defense industries (eight or nine ministries) is conducted by the Council of Ministers Military Industrial Commission, chaired by one of Tikhonov's deputies, Leonid V. Smirnov. He works in close contact with the Central Committee Defense Industries Department (chief Ivan Serbin). Previously the Central Committee used to have a special secretary supervising defense industries. In the late 1950s it was Brezhnev himself, later Ustinov and, more recently, after Ustinov's move to the Ministry of Defense, Yakov Ryabov. However, Ryabov was demoted after a brief tenure to the position of a first deputy chairman of the State Planning Committee (one of five).

The Ministry of Defense, the Ministry of Foreign Affairs and the State Security Committee (KGB) are naturally important actors in national security policy formulation. Officially, all three institutions are subordinate to the Council of Ministers. However, circumstantial evidence suggests that in fact they report directly to the Politburo. First, as full Politburo members (before Andropov's shift to the Secretariat) their respective heads are an integral part of the supreme policymaking body. It is unlikely that one of Tikhonov's several deputies would supervize them.[18] The same is true to some extent even with respect to Tikhonov himself – a life-long industrial manager without any background in foreign policy. The Council of Ministers Presidium has several commissions dealing with economic, defense industry and foreign trade matters. What it essentially appears to be is the headquarters for Soviet economic planning and centralized management with only modest authority over other affairs of state.

The Central Committee Secretariat, on the contrary, has departments – international, international information, liaison with ruling communist parties, cadres abroad and defense industry – which enable it to coordinate and supervize appropriate government national security agencies. However, it may be an oversimplification to suggest that the Central Committee Secretariat formulates decisions while government institutions are entrusted to implement them. The real relationship between the party and government bodies in the national security formulation process is increasingly more of a two-way street with a division of labor rather than a clearcut preponderance of the party as represented by the Secretariat.

To start with, the Politburo status of Andropov, Gromyko and Ustinov created a problem for Central Committee officials responsible for overlapping policy areas. For instance, when International Department chief and Central Committee secretary Boris Ponomarev, who is a Politburo candidate member, dealt with Gromyko, he could hardly ignore the latter's full Politburo rank. Equally important is the fact that the Central Committee departments do not cover some of the most important functions of the government institutions they formally are expected to oversee.

The military is the most obvious case in point. There is no Central Committee unit which would deal with matters of military operations, deployments and infrastructure. The Main Political Administration of the Armed Forces – an integral part of the Ministry of Defense but also associated with the Central Committee – and the Central Committee administrative organs and defense industry departments have responsibilities for political indoctrination, clearing promotions and procurement for the military. But none of them separately and even not all of them together are qualified to give guidance on matters of a purely military nature, for which the marshals are responsible only to the Politburo itself.

In the 1970s the Brezhnev personal secretariat – a small group of top aides to the Secretary-General – gradually emerged as a substitute staff for the Politburo. But while some of these assistants were senior foreign policy experts, none of them was a specialist on defense issues or internal security. There was one major general on Brezhnev's personal staff. However, he was an aide-de-camp without known substantive responsibilities. Accordingly, it appears that Timothy Colton is correct in suggesting that 'although civilian decisions are ultimately shaped by values and perceptions over which the army has no control, civilians do not have the substantial nonmilitary sources of military information found in American politics'. And indeed, as Colton observes, 'there are no Soviet equivalents for the Central Intelligence Agency, the Arms Control and Disarmament Agency, or private consulting firms such as the Rand Corporation'.[19]

In fact, several Soviet foreign affairs thinktanks such as the Institute of World Economy and International Relations, the Institute of the United States and Canada, the Institute of Oriental Studies, the Institute of the International Labor Movement, and several smaller establishments focusing on specific regions, supply the Central Committee and to a lesser extent the Defense and Foreign ministries and the KGB with information and analyses. But the need to know principle, coupled with compartmentalization and secretiveness beyond reason, does not allow Soviet academics access to information about their own country's military capabilities. As a result, Soviet foreign affairs institutes help the leadership to understand the international environment, opportunities for and threats to Soviet activities in the world arena. Such an understanding definitely has a bearing on deliberations regarding the Soviets' own military programs. Still, despite the wide publicity enjoyed by top Soviet officials from these institutes when visiting the United States, their ability to affect seriously Soviet defense debates is questionable at this point.

More influence is probably concentrated in the hands of Soviet scientists associated with defense-oriented research labs and R&D bureaus. Coordinated by the State Committee on Science and Technology and to a lesser extent by the Academy of Sciences, the Soviet scientific community by necessity cannot be denied information about Soviet military technology. But as in the case of foreign affairs, scholars' compartmentalization prevents natural scientists from getting involved in policy debates beyond their immediate, narrowly defined areas of responsibility.

A discussion of who is who in the Soviet national security decisionmaking process would be incomplete without mentioning those who have no relevance or do not exist at all in the Soviet context – the media, Congress and the Arms Control Association – in short, all those groups which assure in the United States that debates are not limited to the search for technically optimal solutions, but offer an alternative perspective to counterbalance the influence of the military, defense industrialists and intelligence enthusiasts. For them, there is no place inside the margins of Soviet policy formulation.

If the institutional/bureaucratic chart of the Soviet national security formulation process is more or less on the record, the rules of the game are far more difficult to identify. However, there is enough evidence to make at least some informed speculations. To start with, it is fairly clear that politics, political maneuvering and the bureaucratic search for advantage are very much present in the Soviet system within the limits discussed above. One could agree with Jerry Hough's suggestion that 'in the Soviet Union too there is unmistakable evidence for the existence of factional and bureaucratic occupational interest group activity'.[20]

However, unlike in the pluralistic system of the United States with its well-known checks and balances and, most importantly, with its vital area of activity outside the government, bureaucratic players in the Soviet Union tend to be very cautious. The price of demotion may be not just a career setback, not just a shift to a less exciting position, but becoming a political nonentity. It is true that there is no fear of execution as under Stalin, and being purged for political disagreement – as long as it is voiced through official channels – is far less likely than it was under Khrushchev, but the record of the Brezhnev years indicates that a consensus style of leadership did not favor those bureaucrats who had strong ideas and were prepared to advocate them in a dynamic manner. A number of former Politburo members who lost their position, such as the forceful opportunist Aleksandr Shelepin, the dogmatic, politically conservative Ukrainian nationalist Petr Shelest, the moderate reformer Gennady Voronov and the alleged sponsor of Russian nationalists Dimitri Polyansky, advocated very different programs and approaches and were dissimilar in their education and personal style. Nevertheless, it seems that it was more than a coincidence that all these officials lost their portfolios while some of their other less colorful and dynamic colleagues survived and prospered. It appears that those who were expelled from the Politburo had at least one thing in common – a positive program, a desire to advocate relatively strong views, to pressure for some form of change. It could not be the only reason for their political misfortunes, but it seems that it was one of them. Consequently, one tends to believe that in the current Soviet political environment, officials arguing for greater allocation of resources or for policy changes tend to be quite conservative in how far they are willing to go in insisting on their views.

In short, political debates in the Soviet Union tend as a rule to gravitate toward the center. Those familiar with Soviet academic literature may find an abundance of evidence to the contrary. Soviet academics disagree widely on important foreign policy matters, including such subjects of crucial significance to the state as whether thermonuclear war would mean the end of civilization or just the end of capitalism. There were heated discussions of how trustworthy are 'American ruling circles' and how much one can rely on them as a partner in détente. Similarly, one can find evidence of Soviet officials arguing about American willingness to go all the way in building an alliance with China. While some Soviet observers suggest that such an alliance is already in effect in existence, others – at least until the crisis over Afghanistan – tend to believe that the United States, although playing the China card, appreciated the basic necessity to have a special relationship with the Soviet Union as the only other superpower.

This list of disagreements could continue. Nevertheless, it would be a mistake to assume that debates among academics and experts necessarily mirror disagreements on the top. Those who climb up to the Soviet leadership tend to be far more cautious than their less disciplined and more opinionated subordinates. Also top leaders like Brezhnev have responsibility for more than one dimension of Soviet foreign policy. This means, for instance, that if the director of the Institute of the USA and Canada, Georgiy Arbatov, might be associated primarily with the cooperative side of the US-Soviet relationship and naturally becomes a kind of spokesman for détente, Brezhnev himself not only presided over Soviet efforts to build bridges to America, but also was well known as a champion of the Soviet military buildup. Accordingly, his position on relations with the United States probably tended to move closer to the center than the position of someone like Arbatov and his colleagues, who have a vested interest in the success of détente with the United States, which in many respects is the foundation of their flourishing careers.

The emerging pluralism in the Soviet decisionmaking process should not obscure the fact that Lenin's notorious democratic centralism is still very much alive. Once the Politburo reaches a decision, all segments of the Soviet bureaucracy are expected to implement it without much discussion, obstruction, or procrastination. Of course, as with any bureaucracy anywhere in the world, this expectation in many cases remains on paper. Still, after the top leadership makes up its mind and speaks out, political debates or even bureaucratic discussions become extremely difficult, if possible at all.

How does the Politburo itself reach its decisions on national security issues? It seems that today the process is far more institutionalized than ever in the past. With the presence of key party and government national security agencies on the Politburo, principal sources of expertise and vested interests are in a position to present their views and recommendations. Most other members of the Politburo involved in political indoctrination, the domestic economy, and so on, probably have relatively little to say on national security subjects. This may be particularly true when there is no national emergency and when foreign policy decisions do not have direct negative domestic implications detrimental for, say, local party officials. One can imagine that the Jackson–Vanik amendment, for instance, which connected American economic benefits to greater freedom of emigration from the Soviet Union, would have been the kind of foreign policy situation which would be of interest to more than just the Politburo resident foreign policy experts.

What are the implications of this consensus-oriented and highly institutionalized style of decisionmaking for the substance of Soviet foreign and defense policies? First, it could be a misconception to assume that an element of pluralism in the policy formulation process always encourages greater restraint in international behavior. History suggests that often the opposite may be the case. Alexander III was a strong tsar willing to accept the responsibilities of the office, and under him, Russian policy toward its neighbors was tough but moderate and fairly unprovocative. His successor, Nikolas II, on the contrary, was open to influences and therefore had difficulty saying no to all kinds of cliques at the imperial court. Eventually he allowed his country without much planning and preparation to engage in Far Eastern adventures which culminated in a disastrous war with Japan.

Nikita Khrushchev, when his position looked reasonably secure, proceeded with a major demobilization of the Soviet armed forces, but earlier as a contender for power, felt compelled to engage in militaristic rhetoric and generally to make an effort to placate the military and their hearty industry allies. More recently Jiri Valenta convincingly demonstrates how bureaucratic politics influenced the Soviet decision to invade Czechoslovakia in 1968.[21] (See also Chapter 7 below.) It obviously would be a fallacy to argue that an emergence of an assertive leader willing and capable of challenging powerful vested interests would assure that the Soviet Union would turn inward and opt for a more moderate foreign policy. But it is safe to assume that in the absence of a strong chief executive, bureaucratic politics Soviet-style provides a considerable structural and psychological edge to the military-industrial complex.

Secondly, a greater opportunity for domestic functional interests to have an input into the formation of national security strategy should not be misperceived – as it unfortunately has been too often in the past – as something generating pressures toward accommodation with the West. Needless to say, the Soviets need foreign credits and technology. What they do not need, however, is an infusion of alien ideas. Thus, the natural instinct of many party apparatchiks would be to treat any sign that the Soviet Union is becoming generally friendly with the West with suspicion.

In the long-term perspective, taking into account the accumulation of Soviet economic difficulties coupled with the costs of global activism, the access of domestic interest groups to the national security formulation process may have a moderating impact, but as Grey Hodnett cautioned: 'In the short run participation probably will heighten conservative tendencies, other things being equal.'[22]

Thirdly, one should take into account an unusual reliance on and fascination with force which for centuries was a pivotal element in Russian political culture. Nobody probably explained the unusual role of the military and military considerations in Russian history better than one of the most formidable statesmen, Sergei Whitte, who served during the last decades of the Old Regime. As he put it:

> In reality what was the Russian Empire based on? Not just primarily, but exclusively on its army. Who created the Russian Empire, transforming the Muscovite Semi-Asiatic tsardom into the most influential, and dominant European power? It was accomplished strictly by the army's bayonets.

> It was not before our culture, bureaucratised church, or wealth and prosperity that the world bowed. It bowed before our power. And when – with a significant degree of exaggeration – it appeared that we were not as strong as everybody thought, and that Russia was the colossus on clay legs – the picture immediately changed. All our enemies – both internal and foreign – raised their heads and the neutrals began to pay no attention to us.[23]

The mindset, articulated so well by the tsarist Prime Minister, remains present in modern communist Russia. Common to the Soviet elite as a whole is a tremendous fear that any perceived military vulnerability will be immediately exploited by all kinds of the regime's opponents. National security requirements are given far greater priority by the Soviet political class than by its Western counterparts.

Fourthly – to paraphrase Whitte – it is not the universal appeal of communist ideology, not the attractiveness of the Soviet model of development, and definitely not the quality and scope of Soviet economic aid that allows Moscow to enjoy the status of a global actor, a superpower second to none. The military tool seems to be the only thing that works among the Kremlin's foreign policy instruments, and as long as the Soviet ruling strata perceives advances in the world arena to be a contribution to the domestic and international legitimacy of the regime, the military is likely to get a sympathetic hearing.

Finally, as I have argued elsewhere, the special privileged position of the military in the Soviet bureaucratic setup is an important factor in shaping Moscow's national security strategy.[24] The absence of alternative sources of expertise in a position to challenge the uniformed military leaves the Politburo no choice but to rely heavily on the judgements of marshals and admirals. Requests of the military have to be treated, of course, within the overall context of: the general economic situation, the availability of resources and technology, the desire not to frustrate consumer expectations too much and also, naturally, the images of the international environment, including threat perceptions. Still, the institutional arrangement, the 'rules of the game' of the decisionmaking process and the mindset of the ruling elite all favor an emphasis not on contractual arrangement – be it with foreign powers or with its own population – but on unilateral efforts to build adequate forces to assure the security and survival of the Soviet regime.

NOTES: CHAPTER 3

1 The Honorable Alexander M. Haig, Jr, Secretary of State. Address before the American Bar Association, New Orleans, Louisiana, USA, 11 August 1981.
2 See for an excellent discussion on this subject, Seweryn Bialer, *Stalin's Successors: Leadership, Stability, and Change in the Soviet Union* (New York: Cambridge University Press, 1980), particularly ch. 15, 'The politics of stringency'.
3 Richard Pipes is one of the more articulate spokesmen for this school. See his 'Mr X revises', *Encounter* (April 1978) and 'Why the Soviet Union thinks it could fight and win a nuclear war', *Commentary* (July 1977).
4 Robert V. Daniels, in John W. Strong (ed.), *Soviet Politics since Khrushchev, in the Soviet Union under Brezhnev and Kosygin* (New York: Van Nostrand Reinhold, 1971), p. 22.
5 Jerry F. Hough, *The Soviet Union and Social Science Theory* (Cambridge, Mass.: Harvard University Press, 1977), 'The Soviet leadership almost seems to have made the Soviet Union closer to the spirit of the pluralist model of American political science than is the United States', p. 10.
6 Arthur J. Alexander, *Decision-Making in Soviet Weapons Procurement*, Adelphi Paper No. 147–8, International Institute for Strategic Studies, London, p. 2.
7 Alexei Kosygin was associated all his life with economic management. The same is true with regard to his successor Nikolai Tikhonov. Defense Minister Dimitri Ustinov while shifting from party to government jobs and back, was inevitably one of the prime leaders for the last forty years of the military-industrial complex. Foreign Minister Andrei Gromyko is a professional diplomat who joined the Soviet foreign service before World War II, etc.
8 '90% of surviving full members of the 1971 Central Committee were re-elected' at the next 25th Party Congress in 1976; see Gail Warshofsky Lapidus, 'The Brezhnev regime and directed social change: depoliticization as political strategy', in Alexander Dallin (ed.), *The 25th Congress of the CPSU: Assessment and Context* (New York: Hoover Institution Press, 1977), p. 35. The same trend continued at the 26th Party Congress in 1981.
9 See, for example, G. K. Zhukov, *Vospominaniyai Rasmyshleniya* (Moscow: Novosti, 1969).
10 *Khrushchev Remembers: The Last Testament*, 2 vols, trans. and ed., Strobe Talbott (Boston, Mass.: Little, Brown, 1970, 1974), pp. 32–3.
11 Thomas W. Wolfe, *The Military Dimension in the Making of Soviet Foreign and Defense Policy*, Rand Paper Series, P-6024, October 1977, p. 6.

12   Robert V. Daniels, in Paul Cocks, Robert B. Daniels and Nancy Whittier Heer (eds), *Office Holding and the Elite Status: The Central Committee of the CPSU in the Dynamics of Soviet Politics* (Cambridge, Mass.: Harvard University Press, 1976), p. 94.
13   See more on this subject in Kenneth A. Myers and Dimitri Simes, 'Soviet decision making, strategic policy and SALT', ACDA/PAB-243, December 1974, pp. 8–11; see also Dimitri K. Simes, *Détente and Conflict: Soviet Foreign Policy, 1972–7* (Beverly Hills, Calif.: Sage, 1978), pp. 46–69.
14   For an excellent discussion of this subject, see the above-mentioned studies by Thomas Wolfe and Arthur Alexander.
15   Harriet Fast Scott and William F. Scott, *The Armed Forces of the USSR* (Boulder, Colo: Westview Press, 1979), p. 99.
16   Konstitutsiya (Osnovnoy Zakon), *Soyusa Sovetskikh Sotsialisticheskikh Respublik*, Moscow, 1977, p. 34.
17   Dimitri K. Simes, 'Deterrence and coercion in Soviet policy', *International Security*, vol. 5, no. 3 (Winter 1980–1), pp. 100–1.
18   Contrary to the usual pattern, Ivan Arkhipov, who replaced Tikhonov as first deputy chairman of the Council of Ministers, was not even given a candidate membership in the Politburo.
19   Timothy J. Colton, *Commissars, Commanders, and Civilian Authority: The Structure of Soviet Military Politics* (Cambridge, Mass.: Harvard University Press, 1979), p. 244.
20   Jerry F. Hough and Merle Fainsod, *How the Soviet Union Is Governed* (Cambridge, Mass.: Harvard University Press, 1979), p. 536.
21   Jiri Valenta, *Soviet Intervention in Czechoslovakia, 1968: Anatomy of a Decision* (Baltimore, Md: Johns Hopkins University Press, 1979).
22   Grey Hodnett, 'The pattern of leadership politics', in Seweryn Bialer (ed.), *The Domestic Context of Soviet Foreign Policy* (Boulder, Colo: Westview Press, 1981), p. 111.
23   S. Ju. Whitte, *Vospominaniya* (Moscow: Politizdat, 1960), Vol. 2, p. 300.
24   Simes, op. cit., pp. 100–2.

Part Two

The Military and Soviet National Security Decisionmaking

4 The Historical Legacy in Soviet Weapons Development

JERRY F. HOUGH

Soviet weapon designers are treated as real heroes in the Soviet Union, as men who are advancing technology and helping with the Soviet effort to catch up with the West militarily. The military men engaged in research and development, by contrast, have remained much more in the shadow. The civilian designers and their shieldbearers have little reason to share their glory with the military, all the more so because the latter have often been on the other side in many types of bureaucratic conflicts. It is, of course, possible that the imbalance in media coverage reflects an actual imbalance in the role the institutions have played. If this is not true, however, we in the West may tend to equate coverage with influence and exaggerate the relative role of the design bureaus in the process of Soviet research and development. This chapter will attempt to round out the picture by pulling together the various pieces of evidence that are available on the role of the military in weapons development.

The information that is available for this task is far from satisfactory. The strict censorship over military-related matters has only been lifted gradually and selectively. The interesting data have not been revealed in balanced scholarly studies about the development of individual weapons, but almost exclusively in biographical and autobiographical form. Either because of the difficulty of obtaining declassification of information from a variety of agencies or simply because of a desire to show their subject in the best light, these books and articles tend to be one-sided.* For these reasons, we will begin our analysis by looking at the role of the military in the period described most comprehensively in the literature, that just prior to World War II. Once we have drawn more reliable conclusions about the bureaucratic relationships at a time when it is more possible to balance different accounts, we will have a baseline against which to judge the continuities and changes suggested by the fewer pieces of information on the postwar period.

THE DEVELOPMENT OF THE COORDINATING INSTITUTIONS

In retrospect, participants in Soviet weapons development in the late 1920s and early 1930s have expressed amazement at the simplicity of it all. A college student could be called upon to design an entire airplane as his

---

* See and cf. biographies of M. Nedelin[1] and S. Korolev,[2] and works by A. Iakovlev[3] and P. Avdeenko.[4]

graduation project,[5] and the only experimental shop for airplane motors was subordinated to the automobile and truck makers and slated for closing until a personal appeal to Stalin saved it.[6] A single Scientific-Technical Committee of the People's Commissariat of Defense handled the evaluation of the broad range of new technical proposals,[7] and the deputy commissar for armaments, Mikhail Tukhachevsky, could become personally involved in setting up a small laboratory for some civilian rocket enthusiasts.[8] Soviet industry was having an extremely difficult time developing tank production, because it did not have an automobile and tractor industry and the trained personnel it would have produced.[9] All heavy industry, including the defense industry, could be supervised by a single commissariat, headed by Sergo Ordzhonikidze.

By the late 1930s, however, the defense establishment had become a much more substantial entity. The armed forces had increased from 100,000 men in 1930 to 3 million in 1939. A decade of rapid industrialization was reflected in the division of the Commissariat of Heavy Industry into a number of independent commissariats, five of them wholly or substantially related to defense: (1) airplane industry; (2) ammunition; (3) armaments (essentially small arms and artillery); (4) medium machinery (essentially trucks and tanks); and (5) shipbuilding. Finally, after the Spanish Civil War, Stalin began to evaluate seriously the kind of artillery, fighter planes and tanks the military really needed.

This growth in the size and complexity of the defense establishment required coordinating mechanisms, and during the purge and immediate postpurge period these were expanded. Khrushchev's memoirs describe Stalin jealously monopolizing all weapons decisions and not even permitting other Politburo members to participate,[10] but this picture is accurate only to the extent of Khrushchev's involvement, as he was largely excluded from this sphere. In fact, Stalin established an elaborate committee structure in which a range of persons, including Politburo members, took part in defense decisionmaking.

Purely military decisionmaking was concentrated within the Commissariat of Defense and the Commissariat of the Navy, with almost no joint discussion of problems between the two institutions.[11] Each commissariat was headed by a Main Military Council (*Glavnyĭ voennyĭ sovet*), which was chaired by the commissar (minister) and contained the deputy commissars and one member of the Politburo among its members. The Politburo member may have changed from time to time. Marshal Zhukov listed Stalin as a member of the Main Military Council of the Army in 1937, but, in 1941, he used the formulation 'one of the members of the Politburo', which could mean the position was rotated.[12] Andrei Zhdanov was the Politburo member on the Main Military Council of the Navy in 1937, but by 1939–40 he was the Politburo member in charge of tanks and in 1941 he was reported to be a member of the Main Military Council of the Commissariat of Defense. At this time he may or may not have retained responsibility for the navy.[13]

The fullest description of the work of the Main Military Council has been provided in the memoirs of Kirill Meretskov. He asserted that the council met two or three times a week and that, as a rule, it heard and discussed

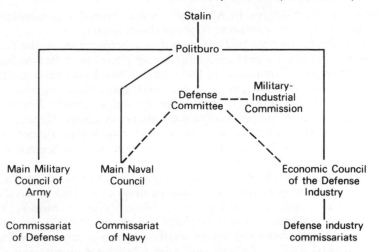

Figure 4.1 The committee structure established by Stalin for defense decision-making.

reports by the commanders of military districts or of kinds of troops. According to Meretskov, a decision was taken on each subject discussed, confirmed by the People's Commissar, and then sent to Stalin. Indeed, Stalin had often already been present during the discussion: 'In these cases, he invited the members [of the council] and the commanders and chiefs of staffs of the districts to his place for dinner in the evening. The conversation often continued there until late at night.'[14]

The Main Military Council was the central place where purely military questions were discussed. It dealt with such questions as the number of troops to be stationed on the Manchurian border, the results at the battle of Lake Khasan, and the structure of the army group conducting the battle at Khalkhin-Gol and the names of the commanders.[15] The Main Military Council was involved in weapons decisions, but its task was to formalize the military position before the final negotiations with the defense industry took place. One source describes a council session devoted to the discussion of competing tank designs, with the designers present to defend their work, and the Commissar of the Navy asserts that questions of ship construction were a frequent subject of discussion at the Main Military Council.[16]

The defense industry originally faced few problems of coordination until early 1939, for the entire industry (except for a small tank industry) was under a single commissariat, headed by Maxim Kaganovich.[17] Then the commissariat was split into three (and ultimately four), and the tank industry became increasingly crucial. At this point, the chairman of Gosplan, Nikolai Voznesensky, was given the responsibility of coordinating the defense industry, and an Economic Council of the Defense Industry was established as the institutional framework in which this was to occur.[18]

A whole series of defense decisions could not, however, be made either by the military or the defense industries alone. This was especially so of decisions on weapons development, where some type of agreement was needed between the producers (the scientists, designers and defense industry), and the consumers (the military). In April 1937 Stalin created a Committee of Defense as the primary institution to serve this function.

In essence the Committee of Defense was a subcommittee of the Politburo. It was chaired by Stalin himself and then by Voroshilov after the latter had been removed as Commissar of Defense in 1940. In addition to these two men, the memoir evidence suggests that Malenkov, Mikoyan, Molotov, Voznesensky and Zhdanov were also members and, no doubt, Beria also served on it. The names of four Politburo members – Andreev, Kaganovich, Kalinin and Khrushchev – never appear in discussions of weapon development, and presumably they (perhaps with the exception of Kaganovich) were not members of the Committee of Defense.

The Committee of Defense had wide-ranging responsibilities in realms where the military interacted with civilian institutions (it had no involvement in the purely military decisions of the Main Military Councils). The committee had to approve all new weapons and modifications in old ones. This jurisdiction included a weapon as small as a pistol or an experimental model of an antiaircraft radar unit, and even a technical question such as whether tank turrets should be cast or stamped out of metal required a Committee of Defense decision.[19] The committee also had to approve the number of weapons produced, and a military-industrial commission (*voenno-promyshlennaia komissiia*) attached to it seems to have handled related questions of supply priorities.[20] One official suggests that in 1940 the committee could have had a key role in allocating sensitive resources between the defense and the nondefense commissariats, in this case means-of-communication items.[21]

The relationship between the Politburo and the Committee of Defense is not clear, all the more so because of the major overlap in their membership. Certainly, however, a distinction was made between the two. Even if the various interested parties were agreed and gave their 'visa' (signature), a Committee of Defense decision normally seems to have required Politburo approval.[22] If one of the parties did not agree with the Committee of Defense, it could appeal the decision to the Politburo – and in one famous case the decision was appealed three times.[23] The literature also contains references to what seem to be preliminary discussion of design decisions before the Politburo.[24]

Particularly after Stalin gave the chairmanship of the body to Voroshilov, the Committee of Defense may have become a more preliminary and technical body in the decisionmaking process. It had a professional staff, whose task seemed to be to draft decisions, to ensure that the necessary documentation was presented, and to provide other staff assistance. The major decisions seemed to be supervised by individual Politburo members – Zhdanov, as has been seen, for tanks, Malenkov, in at least one case, for mortars and apparently Stalin himself for airplanes.[25] The Politburo member would lead much of the discussion and negotiations in his office or in conferences, and the final Committee of Defense decision in these cases would likely be a formality. Similarly, when the artillery decision was appealed three times to the Politburo, Stalin each time created a commission headed by a Politburo member to look into the question – the first headed by Malenkov, the second by Molotov and the third by Zhdanov.

To the extent that key decisions devolved to *ad hoc* conferences and commissions, Stalin probably participated less in Committee of Defense sessions, and the referral of questions to the Politburo may have meant referral to Stalin for final approval. Clearly, Khrushchev was not called in from the Ukraine for these sessions, but the memoir literature suggests that some kind of formal Politburo session did take place. At other times, however, they report meeting with Stalin and 'some Politburo members', and it is conceivable that this kind of session served the function of a Politburo meeting.

There are fewer memoir reports of Politburo sessions on the kind of purely military question which is within the sole province of the Main Military Council, and they tend to be of more formal reviews of past events than operational planning sessions.[26] Stalin may well have felt that many Politburo members needed to participate in weapons decisionmaking because of the implications of weapons for each other and the economy, but that no useful purpose was served by broadening the number of leaders who were exposed to military planning.

MILITARY ORGANIZATION IN THE R&D REALM

In one sense the organization of military participation in weapons decision-making is synonymous with the organization of the military in general. Each type of troop, each type of administrative unit required some type of equipment, and the memoir literature makes it obvious that each demanded greater quantities of weapons and that they were 'quick to make conclusions about design defects'.[27] The military as a collective body could also make an appeal. In one such case, for example, the Main Naval Council petitioned the Committee of Defense to obligate two design bureaus to place torpedo launchers on airplanes.[28]

In circumstances in which the key decisions concerned the characteristics of basic weapons, the military officers in the strongest position to influence the decision were those who would be called upon to use the weapon. Their word was likely to carry great weight on whether to give preference to a new airplane which performed better at one altitude rather than another, to a more maneuverable or a faster airplane, and so forth. Soviet officers actually fought in Spain, in China, on the border with Japanese-controlled China and then in Finland. Some of the leading advisors in Spain were named to key R&D posts in the late 1930s,[29] but the opinions of other participants were frequently solicited – and offered. Thus, Leningrad scientists developed a mine-detector in one day when complaints came in from the Finnish war.[30]

In addition to the general advocacy and expression of opinion coming from all segments of the military, certain officials and administrative units were given special responsibilities in the realm of research and development – or, as the Soviets phrase it, in the realm of 'armaments' (*vooruzhenie*). First, one deputy commissar was named in each commissariat to coordinate weapons development. Tukhachevsky had held this post in the Commissariat of Defense during 1930–6, and in the postpurge period these duties were performed by Grigorii Kulik, an old crony of Stalin from the Civil War.[31] In the Commissariat of Shipbuilding Ivan Isakov had been the deputy commissar for shipbuilding and armament in 1938–40, and he was replaced by L. M. Galler in October 1940.[32]

The deputy commissar for armaments supervised one or more chief administration (*glavnoe upravlenie*) which conducted weapons procurements, a scientific-technical committee, and other independent scientific-technical units (for example, the technical administration in the Commissariat of the Navy and the Artillery Academy in the Commissariat of Defense).[33] Since the scientific-technical committee of the Commissariat of Defense established financial limits on R&D expenditures throughout the commissariat, the deputy commissar inevitably became involved in priority decisions about weaponry for all services, but Kulik is not reported to have been an active participant in decisions about aircraft development.

The most famous and important main administration was the Main Artillery Administration (*Glavnoe artilleriiskoe upravlenie*).[34] Two high officials of the Main Administration explicitly state in their memoirs that it handled almost all the weapons of the ground forces – not only artillery, but small arms, ammunition and tanks as well.[35] Since it was responsible for antiaircraft guns as well as ground artillery, it was concerned with the mechanisms that helped aim the guns and the detection of incoming airplanes, and for this reason it fell into a major role in radar development.[36]

Despite the fact that the Main Artillery Administration was said to exercise responsibility for tanks, the Commissariat of Defense also had a Main-Auto-Armor-Tank Administration (*Glavnoe avtobrontankovoe upravlenie*). The biographical and autobiographical descriptions of the work of the key officials in the tank and armorplate industries repeatedly refer to negotiations with officials of this administration and say almost nothing about the Main Artillery Administration as such.[37] Perhaps the latter just handled the procurement of tanks already produced, or perhaps it concentrated on the guns which were mounted on the tanks.

The Commissariat of the Navy's major subunit for handling R&D was the Main Shipbuilding Administration (*Glavnoe korabl'stroitel'noe upravlenie*). This Main Administration, in turn, contained at a minimum a (naval) artillery administration, a shipbuilding administration, a control-reception apparatus (*kontrol'no-priemnyi apparat*), and (assuming that it was not independent of the Main Administration) a mine and torpedo administration.[38]

Many of the individual services and subservices also had their own armament administrations. In 1940 the development of the airforce was absorbing 40 percent of the appropriations of the Commissariat of Defense budget and, although it is seldom mentioned in the literature, the airforce had a major administrative unit supervising these expenditures – the administration of orders and technical supply of the airforce (*upravlenie zakazov i tekhnicheskogo snabzheniia VVS*).[39] The airforce also had its own research institute (NII VVS) – 'an experimental center in which the final evaluation of the flying and fighting qualities of new airplanes, motors, equipment, and armaments was conducted'.[40] When the designer, Alexander Iakovlev, became deputy commissar of the aviation industry in charge of design and science in 1940, he selected his department heads primarily from airforce generals in the armament sphere, and he named the deputy head of the airforce's research institute as the director of the commissariat's major scientific institute – the Central Hydro-Aerodynamics Institute (TsAGI).[41] Clearly, they had been doing something to prepare them for their new responsibilities.

Subunits within services also often had their armament units. Within the navy, for example, the hydrography administration included a compass section and a compass design bureau, which were deeply involved in the development of magnetic and gyroscope compasses.[42] The Main Military-Engineering Administration of the Army had a department of obstacles and mines in its administration of military-engineering preparation, whose task was 'liquidation of our lag in mines and mine defense'.[43] Such subunits were scattered throughout the military establishment.*

Administrative units of such different power as the Main Artillery Administration and the weapons units of individual services and subservices obviously performed different functions, and these functions changed somewhat as World War II became more imminent. For purposes of simplicity, however, this chapter will use the phrase 'armament administration' to cover all of the units listed above, for it is clear that they all performed much the same functions.

One function of the armament administration was to serve as the primary supply agent for armaments. The Rear Services (*tyl*) was the major arm of the armed forces for handling supply questions, but (except perhaps for providing certain technical services) it was excluded from weapons procurement. Instead, 'the Main Artillery Administration (GAU) bore complete responsibility for leading the many institutions which conducted the placing of orders for the diverse types of artillery and other armament and ammunition for the infantry, which accepted them for the military, and which handled their accumulation, storage, and distribution'.[45] Obviously, the broader planning of the weapons to be delivered to the services involved higher officials and the General Staff as well, but the Main Artillery Administration processed 'the mass of orders for new equipment' and had 'to prepare and conclude the contract' for each of them.[46] It also was responsible for organizing the service and repair of armaments.[47]

A second responsibility assigned the armament administrations was to check on the quality of weapons produced by defense industry plants. Each held the approved blueprints for the weapons within its jurisdiction, and no one – neither the designer nor the defense industry minister nor the plant – could make a change in a weapon without its approval.[48] It had a control-reception apparatus (*kontrol'no-priemnyi apparat*), which supervised a network of military representatives (*voennye predstaviteli* or *voenpredy*) located at the various plants from which it received supplies.[49] These representatives were called upon 'to watch over the quality of production and its correspondence to blueprints and to see that the production processes work according to the strictly-established technology',[50] and their formal power

* Both the commissariats of Defense and the Navy had active scientific-technical committees. The relationships between the committees and the operational armaments administrations is not clear, but the former were more important in purely scientific problems such as the demagnetizing of ships.[44]

was enormous: 'In the case of infringements of the established technology or deviation from the confirmed blueprints, he had the right to refuse to accept delivery and thus to stop production.'[51] Indeed, the military representatives at the plants also had responsibility for 'timely scientific and technological perfecting of military production, the systematic improvement of production, and the introduction of progressive methods of production' at the plant.[52]

The real, as opposed to the formal, duties of the military representatives are, however, not completely clear. The defense plants had their own department of technical control – the OTK – which would seem to have had identical quality-control responsibilities and a very large staff. It seems most improbable that the military representative staff had sufficient manpower to inspect each piece of work on a systematic basis. Perhaps both the OTK and the military representatives received the same inspection report from the factory floor, watched the final testing of major weapons together and then each made its independent judgement.[53]

It would probably be wrong to exaggerate the normal power of the military representative. The status position of these men seems to have been a relatively low one,[54] and a memoir argument about the dangers of leaving the control function entirely to the regular technical control department – and reference to a case where there was no representative at all – suggests some tendency in this direction. Although this latter source reported 'many unnecessary arguments and conflicts' between the military representatives and the industrialists over quality questions,[55] it is likely that the former exercised their full power only in extreme cases.

Particularly in the realm of weapons development, the basic problem with the legal language about the role of the military representatives is that it suggests a neatness in the introduction of new weapons that simply does not exist. It is only in the process of production that bugs are worked out and production problems uncovered – that final blueprints and technological processes emerge. Even then, plant employees and the soldiers are encouraged to make suggestions for improvement in either at any time.

In this process the directors and military representatives often seem to have worked together, and the relationship was often not as antagonistic as appears on the surface. The senior military representative at the Kirov works in Leningrad in 1939–41 has written of his participation in the 'adjustments' (*nalazhivanie*) in production as a new tank (the famous KV) was being introduced,[56] while the Commissar of the Navy reports that ships could be begun before the technical designs were confirmed.[57] A major defense industry administrator at the time suggests in his memoirs that the military representative at the plant normally may have had the *de facto* ability to exercise the authority to deviate from blueprints in minor cases.[58] Of course, the military representative may also have been serving as a communications point, reporting complaints of the troops to the plant and the complaints and proposals of the plant to higher military authorities.

In addition, the military representatives may have been of assistance to the plant when difficulties arose in supplies procurement. During World War II, when military representatives were placed in the important food industry plants, their real-world responsibilities included not only control of the plant's work, but also reporting to higher authorities about supply problems that threatened production: 'Their information gave the possibility of maneuvering resources and overcoming this or that obstacle in time.'[59] This was probably an important part of the military representative's job in the prewar period as well, perhaps necessitated by the difficulties that military secrecy posed for other appeal channels on supply problems (such as the local party organs).[60] An accommodating military representative could also be invaluable to the plant in its drive for plan fulfillment 'in the last days of the month: the 29th, the 30th, the 31st, the 32nd, the 33rd, and even the 34th (thc latter being the days of finishing up production that was already recorded as plan fulfillment in the old month, but completed only in the beginning of the next one)'.[61] Presumably the military representative's signature or at least acquiescence was needed for such machinations.

The third responsibility of the armament administrations was to take a leading role in the modification of weapons or the development of new ones. To some extent the role flowed out of its other duties. Since it held the blueprints of weapons and checked on their strict observance, it naturally became involved in the negotiations to modify them. Since it was the intermediary between the defense industry and the various services in the delivery of weapons, it naturally received the latter's complaints about defects either in production or design.

Nevertheless, the role of the armament administrations in weapons development went far beyond this type of adjusting or intermediary role. In the most basic terms, commanders of the different kinds of troop units were responsible for administering the troops, for training them to use new weapons, for changing the structure of regiments, divisions, and so forth, if new weapons seemed to demand it. The armament administrations – and the deputy minister or deputy commanders of troops which supervise them – are responsible for organizing the development of new weapons – or at least for carrying out the military's duties in this realm.

The clearest statement about the special responsibility of the armament administrations and their supervisors in weapons development comes in the biography of the leading Soviet specialist on rocketry in the 1940s and 1950s, Marshal Mitrofan Nedelin. During November 1948–March 1950 he was head of the Main Artillery Administration, in March 1950–January 1952 commander of the artillery of the armed forces, in January 1952–April 1953 deputy minister for armaments, in April 1953–March 1955 commander of the artillery again and in March 1955–December 1959 once more deputy minister for armaments.[62] His biographer (the present Commander of the Strategic Rocket Forces) asked rhetorically: 'Did such shifts occur by chance?' He answered his own question:

Not at all. When cardinal questions of producing and testing rocket-atomic weapons were being decided then Nedelin became deputy minister for armaments, but in periods when the new weapons were being introduced to the troops, he was entrusted to lead the artillery, in which the first rocket sections were located.[63]

The armament administrations had several different roles in the R&D process. One involved direct supervision of the scientific institutes and laboratories that are subordinated to the military itself. If the institute or laboratory were directly subordinated to the particular armament administration that wanted to promote some project, then the latter could have obligated it to carry out the project.

The important design bureaus, however, were primarily subordinated to the defense industry commissariats (or their plants), and most of the best scientists worked in the institutes of the Academy of Sciences or the industrial ministries. Even the military institutes were spread around the various armament administrations, and any one administration found most of the military institutes administratively independent of itself. In these cases the armament administration had to serve as 'customer' (*zakazchik*). It had to find an institute that would accept a research contract or to persuade a design bureau to modify a weapon or develop a new one. Or perhaps, more typically, it had to participate in committee politics with officials of the relevant military service, leading scientists and designers, officials of the appropriate defense industry, and representatives of the Central Committee and Council of Ministers.

Indeed, until the war (or shortly before it), the Main Artillery Administration (and presumably other armament administrations as well) even served as the general contractor for a new system such as an antiaircraft battery. It made separate contracts with each of the commissariats which were to produce some part of it and then assembled the finished product on its own bases. Only when the scale of work made this system unworkable did the Main Artillery Administration ask for – and receive – the right to compile the general documentation for the system and to give it to the major producer (say, the Commissariat of Armaments). The latter then had the responsibility of ordering what it needed from other commissariats and delivering a finished product to the Main Artillery Administration.[64]

Of course, the crucial question about the role of the military in weapons R&D is the relationship of the armament administrations to the other actors in the system. Whatever the influence of the former, they did not operate by fiat nor did they have exclusive access to the top leadership on weapons questions. For example, the Main Artillery Administration had an artillery committee (*Artkom*) in which 'the tactical-technical data of future modes of artillery armament were examined. The combat commanders, the most prominent scientists, well-known designers, and representatives of the ministries [*sic*] which produced artillery took part in the discussions'.[65] As has been discussed, weapons decisions were also raised in the other collective forums, and Stalin's decisions followed consultation with a variety of officials. In this process what was the relative role and influence of the armament administrations, the services, the defense industry, the designers and the scientists?

THE ARMAMENT ADMINISTRATIONS AND THE MILITARY UNITS

Within the military itself, there were two basic types of actors with which the armament administrations interacted: the General Staff and the services and sub-branches of the services. Of the two, the least important by far seems to have been the General Staff. After the 1935 reorganization at least, the role of the General Staff included 'the planning of orders to industry for military technology and armaments'.[66] The operational administration of the General Staff – the most important subdivision of it – included officers who dealt with each of the services, and in the early 1930s at least the head of the section dealing with the navy participated in weapons decisionmaking with respect to it.[67] Indeed, although very young and not a member of the party, this individual had been appointed to his post by the head of the General Staff, in large part because he had had the temerity to take a position in 'polar' opposition to that of the leading naval officials on a major expenditure decision.[68] (From all indications, he favored a large surface fleet, while they wanted to spend the money exclusively on defensive measures: relocation of the Sevastopol naval base and construction of submarines and small coastal ships alone.)

Nevertheless, a recent description of the inner organizational structure of the General Staff in 1939 and 1941 gives no indication of any administrative section handling technological or weapons questions, nor does a comprehensive memoir about the General Staff during the war.[69] At least during May 1938–July 1940 the head of the General Staff had an assistant 'for organizational-mobilizational and material-technical questions', but a semiautobiographical article by this man suggests that he devoted his major attention to the first three duties specified in his long title.[70] Military intelligence, which was subordinated to the General Staff, had a technical department which sought information about foreign weapons, but it is not clear that it was institutionally integrated with the General Staff.

Although the various heads of the General Staff during this period sometimes attended meetings on new weapons, their biographies and autobiographies do not describe any major involvement in debates about weapons development.[71] The biographer of the head of rocket development in the postwar period reports that the latter 'cleared' (*soglasoval*) the documents that he prepared with the General Staff, and it is likely that this type of overall assurance that the weapons program fit with other programs and with resources was the major role of the General Staff in the prewar period too.[72]

The line officers, by contrast, were very active participants in the details of the weapons development process. On one level their role was quite simple: they wanted more. The head of artillery, Nikolai Voronov, wanted a 100-millimeter gun as well as the construction of two entirely new factories to produce tractors (*tiagachi*) to pull artillery pieces.[73] The commanders of the communications troops – from lower staff officers to top officials in the Commissariat of Defense – were repeatedly complaining about the neglect of the communications system and calling for an improvement.[74] The tank officers were arguing that the shipbuilding program should be cut back so that the armor could be diverted to tanks, while the naval officers were making the opposite case.[75] The head of the military transportation administration asked for 120,000 slow-acting mines (and got 120).[76] Obviously, the services collectively were asking for more than could be produced, and the armament officials were charged with balancing the various pressures.

Of course, the weapons decisionmaking process involved more than decisions about which service requirements to cut and by how much. The major questions were: How much better? At what cost? How fast? A higher-quality and more sophisticated weapon costs more and, given a fixed level of appropriations, the quality is purchased at the price of quantity. Similarly, the more time allocated to the perfection of a weapon, the longer before the services receive it. Conversely, if a new weapon is rushed into production, there is a great danger that the armed services will be equipped in a way that will soon seem obsolete. At a time when the danger of war was very clear, but when it was unclear whether it would occur in one, two, three, or four years, these decisions were excruciatingly difficult.

On this type of question, there seems to have been no consistent differences between the services and the armament administrations. For example, the memoirs of the head of artillery show him taking a variety of positions *vis-à-vis* the Main Artillery Administration and its head, Kulik. In the previously mentioned dispute over the 100-millimeter artillery piece, the government had given Kulik a weight limit for it, but Voronov insisted that only models which were 800–1,000 lb above it were durable. In yet another case it was Kulik who pushed for the 'pretty' model, as Voronov contemptuously (and, no doubt, unfairly) labeled it, and Voronov supported the top defense industry official who argued that 20 percent more guns could be produced if a simpler model were chosen. In a third case he served as the chairman of a state commission charged with deciding whether to accept a new gun, and he refused to accept it, despite the opposition of the defense industry and Commissar of Defense and the silence of the other military officials.[77]

This type of variation in the relationship between the Main Artillery Administration and other bureaucracies on this type of question may well have been typical, for they had reason to be torn between quantity, quality and innovation. On another type of decision, however, the role of the armament administrations seemed more crucial: the development of more unconventional weapons or subtle technological changes in more conventional ones. The need for weapons for airplanes, tanks, artillery and rifles was obvious to everyone, and the tradeoffs involved in decisions about them were not beyond the ability of interested laymen to understand. The feasibility of radar, the best aerodynamic characteristics for airplanes and the right alloys to strengthen armorplate were different matters altogether. A layman could understand the results of tests of such innovations, but a line officer might not be aware that some innovation was possible, let alone desirable.

The armament administrations had the responsibility of filling this gap. In the first place one of the main duties of the Main Artillery Administration was to follow foreign journals carefully – to find ideas that might be adopted and to learn about the West's weapon plans so that countermeasures could be taken.[78] During World War II the specialists of the main administration had to carefully follow the new models of enemy weapons that appeared on the battlefield, so that they could 'react sensitively' and 'take the necessary measures'.[79] They must have done the same for the various military actions in the second half of the 1930s.

In the second place the armament administrations seem to have had a special charge to encourage totally new innovations. Besides their own scientific facilities and test stations, they also had a budget which they could use to support new ideas either directly, or through the signing of contracts with established scientific institutes. The best-documented such case is the development of radar. Although the evidence comes from only one man – the leading officer in the Main Artillery Administration working on airplane detection – and conceivably may exaggerate the relative role of the administration,[80] the nature of the source makes the description of the officer's entrepreneurial role very reliable. And his role was extremely entrepreneurial. He went from scientific institute to institute until he finally found one which was willing to conduct the experiments and then, when the experiment was successful, to take a larger contract. He maintained contact with the scholars in a series of higher-educational institutes, and he fought in bureaucratic politics for the creation of prototypes and eventually an experimental plant and institute. When he felt in a strong enough position during the war, he proposed to the head of the electrotechnical department of the Central Committee that a single state organ be created to develop radar.[81]

With the basic relationship between the armament administrations and the commanders of the services varying with the type of question involved, the relative influence of the two types of officials also surely varied. In fact, Stalin seemed determined to ensure that influence of middle-level officials was not constant. He fully expected his subordinates to defend their institutional interests vigorously, and in at least one case in the early postwar period, he reproached one aviation designer (Lavochkin) for telling him that another designer's (Mikoyan's) plane was better: 'It is not good if a designer does not care for his own machine.'[82] He had the sense that people's judgement could not be trusted when their interests were involved, and he established the norm that the chairman of the state commission which supervised the final testing and reception of a new weapon should not be an 'interested' party.[83] And, of course, he reserved for himself the right to choose between arguments as he wished.

In these circumstances the influence of middle-level officials depended in substantial part on persuasion, and hence was bound to be idiosyncratic and variable. One would have thought that the major armament officials – especially the Main Artillery Administration, which was responsible for a number of weapons – had a natural advantage, for high officials always have a tendency to give the benefit of the doubt to officials charged with balancing the various pressures. Moreover, the head of the Main Artillery Administration, Grigorii Kulik, was an old crony of Stalin from his Civil War days. (He had been chief of artillery of the famous 1st Cavalry army with which Stalin had a close connection.)

Two factors, however, tended to reduce the influence of the armament administrations. First, paradoxically, the very background of Kulik leads one to wonder whether he had the influence suggested by his connections. In the late 1930s Stalin had a very pronounced policy of promoting young, technically qualified men into administrative posts (including military posts) where technical knowledge should be important, but Kulik had no such qualifications. As Khrushchev had told Stalin in calling for Kulik's removal, the post of chief of artillery of the 1st Cavalry army had meant command of two or three cannons,[84] and Kulik has been universally damned in the official memoir literature, despite norms which favor a muting of direct criticism of individuals in these books.[85]

Conceivably the explanation for Kulik's longevity in this post is that, in fact, he was not having as much impact on decisions as appeared to others. Weapons decisions were absorbing much of the attention of the top leadership, and Kulik may primarily have been serving as the 'no man' in the system – the man who was taking the heat for priority decisions that were required by limited funds and that were being taken by Stalin behind his back. Kulik's incompetence made him an ideal lightning-rod for this purpose. The memoirs invariably show him incompetently opposing this or that needed weapon – with the memoirist failing to acknowledge that limited industrial capacity meant that some choice had to be made.[86] Stalin himself is treated much more favorably in this literature, and Kulik may have been one reason.

A second factor that seems to have reduced the role of the staff of the armament administrations was the nature of the weapons problem at the time. The leadership was strongly emphasizing the basic weapons – tanks, artillery, airplanes and (for a period) large ships – and peripheral weapons were neglected in the budgetary squeeze. The development of less dramatic weapons such as mines, mine-detectors and communications equipment was given little priority. Radar too received little support, and the atomic scientists decided that it was hopeless to ask the government for a substantial appropriation to begin work on a reactor.[87]

To the extent that the armament administrations were combing the foreign literature for exotic ideas or supporting such ideas of Soviet scientists or inventors, they had little chance of getting them adopted in the Soviet Union if considerable funds were required. Conceivably the staffs of the armament administration were having a major impact on the microlevel – say, in providing ideas from abroad on a new artillery gear, the best structure of an aileron, or the like – but, unfortunately, the Soviet literature provides little information on this level of development.

At a time when basic weapons were being emphasized and the key decisions involved their characteristics, the military officers who would use the weapons were in a very strong position. This became even truer when war began. In the opening days of the war pilots resolved the long argument between the designers of gasoline airplane engines and those of diesel engines with their complaints about 'the damned diesel engines'.[88] In yet another case a group at the front, unhappy about the vulnerability of the IL-2 airplane to enemy attack, modified one themselves to include space for a tail-gunner as well as a pilot. Sent to Moscow, this plane was tested in front of high officials, and the IL-2 designer was instructed to adopt this modification.[89]

THE MILITARY AND THE DEFENSE INDUSTRY

In overall terms the most powerful civilian participants in weapons development below the Politburo members were the top defense industry administrators. The incentive system under which they worked tended to make them a conservative force in weapons decisionmaking. Essentially they were judged by their ability to fulfill a monthly plan, and hence they had an interest in having a plan that was as low and uncomplicated as possible. Since any change in product is inevitably associated with the type of temporary production problem that can threaten plan fulfillment, the defense industry administrators had every reason to prefer weapons that were simple to produce and that were not being continually changed.

The available evidence suggests that the defense industry administrators did, in fact, have this type of bias. The specific examples of conflict in which they are reported to have been involved almost always centered on their objections to 'unreasonable' quality demands, to excessively 'pretty' weapons, to 'endless' model improvement. The author of the most complete memoirs by a defense industry official of the day – Vasiliĭ Emelianov – is quite open in discussing the tendency of plant managers to protest their inability to accept any new order or task in their plan, and he does not hide his own such behavior. Indeed, when he was new to his post, his superior was careful to warn him against the newcomer's mistake of being too accommodating.*

The most famous battles between the military and the defense industry on the eve of the war concerned the proper characteristics of tanks and artillery. The Commissar of the Tank Industry, Viacheslav Malyshev, became totally exasperated with the tank commanders because of their demands for various types of improvements, and the Commissar of Armaments, Boris Vannikov, objected so 'categorically' to the military proposal to take the 45-millimeter and 76-millimeter artillery pieces out of production and replace them with a more powerful gun that he three times appealed to the Politburo to have the decision favoring the military overturned. It was presumably for his vehemence on this issue that he was arrested, and only after the war started was he summoned from his cell to Stalin's office and restored to high office.

One should, of course, not exaggerate the degree of the conservatism among the defense industry administrators. Planning and development are bargaining processes. An industrial administrator knew that higher officials would demand higher levels of production and that the military would want 'impossible' quality levels. An intelligent industrialist had to overstate his objections and demands so that he would still be in a reasonable position when he made the retreats that he knew were inevitable. The industrial administrators also had their professional pride, and they knew how unprepared the Soviet Union was for an impending war whose loss would be a disaster for their country and for themselves as members of the communist elite. Moreover, the fact that Stalin himself was absorbed in weapons questions and that he had just killed much of the old defense establishment on the ground of treason surely lessened any inclination of the new administrators to drag their feet in a way that might draw similar charges.

One should also not exaggerate the certainty of conflict between the military and the defense industry administrators. Just as the relationship

* For discussion of defense industry–military conflicts, see Goremykin,[90] Nosovsky[91] and Gamburg.[92]

between the military representatives at a plant and the plant manager was ambiguous, so the relationship between higher industrial and military officials was also not one-sided. With the military itself often divided, the industrial administrators were certain to agree with one side or the other, and in conflicts over the priority to be given various types of weapons (for example, tanks vs artillery), the industrialists producing one type of weapon were likely to be allied with the commanders using it against the industrialists and military commanders associated with the other. The cooperation required on this kind of bureaucratic struggle should have muted the tendency toward conflict on other questions.

In practice the literature suggests a good deal of ill-feeling between the tank industry officials and the top tank officers in the army, but, by contrast, the artillery commander, Voronov, reports that he had a very good relationship with the Commissar of Armaments, Vannikov.[93] In early 1940 the new Commissar of the Aviation Industry (Aleksei Shakhurin) and the new Commander of the Airforce (Iakov Smushkevich) also 'found a common language at once'. According to Shakhurin, the two met frequently 'in design bureaus, at experimental plants, and, most often, at airfields . . . Now you cannot find a single protocol of these improvised meetings, but the decisions taken at them were extremely serious'.[94]

If we turn to the question of the relative influence of the military and the defense industry on weapons development, here too we find variability, but probably in the framework of some equality. Vannikov complained about the influence of 'the side which was called upon to guard quality', and, of course, the users of weapons had a major impact on their characteristics, all the more so because they had to make the budgetary commitment to order it. Yet the leadership's desperate desire for quantity in weaponry and the severe restraints on its resources gave great power to any argument that some weapon would be too expensive or difficult to produce.

The basic equality in the power of the military and defense industry administrators is suggested by the frequent consequence of a major conflict between the two: relative inaction. With so many legitimate demands for new weapons, one that could not obtain the approval both of the military and the industrialists tended to languish. The result of the great controversy over artillery was that the Soviet Union entered war with none in production, and the great slowness with which the new KV and T-34 tanks were moved into mass production in the prewar period is probably explained in a similar way.

The normal influence of the defense industry and the military likely varied with the type of question. Ultimately the military had to have the major impact on the basic characteristics of weapons (should the plane be built for altitude or speed? What caliber of weapon was needed?), but the defense industry probably had their greatest impact in determining the general characteristics of all weapons. Westerners have often remarked on the tendency of Soviet weapons to be serviceable and effective, but to be relatively simple and to show little concern for the creature-comfort of the users. The self-interest of the defense industry administrators must have been a major factor in this tendency.

THE MILITARY AND THE SCIENTIFIC-DESIGN COMMUNITY

As indicated earlier, the figures in weapons development who receive by far the most publicity in the Soviet Union are the chief designers. At least in the case of airplanes and many conventional groundforce weapons, their initials – or occasionally their names – even became part of the public name of the weapon.[95] In the everyday jargon of the aviation personnel, the design bureaus are called 'firms' – a word which originally was applied only to capitalist industrial enterprises and which, therefore, suggests entrepreneurial effort.[96] Their powers are described in sweeping terms, and in the space program of the 1950s and early 1960s, the chief designer of each system – the rocket, motor, telemetry, guidance, and so on – was called the 'god' (*bog*) of his activity. For example, Valentin Glushko, the motor designer, was termed 'the god of fire', and the collective meetings of the different chief designers were 'the council of the gods'.[97]

Yet there are nagging worries about the image reported in the previous paragraph. First and foremost, the chief designers who have become the most famous have almost all been subordinated to the defense industry. If the defense industry officials tended to be rather conservative, why did they allow the designers under them to cause trouble by being so innovative?

It may be that, in fact, we have overgeneralized about the innovative role of the designers on the basis of the experience of a few glamorous weapons being developed in unusual circumstances. Each of the major airplane designers of the immediate prewar period has had at least one book dedicated to him but (except for the later rocket designers) the designers of other types of weapons almost never receive this honor.[98] The chief designers of groundforce weapons (even the relatively glamorous T-34 tank and katusha rocket) usually are the subject only of short articles, while those of ships receive even less attention. Conceivably the differences in prestige are related to differences in role.

Even the situation with respect to fighter airplane design may have been peculiar to that time. The major fighter plane designer prior to 1939 had, in fact, ceased to be an innovative force, and Stalin made a deliberate decision to create a competition among young designers, which he personally would oversee. In 1940 when he appointed the 33-year-old Iakovlev to be the deputy commissar of the aviation industry in charge of design, he reassured the protesting Iakovlev that his age was 'not an obstacle but an advantage': 'You are not connected with the mistakes of the past and therefore you can be more objective than old specialists whom we believed very much but who led us up a blind alley.'[99] With the political leadership dissatisfied with the level of innovation, the young designers did, in fact, have every incentive to make a name for themselves by proposing something new, but it was a political decision that gave them the resources and the forum to do so in a dramatic fashion.

The normal relationship between the designers and the military must have varied with the role of the designer. A relatively simple weapon could be the product of a single man or a small team, but ship construction was a far more complex assembly of different systems, and perhaps the personal role of the chief designer was correspondingly low. The relationship between the military and the designers could also vary with the subordination of the latter. Most designers worked in the defense industry, but some worked in institutions directly subordinated to the military. The latter included not only small and narrow units on such things as camouflage and parachute design, but also the Rocket Scientific Research Institute (RNII) that designed the katushas, the Artillery Scientific Research Institute of the Army (ANII RKKA) which worked on shells among other matters, the Scientific Experimental Research Institute of the Army (NIIIS RKKA), the Scientific Research Institute of Armaments and Shipbuilding of the Commissariat of the Navy, the Scientific Research Mine–Torpedo Institute of the Navy (HNMTU), the Scientific Research Naval Institute of Communications (NIIMS), the Naval Artillery Scientific Research Institute (ANIMI) and, no doubt, many others.[100] (The last-mentioned ANIMI had a design staff, in which the young Dimitri Ustinov worked in 1934–8 before becoming director of the major Bolshevik plant in Leningrad.) The designers subordinated to the military were obviously in a very different position than those administratively independent.

In practice the relationship between the military and the designers of the defense industry does, in fact, seem to have varied enormously. The designers of simpler weapons such as guns and artillery seem to have relied heavily on the military for the major specifications, and the latter could describe these designers in quite secondary terms:

> A group of comrades had an occasion to be at the plant that produced 76-millimeter anti-aircraft guns. In conversations with leaders of the plant, the thought arose that it might be possible to take advantage of the great reserve of strength of the gun carriage to mount a larger-caliber barrel on it. The designers liked the idea, and they made the preliminary calculations in our presence. It turned out that it was completely possible to increase the caliber of the barrel. And thus the 1939-model of the 85-millimeter caliber weapon was born.[101]

When weapons were more complex, the designers' role could become more entrepreneurial, but here too their relationship with the military could vary greatly. At one extreme the military and the tank designers seem to have been allied in pushing improvements in the tank, and the top tank industry administrator, who wanted to start mass production, became as annoyed with the designers as he was with the military.[102] At the other extreme the relationship between the military and the aircraft designer seems to have been quite antagonistic on the whole. Fighter design involved a series of tradeoffs. There were choices to be made between maneuverability and speed, as well as between relative performance at different altitudes.[103] More important, armorplating, a tail-gunner, weaponry and larger fueltanks (which were necessary for greater distance) all added weight to a plane and reduced its speed. To the designers, the military came across as men who insisted on ever-greater speed plus more of everything that was incompatible with it.

The military seem to have had considerable influence *vis-à-vis* the designers – or at least they usually seem to have had the ability to block production of a weapon whose design they did not approve. Their ability to influence production decisions on tanks and artillery has already been discussed. The same situation prevailed with respect to aircraft. Thus, even though the troop support plane IL-2 (the plane that was to be the most successful for the Soviet Union in World War II) had been accepted by the state commission, the airforce held up production during February–December 1940 because of disapproval of the plane's armor and speed.[104] Airforce officials were able to force the designer, Lavochkin, to make a change in his LAFF-1 which he thought unwise, and they prevented Iakovlev from providing space for a tail-gunner.[105] The great influence of the airforce on airplane design – and the delays this produced – may well have been one reason that the airforce, alone of the services, had three of its chief commanders killed by Stalin in the postpurge period and a fourth exiled to the Far East.[106]

The relationship of the military to the scientists is more difficult to assess. They do not appear often in Western discussions of Soviet weapons development,[107] and they tend to be peripheral figures in most Soviet discussions. Yet the reasons for the rapid improvement in airplane performance in the 1930s, were improvements in the understanding of aerodynamics, the result of scientific work, not design. In this broader sense the scientific community clearly was having a major impact on weapons development in the Soviet Union in the 1930s.

Conceivably the scientific innovations were being made in the West, were incorporated into Western engineering innovations and then introduced into the Soviet Union by Soviet engineers, but it seems far more likely that the Soviet scientists themselves were a crucial part of this transmission – and creative – process. Certainly, the major Tupovlev design bureau was, for a long time, an actual part of the Central Aero-Hydrodynamics Institute (TsAGI), and all the significant design bureaus had an aerodynamics group within them.[108] Similarly, a coordinating body such as the Scientific Council of the Academy of Sciences for the Problems of Combustion and Explosions must have had considerable contact with those working on detonation and explosives in the military realm.[109]

Although – except perhaps in shipbuilding – scientists may not have had much direct contact with the leadership or often even the military, a number were deeply involved in weapons development as individual entrepreneurs. It has been reported, for example, that the scientist, A. I. Ioffe, 'always was full of new ideas ... He then came to the People's Commissariat of the Defense Industry with a series of new and unusual proposals'.[110] Moreover, when a new scientific idea was involved (as it was in the development of radar), the leading scientists on the subject became powerful authorities. If they said that an idea would not work or if they refused to accept a research contract, their word could be fatal unless the entrepreneurial military officer could find another authoritative scientist with a different view.[111]

THE CHANGING ROLE OF THE MILITARY IN THE POSTWAR PERIOD

The purpose of this chapter has been to try to establish a solid historical baseline against which to judge the evolution of the Soviet R&D process in more recent years. A secondary purpose has been the methodological one of attempting to demonstrate that the unclassified memoir and biographical literature is an extremely rich source for understanding Soviet bureaucratic structure and behavior, even in this sensitive realm.

The limits of space preclude a thorough examination of the evidence on the similarities and differences in the weapons process of the late 1930s and of the present time. The basic relationships between the military and the other actors, however, seem much the same as they were forty years ago. The various services continue to fight for new weapons and for larger quantities of existing ones. The basic relationships between the military, the defense industries, the designers and the scientists also seem much the same as they were in the 1930s. Basically, all of these groups have retained a strong material self-interest in the expansion of the defense establishment. Nevertheless, the old tradeoffs between weapon innovation and ease of production, between quality control and plan fulfillment, between the 'prettiness' of a weapon and the quantity of it to be produced at a given cost continue to exist. The politics of these issues still has the same base of institutional self-interest as before.

Indeed, even the structure of civilian control may be far more similar than the conventional Western image suggests. The notion that coordination between the military, the defense industry and the scientists is provided by a military-industrial commission, headed by the top defense industry administrator, L. V. Smirnov, flies in the face of all bureaucratic logic. The defense industry administrator, who is not even a Politburo member, should not be placed in a position to resolve conflicts between the defense industry and the military. It is far more likely that the military-industrial commission plays the same production and supply priority role that it did in the 1930s (the continued publication in collections of military documents of the decree setting up the commission also suggests this) and that the role attributed to the commission is played by the Council of Defense. (If this is true, the latter probably does not have foreign policy responsibilities.)[112]

The changes in the process of Soviet weapons development are likely to be the product of two factors. First, the nature of Soviet weaponry has changed. The new weapons in the postwar period involved the marriage of such components as nuclear warheads, electronic or targeting systems, radar or other systems of location and computers, and they have become increasingly sophisticated in their technology. The number of participating institutions had to multiply. Thus, when the first relatively long-range rocket (BRDD-1) was designed in 1947, 'the collectives of many scientific research institutes and design bureaus and dozens of industrial plants contributed their work',[113] and this became the rule rather than the exception. In addition, the growth in Soviet military might permitted greater attention to the secondary weapons that were neglected in the 1930s, and this too widened the number of participants in the process.

Secondly, the defense establishment has become much more institutional-ized and stable. The civilians and the military commanders who were thrust upward in the wake of the Great Purge tended to have very long tenures and to dominate the defense establishment into the 1960s, and in some cases (notably Ustinov) even longer. The design community has perhaps been affected most. Iakovlev's bureau began in a bedframe factory and, as he joked later, the plant's plan the first year was 10,000 bedframes and one plane. Now the designers head an institution with several thousand em-ployees, fine accommodations and good equipment, and they themselves inevitably have become more like 'a director of the orchestra'.[114]

The pattern of personnel selection at the top of the design bureaus is even more suggestive of the change from the 1930s. One can find a case in which a chief designer of a rocket design bureau was replaced (although, to be sure, one attached to a plant assigned second-rate work[115]) or in which an Institute of Motors of 1,700 employees, headed by a long-time, 70-year-old designer, was abolished in 1962.[116] Yet such events seem relatively rare – perhaps very rare. The famous airplane chief designers of the 1930s normally retained their posts until their deaths (usually in the 1970s). Their replacements, when known, deepen the impression of a system become ingrained. When Mikoyan died, he was replaced by his long-time first deputy chief designer, R. A. Beliakov,[117] while Tupolev was replaced by his son.[118]

A number of consequences have followed from these two developments:

(1) *An expansion of the system of armament administrations to handle weapons procurement*. Despite the fact that the GAU is now called the Main Rocket Artillery Administration,[119] many of the 'modern' weapons have been taken from it and given to new main administrations. (The rocket in its title refers to ground force rockets like the katushas.) Judging by signatures to obituaries, two main administrations may have been created to deal with long-range rockets – one that focuses primarily on atomic warheads, the other on strategic rockets and launch sites.[120] At least one other main administration also was formed to handle some aspects of electronics or air defense weaponry (perhaps SAM missiles).[121] This may well be an incom-plete list.

(2) *A greater coordinating problem in weapons development and an expan-sion in the coordinating mechanisms*. Within the military, a second deputy minister for armaments was established over at least 1949–64 – a deputy minister for electronics – and then apparently recreated during 1977–80.[122] The role of the General Staff in weapons development was also greatly increased. During 1964–70, in particular, there was no deputy minister for armaments, and the first deputy head of the General Staff served as the top military official in armaments development. In 1970 the post of deputy minister for armaments was reestablished, and the top coordinating official in the General Staff was demoted from first deputy head to deputy head,[123] but even this post did not exist in the 1930s.

In the civilian sphere the most visible expansion in the coordinating mechanisms occurred within Gosplan. A special first deputy chairman of Gosplan was named to coordinate security planning – first of all, defense industry and military spending, but also that for the police.[124] One would think that a single Council of Defense would have become overburdened with the proliferation of new weapons and that much of the actual authority to approve weapons changes and innovations would have passed to *ad hoc* interagency committees, but, if so, no information has emerged about them.

(3) *Some lessening of the competitive atmosphere in weapons design that featured fighter plane development at the end of the 1930s.* Part of this is the inevitable product of the change in weaponry. It was extremely wasteful to ask several design bureaus to produce models of rifles or even a World War II fighter plane and then to have the winner selected in a performance competition. Such a process would have been economically unthinkable in the development of the atomic bomb and, in practice, it was not followed. As weapons become more complex and expensive, it is likely that the Soviet Union has been moving increasingly to a pattern of decisionmaking in which key decisions are taken at an earlier stage than in the famous airplane decisions. Even in a realm such as fighter planes, the airforce has concentrated its purchasing on the gradually evolving product of the Mikoyan bureau for thirty years.

A number of Western observers have noted on the gradualism that seems to have crept into the design of a number of Soviet weapons,[125] and the explanation may go beyond the growing complexity of weaponry. The institutionalization of the design process and the stability in the network of major bureaus would also produce this effect and surely has to some extent. In addition, the institutionalization almost surely has made the design bureaus much more a part of the defense industry to which they are subordinated. That is, one suspects that the developments in the design bureaus are not unrelated to the structure of self-interest of their defense industry superiors and that, as a result, the design bureaus have taken on some of the conservatism of the latter.

(4) *A larger role for scientists and scientific institutes in the development of weaponry.* The relationship between the natural scientists and the political-economic elite seems to have been marked by social distance and mutual suspicion in the prewar period, and this must have had an impact on their role. This changed during and after the war. The proportion of scientists who joined the Communist Party gradually increased,[126] and the young graduates of the engineering institutes of the 1930s, especially those of white-collar origins, had a tendency to flee from production into science and design.[127] As they aged and rose in responsibility, they were much more integrated into the Soviet system than had been the previous generation of scientists.

More important, as the leading Soviet military theorist on science has emphasized, the changing nature of weapons has had a major impact on the role of the scientists:

> For a long time the mutual relationship between [science and military affairs] was built on the model: from the military sphere to science and back from it to the military. At a certain stage the military recognized a need and formulated it in a concrete inquiry to the competent scientific institutions . . . With the development of science and the growing complexity of the problems of strengthening the defense might of the country, a different type of connection began to be more widespread – from science

to the military . . . To a greater degree, the development of science led that of the military sphere.[128]

The clearest example of the model 'from science to the military' arose in the nuclear realm. The military could ask the scientists for more resistant armorplate for tanks, but they did not even dream that a splitting of the atom would have important military consequences. The scientists had to tell them. Then once the atomic program was established, the government knew that it had to expand the amount of nuclear research so that scientists might learn other unanticipated facts.[129] With the development of electronic, biological and chemical weapons, there is almost no branch of science that is not of direct relevance to the military, and even mathematicians became vital for computer and rocket development. (The director of the Institute of Applied Mathematics of the Academy of Sciences, Mstislav V. Keldysh, was named 'the chief theoretician' of the space program, heading 'the work of coordinating the activity of the institutes and design bureaus aimed at creating the first artificial satellite of the Earth'.)[130]

(5) *A likely increase in the initiating and innovative role of the military in weapons development, especially* vis-á-vis *the designers.* During the 1930s the military had an especially great innovating role in radar, where it was necessary to deal with the scientific community and stimulate new research. It is probable that the military study of foreign material has expanded enormously, as has the military pressure for parallel work in the Soviet Union. It is highly significant that the deputy commander of the airforce for armaments (Mishuk) has close connections with the director of the Central Hydro-Aerodynamics Institute, but weak ones with the design bureaus.[131] With the scientists preferring basic or at least nonclassified research, the military's pressure for applied military work may be quite necessary, and the major expansion in the network of purely military institutes increases their ability to push through what they want.[132]

(6) *The most interesting question about change concerns not the recent past, but the future.* The Soviet defense sphere under Brezhnev took on a somewhat relentless but rigid appearance. Weapons continue to be produced beyond the point of rationality. New models are developed which are but minor improvements upon old models. One could explain these developments as the response to a planned drive for superiority, but they are also consistent with a model of bureaucratic incrementalism in which the leadership passively ratifies decisions within the framework of a 4–5 percent budgetary increase. The debate about these rival explanations is really unresolvable on the basis of current knowledge, but a change in leadership at a time of great policy dilemmas should provide the opportunity for greater leadership control over the defense establishment if there is a will. Despite the program of the Reagan administration, the opportunity to put enormous strains on the NATO alliance will give the new leaders ample incentive to make significant changes in the defense realm if the pattern of decisions which seem so threatening to us have merely been the result of bureaucratic inertia.

NOTES: CHAPTER 4

1 V. Tolubko, *Nedelin. Pervyi glavkom strategicheskikh* (Moscow: Molodaia gvardiia, 1979), p. 188.

2 P. T. Astashenkov, *Akademik S. P. Korolev* (Moscow: Mashinostroenie, 1969).

3 For example, see A. Iakovlev, *Tsel zhizni (Zapiski aviakonstruktor)*, 3rd edn (Moscow: Politizdat, 1972), pp. 210, 239, 252. In one case the military held up the IL-2 support plane in January–December 1940, even though it had passed state inspection, for they were dissatisfied with the thickness of its armor. In another the head of the airforce strongly resisted the designers' efforts to remove skis from fighters because he believed that northern fields could not be kept clear of snow. And, finally, unnamed influential airforce officers were said to underevaluate fighter planes in comparison with bombers. However, Iakovlev did acknowledge that an earlier head of the airforce, Iakov Smush-kevich, had liked a sports plane Iakovlev had designed and had reported about it to Stalin; see ibid., p. 163. (In general, Iakovlev goes out of his way to include as many conversations with Stalin as possible in the third edition, and for this reason it is usually the most useful for the historian.)

4 Thus, an airforce colonel attributes the delay in the IL-2 not simply to the airforce, but to arguments between the airforce and the People's Commissariat of the Aviation Industry. P. Avdeenko, 'Sovetskoe samoletostroenie v gody predvoennykh piatiletok (1929–40 gg.)', *Voenno-istoricheskiĭ zhurnal*, no. 7 (1974), p. 89. An airforce general specifically criticizes Iakovlev for saying almost nothing about the role of military testing of planes in their development and accuses the designer of sometimes charging others with mistakes that were his own. N. Sbytov, 'Vazhnyi vklad v istoriiu razvitiia otechestvennoi aviatsiĭ', *Voenno-istoricheskiĭ zhurnal*, no. 10 (1967), pp. 105–6.

5 Astashenkov, op. cit., p. 101.

6 A. D. Charomskii, 'Pervye shagi sovetskogo aviatsionnogo motorostroeniia', in I. M. Danishevskii (ed.), *Byli industrialnye (Ocherki i vospominaniia)*, 2nd edn (Moscow: Politizdat, 1973), pp. 110–17.

7 M. M. Lobanov, *My-voennye inzhenery* (Moscow: Voenizdat, 1977), pp. 95–6.

8 A. P. Romanov, *Raketam poskoriatsia prostranstvo* (Moscow: Politizdat, 1976), pp. 34–9; Iaroslav Golovanov, *Korolev* (Moscow: Molodaia gvardiia, 1973), pp. 210–29; and Astashenkov, op. cit., pp. 53–5.

9 John Erickson, *The Soviet High Command* (London: Macmillan, 1962), pp. 302–3.

10 Nikita S. Khrushchev, *Khrushchev Remembers*, 2 vols, trans. and ed., Strobe Talbott (Boston, Mass.: Little, Brown, 1970), pp. 158–9, 174.

11 G. K. Zhukov, *Vospominaniia i razmyshleniia*, Vol. 1, 2nd edn (Moscow: Novosti, 1974), p. 229.

12 ibid., pp. 117, 217.

13 For 1937, see ibid., p. 117; for 1941, ibid., p. 236; and for 1939–40, V. Emelianov, *O vremeni, o tovarishchakh, o sebe*, 2nd edn (Moscow: Sovetskaia Rossiia, 1974), p. 499. Tanks and ships were not an unnatural combination. They were the big competitors for scarce armorplate, much of which was produced at 'Northern Works' in Zhdanov's Leningrad.

14 K. A. Meretskov, *Na sluzhbe narodu: Stranitsy vospominanii* (Moscow: Gospolitizdat, 1968), pp. 168–9.

15 M. V. Zakharov, 'Nakanune vtoroi mirovoi voiny (mai 1938 g.–sentiabr' 1939 g.)', *Novaia i noveishaia istoriia*, no. 5 (September–October 1970), pp. 13, 17, 23.

16 V. A. Vishniakov, *Tank na pedestale* (Moscow: Voenizdat, 1970), pp. 48–50; and N. G. Kuznetsov, *Nakanune* (Moscow: Voenizdat, 1969), p. 226.

17 Kaganovich was not very competent, and in practice his three deputy commissars are said to have handled matters largely by themselves; see Emelianov, *O vremeni, o tovarish-chakh, o sebe*, op. cit., p. 358.

18 V. Chalmaev, *Malyshev* (Moscow: Molodaia gvardiia, 1978), p. 100; and B. Vannikov, 'Iz zapisok Narkoma vooruzheniia', *Voenno-istoricheskiĭ zhurnal*, no. 2 (1962), p. 81.

19 V. V. Bakhirev and I. I. Kirillov, *Konstruktor V. A. Degtiarev: Za strokami biografii* (Moscow: Voenizdat, 1979), pp. 108, 109; Lobanov, *My-voennye inzhenery*, op. cit., p. 152; and Emelianov, *O vremeni, o tovarishchakh, o sebe*, op. cit., pp. 515–18.

20 The memoir literature, which does not hesitate to discuss or at least mention all of the other high-level collective bodies, does not, so far as I have discovered, contain a single

concrete reference to the commission. (Emelianov does mention it in the most general of terms, *O vremeni, o tovarishchakh, o sebe* op. cit., p. 568.) However, the decision creating the commission has been republished in *KPSS o vooruzhennykh silakh Sovetskogo Soiuza* (Moscow: Voenizdat, 1969), p. 278.

21 N. Gapich, 'Nekotorye mysli po voprosam upravlenii i sviazi', *Voenno-istoricheskii zhurnal*, no. 7 (1965), p. 49.

22 Emelianov, *O vremeni, o tovarishchakh, o sebe*, op. cit., pp. 518–22.

23 P. N. Goremykin, 'O proizvodstve vooruzheniia i boepripasov', in P. N. Pospelov (ed.), *Sovetskii tyl v velikoi otechestvennoi voine* (Moscow: Mysl, 1974), Vol. 2, p. 121. A report about the third commission and its work is found in B. Vannikov, op. cit., p. 81.

24 Chalmaev, op. cit., p. 113.

25 For the mortar case, see Emelianov, *O vremeni, o tovarishchakh, o sebe*, op. cit., p. 506. Zhukov reports that aviation was 'to a certain extent, a passion' of Stalin, and the memoirs do, in fact, report continual contact between him and the airplane designers and little consistent involvement of other Politburo members; see Zhukov, op. cit., Vol. 1, p. 225. Either just before or at the beginning of the war, Stalin shifted the duties of his lieutenants. Zhdanov was stationed at the Leningrad front until 1944, and Molotov took over responsibility for tanks. Malenkov supervised airplane production, and Beria seems to have handled small arms, artillery and ammunition.

26 See, for example, A. Vasilevsky, *Delo vsei zhizni*, 2nd edn (Moscow: Politizdat, 1975), pp. 96–7, 104; for an exception, see Zakharov, 'Nakanune vtoroi mirovoi voiny', op. cit., p. 15.

27 Lobanov, *My-voennye inzhenery*, op. cit., p. 143.

28 P. N. Ivanov, *Krylia nad morem* (Moscow: Voenizdat, 1973), p. 58.

29 D. G. Pavlov became head of the Chief Auto-Armor-Tank Administration, N. N. Voronov became head of artillery and Ia. V. Smushkevich was named deputy head of the airforce; N. N. Voronov, *Na sluzhbe voennoi* (Moscow: Voenizdat, 1963), p. 157.

30 Meretskov, op. cit., p. 183.

31 Kulik did not actually become deputy commissar until January 1939, but he had been head of the Artillery Administration since May 1937 and the evidence suggests that he had general responsibilities from the beginning; for his biography, see *Sovetskaia voennaia entsiklopediia* (Moscow: Voenizdat, 1977), Vol. IV, p. 517.

32 Isakov clearly supervised the Main Shipbuilding Administration, for, like every communist, he had to be included in a primary party organization at his place of work, and in 1938 he was enrolled in the one in this main administration; see A. O. Ariutinian and O. S. Balikian (eds), *Ivan Stepanovich Isakov: Sbornik dokumentov i materialov* (Erevan: Izdatelstvo Akademii Nauk Armenskoi SSR, 1975), p. 61. For Galler, including the assertion that he supervised 'all the technical organs' of the commissariat, see N. Kuznetsov, 'Vsia zhizn' flotu', *Voenno-istoricheskii zhurnal*, no. 3 (1963), p. 75.

33 Zhukov, op. cit., Vol. 1, p. 217.

34 *Sovetskaia voennaia entsiklopediia*, Vol. II, pp. 560–1.

35 Lobanov, *My-voennye inzhenery*, op. cit., p. 163; and Voronov, *Na sluzhbe voennoi* op. cit., p. 157.

36 This is best described in Lobanov, *My-voennye inzhenery*, op. cit.

37 Chalmaev, op. cit., pp. 129, 135–6, 152–3; Emelianov, *O vremeni, o tovarishchakh, o sebe* op. cit., pp. 415–27. Indeed, Emelianov explicitly states that he only knew Kulik a little; see ibid., p. 482.

38 For references to these units, see *Sudostroenie*, no. 4 (April 1975), pp. 68, 73, 74; V. Kostygov and A. Shorygin, 'Vklad v pobedu', *Morskoi sbornik*, no. 7 (July 1973), p. 84; A. Iurkovsky, 'Morskaia artilleriia gotovilas' k boiam', *Morskoi sbornik*, no. 11 (November 1976), pp. 67, 68; M. N. Surguchev, *Korabli vozvrashchaiutsia v stroi* (Simferopol: Tavriia, 1972), pp. 46, 60, 153; and Iu. A. Panteleev, *Polveka na flote* (Moscow: Voenizdat, 1974), p. 245.

39 M. V. Kozhevnikov, *Komandovanie shtaba VVS Sovetskoi Armii v Velikoi otechestvennoi voine, 1941–1945 gg.* (Moscow: Nauka, 1977), p. 59.

40 D. Ia. Zilmanovich, *Na orbite bolshoi zhizni* (Vilnius: Mintus, 1971), p. 210.

41 Iakovlev, op. cit., pp. 202–3.

42 A. Fedotov, 'Razvitie tekhnicheskikh sredstv korablevozhdeniia na sovremennom etape', *Morskoi sbornik*, no. 9 (1977), p. 29.

43 I. T. Starinov, *Miny zhdut svoego chasa* (Moscow: Voenizdat, 1964), p. 173.

44   See ibid., p. 177; and B. Tkachenko, 'Pobeda nad magnitnoi miny', *Tekhnika i vooruzheniia*, no. 10 (1971), p. 11.
45   Tolubko, op. cit., p. 156.
46   Lobanov, *My-voennye inzhenery*, op. cit., p. 143.
47   *Tyl sovetskikh vooruzhennykh sil v velikoi otechestvennoi voine, 1941–1945 gg.* (Moscow: Voenizdat, 1977), p. 66.
48   Lobanov, *My-voennye inzhenery*, op. cit., p. 163.
49   I have identified the title '*kontrol'no-priemnyi apparat*' only in the navy. The Commissar of Armaments in the 1930s used the term 'military reception' (*voennaia priemka*) in a colloquial sense, but 'control reception' accurately describes the functions and was probably the formal title everywhere; see Vannikov, op. cit., pp. 86–8.
50   Mikhail Arlazorov, *Artem Mikoian* (Moscow: Molodaia gvardiia, 1978), p. 43. This statement refers to a military representative on an aviation plant, but the situation was identical in other industries.
51   Vannikov, op. cit., pp. 86–7.
52   ibid., pp. 86–7.
53   For references to joint inspections by the OTK and the military representative at a plant, see N. E. Nosovsky, 'Pushki na konveire', in Danishevsky, *Byli industrialnye*, op. cit., pp. 137, 140.
54   Vannikov, op. cit., p. 87; and Arlazorov, *Artem Mikoian*, op. cit., p. 43.
55   Vannikov, op. cit., pp. 87–8.
56   *Voenno-istoricheskii zhurnal*, no. 12 (1979), p. 81.
57   Kuznetsov, 'Vsia zhizn' flotu, op. cit., p. 73.
58   Emelianov, *O vremeni, o tovarishchakh, o sebe*, op. cit., pp. 515–18. Actually in the case cited by Emelianov, head of the armor-steel production of the Commissariat of Ship-building, he and the senior military representative at the plant usurped the authority of the Committee of Defense to make a major change in the way tanks were produced, but surely they would not have done this if they had not been accustomed to making small changes on their own.
59   D. V. Pavlov, *Stoikost* (Moscow: Politizdat, 1979), p. 132.
60   See the discussion in Jerry F. Hough, *The Soviet Prefects* (Cambridge, Mass.: Harvard University Press, 1969), pp. 224–34. In his memoirs Khrushchev reports that, even though a Politburo member, he often had little knowledge of the Kharkov Tractor Works and that special permission was needed to go there; see Khrushchev, *Khrushchev Remembers*, op. cit., pp. 158–9.
61   M. Gallai, *Cherez nevidimye barery. Ispytano v nebe: Iz zapisok letchika ispytatelia* (Moscow: Molodaia gvardiia, 1965), p. 189.
62   Tolubko, op. cit., pp. 215–16.
63   ibid., p. 181.
64   Lobanov, *My-voennye inzhenery*, op. cit., pp. 192–3.
65   Voronov, *Na sluzhbe voennoi* op. cit., p. 113.
66   V. Danilov, 'Generalnyi shtab RKKA i predvoennye gody (1936–iun 1941g.)', *Voenno-istoricheskii zhurnal*, no. 3 (March 1980), p. 68.
67   The section was called the ninth section of the first administration; see Ariutinian and Balikian, op. cit., pp. 48, 340. In World War II the operational administration still contained officers for each kind of troop; see S. M. Shtemenko, *Generalnyi shtab v gody voiny* (Moscow: Voenizdat, 1968), pp. 132–3.
68   See Vladimir Rudnyi, *Dolgoe, dolgoe plavanie* (Moscow: Politizdat, 1974), pp. 98–100; and A. M. Arzumanian, *Admiral* (Moscow: Voenizdat, 1976), pp. 377–80, 386. An earlier version of this latter biography of I. S. Isakov was published in Erevan, Armenia, by the Aiastan publishing house in 1973. The latter includes some 'negative' detail that was excised from the Moscow edition, and it is organized somewhat differently. On this issue, however, the reports are virtually identical.
69   Danilov, 'Generalnyi shtab RKKA i predvoennye gody (1936–iun 1941 g.)', op. cit., pp. 69, 70; and S. M. Shtemenko, *Generalnyi shtab v gody voiny, Kniga vtoraia* (Moscow: Voenizdat, 1973), pp. 5–21.
70   Zakharov, 'Nakanune vtoroi mirovoi voiny', op. cit., pp. 3–27.
71   M. V. Zakharov, *Uchenyi i voin*, 2nd edn (Moscow: Politizdat, 1978), pp. 77–90; Meretskov, op. cit., pp. 166–70, 195–200; Zhukov, op. cit., Vol. I, pp. 210–63; and Vasilevsky, op. cit., pp. 91–114.

72 Tolubko, op. cit., p. 175.
73 Voronov, *Na sluzhbe voennoi*, op. cit., pp. 116–17.
74 Gapich, op. cit., pp. 47–50.
75 Emelianov, *O vremeni, o tovarishchakh, o sebe,* op. cit., p. 437.
76 Starinov, op. cit., p. 186.
77 Voronov, *Na sluzhbe voennoi,* op. cit., p. 115.
78 Lobanov, *My-voennye inzhenery,* op. cit., pp. 143, 191.
79 A. N. Latukhin (ed.), *Bog voiny* (Moscow: Molodaia gvardiia, 1979), pp. 86–7.
80 In a note attached to Lobanov's first article on the subject, the editors warned that the analysis might be contentious; see M. Lobanov, 'K voprosu vozniknoveniia i razvitiia otechestvennoi radiolokatsii', *Voenno-istoricheskii zhurnal*, no. 8 (1962), p. 13.
81 Lobanov, *My-voennye inzhenery,* op. cit., *passim*.
82 Mikhail Alazorov, *Front idet cherez KB* (Moscow: Znanie, 1969), p. 127.
83 Emelianov, *O vremeni, o tovarishchakh, o sebe,* op. cit., p. 424. Every rule has its exception. In 1947 Stalin was extremely eager to have twenty bombers, so that he would have an atomic delivery system. The Minister of the Aviation Industry was told to have them by 1 May, or he would 'personally answer' for it. He insisted that in such a case he should be chairman of the state accepting committee (so that the military could not hold things up), and in the circumstances was granted his wish. Igor Shelest, *Lechtu za mechtoi* (Moscow: Molodaia gvardiia, 1973), p. 253. For the extraordinary testing procedures for these planes, see Gallai, *Cherez nevidimye barery. Ispytano v nebe,* op. cit., pp. 162–230.
84 Khrushchev, op. cit., p. 174.
85 The most damning picture of Kulik has come from the man who served as first deputy head of the Main Artillery Administration under him: 'G. I. Kulik was a man who was unorganized, who thought too much of himself, who considered all his actions infallible. He believed that the best method of work was to hold his subordinates in terror. His favorite saying in setting a task or giving an instruction was 'prison or a decoration'. In the morning he usually called a multitude of subordinates, assigned tasks in a very foggy manner, and asked in a threatening way "Understood?". Those who received tasks usually came to me and asked explanations and instructions'; see Voronov, *Na sluzhbe voennoi,* op. cit., p. 166.
86 Thus, four pages after damning Kulik, Zhukov admitted that the military had demanded too much; see Zhukov, op. cit., pp. 209–10.
87 David Holloway, 'Entering the nuclear arms race: the Soviet decision to build the atomic bomb, 1939–45', in *Social Studies of Science* (Beverly Hills, Calif.: Sage, 1981), Vol. 2, pp. 159–97.
88 Mikhail I. Vodopianov, *Druzia v nebe* (Moscow: Sovetskaia Rossiia, 1967), p. 215.
89 *Voenno-istoricheskii zhurnal*, no. 9 (1965). It is possible that this story is more complex than this article indicates. The designer of the IL-2, Sergei Iliushin, had originally wanted a tail-gunner and had included a place for one in his first model. 'Specialists' from an unspecified institution objected for unspecified reasons, and Iliushin lost in this dispute; see P. Astashenkov, *Konstruktor legendarnykh ilov* (Moscow: Politizdat, 1970), p. 53.
90 Goremykin, 'O proizvodstve vooruzheniia i boepripasov', op. cit., p. 121. A report about the third commission and its work is found in Vannikov, op. cit., p. 81.
91 In one case a simple error in copying blueprints resulted in a tolerance of 0·02 being changed to 0·2 on a part and led to a major malfunctioning of the weapon and a major bureaucratic scandal before the cause of the problem was discovered; see Nosovsky, op. cit., pp. 140–1.
92 I. Gamburg, 'Nezabyvaemye vstrechi', *Voenno-istoricheskii zhurnal*, no. 11 (1962), p. 76.
93 Voronov, *Na sluzhbe voennoi,* op. cit., p. 114.
94 Arlazorov, *Front idet cherez KB,* op. cit., p. 61.
95 For example, the letters of the MIG fighters represent their designers, Mikoyan and Gurevich ('i' is Russian for 'and'), while the larger TU- and IL- planes are named for Tupolev and Iliushin, respectively. The designer of the famous Kalashnikov rifle is obvious.
96 Arlazorov, *Artem Mikoyan,* op. cit., p. 62. The term is regularly applied to the bureaus of all the major plane designers in the biographies and autobiographies of designers and test pilots; see ibid., p. 97; Shelest, op. cit., p. 385; and Gallai, op. cit., pp. 96, 274.
97 N. P. Kamanin, *Letchiki i kosmonavty* (Moscow: Politizdat, 1972), op. cit., pp. 345–6.

98   An exception is a 1979 biography of the machine-gun designer, Degtiarev; see Bakhirev and Kirillov, op. cit.
99   Iakovlev, op. cit., pp. 191, 199.
100   Iurovsky, 'Morskaia artilleriia gotovilas k boiam', op. cit., p. 70; Lobanov, *My-voennye inzhenery*, op. cit., p. 120; *Morskoi sbornik*, no. 12 (1974), p. 77; and B. A. Tkachenko, *Istoria razmagnichivaniia korablei sovetskogo voenno morskogo flota* (Leningrad: Navka, 1981), p. 21.
101   N. N. Voronov, 'Tak my gotovilas k trudnym ispytaniiam', *Vestnik protivovozdushnoi oborony*, no. 10 (1967), p. 64.
102   Chalmaev, op. cit., p. 116.
103   Arlazorov, *Artem Mikoyan*, op. cit., p. 96; Shesterin, op. cit., pp. 38–9; Iakovlev, op. cit., p. 192.
104   Astashenkov, op. cit., p. 52.
105   Arlazorov, *Front idet cherez KB*, op. cit., p. 60.
106   A. D. Loktionov served from 1937 to November 1939, Ia. V. Smushkevich from November 1939 to August 1940, P. N. Rychagov from August 1940 to April 1941 and P. F. Zhigarev from April 1941. The air defense forces, which used antiaircraft guns and fighter planes, had similar rates of turnover among their commanders.
107   An exception is Holloway, op. cit.
108   The biographer of Artem Mikoyan speaks of his 'intimate collaboration' with his 'multi-year partners – the scholars from TsAGI'; see Arlazorov, *Artem Mikoyan*, op. cit., p. 128.
109   B. Konovalov, 'Gorenie', in A. M. Sinitsyn (ed.), *Schast'e tvorcheskikh pobed. Ocherki o geroiakh trudakh* (Moscow: Politizdat, 1979), p. 87.
110   Emelianov, *O vremeni, o tovarishchakh, o sebe*, op. cit., pp. 372–3.
111   M. M. Lobanov (cited earlier) is the best source on these relationships.
112   James M. McConnell's thesis about the distinction between 'military' (*voennyi*) and 'oboronnyi' (defense) in Soviet usage seems absolutely right and of crucial importance in understanding the higher Soviet institutions: McConnell, *Military-Political and Military-Strategic Leadership in the USSR* (Alexandria, Virg.: Center for Naval Analysis, memorandum no. 1129-75. 09, 28 July 1975).
113   Romanov, op. cit., p. 52.
114   'U aviakonstruktora A. S. Iakovleva', *Voenno-istoricheskii zhurnal*, no. 8 (1978), pp. 70, 73.
115   In the mid-1950s Mikhail Iangel was one of Korolev's top assistants (apparently his first deputy, judging by the way the case is described), and they perpetually disagreed. Iangel was finally named to replace the chief designer of another bureau, and he turned it into a major one; see V. Gubarev, *Konstruktor: Neskol'ko stranits iz zhizni Mikhaila Kuzmicha Iangela* (Moscow: Politizdat, 1977), pp. 72–80.
116   Feliks Chuev, *Stechkin* (Moscow: Molodaia gvardiia, 1978), p. 231.
117   His biography is published in *Deputaty Verkhovnogo Soveta SSSR* (Moscow: Izdatelstvo Izvestiia, 1979), op. cit., p. 61. Also see Arlazorov, *Artem Mikoyan*, op. cit., p. 256.
118   V. Airdarov, 'A. N. Tupolev', *Soviet Military Review*, no. 10 (1978), p. 36.
119   *Krasnaia zvezda*, 31 May 1981, p. 4.
120   V. A. Boliatko, head of a main administration until his death in 1965, and N. P. Egorov, head of a main administration in the mid-1970s and perhaps earlier, had a similar set of signatures on their obituaries, including a number of rocket officials and the Minister of Medium Machinery (the atomic energy program) as the only industrial minister; see *Krasnaia zvezda*, 28 November 1965, p. 3, and 11 February 1976, p. 3, for Boliatko's and Egorov's obituaries. The location of Egorov's signature on the obituary of another official in *Krasnaia zvezda*, 21 June 1967, suggested that he must already have been head of a main administration at that time. If so, he was almost surely Boliatko's successor. The obituary of A. G. Karas, which was signed by strategic rocket officials but not the Minister of Medium Machinery, stated that he had been head of a main administration in 1965–79 (thereby overlapping Egorov); see *Krasnaia zvezda*, 4 January 1979, p. 3.
121   E. G. Iurasov was said to have 'for a long time' been head of a chief administration of the Ministry of Defense before he became first deputy commander of the air defense troops in 1978; see *Kalininskaia pravda*, 20 February 1980, p. 1.

122   M. M. Lobanov was identified as a 'deputy minister of war', without any specification as to date, but the precise wording of his title indicated that he held the post sometime during 1946–53. It is likely that he assumed the post in 1949 upon leaving the Main Artillery Administration. It is likely that he supplemented the regular deputy minister for armament; see M. Lobanov, 'K voprosu vozniknoveniia i razvitiia otechestvennoi radiolokatsii', op. cit., p. 13. Lobanov, *Iz proshlogo radiolokatsii*, op. cit., pp. 166, 172–3. In 1953–60 there definitely was a second deputy minister in the armaments realm, although the post was so sensitive that it was not even mentioned in the press at the time. However, the biographical entries of A. I. Berg and A. V. Gerasimov in the *Soviet Military Encyclopedia* revealed that they had been deputy ministers in 1953–7 and 1957–64, respectively. Gerasimov was specifically listed as a deputy minister 'for radio-electronics' (although conceivably he took over the whole armaments portfolio when Nedelin died in 1960), and Berg must have had the same responsibilities since he had been a top scientist in the development of radar; *Sovetskaia voennaia entsiklopediia*, Vol. I, op. cit., p. 444, and Vol. II, p. 525. Twice in the 1970s another deputy minister was appointed whose function was unclear (N. V. Ogarkov in 1974–7 and V. M. Shabanov in 1978–80). Judging by the functions he attended, Ogarkov is far more likely to have been in charge of foreign weapon deliveries than weapons development, but he must have had some role in general discussions of the latter because of his SALT involvement. Shabanov did not appear at foreign functions, but since he became the deputy minister for armaments when the previous one (N. N. Alekseev) died, he must have already been working in this realm beforehand; see *Krasnaia zvezda*, 26 June 1981, p. 2.

123   Actually the old first deputy head, A. V. Gerasimov, retired, the old head of the Scientific-Technical Committee (N. N. Alekseev) became deputy minister for armaments and Gerasimov's replacement, V. V. Druzhinin, was only given the title of deputy head of the General Staff.

124   The three most recent holders of this post have been V. M. Riabikov, G. A. Titov and L. A. Voronin.

125   Arthur J. Alexander, *Decision-Making in Soviet Weapons Procurement*, Adelphi Paper No. 147/8 (1978), pp. 24–6, 41–2.

126   See Jerry F. Hough and Merle Fainsod, *How the Soviet Union Is Governed* (Cambridge, Mass.: Harvard University Press, 1979), p. 348.

127   Kendall E. Bailes, *Technology and Society under Lenin and Stalin* (Princeton, N.J.: Princeton University Press, 1978).

128   V. M. Bondarenko, *Sovremennaia voina i razvitie voennogo dela* (Moscow: Voenizdat, 1976), pp. 39–40.

129   V. S. Emelianov, *S chego nachinalos* (Moscow: Sovetskaia Rossiia, 1979), pp. 161–2, 257.

130   V. Kotelnikov, B. Petrov and A. Tikhonov, 'Glavnyi teoretik kosmonavtiki', in Sinitsyn (ed.), op. cit., pp. 108–20; the quotation is from p. 109.

131   Alexander, op. cit., p. 18.

132   Bondarenko, op. cit., p. 43.

5 Defense R&D Policymaking in the USSR

ELLEN JONES

Western observers of Soviet military trends are concentrating increased interest on what has come to be known as the Soviet military buildup. Indicators of Soviet military activity reveal an increase in the range and scope of defense commitments. As the overall direction of Soviet military activity became clearer, attention has focused not on the existence of a sustained buildup in military force, but rather on the explanation for it. A key issue in the search for explanations is the extent to which the observed trends can be traced to Soviet policy goals.

The role of policy in shaping Soviet force posture is crucial in determining how one goes about assessing Soviet intentions. Suppose we conclude, for example, that observed outputs can be traced primarily to efforts of Soviet bureaucratic entities to preserve their turf. According to this approach, the sustained output of tanks and the steady appearance of improved models are results of the complex organizational interplay between the Ministry of Defense Industry (which produces conventional weapons), and the high-level party–government officials who ultimately referee the struggle for scarce resources. Tank production continues at a high rate not because the top political leaders want more tanks, but because the policy process naturally seeks a compromise between the various contenders for resources. In this model of the Soviet weapons acquisition process policy goals are largely irrelevant to output. One need not inquire why Soviet political leaders have chosen to underwrite a sustained output of high-quality tanks, because tank production levels are a result of the bureaucratic process itself and not primarily a matter of deliberate leadership choice.

Suppose, on the other hand, we conclude that the observed numbers and quality of Soviet tanks can be explained largely by policy goals; that is, Soviet tank programs are primarily a means to an end. In this case the analysis cannot begin and end with an explanation of observed output. The field of inquiry must be broadened to include a discussion of Soviet goals, what these goals may mean for Soviet foreign policy activities, and ultimately what challenges these goals represent for US policy.

Western discussions of Soviet military activities tend, implicitly or explicitly, to assign varying weight to the role of policy choice in weapons output. For analytical purposes, one may construct a continuum along which various Western models of the Soviet process can be placed. At one end of this spectrum is a hypothetical model which explains Soviet R&D behavior solely by reference to broader policy goals; environmental factors such as the bureaucratic process mentioned above play no role. At the other end of the spectrum is a model which dismisses policymaker intentions as totally

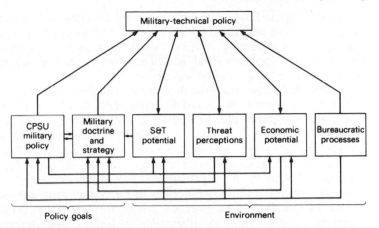

Figure 5.1 Decisionmaking model relating policy goals and environmental constraints to military R&D outputs.

irrelevant and assigns varying importance to environmental factors such as the policymaking process itself, technology levels, economic constraints and threat perceptions.

A decisionmaking model relating both policy goals and environmental constraints to military R&D outputs is shown in Figure 5.1. The analytical challenge is to isolate evidence which would provide insight into the relative weight of policy and environmental factors in explaining Soviet force posture. This chapter examines the impact of policy goals on military R&D and how these outputs are modified by one key environmental factor – the organizational setting in which these policies are made and implemented. It is based partly on limited descriptions of the current Soviet military-political policymaking system found in the Soviet press, and on the more forthcoming treatments of past military policy choices. It also draws on the much richer legal and administrative literature on the Soviet political system itself – a literature that not only describes the normative process (the legal regulations defining levels of authority and procedures for decision formulation and implementation), but also how actual decisionmaking and implementing deviates from the normative process. Finally, the chapter uses the fragmentary bits of evidence emanating from former participants in the process whose testimony has been related in the Western press. It is argued here that policy goals drive the defense policy process far more than has been acknowledged by many Western observers who stress the role of organizational momentum or bureaucratic inertia to explain the Soviet military buildup.

DEFENSE POLICY GOALS

The Soviet description of the military R&D decisionmaking process ascribes paramount importance to the role of policy goals formulated by the central party decisionmaking bodies. Defense policy, 'CPSU military policy', provides the overall guidelines for Soviet military doctrine and, in turn, for weapons procurement activities. CPSU military policy sets basic resource allocation priorities affecting defense allocations and determines the necessary supporting policies (that is, science and economic policies) to implement overall national security goals.[1]

Military policy also determines the main functions of the armed forces and defines the requisite force structure to discharge these functions. The Soviet military's most important role, according to CPSU military policy, is to ensure the USSR's national security.[2] A formulation underlining the pivotal role of Soviet military power was incorporated in the 1961 Party Program, and was still considered relevant in the heyday of détente, 'because there still exist forces who deviate from the principle of peaceful coexistence'.[3] Additional 'external' (purely military) functions of the Soviet armed forces are the defense of the WTO, support of Soviet foreign policy goals (in Soviet parlance, aid to national liberation struggles), and deterrence.[4] Flowing from these overall objectives, the priorities implicit in CPSU military policy are incorporated in economic and scientific plans, 'military development' plans (about which more will be said below), and contingency plans for the transition from peace to war.[5] The goals embedded in CPSU military policy are thus said to affect weapons and force structure choices in these ways: directly through long-term defense plans and indirectly through economic and scientific plans.

The military priorities set by CPSU military policy do not, of course, provide an unambiguous guide to actual program choices. The perceptual filter through which purposeful policy goals (as embodied in CPSU military policy) are translated into broad military objectives and requisite force postures is provided by Soviet military doctrine: 'a system of views accepted by a government at a given time on the goals and character of a possible war, on the preparation of the country and armed forces for it, and the capabilities for prosecuting it.'[6] The Soviets describe their doctrine as generated from military requirements (determined by strategy), coupled with the current levels of economic and scientific development, existing military technology and threat perceptions.[7] That is, overall defense goals are not formulated in isolation from economic or technical constraints or the perceived threat.

A key issue in an assessment of the role of policy goals in military R&D outcomes is the relevance of military doctrine for weapons procurement. It may be argued that doctrine has little impact on actual weapons choices and that individual program decisions are made on a case-by-case basis with no relationship to overall goals. One way to evaluate the influence of doctrine is to examine the various factors influencing the development of a single system.

One example of the interplay between military doctrine, on the one hand, and the development of military equipment, on the other, is provided by the ongoing Soviet efforts to develop an automated troop control system. The Soviet term for such a system is 'avtomatizirovannaiia sistema upravleniia voiskami' (ASUV). Improvement of control methods through an automated command system is one of the five 'major tasks' of the Soviet unified military technical policy.[8] Perceived need for the system preceded actual application of computer technology to battlefield management and was based on Soviet perceptions of the nature of the next war, one aspect of Soviet military doctrine. Soviet military theorists indicate that the 'revolution in military affairs' has placed an increasing burden on command decisionmaking due to increases in the scale of combat, and the range, speed and destructive capabilities of weapons.[9] These changes have brought about an increase in the volume of information that staffs must process. At the same time, the increased pace of combat means that the commander has even less time than he previously did to process incoming information and make decisions.[10]

One possible solution to this problem is a decentralization of control authority, increasing the decisionmaking flexibility of lower-level units. Such a solution, however, was unpalatable to the Soviet military and political leadership, since it violates a basic principle of armed forces development: a centralized command structure.[11] A second, and from the Soviet standpoint, much more desirable solution, is to facilitate the command decisionmaking process through the application of quantitative and automated aids for situation analysis and decisionmaking. Soviet operations research (OR) specialists who advocated this solution to the command and control problem found ample support for their convictions in the Soviet doctrinal stress on 'scientific' problemsolving and in Western military literature extolling the utility of battlefield computers. In fact, the concepts of Soviet automated troop control systems, which are now in a test phase, are based in part on Western developments, although the actual Soviet applications have been much different from those of the West.

The Soviets have attempted to promote their articulated goal – the use of OR methods in command decisionmaking – by developing special procedures to promote the use of combat calculations such as correlation of forces computations. These procedures range from simple charts and nomograms presenting the results of an individual calculation over a typical range of input values,[12] to complex automated control systems. Such a system (ASUV) is defined as: 'a man–machine system providing automated collection and processing of information needed for optimizing troop control with the goal of more effective use of troops'.[13]

ASUV involves four interrelated functions: information storage and retrieval, operational planning calculations, decision evaluation and transmission of commands.[14] Interestingly, the emphasis in Soviet ASUV is on the analytical function (operational planning and decision evaluation), providing a marked contrast with US efforts to develop an information storage and retrieval capacity on the battlefield. The Soviets apparently see ASUV primarily as a way of performing more sophisticated combat calculations,[15] partly because current Soviet deficiencies in computer technology limit storage capacities and partly because such calculations were already part of the operating procedures for command staffs and must have seemed an obvious candidate for automation.

The Soviet approach to automated command systems, then, is a result of the interplay of several factors (see Figure 5.2). Soviet military doctrine, stressing the rapid tempo of modern warfare, isolated the problem: how to facilitate the tactical commander's ability to make rapid operational decisions. The principle of command centralization precluded a substantial

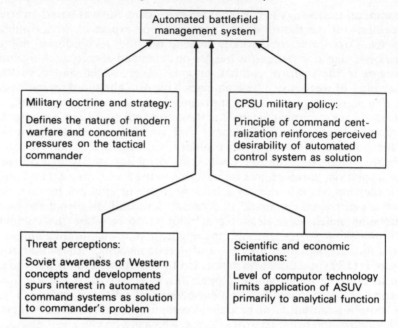

Figure 5.2 Factors influencing Soviet approach to automated command systems.

decentralization of command authority. Soviet awareness of Western operations research (OR) developments underlined the possibilities of an alternate solution to the problem – an automated command system. Existing levels of computer technology led to a Soviet stress on the analytical (as opposed to information storage and retrieval) function, since the use of OR techniques for analytical purposes on the battlefield was more compatible with a lower level of computer technology. This solution was also in line with the growing doctrinal emphasis on quantitative and 'scientific' approaches to problemsolving. With regard to automated command systems, environmental constraints modified the outcome, but Soviet military doctrine pinpointed the need and significantly limited the options.

Articulated doctrine has also influenced observed Soviet design 'style'. The Soviet military press reveals an articulated design philosophy which includes simplicity of design and manufacture; frequent use of proven components; relative ease of maintenance; modernization and modification of existing designs; and high levels of reliability. Observed Soviet design choices are consistent with these aspects of the articulated 'design thought'. As compared with equivalent Western systems or techniques, Soviet weapons tend to be relatively straightforward and easy to manufacture, a principle that the Soviets feel is well supported by the experience of World War II: 'Combat experience has underlined the validity of the basic directions of the development of Soviet design thought, in particular, the attempt to guarantee maximum rationality of design, production and repair technology, unification of components and aggregates, and simplicity of maintenance.'[16]

Soviet tank development provides an example of the Soviet preference for evolutionary (or incremental) weapons development using proven system components – or in the Soviet terminology 'modernization of weapons equipment'.[17] The baseline for the current generation of Soviet tanks is the T-34, developed in 1939. Later Soviet tanks were largely improvements on that basic design.[18]

A related aspect of Soviet design philosophy is the commitment to modification as opposed to replacement:

> It can be stated in advance that the technical level of armament in the hands of the troops will always lag behind current scientific and technical achievements. However, this does not mean that it is necessary to reject available weapons entirely and replace them with new weapons. In a number of cases, relatively minor modifications of already available armament turns out to be more advantageous than the development of new models, mastering their production and rearming the troops with them. In such cases, economic considerations acquire great weight, as well as the maintenance of the appropriate level of combat readiness of troops in each given segment of time.[19]

Soviet equipment practices have been consistent with this principle.[20] Whenever possible, existing equipment is upgraded rather than replaced. In part, this policy is related to cost factors; the Soviet stress on quantity has resulted in large accumulations of equipment; as a result, the cost of weapons obsolesence is magnified. Another consideration, as suggested in the citation above, is the temporary deleterious effect on combat readiness related to the introduction of new weapons in the field.

Soviet efforts to increase such factors as ease of maintenance and system lifetimes – efforts that are evident both in Soviet design choices which favor relatively simple and rugged designs as well as in Soviet articulations of desirable weapons characteristics – are closely connected with achieving high indices in weapons reliability.[21] Given the generally limited mechanical and technical capabilities of the typical Soviet conscript, this principle has been translated into relatively tough, durable designs, simple and sturdy controls and maintenance routines which minimize mechanical demands on the weapons crews. Observed Soviet weapons design choices, then, are consistent with an articulated 'design philosophy'.

ORGANIZATIONAL ENVIRONMENT

Articulated policy goals provide a good deal of insight into military R&D choices. The formulation of policy goals, however, represents only one stage in the policy process. For military policy, as for other policy areas, policy statements must be broken down into concrete, detailed programs and put into practice. Like all large organizations, congruence in the Soviet system between policymaker intentions and the reality of how policies are implemented in practice is far from perfect. The image of a command economy in which subordinate governmental bodies passively transmit and

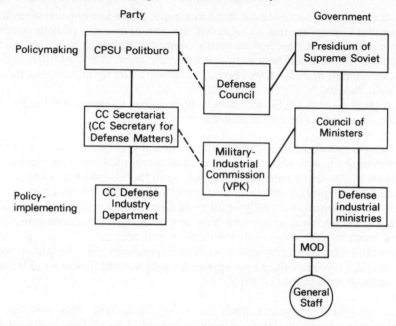

Figure 5.3   Soviet military-political decisionmaking bodies (formal administrative bodies).

execute the dictates of national policymakers is a distorted one. In the national security area, however, the Soviets have shaped their decision-making structure to maximize the party leadership's ability to translate overall priorities into more specific programs and to oversee their implementation by the government apparatus.

Military policy is formulated and implemented within a dual party–government structure, as depicted in Figure 5.3. The respective responsibilities of each component of this structure are spelled out in Soviet legal regulations and party decrees. In general, the party (and more specifically, the top-level party leadership in the Politburo and CC Secretariat) has the authority to formulate policy and to oversee its execution; the government role is to ratify party policy through laws and administrative acts and to implement it. Major military policy decisions providing guidelines for military and armed forces development are approved by the Politburo, as is Soviet military doctrine.[22] The Ministry of Defense (MOD) is currently represented in the Politburo by Minister of Defense D. F. Ustinov. Prior to Ustinov's appointment in April 1976, the Minister of Defense (Marshal Grechko) had been a professional military officer, providing the professional military with a representative on the highest policymaking body in the Soviet Union. Although Grechko's successor Ustinov does not come from the ranks of the professional military, his previous experience included over thirty-five years as the single leading individual in the national-level weapons acquisition management.

While final approval of major policy decisions is reserved for the Politburo, policy recommendations on national security issues are probably formulated in the Defense Council, a joint party-military body that is legally subordinate to the Presidium of the Supreme Soviet, but which apparently operates more as a subcommittee of the Politburo.[23] The Defense Council, described in Soviet legal literature as a 'collegial, interdepartmental body of state administration' which determines 'the basic directions of military development of the USSR', apparently reviews recommendations on CPSU military policy and Soviet military doctrine, with important substantive inputs from the MOD, the General Staff, and top officials from the defense industrial community.[24] The only publicly acknowledged member of the council was former Secretary-General Leonid Brezhnev, who served as chairman from 1964.[25] Brezhnev's successor as secretary-general, Yuri Andropov, has now been officially acknowledged as Defense Council chairman. Historical analogy and analogy with East European defense councils suggest that Defense Minister Ustinov, Premier Tikhonov, Foreign Minister Andrey Gromyko, and L. I. Smirnov (the head of the Military Industrial Commission) may also be Defense Council members.[26] Other probable participants in Defense Council activities are Chief of the General Staff Ogarkov and other senior military leaders, providing the military professionals with direct institutional access to the top forum for political-military recommendations. This high-level membership suggests that Defense Council recommendations dominate Politburo decisions.

The military policies reviewed and approved by the Politburo and Defense Council are executed by government organizations, under close party scrutiny.[27] Soviet legislative and administrative procedures are carefully designed to ensure party domination of the government apparatus.[28] The most important and far-reaching of party policies are embodied in laws (*zakony*) approved by the Supreme Soviet – the highest legislative organ in the Soviet Union.[29] Formal Supreme Soviet ratification is legally required for all major policy decisions, including the level of defense expenditures and the organization of the armed forces high command.[30] The Presidium of the Supreme Soviet is the Supreme Soviet's standing executive committee. Like the Supreme Soviet itself, the Presidium endorses party policy, endowing it with legitimacy. Defense-related issues which require Presidium ratification include approval of Defense Council composition, appointments to the military high command and other military development issues. The Presidium, like the Supreme Soviet, essentially rubber-stamps important policy decisions previously reviewed by the party leadership. Both bodies play a largely symbolic role. The legal acts promulgated in their name, however, are very real, for they provide the legal form for key party leadership decisions. The legal activities of the Supreme Soviet and the Presidium thus provide additional insight into those aspects of military policy which the party leadership considers so crucial as to warrant the highest-level attention.

The Supreme Soviet and its Presidium endow the most far-reaching of the party's policies with legislative form. Actual implementation of policy is the responsibility of the government's administrative apparatus, legally subordinate to the Council of Ministers. Under the Council of Ministers' law of July 1978, the Council is charged with 'guaranteeing the security and defense capability of the country with the goal of defending socialist achievements and the peaceful labor of the Soviet people'.[31] The Council itself is a large body required to meet only once per quarter. As a collective body, its actual policymaking role may be quite limited. However, legal acts executed in its name are very important for they provide the legal authority to execute party military policy. Moreover, the Council's chairman, currently Tikhonov (a full Politburo member) and his closest advisors on the Council of Ministers Presidium wield a great deal of political power and probably have at least some influence in determining how party military policy is executed. The Council is legally tasked with exercising general direction over armed forces development; directing the activities of the Ministry of Defense; and insuring that the armed forces are equipped with 'all that is necessary' to fulfill their mission and that defense needs will be considered in the formulation of economic plans and the budget.[32]

The primary government organization responsible for implementing CPSU military policy and Soviet military doctrine is the Ministry of Defense.[33] MOD responsibilities include formulating plans for the development of the armed forces; improving weapons and military equipment; planning the supply of troops with weapons; and coordinating research and design work in the services.[34] It might be worthwhile here to summarize what is meant by the term military development (*voennoe stroitel'stvo*) and armed forces development (*stroitelstvo vooruzhennykh sil*). The Soviets make a careful distinction between the kinds of responsibilities embraced by these two terms and between the various party and government bodies charged with approval or execution of each. 'Military development' is the broader area of authority; it includes economic, social-political and purely military measures taken by a government to enhance its military power. Military development decisions define the organization and missions of the armed forces, its basic command structure and the manpower procurement system.[35]

Armed forces development, on the other hand, is a component of military development. Armed forces development includes measures relating to the organizational structure of the military, the balance between the various services and branches of service, weapons procurement, manpower procurement procedures, force deployment and supply.[36] It is interesting to note that the party leadership and Defense Council are credited with involvement in both military and armed forces development. At somewhat lower policy level the MOD is charged with formulating armed forces development plans; the Council of Ministers with providing 'general direction' over armed forces development. It is tempting to speculate that the broader issues of military development, which would necessarily impinge on economic, science, language and education policy, are reserved primarily for Defense Council and Politburo approval, with the MOD playing the key role in formulating the more narrowly focused armed forces development plans.

Aiding the Defense Minister in preparing armed forces development plans is the MOD Collegium, a consultative organ roughly analogous to those of nonmilitary ministries.[37] Chief of the General Staff Ogarkov, as the number-two man in the MOD and Ustinov's closest advisor, probably plays a key role in Collegium deliberation. The General Staff headed by Ogarkov is the single most important military staff supporting the MOD and the

Defense Council, and a focal point for military decisionmaking with the MOD.[38] It provides military inputs to Soviet threat assessments, formulates military strategy and evaluates potential military applications of new technology.[39] These responsibilities involve the Soviet General Staff in a variety of activities relating to peacetime military planning, including an important role in arms control negotiations and weapons acquisition.[40] Much of the Staff's influence is related to its role in preparing decision options relating to doctrine, strategy and defense structure planning and in implementing policy decisions approved at higher levels. The Staff's control of military information permits it to exert significant influence on national military policy by presenting issues and options to major decisionmaking forums in ways which favor preferred outcomes.

Another key post in military R&D management and weapons acquisition is that of Deputy Minister of Defense for Armaments, a post currently held by Army General Vitaliy Shabanov. Shabanov, a former Deputy Minister of the Radio Industry, was named deputy MOD in 1978 and formally identified in the armaments post in June 1981. He succeeds Marshal Nikolay Alekseev, who died in 1981 after a ten-year tenure as Deputy MOD for Armaments.[41] An analysis of Alekseev's public statements during his tenure suggests a portfolio of responsibilities which involves management of MOD-wide military R&D efforts, coordination of the R&D activities of the services and direction of other MOD agencies dealing with military R&D management.[42] Shabanov's public appearances during his tenure in the post suggest a similar range of responsibilities.[43]

Each of the service commands has charge of the overall direction of weapons and equipment development within the service; the service commands are also responsible for oversight of the developmental process by factories, research institutes and design organizations.[44] Positions analogous to the deputy MOD for armaments have been identified in several of the services: PVO (air defense), deputy CINC for armaments N. D. Grebennikov and navy deputy CINC for shipbuilding Engr-Admiral P. Kotov. The incumbents of these positions are apparently charged with assisting the service commander in his weapons development functions, coordinating and managing the weapons acquisition process within the relevant service and providing guidance to the service technical directorates.

The major R&D and production performers for armaments and military equipment are not organic to the MOD, but are legally subordinate to the civilian defense industrial ministries; the MOD in effect must 'contract out' individual weapons programs. The primary interface between the MOD consumer and the developer/producer is the technical directorate. One technical directorate which was reorganized in the early 1950s to accommodate nuclear and rocket technology is the Main Rocket and Artillery Directorate (GRAU). GRAU's functions, based on analogy with those of its predecessor, the Main Artillery Directorate, include formulation of the tactical-technical requirements (TTTs) for weapons and military equipment and oversight of weapons system production.[45] Similar missions are performed by the Main Armor Directorate (GBTU), headed by Col. General Yuri Potapov.[46] The technical directorates like GRAU and GBTU administer the MOD's contract (*zakaz*) with the defense industrial ministries and provide military representatives (essentially contract monitors) to ensure the timeliness and quality of the product.[47] These onsite military representatives provide the military consumer with a direct agent at design bureau and enterprise level. Military representative responsibilities include monitoring military production, quality control (testing and acceptance of military design and products) and price calculations.[48]

The close involvement of military representatives at every stage of the design, development and production process ensures a measure of performer responsiveness to the MOD as consumer which is almost totally absent in the nonmilitary sector of the Soviet economy. This difference helps to explain the remarkable contrast between the level of Soviet military and civilian technology. Civilian goods, both producer and consumer, are subject to the producer's inhouse quality control checks; but the quality controllers work for the institute or factory director. If achievement of both production norms and high quality is impossible, the latter is often sacrificed for the former. The result is sometimes shoddy goods; the customer organization (regardless of whether it is another plant or design bureau or a wholesale trade outfit) has little power to enforce high quality. In short, the civilian customer is a captive consumer; the power equation is weighted to the advantage of the supplier. The military representative system operates to help change the producer–consumer relationship, tipping the power balance in favor of the MOD consumer. The military representative quality-control screening is notoriously more stringent than the inhouse checks. New weapons are subjected to rigorous testing prior to official acceptance and performance specifications are rigidly enforced.[49] The high level at which these decisions are apparently approved is suggestive of the power wielded by the military consumer.

Another factor which helps to explain the military consumer's influence over the designer and producer is the special attention devoted to monitoring defense programs. The primary government office that mediates between the various organizations involved in the development of a particular weapon is the Military Industrial Commission (VPK). VPK responsibilities apparently include the guidance and monitoring of weapons development and production. VPK officials have also figured prominently in the strategic arms limitation negotiations.

Although the precise portfolio of VPK duties is not known, its duties in regard to weapons R&D may be roughly analogous to that of the State Committee for Science and Technology (GKNT), which is charged with coordinating nonmilitary scientific development. The following discussion of probable VPK responsibilities in the area of military R&D is based directly on analogy with the legally defined responsibilities of the GKNT in civilian R&D management.[50] This analogy would suggest a mission which includes helping to define the 'basic directions' of military R&D; coordinating military R&D projects that cross ministry lines; organizing military S&T information; and establishing links with WTO countries in the area of military R&D cooperation. The VPK, like its nonmilitary analogue, may also participate in the formulation of *predlozheniia* ('proposals') on the basic directions' of military R&D development and coordinate with the defense production ministries and the MOD in drafting long-term economic plans.

Another apparent VPK function, roughly analogous to that performed by the GKNT for civilian R&D, is that of 'kontrol' ' (literally, checking) on the fulfillment of assigned projects, intervening to mediate interministerial disagreements.

Of course, the VPK portfolio goes beyond that of R&D and apparently includes matters relating to production and delivery as well. Moreover, it also appears to occupy a higher status in the legal hierarchy than the GKNT – that of a Council of Ministers Presidium commission.[51] This supraminister-ial position would likely endow the VPK with greater legal authority and political power than the GKNT.

Shadowing the government organization charged with defense industrial management (the VPK) is a top-level party secretariat department – the Central Committee Defense Industry Department. The Defense Industry Department provides top party oversight of the weapons R&D and pro-curement process; and is responsive to the Central Committee secretary for defense matters. This post was formerly held by long-time top defense industrial manager D. F. Ustinov. At some time following his 1976 appointment as Minister of Defense, Ustinov's tenure as a Central Commit-tee secretary ended, although he was never formally and officially released from duty. In October 1976 Ia. P. Riabov, former first secretary of Sverd-lovsk *oblast'*, was elected to the Central Committee Secretariat; his public activities indicated that he had assumed some (if not most) of Ustinov's previous secretariat responsibilities in the area of defense industrial man-agement. In early March 1979 Riabov was appointed a first deputy chairman of the State Planning Committee (Gosplan), an apparent demotion which was followed by his official release from the Central Committee Secretariat in April 1979.[52] Riabov's successor to the defense industry post on the Secretariat is not known. It is possible that these duties are currently being handled by the CC Defense Industry Department under former supervisor Ustinov's watchful eye.

While little direct information on the activities of the Defense Industry Department is available, its mission is analogous to party committee departments at *krai* and *oblast* level, about which considerably more is known.[53] Its major tasks appear to be those of monitoring defense industrial compliance with party policies and providing a national-level party rep-resentative of defense/defense industrial interests. Department officials thus provide a supplement to the MOD and VPK monitor and review systems.

This survey of the organizational environment in which defense R&D policy is implemented would suggest that the parameters for independent action either by the defense industrial ministries, or individual research, design and production elements within them, have been deliberately limited by the existence of a series of party/government/MOD consumer monitor networks, which share the basic goal of ensuring maximum developer/ producer responsiveness to the military consumer. The institutional arrangements supporting the MOD's weapons procurement activities pro-vide the MOD with the potential for a very active role in the military R&D process. The MOD controls an extensive system of military representatives who ensure that the developer/producer complies with specified schedules and military requirements. The military consumer also benefits from pressure exerted on the producer by the party and government R&D and production monitors.

THE DEFENSE PLANNING PROCESS

The organizational environment supporting military R&D management, then, is a highly centralized one. This high level of centralization in the national security area is particularly dramatic when compared to relatively decentralized areas such as health care and retail trade. The defense planning process that takes place within the environment is also highly centralized. The planning procedures – which translate the policies embedded in CPSU military policy into specific weapons programs, development and production performers, technical specifications and schedules – have been deliberately designed to maximize the ability of the political and military leadership to control and dominate the defense procurement process.

Like nonmilitary planning, the process begins with a top-level party review and state ratification of basic defense priorities. Historical data from the interwar period would suggest that these priorities are embedded in five-year defense plans paralleling the state economic and RDI plans. The basic guidelines for the first five-year plan for military development were established by the Politburo resolution of 15 July 1929, which prescribed a two-year weapons modernization program, covering artillery, large-caliber machine guns, chemical defense and aircraft production.[54] The second five-year plan for military development (1934–8) was formulated in 1933 on the basis of a Central Committee requirement calling for the achievement of superiority over the capitalist states in three major areas: aviation, tanks and artillery.[55] The third five-year plan, which began in 1938, envisioned a general improvement in the striking force and maneuverability of the army through an increase in deployed ground, artillery, air and navy forces, the creation of large armored units and further motorization of troops and the rear services. The plan also involved a 70 percent increase in capital investment for defense industry and a plan to enhance scientific and research capabilities in all military areas with special emphasis on long-term development of new forms of weapons.[56]

The mechanism for translating the general guidelines implicit in 'military development' goals into general R&D goals for the civilian defense industrial performers is not known. The existence of the MOD as an institutionally powerful and sole consumer of military R&D, however, would suggest that the military hierarchy itself plays a major role in translating the military goals into basic military R&D problems, with participation by the VPK and the State Planning Committee (Gosplan). The mechanism for integrating military R&D problems with other components of the national and branch five-year plans is also not known.

Similarly, very little is known about how military development plans (which affect the civilian defense product ministries and other parts of the economy) are broken down into more precise plans for armed forces development, then into service-specific plans and, finally, into individual weapons programs. The available historical data, however, suggest that the mechanisms for accomplishing these steps consisted of a series of high-level party or party–government resolutions. Historical analogy would also suggest a key integrating and coordinating role for the General Staff in all steps of the process.[57] In the 1930s, for example, the Staff worked closely with the armaments chiefs and their subordinate armaments directorates (artillery, chemical, communications and control) to develop a plan for the Development of the Red Army, which executed the five-year military development plan. In 1936 the armaments directorates were reorganized into the Main Directorate for Armaments and Technical Supply, which was subordinated to the Defense Ministry, but responsive to directives from the General Staff. The Main Directorate's mission was to provide oversight for the implementation of the army's armaments plans; to facilitate and unify plans for scientific research, design and inventions activities relating to new military weapons and equipment; and to review weapons repair and employment practices.[58] It is quite likely that many of these functions are now served by the technical directorates at MOD and service level, responding, as before, to General Staff directives.

High-level approval was also required for the activities which executed the armed forces development plans. In the 1930s, the five-year plans were broken down further into service-specific programs, approved by the Council of Labor and Defense. In June 1933 the Council approved a resolution 'on a program for naval development, 1933–1938'.[59] This was a follow-on to a December 1926 Council-approved program of shipbuilding covering the years 1926–32, which authorized the construction of twelve submarines, eighteen escort vessels and thirty-six torpedo boats.[60] A plan for the development of the airforces covering 1935–7 was approved on 25 April 1935. Groundforces programs were also scrutinized by the top-level leadership. On 22 March 1934 the Council of Labor and Defense approved another resolution, this time 'on a system of artillery weaponry for the Red Army in the Second Five Year Plan'.[61] This was implemented by a series of Central Committee and Defense Committee measures involving the transformation of several large machine-building plants into artillery plants.[62] The Main Artillery Directorate played a key role in devising programs to implement this series of Central Committee directives on artillery development.[63] Tank development was also a subject of concern to the Soviet leadership. In 1938 Soviet authorities asked the tank designers to create a design incorporating improved armor and firepower, high maneuverability and reliability. Tactical-technical parameters incorporating the desired performance levels were formalized by a 'special resolution of the Central Committee and Soviet Government'. The party leadership also voiced disapproval over what they saw as an unnecessarily slow pace of series production. In 1940 another special Central Committee/Council of Ministers joint resolution was passed calling for performance improvements in the T-34 tank.[64]

The historical record suggests, then, that the process of translating plans for military development into more specific plans and programs was one which went forward under close high-level attention. Not only service-specific plans but also individual weapons programs which implemented these plans were executed via high-level party–government resolutions.

Assuming this pattern holds in the current system, it is quite likely that this high-level scrutiny operates to restrict the autonomy of both the designer and the MOD consumer, maximizing the responsiveness of both groups to policymaker intentions.

CONCLUSIONS

The Soviet description of their own military R&D process emphasizes the salience of policy goals in shaping military R&D priorities. While it is difficult within existing data limitations to determine with precision the motivating factors behind specific program decisions, the Soviet model of a policy-driven R&D environment appears to be a fairly valid one. The defense planning, policy implementation and program decisionmaking process that the Soviets have constructed to support their military R&D activities maximizes the party leadership's ability to shape these activities.

One reflection of the organizational and procedural arrangements designed to promote leadership control of the defense policy process is the higher levels of centralization in defense management. The Soviet political system is designed to permit various levels of centralization according to function, with functions of highest priority assigned a greater degree of centralization. In the USSR, as elsewhere, organizational arrangements are not neutral. The organizations and procedures used to implement policy vary substantially from sector to sector, reflecting clear choices about which goals are of highest priority. The importance accorded to each sector can be roughly gauged by its level of centralization, with frequent high-level intervention (or threats thereof) to ensure priority treatment of the most important goals. National security-related activities are among the most highly centralized of Soviet policy areas. This high degree of centralization means that the government bureaucracy which implements party military decisions is far more responsive to top-level policy choices than in areas of lower priority and lower centralization.

One manifestation of the highly centralized institutional arrangements supporting military policymaking is the Defense Council. By bringing together the top political, military and economic leaders, the council provides a top-level forum to systematize and legitimize the priority of military interests in other policy areas. Management arrangements within the Ministry of Defense itself, as well as the eight major defense industrial ministries, represent the more centralized end of the USSR's management continuum. As 'all-union' ministries, these organizations operate in a far more centralized fashion than either union republic or republic ministries.

Another reflection of the higher level of centralization in defense management is the more centralized review process for planning documentation revealed in the historical record of interwar defense planning. An example drawn from the Soviet legal press suggests that the special status of defense programs in Soviet planning, as revealed by the historical record, is characteristic of current planning procedures as well. Defense contracts are legally excluded from the review by republic, regional and local governments which is required of plans for civilian programs.[65] Republic and regional government officials can mount a determined (and sometimes very effective) opposition to civilian programs involving new facilities or expansion of existing ones, if, for example, they object to the environmental impact of a new factory, or feel that the ministry's arrangements for housing provisions for the new workers is inadequate. If the project is military-related, however, they have no voice in the decision.

The legal provisions excluding local government officials from a role in defense-related programs are paralleled by the special procedures for oversight by the party and military leadership. The redundant oversight systems are deliberately framed to facilitate fairly detailed top-level scrutiny of military investment activities and to increase developer/producer responsiveness to military requirements in a high-priority area. Such high-level attention has the effect of mitigating environmental constraints, as financial and technical resources are concentrated to meet high-level demands.

The importance of top-level party management and consumer control notwithstanding, there are several factors which operate as constraints on the ability of the national political and military policymakers and executors to shape the weapons procurement process. One factor is the diversity of low- and middle-level participants in the process. Many of the routine design and technological decisions, which cumulatively have an impact on the R&D investment pattern as a whole, are probably made in the coordination process between relatively low-level actors – between, for example, design personnel from the defense industrial design bureaus and military representatives from the MOD's technical directorates.

Another factor that acts as a constraint on the ability of national-level political and military managers to significantly influence the military R&D process is the inertia in the incentive systems inherent in the Soviet economic system. Many of the factors impeding more effective production of non-military items can be traced to a dysfunctional incentive and pricing system, which inhibits the application of advanced technology to industrial processes and creates a situation in which the producer of consumer items is remarkably unreceptive to the needs and desires of the consumer. The various mechanisms for controlling defense R&D are designed to overcome these problems in a high-priority area. The combination of high-level attention and a resource allocation which has favored military and heavy-industrial production has achieved impressive results in terms of the military product output, but the institutional disadvantages of the Soviet 'administered economy' – the lack of a competitive economic base, resistance to innovation and difficulties in assimilating new technological development – still present a challenge to the national-level management's ability to shape the defense industrial output to the directions intended by the policymaker.

On the whole, however, the high priority Soviet leadership has placed on defense programs has brought with it a corresponding reduction in the role played by organizational and management inefficiency. Indeed, much of the ineffectiveness so apparent in the consumer goods sectors is due precisely to the low priority it has been assigned by the Soviet leadership. The Soviet 'administered' economy works for military programs because of its favored status – a status which exempts military projects from the effects of many of the more dysfunctional aspects of the Soviet system and makes the military R&D process much more responsive to high-level direction.

An examination of the Soviet military R&D process would suggest, then, that policy goals drive the weapons acquisition process far more than has been acknowledged by many Western observers who stress the role of organizational momentum or bureaucratic inertia to explain Soviet military developments. The existence of an articulated military policy exerts a strong influence on defense planning and weapons acquisition decisionmaking. It may be argued that such policy is merely a formalization of existing decisions intended to provide an *ex post facto* justification for programs undertaken for very different reasons. Indeed, to argue the policy is the sole determinant of observable programs is to ignore the very real influence of environmental constraints and personalized decisionmaking on the outputs of the defense planning process. However, a comparison of key doctrinal and policy statements with observed defense outputs reveals a strong congruence between articulated goals and observable choices. These findings suggest that the Soviet military R&D environment is, at least to some degree, a policy-driven one. Observed program choices can be adequately explained only within the broader context of CPSU military policy and Soviet military doctrine.

NOTES: CHAPTER 5

1 A. A. Epishev, 'Voennaia politika KPSS', *Sovetskaia voennaia entsiklopediia*, Vol. II, pp. 191–3 (hereafter cited as *SVE*); see also P. Efimov, 'The communist party – organizer of the defense of the USSR', *Voenno-istoricheskii zhurnal*, no. 11 (1972), pp. 3–11.
2 *SVE*, Vol. II, p. 192.
3 *Materialy XXV s''ezda KPSS* (Moscow: Voenizdat, 1976), p. 154.
4 Colonel V. Tretiakov, 'The armed forces in the political organization of developed socialism', *Vestnik Protivovozdushnoi Oboroni*, no. 1 (1973), pp. 16–23 (hereafter cited as *VPO*); see also Colonel B. Kanevskii, 'Leninist concepts in CPSU military policy', *Krasnaia zvezda*, 20 January 1979, pp. 2–3; and Colonel D. Volkogonov, 'Actual questions of Soviet military development', *Kommunist vooruzhennykh sil*, no. 11 (1972), pp. 10–20.
5 E. Nikitin and B. Kanevskii, 'Problems of defense capability of the country and combat readiness of the Soviet armed forces in CPSU military policy', *Voenno-istoricheskii zhurnal*, no. 9 (1978), pp. 3–10.
6 'Doktrina voennaia', *SVE*, Vol. III, p. 225.
7 *Slovar' osnovnykh voennykh terminov* (Moscow: Voenizdat, 1965), trans. by the US Airforce as *Dictionary of Basic Military Terms*, p. 37.
8 A. A. Grechko, *Vooruzhennye sily sovetskogo gosudarstva* (Moscow: Voenizdat, 1974), p. 180. High-level support for the program was underlined by General Staff Chief Ogarkov. See N. V. Ogarkov, *Vsegda v gotovnosti k zashchite otechestva* (Moscow: Voenizdat, 1982), pp. 36–7.
9 A. B. Pupko, *Sistema; Chelovek i voennaia tekhnika* (Moscow: Voenizdat, 1976), p. 156; S. P. Ivanov, *O Nauchnykh osnovakh upravleniia voiskami* (Moscow: Voenizdat), pp. 70–2; V. Sinyak, 'Electronic machines at the command post', in *Matematika v boiu* (Moscow: Voenizdat, 1965). pp. 76–85; Yu. Pivovar, 'Surprise in combat', *Voennyi Vestnik*, no. 4 (1971), pp. 77–80; V. Savkin, 'The time factor in battle', *Voennyi Vestnik*, no. 2 (1976), pp. 30–4; V. Savkin, 'Features of modern combat', *Voennyi Vestnik*, no. 2 (1977), pp. 44–8; and V. Savkin, 'High tempos of attack', *Voennyi Vestnik*, no. 2 (1977), pp. 44–8.
10 N. A. Lomov, *Nauchno-Tekhnicheskii progress i revolyutsiia v sovetskikh vooruzhennykh silakh* (Moscow: Voenizdat, 1974), p. 102.

11 General Lt M. G. Sobolev, *Partiino-politicheskaia rabota v sovetskikh vooruzhënnykh silakh* (Moscow: Voenizdat, 1974), p. 102.

12 D. A. Ivanov, *Osnovy upravleniia voiskami* (Moscow: Voenizdat, 1971), pp. 121–3; and A. Ia. Vainer, *Takticheskie raschety* (Moscow: Voenizdat, 1977), pp. 15–17.

13 V. V. Druzhinin, 'Avtomatizirovannaia sistema upravleniia voiskami', *SVE*, Vol. I, pp. 78–81.

14 ibid.

15 Iu. Sushkov, *Kibernetika v boiu* (Moscow: Voenizdat, 1972), p. 103; A. Volkov, 'Man and computer in automated systems of troop control', *Vestnik protivovozdushnoi oborony*, no. 7 (1976), p. 13; Vainer, op. cit., pp. 13–14, and *Voprosy nauchnogo rukovodstva v sovetskikh vooruzhennykh silakh* (Moscow: Voenizdat, 1973), pp. 243–4.

16 General Eng. I. Tsygankov, 'Soviet military technology: the development of design thought', *Tekhnika i vooruzhenie*, no. 11 (1974), p. 6.

17 A. N. Volzhin, 'Modernizatsiia voennoi tekhniki', *SVE*, Vol. V, pp. 351–2.

18 E. A. Kosyrev, E. M. Orekov and N. N. Fomin, *Tanki* (Moscow: DOSAAF, 1973), pp. 14–60; P. A. Rotmistrov, *Vremia i tanki* (Moscow: Voenizdat, 1972), pp. 220–1; and John Missom, *Russian Tanks, 1900–1970* (Harrisburg, Pa: Stackpole, 1970), *passim*.

19 Major General Eng. Tech. Service A. Parkhomenko, 'The analysis of armament systems', *Voennaia mysl'*, no. 1 (1968); and A. N. Volzhin, 'Modifikatsiia voennoi tekhniki', *SVE*, Vol. V, p. 352.

20 'Allocation of resources in the Soviet Union and China – 1978', statement of Lt General Harold R. Aaron (DIA), 14 July 1978; and *Hearings before the Subcommittee on Priorities and Economies in Government of the JEC, Part 4: The Soviet Union*, pp. 206–7.

21 V. E. Zotkin, 'Nadezhnost' voennoi tekhniki', *SVE*, Vol. V, pp. 476–7.

22 A. A. Epishev, 'Voennaia politika KPSS', *Sovetskaia voennaia entsiklopediia*, Vol. II, pp. 191–3; E. Nikitin and B. Kanevskii, 'Problems of defense capability of the country and the combat readiness of the Soviet armed forces in CPSU military policy', *Voenno-istoricheskii zhurnal*, no. 9 (1978), pp. 3–10; *SVE*, Vol. III, p. 225; N. Lomov and S. Alfirov, 'To the question of Soviet military doctrine', *Voenno-istoricheskii zhurnal*, no. 7 (1978), pp. 21–30; and G. Sredin, 'The bases of Soviet military development', *Voenno-istoricheskii zhurnal*, no. 2 (1978), pp. 3–15.

23 A. A. Epishev, 'Mighty shield of the socialist fatherland', *Krasnaia zvezda*, 1 November 1977, pp. 1, 3; *Konstitutsya Soiuza Sovetskikh Sotsialisticheskikh Respublik* (Moscow: Politizdat, 1977), p. 43; Army General Shkadov, 'Sacred duty', *Kommunist vooruzhennykh sil*, no. 23 (December 1977), pp. 15–23; 'L. I. Brezhnev', *SVE*, Vol. I, pp. 586–9; Lt Colonel A. Kostin and Lt Colonel I. Shatilo, 'Armed forces of the multinational state', *Krasnaia zvezda*, 11 August 1977, pp. 2, 3; and S. A. Tyushkevich, *Sovetskie vooruzhën-nye sily* (Moscow: Voenizdat, 1978), p. 464. Discussions of this body by Western analysts are available in: Harriet Fast Scott, 'The Soviet high command', *Air Force*, Vol. LX, no. 3 (March 1977), pp. 52–6; and M. P. Gallagher and K. Spielmann, *Soviet Decisionmaking for Defense* (New York: Praeger, 1972), p. 19.

24 *Sovetskoe administrativnoe pravo* (Moscow: Iuridicheskaia Literatura, 1981), p. 375; Iu. M. Kozlov, *Upravlenie v oblasti administrativno-politicheskoi deiatel'nost'* (Moscow: Iuridicheskaia Literatura, 1979), p. 36; 'Concern of the Communist Party for the security of the socialist fatherland', *Voenno-istoricheskii zhurnal*, no. 12 (1981), pp. 5–12; M. Naumenko. 'Main source of our defensive might', *Kommunist vooruzhënnykh sil*, no. 19 (1980), pp. 9–17; M. G. Sobolev and I. S. Mareev (eds), *Partiino-politicheskaia rabota v Sovetskoi armii i Flote* (Moscow: Voenizdat, 1979), p. 13.

25 'Leonid Ilich Brezhnev', *Pravda*, 12 November 1982, p. 2.

26 D. Garthoff, 'The Soviet military and arms control', *Survival*, Vol. XIX, no. 6 (November–December 1977), pp. 242–50. The Romanian Defense Council includes the Secretary-General of the Romanian Communist Party, who is also the President of Romania and Supreme Commander of the Armed Forces; the chairman of the Council of Ministers; the Minister of National Defense; the Foreign Minister; the Minister of Internal Affairs; the chairman of the State Planning Committee; and the Chief of the General Staff. I. I. Iakubovskii, *Boevoe sodruzhestvo bratskikh narodov i armii* (Moscow: Voenizdat, 1975), p. 199. Historical material on the role of Lenin's Defense Council in the early years of Soviet rule is available in A. Lagovskii, *Strategiya i ekonomika* (Moscow: Voenizdat, 1961), pp. 14–19.

27 Article 6 of the new Soviet constitution states: 'The directing and guiding strength of

Soviet society, the nucleus of its political system and social organizations is the CPSU . . . the Communist Party defines the general perspective development of society, the lines of internal and external Soviet policy, heads the great creative work of the Soviet peoples', *Konstitutsiia (osnovnoi zakon) soiuza sovetskikh sotsialisticheskikh respublik* (Moscow: Politizdat, 1977).

28 'The Communist Party directs the activities of the Supreme Soviet and all Soviet workers' deputies. The decisions of Party Congresses and the central committee are the ideological-political bases of laws and other acts approved by the Supreme Soviet of the USSR', *Verkhovnyi Sovet SSSR* (Moscow: Izvestiia sovetov deputatov trudiashchikhsia, 1975), p. 27.

29 S. S. Maksimov, *Osnovy Sovetskogo voennogo zakonodatel'stva* (Moscow: Voenizdat, 1978), p. 51; see also A. G. Gornyi, *Sotsialisticheskaia zakonnost' i voinskiy pravoporyadok* (Moscow: Voenizdat, 1973), p. 51.

30 Maksimov, op. cit., p. 51; P. I. Romanov and V. G. Beliavskii, *Konstitutsiya SSSR i Zashchita Otechestva* (Moscow: Voenizdat, 1979), pp. 51–8; *Verkhovnyi Sovet SSSR*, op. cit., p. 86; Ia. N. Umanskiy, *Sovetskoe gosudarstvennoe pravo* (Moscow: Vyshaya shkola, 1970), pp. 364–80.

31 'Zakon o sovete ministrov SSR', *Izvestiia*, 6 July 1978, pp. 1, 2.

32 Maksimov, op. cit., pp. 51–2.

33 I. Lepeshkin (ed.), *Osnovy Sovetsk'ogo voennogo zakonodatel'stva* (Moscow: Voenizdat, 1973), p. 91; see also A. G. Gornyi (ed.), *Osnovy Sovetskogo voennogo zakonodatel'stva* (Moscow: Voenizdat, 1966), pp. 66–8. Administrative procedures within the MOD are regulated by the MOD's legal charter and the general regulations governing ministerial procedures; see Iu. M. Kozlov (ed.), *Pravovoe polozhenie ministerstv SSSR* (Moscow: Iuridicheskaya Literatura, 1971), *passim*.

34 'Ministerstvo oborony SSSR', *SVE*, Vol. V, pp. 294–6; and Iu. M. Kozlov (ed.), *Sovetskoe administrativnoe pravo* (Moscow: Iuridicheskaya Literatura, 1973), pp. 521–3.

35 Sobolev, *Partiyno-politicheskaia*, op. cit., pp. 101–2; and V. I. Oskin, 'Voennoe stroitel'stvo', *SVE*, Vol. II, p. 219.

36 A. A. Babakov, 'Stroitel'stvo vooruzhënnykh sil', *SVE*, Vol. VII, p. 580.

37 Lepeshkin, op. cit., p. 91; 'Kollegiia ministerstva oborony SSSR', *SVE*, Vol. IV, pp. 235–6; and *Krasnaia zvezda*, 7 July 1978. On nonmilitary counterparts of the MOD Collegium, see I. L. Davitnidze, *Kollegii Ministerstv* (Moscow: Iuridicheskaya Literatura, 1972); and I. L. Davitnidze, *Kollegial'nost' i edinonachalie v Sovetskom gosudarstvennom upravlenii* (Moscow: Znanie, 1974).

38 'Glavnye i tsentral'nye upravleniia', *SVE*, Vol. II, p. 565.

39 V. G. Kulikov, 'General'nyi Shtab', *SVE*, Vol. II, pp. 510–13; see also M. A. Gareev and A. I. Evseev, 'Voenno-nauchnaia rabota', *SVE*, Vol. II, pp. 243–4. This task probably involves the Staff closely in the formulation of mobilization plans; see 'Mobilizatsionnyi plan', *SVE*, Vol. V, pp. 341–2.

40 V. G. Kulikov, 'Soviet military science today', *Kommunist*, no. 7 (1976), pp. 38–47.

41 'N. N. Alekseev', *SVE*, Vol. I, p. 145; *Krasnaia zvezda*, 14 November 1980, p. 3; and 'V. M. Shabanov', *SVE*, Vol. VIII, p. 488.

42 This model of Alekseev's relationship with the service armament deputy CINCs is based on an analogy with the legal administrative relationships between the deputy MOD for Rear Services and the deputy service CINCs for Rear Services. Additional insight into Alekseev's responsibilities was provided by his periodic articles in *Tekhnika i Vooruzhenie* (*TIV*): *TIV*, no. 2 (1977), pp. 2–6; *TIV*, no. 1 (1976), p. 106; *TIV*, no. 8 (1976), pp. 1–4; *TIV*, no. 1 (1975), p. 104; *TIV*, no. 1 (1974), p. 103; *TIV*, no. 8 (1974), p. 104; *TIV*, no. 1 (1972), p. 24; see also *Azbuka Izobretatel'stva* (Moscow: Voenizdat, 1978), pp. 88–9; and *SVE*, Vol. III, p. 504.

43 V. Shabanov, 'High technical equipment', *Kraznaia zvezda*, 26 June 1981, pp. 2, 3.

44 A. I. Tabak, 'Glavnokomanduiushchii vidom vooruzhënnykh sil', *SVE*, Vol. II, pp. 564–5.

45 'Glavnye i tsentral'nye upravleniia MO SSR', *SVE*, Vol. II, p. 565; see also *KVS*, no. 17 (1976), p. 93; B. V. Livshin, 'The role of Soviet science in the material-technical safeguarding of the country's defense', *Istoriia SSR*, no. 3 (1975), pp. 45–62; and P. N. Kuleshov, 'GAU', *SVE*, Vol. II, p. 561.

46 Until late 1981 Potapov had been identified as chief of the tank troops; see *Kraznaia zvezda*, 14 December 1979, p. 2, 12 September 1981, p. 1 and 13 September 1981, p. 3.

47 Contractual relationships (dogovor) between military units and civilian organizations for

food, material supplies, construction and transportation are regulated by civil law; see 'Dogovor', *SVE*, Vol. III, pp. 215–16.

48 V. A. Silinskii, 'Voennyi Predstavitel'', *SVE*, Vol. II, pp. 271–2. Information on current activities of the *voenpred* is quite limited. Historical data, however, indicate that one contingent of *voenpred*, working out of the Main Artillery Directorate, monitored defense production in over 1,000 plants; see P. N. Kuleshov, 'GAU', *SVE*, Vol. II, pp. 560–1.

49 Arthur Alexander, *Decisionmaking in Soviet Weapons Procurement*, Adelphi Papers, no. 147/148 (International Institute for Strategic Studies, 1979), pp. 18–19, 23; see also M. Agursky, *Nauchno-issledovatel'skii institut tekhnologii mashinostroeniia kak chast' Sovetskogo voenno-promyshlennogo kompleksa* (Jerusalem: Hebrew University of Jerusalem/Soviet and East European Research Center, 1976), pp. 8–12.

50 'Polozhenie o gosudarstvennom komitete soveta ministrov SSSR po nauke i tekhnike', *Spravochnik Partiinogo Rabotnika*, op. cit., pp. 272–8; see also V. A. Rassudovskii, *Gosudarstvennaia organizatsiia nauki v SSSR* (Moscow: Iuridicheskaia Literatura, 1971), pp. 25–30, 68–79, 95–107; and *Pravovoe polozhenie ministerstv SSSR* (Moscow: Iuridicheskaya Literatura, 1971), pp. 128–9.

51 Georgy Titov, first deputy Gosplan chief who died in late 1980, was 'first deputy chairman of the Commission of the Presidium of the Council of Ministers' in 1958–74. Given Titov's strong association with defense industry – a connection stressed in his obituary – it is likely that the unidentified commission was the VPK; see *Pravda*, 21 October 1980, p. 2.

52 'Iakov Petrovich Riabov', in *Deputaty verkhovnogo soveta SSSR* (Moscow, 1979), p. 386.

53 Jerry F. Hough, *The Soviet Prefects: The Local Party Organs in Industrial Decisionmaking* (Cambridge, Mass.: Harvard University Press, 1969).

54 'O sostoianii oborony SSSR' (from the Central Committee Resolution of 15 July 1929), excerpted in *KPSS o vooruzhennykh silakh sovetskogo soyuza: dokumenty, 1917–1968* (Moscow: Voenizdat, 1969), pp. 264–6; Tiushkevich, *Sovetskie vooruzhënnye sily*, op. cit., pp. 190–5; *KPSS i stroitel'stvo sovetskikh vooruzhënnykh sil* (Moscow: Voenizdat, 1967), pp. 170–2.

55 Marshal M. Zakharov, 'The Communist Party and the technical rearmament of the army and navy in the years of the pre-war five year plans', *Voenno-istoricheskii zhurnal*, no. 2, (1971), pp. 3–12.

56 ibid.

57 Tiushkevich, *Sovetskie vooruzhennye sily*, op. cit., p. 185.

58 Zakharov, op. cit., pp. 3–12.

59 ibid.

60 Tiushkevich, *Sovetskie vooruzhennye sily*, op. cit., p. 165.

61 Zakharov, op. cit.

62 *KPSS i Stroitel'stva Vooruzhënnykh sil*, op. cit., p. 181.

63 *SVE*, Vol. II, p. 561.

64 *KPSS i Stroitel'stva Vooruzhënnykh sil*, op. cit., pp. 183–4.

65 On the role of republic government in reviewing selected portions of nondefense plans, see 'Polozhenie of Ministerstvakh SSSR', *Sobranie Postanovlenie SSSR*, No. 17 (1967). On regional government functions in this area, see 'Zakon SSSR ob osnovnykh polnomochiiakh kraevykh, oblastnykh sovetov narodnykh deputatov, sovetov narodnykh deputatov avtonomnykh oblastei i avtonomnykh okrugov', *Pravda*, 26 June 1980, pp. 1–3.

6 The Soviet Military and SALT*

RAYMOND L. GARTHOFF

The Strategic Arms Limitation Talks (SALT) in 1969–79 were a familiar feature in the international political landscape and an important element in US-USSR relations. Much more than any other arms control and disarmament measure negotiated to date, SALT dealt with the most vitally important elements of national power of the two countries. More than any other, it engaged the alert and active attention and participation of the senior military authorities of both countries. The present discussion deals with attitudes of the Soviet military toward SALT, Soviet military objectives in SALT decisionmaking and negotiation, the role of the Soviet military in SALT, the interaction of SALT with the Soviet military posture and military thinking, and some effects of SALT on evolving Soviet political-military relationships over that decade.

SOVIET ATTITUDES TOWARD SALT

In December 1966 and January 1967 the United States advanced, in private, a proposal for bilateral talks on limiting strategic arms, specifically antiballistic missile (ABM) systems. The Soviet response was cautious, noting that the question deserved attention, and not rejecting the idea, but couched in terms which left open options either for serious negotiation, or for retreat to a propagandistic embrace of drastic reductions by both sides down to a minimum deterrent 'nuclear umbrella' (an idea earlier championed by the Soviets in Geneva). For the next eighteen months, the Soviet side declined to agree on a time and place for beginning substantive discussions, despite repeated American importuning, including a personal argument for SALT by Secretary of Defense McNamara to Soviet Prime Minister Kosygin at Glassboro in June 1967.[1]

The precise role of the Soviet military leaders in this initial pre-SALT phase is not known, but it is highly likely (and in accordance with published Soviet military statements) that their predominant reaction was a compound of suspicions – suspicion both of disarmament and of arms control; suspicion

* Earlier versions of this chapter appeared as 'SALT and the Soviet military', *Problems of Communism*, vol. XXIV, no. 1 (January–February 1975); and as a chapter in John Baylis and Gerald Segal (eds), *Soviet Strategy* (Montclair, NJ: Allanheld, Osmun, 1981); this chapter is a revised, updated and expanded discussion. The author was a direct participant in the American-Soviet discussions in 1967–9 leading up to the formal SALT negotiations, and served as senior Department of State advisor and the executive officer of the SALT I delegation in 1969–72.

of the United States in general, and in particular what it was up to in proposing SALT; suspicion that arms budgets would be reduced; and suspicion of likely further involvement of Soviet political leaders and political considerations in decisions on military programs. These military attitudes reinforced the wariness of the Soviet political leaders, but did not override the readiness of the latter to keep the possibility of SALT open and under continuing consideration.

The first substantive position taken by the Soviet side was a firm statement at the very outset of the exchanges that strategic offensive arms, as well as antiballistic missile systems, must be included in any talks. This position, made known in January 1967, was promptly accepted by the USA – perhaps to the surprise of the Soviet side. We do not know whether this position was advanced by the Soviet military or (as the author believes more likely) by the political leaders to provide a basis for 'outbidding' the USA in moving to the propaganda high ground of proposing drastic nuclear disarmament in case the course of the talks threatened to reveal Soviet unreadiness to agree on apparently reasonable limitations, owing to the relative weakness of Soviet strategic forces at that time.

A second Soviet position which became clear in the 1967 diplomatic exchange was a strong stand eschewing an approach based on freezing the existing strategic balance. The Soviet leaders, political and military, were wary that the USA might call for a rigid 'freeze' of force levels, at a time when the USA had a heavy strategic preponderance in all categories of intercontinental forces – ICBMs, SLBMs and heavy bombers. In January 1967, when SALT was proposed, the USA had operational 1,054 ICBMs, 576 SLBMs, and 650 B-52 heavy bombers while the USSR had only 500 ICBMs (many in 'soft' deployment), 100 old short-range SLBMs and 155 inferior heavy bombers.[2] The US total of 2,280 was thus three times the Soviet total of 750 operational units (and still nearly twice the Soviet total of 1,200, if the additional ICBM and SLBM launchers then under construction in the USSR were counted).

Concerning strategic defensive systems, the problem from the standpoint of the Soviet military and political leaders was different: they were reluctant to accept limitations on their own freedom of action. The ABM deployment around Moscow was not yet operational, although it had been under construction for over two years. The Soviet ABM system was cumbersome and costly; hence, it was being deployed only around Moscow. But Soviet military doctrine and related political-military commentary in the press (such as the late Major General Nikolai A. Talensky's articles after 1964),[3] was based on the assumption that deployment of all means of strategic defense was morally and politically justified, and strategically sound and stabilizing. Moreover, a ban or sharp limitation on ABM deployment, coupled with growing American strategic offensive superiority (or an arms control freeze of the existing US superiority), would have consigned the Soviet Union to permanent inferiority and one-sided vulnerability. In an unconstrained arms race, at least the Soviet Union had a good chance of achieving *mutual* vulnerability, and of mitigating the near-complete nakedness of the Soviet Union to American missile attack. Hence, the Soviet military insistence on coupling possible strategic offensive limitations with

ABM limitations, and hence, too, the Soviet reluctance to become committed to SALT until their own strategic offensive force buildup had at least brought the Soviet Union within sight of parity with the United States in intercontinental capabilities.

The US decision in September 1967 to deploy a nationwide ABM defense compelled the Soviet leaders to stop and calculate seriously the impact on the strategic balance of a major US ABM deployment. The prior Soviet testing and developing of an ICBM had not prevented the USA from leaping far ahead of the USSR in deploying a much larger and much more capable strategic offensive force, and if the same thing were to be repeated with ABM systems as well, it would seriously prejudice and could confound Soviet aspirations to achieve strategic parity with the United States.

By mid-1968 the Soviet leaders decided to enter SALT and see what it could offer as against the alternative of an unrestricted strategic arms competition with the United States. By the time SALT was originally scheduled to convene, on 30 September 1968, the American strategic offensive force levels had long ago leveled off, while the Soviet buildup of modern silo-protected ICBMs was proceeding apace, and a modern SLBM production program was underway. Accordingly, in some contrast to the situation at the time SALT had first been proposed, by September 1968 the USA had 1,054 ICBMs, 656 SLBMs and 565 B-52s, while the USSR had operational about 875 ICBMs, 110 SLBMs and 155 heavy bombers. Counting additional Soviet ICBM and SLBM launchers under construction, the totals overall were 2,275 for the USA and 1,650 for the USSR.

SALT was postponed for slightly over a year as a consequence of the Soviet invasion of Czechoslovakia (on 20 August 1968, literally on the eve of the planned announcement of a forthcoming US-USSR summit meeting in Leningrad and the commencement of SALT), then the advent of a new American administration, the decision of that administration to review its military policy and SALT position and other delaying factors. But throughout that year the Soviet side reaffirmed its readiness to begin SALT. From the standpoint of developments affecting the strategic balance, the difference of that year was of some significance in two respects: first, the USA moved from initial testing (beginning in August 1968) to development of deployable multiple independently targetable reentry vehicles (MIRVs); and secondly, the Soviet ICBM and SLBM buildup had proceeded to an extent that now virtually assured parity in the bilateral strategic balance in numbers of missile launchers.

As of November 1969, when SALT actually got underway, the US force levels remained unchanged from September 1968 except for a slight decline in the number of B-52 bombers, while the USSR then had 1,140 ICBMs operational and some 380 more under construction, about 185 SLBMs operational and 175 more under construction, and 155 heavy bombers. Thus the totals, including Soviet ICBMs and SLBMs under construction, stood at 2,235 for the USA and 2,035 for the USSR. Meanwhile, the Soviet Union had virtually completed its ABM deployment underway with 64 ABM launchers at Moscow, while the US was launched on a major ABM program now called 'Safeguard', somewhat reoriented from the 'Sentinel' program of 1967 to stress defense of ICBMs, but still nationwide and with well over ten times the number of ABM launchers and interceptors comprising the Soviet deployment.

The Soviet military leaders do not limit their view of 'the strategic balance' to a comparison of US and Soviet intercontinental strategic forces. As we have learned in SALT, they insist on considering in conjunction with these elements other US and Allied nuclear forces capable of striking the Soviet Union. In this respect it may be somewhat misleading to list only these intercontinental forces in comparing force levels. None the less, the Soviets have recognized in the SALT I and II agreements the key role these elements have in the strategic equation, and it is important to bear in mind these developments in the changing intercontinental strategic balance, even though this summary does not cover many other important aspects of, and factors affecting, the overall strategic balance. Both the reality and perceptions of the strategic balance are, and have been recognized to be, important in military and in political terms.

During the critical gestation period of SALT in 1967–9 the Soviet military leaders (as well as political leaders) came to realize several important things affecting their approach to SALT.

(1)   The United States remained interested in SALT under conditions of near-parity, and not only when it had a three-to-one superiority in strategic offensive forces.
(2)   The United States had demonstrated its capability and will to build up qualitatively and quantitatively superior forces rapidly in strategic bombers in the 1950s, and in ICBMs and SLBMs in the 1960s, and it could do so again with ABMs and MIRVs in the 1970s if strategic arms competition remained unrestrained.
(3)   The United States had indicated it was prepared to place maximum reliance on unilateral means of verification, in contrast to its earlier demands for onsite inspections to verify strategic arms limitation agreements.
(4)   Bilateral strategic arms limitations, if mutually acceptable terms could be negotiated, would contribute to a general lessening of tensions between the Soviet Union and the United States, particularly important given increased Sino-Soviet tensions, and consonant with Soviet political strategy in Europe as well.
(5)   There were measures which the Soviet Union and the United States could take that would reduce the possibility of the outbreak of nuclear war, and SALT could serve as a useful and appropriate forum to raise and consider such matters.

Of these, the second point was undoubtedly of highest importance to the Soviet military leaders. They remained suspicious of US intentions in SALT, but saw a possible advantage if strategic parity would be accepted by the United States and if limitations could be agreed upon which would prevent a new US surge in strategic deployments threatening this newly won and still precarious Soviet prospect of achieving strategic parity.

Throughout the SALT negotiations (including the period since the 1972 SALT I agreements were reached) foreign analysts have cited Soviet military statements warning of the possibility of nuclear war, of American aggressive intentions, and of the need for vigilance and for continued efforts to maintain Soviet military might.[4] Soviet authors have done the same in reverse, the most extensive being a 1971 book called *First Strike*,[5] reviewing American military statements and weapons programs and alleging a US proclivity to seek a first-strike capability. These Soviet statements in support of the Soviet military effort no doubt in part reflect real continuing Soviet military concerns; in part they probably are rationalization for desired programs; and in part they may represent instruments in bureaucratic man-euver by those opposed to SALT or at least to far-reaching Soviet moves in SALT.

It is evident from the virtual absence of references to SALT in Soviet military publications and in most statements by military leaders in the early 1970s that there has been a strong current of reserve and reluctance toward SALT among the military. There has been more, and more favorable, reference since the mid-1970s. Much of the explanation may lie simply in concern at undercutting the case for maintaining a strong military posture – a concern which continues since the SALT agreements have been reached. When Chief of the General Staff and First Deputy Minister of Defense Army General Viktor G. Kulikov endorsed the SALT I agreements before the Supreme Soviet in August 1972, he coupled with this support reference to the fact that the party and government at the same time 'display constant concern for raising the defense capability of the Soviet Union', affirming that 'the Soviet Armed Forces possess everything necessary to reliably defend the state interests of our Motherland'. He also noted (as did other speakers) that 'the ABM Treaty halts the further buildup of ABM systems in the USSR and the USA, preventing the emergence of a chain reaction of competition between offensive and defensive arms'.[6] Marshal Grechko stressed this same point on the occasion of the ratification of the ABM Treaty by the Presidium of the Supreme Soviet a month later,[7] underlining the arms control aspect of greatest significance to the Soviet military (as well as political) leaders.

SOVIET OBJECTIVES IN SALT

A number of foreign policy, economic, strategic – and bureaucratic – considerations have been noted by various observers as contributing to the formulation of Soviet positions and objectives in entering SALT.[8]

The Soviet political leaders have been particularly concerned with politi-cal, economic and diplomatic objectives, but they have also shared the interest of the military leaders in military considerations and objectives. The most fundamental political objective has been American recognition of parity of the USSR with the USA – parity in the broadest political and political-military as well as strategic sense, spelling an end to Soviet inferior-ity in its relations with the United States. The SALT agreements reached in May 1972 reinforced in Soviet eyes the Basic Principles on Relations bet-ween the USA and the USSR, signed by the President in Moscow at that same time.[9] In a political-military context these agreements reflected and bore witness to American recognition of the fact that there exists a military parity in the broad sense of inability of either side to prevail militarily over the other and hence an inability to coerce the other side; in terms more familiar in the West, it reflects an equal vulnerability of both sides and therefore a state of mutual deterrence of nuclear war.

As early as 1968 the Soviet side had agreed that the main objective of SALT would be to achieve and to maintain stable US-Soviet strategic deterrence through agreed limitations on the deployment of strategic offensive and defensive arms. Soviet representatives stressed then, and throughout SALT, that limitations must be so balanced that neither side could obtain military advantage and that equal security should be assured for both sides.

The military leaders in Moscow, while sharing or at least accepting these political and political-military strategic objectives, also continue to hold to a military doctrine which calls for preparing to wage war if deterrence should fail. Also they are naturally more concerned with the specifics of the strategic military balance notwithstanding overall parity in a broad military-political sense.

Among the considerations leading to serious Soviet interest in SALT has been the pressure of an economic pinch.[10] The Soviet leaders have not been compelled by economic pressures to become interested in SALT or to reach any particular arms limitations. But they have found an important economic incentive for dampening down unlimited military competition with the USA. And the Soviet military leaders realistically recognize the constraints which competing economic needs have always placed on military programs in the Soviet Union.

It is important to bear in mind that there are varied and sometimes competing interests among the military leaders (and among civilian military-industrial chiefs), since they have differing stakes in particular weapons programs and military forces. The 'military' by no means always speaks with one voice.[11] But overall, the principal basic objectives of the Soviet military in SALT have been:

(1) to assure that the terms of any negotiated strategic arms limitation would result in no military disadvantage and, if possible, some advantage to the USSR;
(2) to preserve maximum leeway for Soviet military research and development and deployment programs, except when specific limitations are justified by limitations of comparable value placed on US military programs;
(3) to forestall an extensive US deployment of ABM systems, even at the cost of forgoing comparable Soviet ABM defense;
(4) to preserve the right to maintain Soviet offensive and defensive forces required to counter third country forces, excepting only special cases where a US-Soviet limitation was deemed paramount (for example, ABM limitation).

In engaging in SALT the Soviet military have also had certain specific second-order objectives:

(1)   to avoid any onsite inspection in the USSR and to obtain agreement instead to rely on national technical means of verification;

(2)   to obtain, if possible, inclusion of the full range of American nuclear delivery forces deployed within striking range of the Soviet Union in the forces subject to limitation;

(3)   to ensure that the SALT negotiations do not become an opening which would compromise Soviet military secrets, in the first instance to the USA, and for an even wider range of matters on which the USA was informed to third countries and the world at large (and, for that matter, to the Soviet public).

The Soviet side, probably at the insistence of the political leadership, also decided some time prior to the beginning of SALT to pursue in that forum the tangential but significant objective of seeking agreement with the USA on measures to reduce the possibility of the outbreak of nuclear war between the two countries as a result of accident, unauthorized use of nuclear weapons, misconstruction of some technical development or weapons test, or provocative action by a third nuclear country. It is likely that the military agreed on this objective with the proviso that it did not involve intrusion into the secrecy surrounding Soviet military command and control arrangements.

The strong preference of the Soviet military for caution in disclosure of Soviet military interests and concerns clearly contributed to the generally passive and reactive Soviet stance with respect to concrete proposals for arms limitation. As a consequence, the United States took most initiatives in raising propositions and advancing proposals. The Soviet military seemed to be on guard against revealing their own concerns and weaknesses. Particularly with respect to possible MIRV limitation in SALT I this was unfortunate. More generally, while American views on this question have been divided, the advantages of staking out the ground in proposals was probably an advantage to the American side.

ROLE OF THE SOVIET MILITARY IN SALT DECISIONMAKING AND NEGOTIATIONS

SALT represented the first arms limitation negotiation in which the Soviet military played a direct and major role. Soviet military representatives and experts have attended other disarmament and arms control negotiations as advisors (particularly the conference on measures to avert surprise attack in 1958), but never with the seniority of direct participation represented in SALT.

The Soviet leaders initially (in 1968) contemplated having a senior military man, possibly Marshal Matvei V. Zakharov, then Chief of the General Staff, head their delegation, but they decided instead to follow the pattern they understood the USA had in mind of having a senior civilian official as chief negotiator, and to make a senior military representative the deputy chief of their delegation.

During the first three 'rounds' of SALT I, in late 1969–end-1970 the second-ranking member of the Soviet SALT delegation was Colonel General

Nikolai V. Ogarkov, then first deputy chief of the General Staff of the USSR Armed Forces. (Since 1977 he has been Chief of the General Staff and First Deputy Minister of Defense and a Marshal of the Soviet Union.) For a man with this position and broad responsibilities to devote eight months in a fourteen-month period to service on a delegation abroad – in addition to time spent in Moscow in preparation for each round of negotiation – demonstrates the seriousness which the Soviet government and the Soviet military ascribed to SALT.

In addition to General Ogarkov, Colonel General of the Engineering Technical Service Nikolai N. Alekseyev was a member of the Soviet SALT delegation in the first two rounds of negotiation in 1969 and 1970. Succeeding Generals Ogarkov and Alekseyev as the senior Soviet military representatives on the SALT delegation were Lt General Konstantin A. Trusov, a senior General Staff officer with a background of work overseeing advanced weapons development, and Lt General Ivan I. Beletsky.

Colonel General Anatoly A. Gryzlov, a seasoned General Staff officer since World War II, had been assigned to disarmament and arms control matters in the late 1950s, and attended all significant disarmament conferences from the Surprise Attack Conference in 1958 through SALT (attending SALT I sessions in 1969–late 1971). General Gryzlov also headed an Arms Control Section of the Main Operations Directorate of the General Staff, which coordinated working-level preparations for SALT in the Soviet military establishment. General Gryzlov's successor, Lt General Ivan I. Beletsky, appeared as an 'advisor' on the Soviet delegation at the beginning of SALT II in November 1972. In all subsequent SALT sessions, by then a Colonel General, he served as a full 'member' of the delegation. Both he and General Trusov (also a Colonel General) seem to have had virtually full-time SALT responsibilities throughout SALT II. After General Trusov left the delegation in 1978, he was succeeded by Major General Viktor P. Starodurov, a strategic missile forces officer who had earlier served as an advisor on the SALT delegation, as a colonel, in 1972–4.

Among the key military men also deeply involved in SALT in Moscow have been Generals Kozlov and Akhromeyev. Colonel General (later Army General) Mikhail M. Kozlov was involved in SALT from its inception by virtue of his position as chief of the Main Operations Directorate and deputy chief of the General Staff. When General Ogarkov became a deputy minister of defense in December 1973, Kozlov succeeded him as first deputy chief of the General Staff. In that capacity he played a prominent part in the two SALT-involved summit meetings of 1974, especially at Vladivostok. In the spring of 1979 General Kozlov was succeeded as first deputy Chief of Staff by Colonel General (soon Army General) Sergei F. Akhromeyev (who had probably earlier succeeded to Kozlov's former position as chief of the Main Operations Directorate). These key generals also met with three delegations of American senators visiting Moscow in November 1978 and January 1979 (Kozlov), and August 1979 (Akhromeyev), after the delegations had expressed the wish to discuss the SALT II Treaty with authoritative military as well as political officials.

A number of other Soviet officers, some of flag rank, have participated directly in the SALT talks as 'advisors' or (a less-prestigious category) as 'experts'.[12] As one would expect for a serious negotiation, the Soviet side has sent highly qualified specialists in the key areas under discussion: strategic missile experts, ABM experts, submarine and ASW specialists and strategic bomber officers, all working (as we have seen) under senior officers of the General Staff concerned with advanced weapons development and procurement.

The US has throughout SALT been represented by capable senior military officers with excellent staffs, but the scale of military representation has been more limited. As a member of the US delegation, in 1969–72, Lt General Royal Allison (USAF) and in 1973–mid-1979, Lt General Edward Rowny (USA) represented the JCS; there have been no other general officers and relatively fewer other military advisors on the American side.[13] (In addition, the US delegation included a senior civilian representative of the Secretary of Defense, in 1969–74 Paul Nitze, for whom there is no Soviet civilian equivalent.)

In addition to military representatives, the USSR included in its delegation two senior figures from the scientific-technological-military production field. Academician Aleksandr N. Shchukin, a highly respected 'elder statesman' in military applications of science and technology, was active throughout *all* SALT I and II sessions, in 1969–79. A reserve major general in the engineering-technical service, he played a key role as the representative on the delegation of the Military-Industrial Commission, of which he is a deputy chairman. Petr S. Pleshakov also served throughout SALT I and into SALT II in 1969–74, despite his other responsibilities initially as a deputy minister, and after 1973, Minister of Radio Industry (producing radars, computers, electronics and communications equipment for military as well as civilian uses). He, too, is a reserve officer, as are many Soviet scientific and industrial production personnel; his reserve rank is lieutenant general of the engineering-technical service. (On the US delegation, there has been one equivalent representative, Dr Harold Brown, in 1969–76.)

SALT led to the establishment of direct coordination between the Ministry of Defense and the Ministry of Foreign Affairs, also with participation of Academy of Sciences political and technical institutes and of representatives of the industrial production ministries. Appropriate sections of the Central Committee apparatus, and of the personal staff of the secretary-general, also play an important coordinating and tasking role. The participation of senior levels of elements in addition to the Ministries of Defense and Foreign Affairs was manifest in the SALT negotiations at the first Moscow Summit meeting in May 1972, when Deputy Prime Minister Leonid V. Smirnov played an important direct part in the final negotiation of the SALT I Interim Agreement limiting strategic offensive arms. Smirnov has for years chaired the important Military-Industrial Commission (VPK), which handles coordination between the Defense Ministry, ministries concerned with military production, and Academy of Science institutes contributing to military research and development.

The highest body dealing specifically with military and defense matters is the Defense Council. Although formally acknowledged only in the new Soviet Constitution in 1977, and nominally responsible to the Presidium of the Supreme Soviet, the Defense Council has existed at least since 1964 and in practice represents an elite national security committee of Politburo members.

The highest authority is the Politburo of the Central Committee of the Communist Party of the Soviet Union. The key Soviet decisions on entering SALT, and all major positions in SALT, were determined by the Politburo. This body includes the other political leaders who do not usually concern themselves with defense or foreign affairs. In an unusual circumstance, as during the intensive five days of negotiations on SALT at the first Nixon–Brezhnev summit conference in Moscow in May 1972, the Politburo (which normally meets weekly) met at least four times.

In April 1973 then Defense Minister Marshal Grechko (along with Foreign Minister Gromyko and then KGB chief Andropov) was added to the Politburo. Previously he had attended not as a member, but rather by special invitation, on occasions when policy questions under discussion directly concerned him – which occurred increasingly often. His successor in 1976, Dimitri Ustinov, was also promoted from candidate membership he already held as a party secretary to full (voting) membership in the Politburo. Also, soon after Marshal Grechko's death and replacement by Ustinov, Brezhnev was promoted to Marshal of the Soviet Union (in May 1976), followed by Ustinov (in July 1976).

An illustration of the role played by Marshal Grechko as a Politburo member centrally concerned with SALT was his recall from a visit to Iraq in March 1974 to participate in a meeting of the Politburo (or of the Defense Council, it is not certain which) convened to consider a key proposal for a MIRV limitation in SALT II. (The urgency stemmed from the fact Dr Kissinger was in Moscow negotiating in preparation for the forthcoming third summit meeting with President Nixon.) Marshal Grechko's death and replacement by the essentially civilian (if veteran member of the 'military-industrial complex') party secretary Dimitri Ustinov did not affect the general role of the military in Soviet policymaking, or decisionmaking on SALT in particular. As we have noted, Grechko had been raised to voting membership on the Politburo. Of greater importance had been the institutional experience of SALT, in which a number of senior military men participated and through which a number of the political leaders became more involved in military matters which they had not addressed in previous experience in the overall budget allocation process.

Moreover, on the part of the military itself, there had been an increasing acceptance of SALT and better understanding of its requirements as well as its results. Thus, even during Marshal Grechko's tenure the Soviet military loosened up somewhat its constraints on discussing Soviet weaponry, and also its insistence on covering all American offensive arms capable of striking the Soviet Union. Indeed, in 1974 at the third Soviet-American summit involving SALT, a senior Soviet general went so far as to inform an American general that the United States in its published evaluations was *underestimating* the accuracy of Soviet ICBMs and to provide some substantiating data (in an evident, if misguided, attempt to dissuade the Americans of the feasibility of gaining from an intensified arms race).[14]

Military men did not directly participate in the summit meetings of Soviet and American leaders dealing with SALT in 1972 and 1973, but senior

Soviet military representatives (including General Kozlov) did participate in certain of the summit SALT discussions at Yalta and Vladivostok in June and November of 1974. Others, including Marshal Ogarkov (and VPK chairman Smirnov), participated in Moscow SALT negotiations by Secretary Vance in March 1977 and October 1978. At the Vienna Summit in June 1979 senior military men of the two sides met for the first time. The meetings between Defense Minister Ustinov and Defense Secretary Brown, while useful, did not address concrete issues. (No American military representatives or Defense Department officials participated directly in any of the summit meetings until 1979, except for a non-SALT role for Secretary of the Navy John Warner in 1972.)

Following the third SALT summit at Moscow, in July 1974 Secretary Henry Kissinger offered a public comment, probably reflecting a sincere judgement on his part, that 'both sides have to convince their military establishments of the benefits of [arms control] restraint, and this is not a thought that comes naturally to military people on either side'.[15] It is not clear if his remark was directed more at the American or at the Soviet military.

Another sidelight on Soviet military participation in SALT summit meetings has been unintentionally disclosed. In a news conference in December 1974 on 'deep background' – not only not for attribution, but also not for publication – Kissinger commented (indiscreetly) on a collusion with Ambassador Dobrynin to slim down attendance at some of the meetings at Vladivostok and cut out the Soviet generals there. After six years of judicial proceedings, the item was recently reluctantly released as unclassified by the Department of State. An excerpt is worth citing:

> The meeting started with two generals sitting behind Brezhnev – and whenever we started getting concrete they started slipping little pieces of paper to him, or butting into the conversation one way or the other. So, at the first break, Dobrynin came to me and asked whether we couldn't confine the meeting to three people on each side – which got rid of the two generals. So after that, whenever numbers came up, we would explore the numbers, and then he would take about a forty-five minutes break, either to consult the two generals and, on at least two occasions, to consult Moscow.[16]

Soviet military participation in the SALT planning and decisionmaking, and in the actual negotiations, has been active and vigorous at all levels. The effect of this active role has probably been to exert a conservative and cautious influence on Soviet positions, but it has not precluded reaching a number of significant agreements.

SALT AND SOVIET MILITARY POLICY AND PROGRAMS

The first significant effects of SALT on Soviet military programs were felt long before the representatives of the two sides appeared at the green negotiating table. The Soviet political and military leaders were led by the persistent high-level American request for SALT throughout 1967 and 1968 to give the idea careful consideration. And even the prospect of Soviet entry into SALT had an impact in certain instances – particularly with respect to the Soviet ICBM buildup.

As we have noted, US strategic offensive forces had leveled off by mid-1967, and each step toward deployment of an ABM system was accompanied by private as well as public urging of strategic arms limitation talks. At the same time, as the Soviet ICBM deployment program moved toward numerical equality with the US and the SLBM program got underway, Soviet ABM development continued to yield disappointing results.

In 1967 the Soviet leaders decided to curtail by one-third the originally planned deployment of ninety-six ABM launchers in twelve complexes around Moscow, even abandoning some construction already underway. It is unlikely that this move was intended to signal restraint to the USA; rather, it appears to have represented a decision, based on the relatively poor performance of the existing ABM system, to cut back on even the modest original deployment around Moscow. (Work on the other eight complexes with a total of sixty-four launchers and associated battle engagement radars continued, reaching completion shortly before SALT began in late 1969.) This pattern of ABM deployment suggested, as early as 1968, that the Soviet side might be prepared to agree, in SALT, to an ABM limitation at 75–100 launchers for defense of Moscow.

Reflecting these developments there was a sharp drop in 1968 in the frequency of claims to an effective ABM defense of the USSR – a claim for years routinely sounded by Soviet military spokesmen. This change clearly reflected Soviet reconsideration of their originally more or less automatic commitment to ABM deployment. Following the US 'Safeguard' deployment debate, reference to Soviet ABM defense capability resumed in 1970, but again, as agreement on an ABM treaty became more likely in 1971, virtually all references to a Soviet ABM capability ceased, not to be resumed again.

During the period 1966–9, as we have seen, the Soviet ICBM force was growing by about 300 new silo launchers per year. The Soviet military and political leaders were determined that the Soviet Union should equal the USA at least in number of ICBM silos, and preferably in modern ICBMs and SLBMs combined. By the time the Soviets were prepared to begin SALT in 1968, the USSR had more ICBM launchers operational and under construction than did the USA (although slightly fewer in protective silos). The USSR was, however, still lagging badly in SLBMs, just beginning deployment of a Polaris-class submarine (the nuclear-powered Yankee class, with sixteen launchers).

The delay of SALT in September 1968–November 1969 gave the Soviet Union the advantage of having an additional 375 ICBM and SLBM launchers operational and under construction. At this point, having surpassed the USA in numbers of ICBMs, the Soviet leaders decided to stop the buildup of ICBM launchers. After SALT began, no additional groups of ICBM silos were begun for a year. (Indeed, three groups of SS-9s with eighteen launchers, in early construction were abandoned in 1970.)

Construction of Yankee-class submarines with SLBM launchers continued apace, as the Soviet navy still had very few.

The Soviet cessation of its ICBM buildup was, in my view, intended as a 'signal' in SALT, although it also reflected Soviet intention to shift to a new generation of improved ICBMs, if SALT did not preclude having more and the ICBM buildup resumed. One can only surmise, but it seems likely that the Soviet decision at that time was a contingent one, designed to seek the benefit for SALT purposes of a display of restraint, while keeping the door open for a renewed buildup if SALT did not result in a timely agreement limiting ICBMs. The 'signal' in SALT was gently prompted by some unofficial Soviet spokesmen, but did not really 'catch' until well into 1970, partly owing to seasonal construction patterns but mainly because of the usual caution in reporting favorable intelligence. The Soviet side did not receive a response to this signal.

About a year after the first signal, as the SALT talks began to stalemate, a new 'signal' of a different kind was made as a limited deployment of additional missile silos was undertaken – construction began on some eighty new ICBM launcher silos (and some new underground control chambers). This signal hit a little more rapidly, in the early spring of 1971, just before agreement was reached by the highest US and Soviet government leaders on a new approach in SALT. Probably as a consequence of the agreement of 20 May 1971 on new guidelines for the talks, no additional ICBM launchers were begun thereafter – again a positive signal by the Soviet leaders, unilaterally restraining their own deployment for the year until actual agreement on ICBM limitations was reached in SALT I.

Skeptics of the value of the SALT accords suggest that the Soviet Union probably had no intention to build more ICBMs in any case. While conceivably this was so, it may be observed that these skeptics were often the same people who had projected much higher levels of Soviet ICBM deployment, had doubted the 'signals' of 1969–70 and 1971–2, and had most ardently during those years argued the need for limiting Soviet ICBM (and particularly SS-9) deployment. In fact, as we have noted, during the two and a half years of SALT negotiations leading up to the Interim Agreement of 26 May 1972 on strategic offensive arms, the Soviet ICBM buildup was unilaterally limited to eighty additional ICBM launchers, in contrast to the 300–350 built each year during the preceding three years. Additionally, the Soviets agreed to build no additional ICBM silos over the five years duration of the Interim Agreement.

The Soviet ICBM force buildup, restraints and limitation should be considered in light of the fact that this matter was also viewed by the Soviet military in terms of requirements *vis-à-vis* third-party countries. Both the USSR and the USA would need to consider possible use of some portion of their ICBM forces against China. But for the Soviet military that possibility, as well as possible use against yet other countries, and against US bases in Eurasia, required balancing ICBMs for these roles against MRBMs and IRBMs. In 1969 it became publicly known that the USSR was deploying 120 SS-11 missiles capable of being fired at targets either in the United States, or in the Eurasian periphery. Shortly thereafter, it became clear that a number of MRBMs and IRBMs were being phased out; in all, over 100 MRBM and

IRBM launchers were deactivated by 1972. In all, probably more than 300 ICBMs were deployed primarily for potential use against peripheral continental, rather than intercontinental, targets. (Some sixty of the eighty new launchers begun in 1971, incidentally, were for SS-19 missiles in an expansion of two SS-11 deployment fields oriented toward peripheral targets in Eurasia rather than toward the United States.) In the SALT negotiations the Soviet side none the less agreed to count launchers for all such missiles as ICBM launchers, recognizing that the USA could not agree to exempt weapons which could be fired at targets in the United States.

Thus, we see that the very proposal for SALT, and then the two and a half years of negotiations leading to the May 1972 SALT I accords, almost certainly *did* have a restraining effect on Soviet ICBM deployment, and may have reinforced other considerations leading to an early leveling off at a very low level of ABM deployment. On the other hand, a steady SLBM buildup continued.

The SALT II negotiations also were reflected in, and influenced in at least a modest way, actual Soviet missile deployments. Throughout the SALT II negotiations the United States was well in advance of the Soviet Union in MIRV deployment. Indeed, Soviet MIRV development and deployment in the 1970s lagged behind US expectations. Contrary to the contention of some critics of SALT, the United States had in 1972 projected a Soviet initial MIRV deployment *earlier* than the actual 1975 start, and also a faster deployment rate. (American estimates on Soviet MIRV accuracy were, on the other hand, behind the actual pace of development.) As a consequence of the American lead in MIRV deployment, it was the United States which set the relatively high MIRVed missile sublimits (1,320 at Vladivostok, later modified to include strategic cruise missile (ALCM) and MIRVed airborne ballistic missile (ASBM) carrying heavy bombers in that total along with MIRVed ICBMs and SLBMs, with a new 1,200 ceiling for MIRVed ballistic missile launchers). The United States later pressed for a MIRVed ICBM sublimit as well, which would pinch the Soviets more than the USA, and a MIRVed ICBM launcher limit of 820 was finally agreed. The Soviet Union had planned (in line with the Vladivostok agreement), and had begun construction, of about 100 launchers of MIRVed ICBMs *above* the 820 limit, and they accordingly abandoned that construction. So SALT II did impose direct limits of at least 100 (fifty SS-17 and fifty SS-19 launchers) on the Soviet MIRVed ICBM silo deployment program. This example again clearly disproves the contention that SALT has never required the Soviet Union to modify and restrain its existing buildup, although it remains true that both the United States and the Soviet Union have preferred as a general rule to set limits at or above existing and even currently programmed force levels.

We do not know in detail what the views of the Soviet military were on the pace and levels of strategic force buildup at various stages of the SALT process. It is very likely that particular services had their own advocacies. The air defense forces probably lobbied for higher levels of ABM deployment in SALT I, but even the military leadership probably was prepared to agree to forgo Soviet ABM deployments if the USA also would do so. It seems clear that the Soviet military leaders (and probably the political leaders, too) preferred to keep the Moscow ABM deployment, particularly to provide defense against small third-country strikes and accidental launchings (remote though the latter possibility would be), and perhaps also to have the benefit of some operational experience with an ABM system. But it is not clear that a complete ABM ban could not have been negotiated; the possibility was not fully explored. (In 1980 the Soviets reduced the number of ABM launchers they had maintained since 1969 from sixty-four to thirty-two, probably temporarily pending modernization.)

The Soviet military, not unlike the American, was evidently inclined to prefer specific deployment limitations, but no more than minimal restraints on R&D and on system modifications and improvements. None the less, initial opposition was overcome to such limitations as a ban on deployment of future 'exotic' types of antiballistic missile systems, as well as to development and testing of various ABM systems, such as space, air, sea and land-mobile based, and rapid-refire systems.

The strongest military consideration pressed by the Soviet side, and one representing a major difference with the USA, was the insistence that strategic offensive arms for purposes of SALT include all nuclear delivery means capable by virtue of their deployment location of striking the USSR or the United States. This position underlay their opposition to early US proposals in 1970 to limit Soviet MRBMs and IRBMs deployed against targets in Europe, the Middle East and Asia, but the US did not press this proposal. Much more difficult has been the persistent Soviet attempt to include in some manner US forward-based systems (FBS) deployed within nuclear strike range of the USSR. These are mostly aircraft dual-capable (for nuclear or nonnuclear attack) based on US airbases in Allied territory or on US attack aircraftcarriers. It is not necessary to discuss this issue – which bedeviled SALT I until May 1971, SALT II until Vladivostok in 1974 and remains active in strategic arms reduction talks (START) and intermediate-range nuclear forces (INF) negotiations – save to note that the issue was probably posed by real concerns, exaggerated in their own minds, on the part of the Soviet military. The political leaders probably found these arguments convincing but not overriding in the context of the SALT I accord or in the Vladivostok formula for a ten-year SALT II agreement on strategic offensive arms. If the matter had been raised primarily to cause the US difficulties with its allies, or for tactical negotiating reasons, it would have been much more readily disposed of.

The FBS issue represents, but does not exhaust, the category of 'worst-case' calculations which each side can conjure up to justify hedges in limitations favorable to itself as counterweights to these conceivable advantages to the other. The USA has had its share, including the exaggerated concerns of some American officials during the SALT I negotiations over so-called 'SAM upgrade', the possible upgrading of components of surface-to-air missile (SAM) antiaircraft systems converting them into low-grade ABM systems. Despite strong Soviet military (and political) suspicions that this concern was both fraudulent and involved unwarranted attempts to impinge on air defense systems, the strength of the American concern did lead the Soviet side to accept obligations not to convert or upgrade SAM missiles, launchers and radars to ABM missiles, launchers and radars, and to agree not to test such SAM components against strategic ballistic missiles, and not to deploy SAM or other phased-array radars of a certain power (except for agreed special and limited purposes). Real concerns were met without undue impingement on Soviet air defenses once exaggerations of concern were set aside.

Perhaps the chief instance of Soviet refusal to accept an American proposed limitation in the SALT I Interim Agreement was the definition of 'heavy' ICBMs. In retrospect, it is clear that the Soviet SS-19 (and possibly the SS-17) would not have been allowable within the US proposed limit, and the Soviet military could never have accepted a limitation which precluded their deployment of the long-awaited MIRVed ICBM counterpart to the US Minuteman III. The no 'significant increase' in silo size was less constraining and thus permitted a compromise wherein the Soviets agreed not to retrofit SS-9-class missiles in the SS-11 silos (the main American concern at the time), but kept the opportunity to deploy the SS-17 and the SS-19 in modified SS-11 silos, and the SS-18 in SS-9 silos.

In the SALT negotiations each side has of course presented national positions, so that it would usually only be possible to infer which positions were adopted because of 'military' concerns and preferences, as distinguished from those of nonmilitary leaders and negotiators. But the examples above illustrate some of the particular interests of the Soviet military as reflected in the SALT negotiations.[17]

It is reasonable to assume that Soviet military men may have sought to couple with their approval of the SALT limitations commitments by the political leaders to continuation or intensification of some other nonlimited military programs, although we can only infer from what has been happening in the Soviet military forces since the SALT accords of 1972. It is, for example, quite possible that the powerful PVO (Air Defense Command) 'lobby' sought and secured an assurance that forgoing ABM defenses would not be followed by unilateral or negotiated cutbacks in air defenses – notwithstanding the gap in logic for maintaining costly (and relatively ineffective) strategic air defenses when the massive missile forces of the potential opponent would be unopposed. (Of course, the Soviet Air Defense and other military leaders do make a case for maintaining extensive air defenses against possible air attack by other powers on the Eurasian periphery.) Similarly, the military leaders doubtless secured agreement to proceed with MIRVing much of the ICBM force by modifying existing launchers for new MIRVed missiles, and with deploying the additional modern SLBMs allowed under the Interim Agreement.

There is strong basis to conclude that the Soviet military leadership has seen its programs to improve the SLBM force and, above all, to replace about half of the SS-11 force with MIRVed SS-17s and SS-19s and all of the SS-9 force with SS-18s, as necessary and prudent actions in order to preserve parity by matching the buildup of US Minuteman III, Poseidon and Trident strategic forces. (Also the SS-20 mobile IRBM deployment permits returning to intercontinental missions the several hundred SS-11 and SS-19 ICBMs assigned to peripheral theater missions in the 1970s.) These Soviet efforts to catch up and then keep up with the USA are, however, seen by many in the United States as threatening to move *ahead* of the USA in strategic offensive strength. These conflicting perspectives of the two sides have posed a major problem for the SALT negotiations. Turning now from discussions of some interacting influences of Soviet deployment programs on SALT and *vice versa*, it may be useful to consider some aspects of doctrine and military thinking particularly pertinent to SALT and also interacting with it.

MILITARY DOCTRINE AND THE SALT DIALOGUE

By 1969 the Soviet military leadership had reached the conclusion that strategic superiority in the sense of a first-strike option permitting escape from a crushing retaliatory strike was not possible for either side in contemporary conditions, and that a kind of 'nuclear balance' in terms of capabilities for mutual destruction had come into being. At the same time the military leaders were concerned that this balance could be threatened if one side – the USA – achieved a highly effective antiballistic missile defense while the other side – the USSR – did not have such a defense. Hence, their willingness to support the political leadership in its desire to avoid heavy expenditures on an unpromising and even dangerous further round of the strategic arms race caused by extensive ABM deployments – if a mutually equitable limitation could be reached with the United States.[18]

These views came slowly, in part because they were not self-evidently consistent with the standard military statements implying Soviet victory in a nuclear world war if one should come. Such public statements in the military press and on national military commemoration days have a number of purposes, prominently including indoctrination and morale-boosting of the armed forces and the public. Also, specifically with respect to ABM defenses, since the early 1960s it had been standard military litany to claim in a general implied way the *existence* of reliable antimissile defenses (although beginning in 1967 a muted countercurrent to this view began to be expressed). Moreover, as noted earlier, it had been the established Soviet view that ABM defenses were naturally 'good' – a position still publicly echoed by Prime Minister Kosygin in London in February 1967, and privately during his visit to the United States in June of the same year.[19] By 1969, however, claims that ABM defense was 'good' while offensive weapons were 'bad' had ceased, and by early 1971 claims to an ABM defense of the Soviet Union had quietly been dropped.

Some controversy has arisen in Western commentaries over the significance of the Soviet agreement to the 1972 ABM Treaty with its clear acceptance for the indefinite future of assured vulnerability of the USSR (as well as the USA) to missile attack. Some commentators who are opposed to the idea of 'mutual assured destruction' (calling it 'MAD') are also reluctant to conclude that the Soviet leaders subscribe to such a doctrine. They rightly note that Soviet military doctrine has long stressed 'damage limitation', and that the USSR continues to maintain extensive strategic antiaircraft defenses. Moreover, a comment by Marshal Grechko in 1972 that 'research and development directed toward resolving the problems of the defense of the country against nuclear missile attack' is not limited[20] suggests that the military did not originate, and may have been cool toward, the Soviet position in favor of an explicit ban on deployment of a ballistic missile defense of the territory of the country. However, these considerations do not negate the fact of the Soviet acceptance in the ABM Treaty of mutual assured vulnerability of the Soviet Union and the United States to missile attack. The Soviet leaders value doctrine, but they are not doctrinaire.

The SALT negotiations thus far have not led to the kind of far-reaching dialogue on military concepts that some of us hoped to see emerge from SALT. There was early significant agreement on certain basic concepts such as mutual deterrence, equal security and strategic stability. But views on specific prescriptions for 'strategic stability' in particular have differed significantly. Moreover, each side has stressed those aspects of stability of greatest concern to it and in terms of support for its current proposals. (This has led to some interesting reverse field running by both sides at different stages of the negotiation.) But the net result has been to negotiate in a classical bargaining fashion as much as to persuade by debates over doctrine and strategic concepts.

An example from SALT I can illustrate the difficulty in engaging in discussion of doctrine. During an exchange on strategic stability in the SALT plenary meetings in the spring of 1970 the Soviet side referred to the possibility that ICBM silos might be empty by the time of an enemy strike, since the ICBMs in them could already be in flight owing to information gained from technical early-warning systems. The US delegation took the occasion of this remark to make clear that the US held any 'launch on warning' doctrine abhorrent, and a statement to that effect by the Secretary of Defense was subsequently placed on the SALT plenary record. The Soviet side declined, however, to pick up a suggestion that it too make an official statement of the Soviet position, because the Soviet military were consistently adamant against any discussion of such matters of operational doctrine. Indeed, this discussion was the occasion on which General Ogarkov took aside his counterpart, General Allison, and suggested that it was not necessary or appropriate to talk about such military concepts in an arms limitation negotiation. He went on to say: 'As a military man you should understand the answer to that question [on launch on warning]' – implying a positive answer. This incident has been widely cited, with varying degrees of error, based on a published reference which had erroneously indicated that the context was discussion of Soviet military 'hardware', attributing to Ogarkov the comment that such matters 'need not concern his civilian colleagues', in an unintended distortion of what Ogarkov really said.[21] In one sense it is true, the Soviet military did *not* wish to have such matters discussed (nor, though not relevant in this incident, to disclose details of Soviet military 'hardware'); but the real import of Ogarkov's remark was that the Soviet side did not consider military operational concepts and doctrine subject to discussion in SALT. (In addition, with respect to the specific subject, there is now considerable evidence from Soviet internal military discussions and other sources that the Soviet Union had adopted a launch-under-attack contingency concept.[22])

One hazard of a strategic dialogue between adversaries was also illustrated in SALT. In the SALT I discussions the Soviet delegation expressed concern over possible American programs for improving accuracy of missiles to the point of providing counterforce capabilities. In accordance with authoritative American policy, and citing a publicly released letter from President Nixon to Senator Brooke reaffirming that the United States would *not* develop such capabilities, the US delegation vigorously argued that such action would not be taken because it would be destabilizing. Three years later, in 1974, that same president reversed policy, and announced publicly programs to attain those capabilities.

At the June 1979 summit meeting at which the SALT II Treaty was signed, on American initiative the respective military leaders attended the conference and also met alone. Secretary of Defense Harold Brown and General David Jones, Chairman of the Joint Chiefs of Staff, met for several hours with Marshal Dimitri Ustinov, Minister of Defense, and Marshal Nikolai Ogarkov, Chief of the General Staff and First Deputy Minister of Defense. This was the first such meeting ever to occur, and the first involving military men of this standing since the wartime Yalta conference. It was sought by the American side to serve as the beginning of what it was hoped would become a dialogue over strategic issues, and was intended to deal in a general way with anticipated strategic and related arms control problems, rather than negotiating on a current basis. (The SALT II Treaty had been completed; the military men were not directly involved in resolving the one issue remaining, namely, the form of an agreed assurance by Brezhnev with respect to limiting the production rate of the backfire bomber – although involving a military matter, the problem at this stage was essentially political.) The Soviet side was receptive, and Marshal Ogarkov in particular was clearly in favor of developing 'military-to-military' talks of this kind. Ustinov did use the occasion to object to the MX ICBM deployment recently announced by the United States if it involved a basing mode inconsistent with SALT verification provisions. Incidentally, at the close of the summit meetings, Brezhnev made a point of praising Brown and Ustinov, as well as Vance and Gromyko, for their contributions to the SALT II Treaty.[23]

Unfortunately, subsequent events leading to the sharp deterioration of Soviet-American relations, and the American decision not to ratify the SALT II Treaty, made any continuation of this military dialogue out of the question. The attempt at the June 1979 summit to launch a high-level dialogue came too late, at the very end of the decade of détente.

SALT AND SOVIET POLITICAL-MILITARY RELATIONS

SALT has affected political-military relations in the USSR in a number of ways.[24] Probably both the political and the military leaders have gained broadened perspectives, the former through acquainting themselves with military matters in ways other than those familiar from Politburo reviews of the military budget, and the latter through thinking more in terms of political uses – and limits of uses – of strategic forces rather than exclusively in terms of deterrence and contingent war-waging requirements. This development should probably be regarded as a significant dividend from SALT; so, too, should the introduction of Soviet military leaders into a bilateral US-Soviet dialogue on strategic matters.

As noted earlier, SALT was reportedly responsible for the establishment in the late 1960s at the 'working level' of a Ministry of Foreign Affairs and Ministry of Defense joint working group to study the issues and to draft positions for higher-level review. Politico-military matters have traditionally been handled only through occasional *ad hoc* meetings, so this has led to greater contact and probably better mutual understanding. Similarly, SALT has contributed to drawing members of the staffs of research institutes – especially the Institute on World Economics and International Relations, and the USA Institute – including a number of retired military officers, into writing and publishing commentaries on a wide variety of political-military and strategic themes. Many of these articles display high professional competence. The role of these institutes in influencing Soviet policy decisions on SALT has probably been limited, but their indirect influence may be appreciable.

In general, the Soviet military has had a very strong voice in SALT not only owing to its responsibilities for security, but also owing to a near-monopoly of expertise and relevant information. Soviet military leaders, well aware of this advantage, will not easily share this source of power. None the less, there will probably continue to be some greater diffusion of information and opportunity to comment on political-military issues.

In the negotiations the Soviet military were initially very conservative and restrictive, and displayed traditional suspicion of Western intelligence 'fishing'; they even objected to discussion of matters involving military secrecy in the presence of *Soviet* civilian officials engaged in SALT. Marshal Grechko at the beginning of SALT in 1969 ordered the Soviet delegation to provide no quantitative or qualitative information on Soviet military and technical capabilities. As SALT progressed, the Soviet military gradually relaxed their intense security concerns somewhat. By the conclusion of SALT II in June 1979 the formal documentation actually provided many details of Soviet force levels and weapons designations never before publicly revealed. For example: the 'Bear' bomber is designated the Tu-95, the 'SS-18' is the RS-20 and the 'SS-N-18' SLBM is the RSM-50, and it has seven MIRV warheads; the Soviet Union as of June 1979 had 156 Bear and Bison heavy bombers (rather than the 135–140 previously estimated by the Institute of International and Strategic Studies (IISS) and others); and the Soviet Union had 576 launchers for MIRVed ICBMs in November 1978 and 608 in June 1979.[25]

It should be observed that for some time the Soviet commitment to SALT was highly tentative – not only prior to the actual beginning of the talks in November 1969, but until April 1971. By the end of the first round of talks, in December 1969, the Soviet military (as well as political) leaders had concluded that the US was indeed serious about SALT, and after high-level correspondence between President Nixon and Prime Minister Kosygin, and Kissinger–Dobrynin discussions, over the period January–May 1971, they concluded that a mutually acceptable limitation *could* be negotiated. The critical juncture was reached in deliberations in Moscow at the time of the 24th Communist Party Congress in April 1971. Marshal Grechko supported

Brezhnev in these discussions. And from that time on, the highest-level role in SALT on the Soviet side was assumed directly by Secretary-General Brezhnev, now the champion of détente.

There were signs during SALT I that the Foreign Ministry negotiators did not always appreciate fully the depth of certain military concerns, and this may also have been true among higher-level political leaders. Certainly, by the time of the April 1972 visit of Dr Kissinger to Moscow and the first summit meeting a month later, Brezhnev and several other senior civilian leaders were deeply involved in detailed negotiation. (To a lesser extent, because the initial gap generally was less, SALT has probably also helped to bring some American civilian leaders more deeply into strategic matters.)

Soviet presentation of its own 'scare' picture of American strategic capabilities at the third summit in June 1974 represented a step forward in civilian engagement with military evaluations, and in frankness in the dialogue between the two sides. On that occasion, Colonel General Kozlov and other Soviet General Staff representatives (including General Afonsky, who had served as an advisor on the Soviet SALT delegation) assisted Brezhnev in presenting an impressive picture of American strategic forces and capabilities (including FBS, as well as intercontinental forces), operational and planned under current programs, of overwhelming superiority. The Soviet military may have overstated their case in order to stress their point, but they – and the Soviet political leaders – evidently believed that there was a valid point to be made. Marshal Grechko personally stressed this case to Secretary Kissinger at that time. And some of the Americans were, indeed, impressed, if not convinced of the Soviet conclusion. It was significant that the Soviet military were allowed to have their say directly in negotiations at the summit.[26]

In general, frank exchanges could lead to a more healthy awareness by each side of the differences in perspective and inherent biases both sides display in their military evaluations. In evaluating the 'threat' from the other side, each side tends to hedge by conservative estimates of its own capabilities in a retaliatory situation, while judging the maximum capability of the other side in an initial surprise attack. Moreover, each side in its military evaluations looks ahead at what the other side *may* have the capability to do in the next several years, but again is conservative about its own prospects. Such biases in the military evaluation process make much more difficult the process of agreeing on equitable and mutually acceptable asymmetrical limitations on the strategic forces of the two sides. But recognition of the problem, and that it does not (at least not entirely) spring from intentional attempts of the other side to gain unilateral advantage is at least a step toward facilitating a solution. Other factors, such as public ventilation of 'worst-case' threats, and also attempts to build 'bargaining chips' through additional military programs (or worse, so labeling new programs which it is *not* intended or desired to 'cash in' in negotiated tradeoffs and limitations) further compound the problem. But the direct involvement of the military on both sides may help to gain mutual respect and confidence in negotiations seriously pursued.

As the negotiation of the SALT II Treaty was being concluded, it was evident that the military on both sides had found it necessary to compromise on a number of sensitive points. On both sides, for example, there was less than complete satisfaction with the extent of impingement of verification requirements on freedom of encryption of telemetry in missile testing – the American side (although there were divided views) felt the constraints did not go far enough, and the Soviet military had been reluctant to place any constraints at all. The Soviet Backfire bomber posed another issue of special concern to both sides: the American Joint Chiefs of Staff pressed very strongly for inclusion of the Backfire bomber because it could have some strategic intercontinental capability, while the Soviet General Staff and airforce were adamant because in fact they regarded it as intended, and truly capable, only for continental theater and naval employment. Finally, the American side reluctantly accepted formal assurances that the Soviets would not upgrade and provide intercontinental capabilities to the Backfire bomber by refueling and design changes, and would not increase the rate of production (above the current level of thirty per year). The Soviets were prepared to agree to the terms but objected in principle to formal assurances on the grounds that the Backfire was not truly intercontinental, and that American forward-based aircraft capable of strategic strikes on the Soviet Union were not limited. Eventually the issue was resolved only when President Carter personally pressed the matter with Brezhnev at the Vienna Summit.[27]

On many occasions Soviet and American military representatives in SALT attempted to persuade their counterparts of the basis for various positions. For whatever reasons, there has been much less success than in similar discussions between diplomats on the two sides. Relations have tended to be more stiff and reserved, with less readiness to 'empathize' with the other side and less development of personal rapport. None the less, SALT marked a beginning. On the level of *political* recognition of the military concerns of the other side, there was (at least for a time) somewhat greater success.

Several important achievements in SALT were facilitated by recognition of common political-military interests of the two sides. One important example was the agreement to rely on national technical means of verification, and its highly significant corollary commitment not to interfere actively or passively with the other side's operation of its means of verification. Similarly, notwithstanding the reluctance of the military on both sides to be drawn into discussions of traditionally secret procedures concerning security of means of command and control, both also were prepared to seek agreement on the measures included in the 'Agreement on measures to reduce the risk of the outbreak of nuclear war between the USA and the USSR', and the companion 'Agreement on measures to improve the USA–USSR direct communications link', both negotiated at SALT and signed on 30 September 1971 (and the 'USA–USSR Agreement on the prevention of incidents on and over the high seas', negotiated in separate parallel talks involving naval officers on both sides and signed on 25 May 1972). Finally, there was no difficulty in agreeing on the establishment of a standing consultative commission to deal with details of implementation of the SALT agreements. This body has considerable potential, and has proved useful to date in working out detailed implementing procedures on dismantling systems being reduced, and in clarifying uncertainties over compliance with the SALT agreements. Its composition is mixed civilian and military personnel on both sides.

CONCLUDING OBSERVATIONS

The Soviet military approached SALT warily. Its active participation in the negotiation probably contributed to a constructive, if conservative, approach. Public statements of Soviet military leaders and other articles in the Soviet military press have practically ignored SALT; they have continued to stress the requirements for deterrence and for waging war if deterrence should fail; and they have criticized new American military programs. None the less, they have refrained from taking positions that would preclude agreements, and have supported the SALT agreements reached.

In SALT the Soviets have accepted mutual deterrence, both through advocacy of equal security for the USA and the USSR and even more tellingly through sponsoring an ABM limitation specifically precluding a defense of the country against overwhelming strategic missile attack and thus ensuring mutual vulnerability. They have accepted strategic parity as reflected in the SALT agreements, and as a goal for further agreements. They have acknowledged the strategic offensive-defensive and action–reaction interrelationships. They have recognized the importance of crisis management, agreed on specific measures to deal with possible nuclear accidents or unauthorized nuclear or missile firings, advocated defense of the national command authorities of both sides, agreed on upgrading the 'hotline' Moscow–Washington direct communications link through satellite communication and agreed on consultations in crisis situations to avoid the outbreak of nuclear war.[28]

SALT led Soviet military and political leaders both to understand as never before the indivisibility of strategy and arms control, and therefore of certain political-military considerations which impact on internal Soviet decision-making on military affairs. SALT has also led to recognition of the importance of both strategic and 'political-military' interaction between the USA and the USSR and indeed has enhanced considerably the importance of that interrelationship.

Despite the collapse of the Soviet-American détente to the 1970s and the shelving of SALT II, and the unpromising prospects for START and indeed for revival of an 'era of negotiation', the SALT experience may have led some on each side to the beginning of a more realistic common understanding of the strategic military balance and of a stabilizing role for strategic military power, as well as of agreed limitations on that power. That legacy may prove a useful point of departure if relations between the adversaries improve, and for better unilateral understanding even in the absence of efforts to find agreed restraints.

NOTES: CHAPTER 6

1 For accounts of the US proposal, its background and origin, and initial Soviet reactions, see John Newhouse, *Cold Dawn: The Story of SALT* (New York: Holt, Rinehart & Winston, 1973), pp. 86–95; and Raymond L. Garthoff, 'SALT I: an evaluation', *World Politics*, Vol. XXXI, no. 1 (October 1978), pp. 1–25.

2 These figures on US and Soviet strategic force levels, and others cited later, are drawn from authoritative sources including not only the unclassified versions of the Annual Reports (or 'Posture Statements') of the US Secretary of Defense, but also later declassified 'sanitized' versions of the classified reports, and the unofficial but well-informed annual *Strategic Balance* publication of the International Institute for Strategic Studies in London, including refinements and corrections presented in later years as well as those current for the dates indicated.

3 See, for example, Major General Nikolai A. Talensky, 'Anti-missile systems and disarmament', *International Affairs* (Moscow), no. 10 (October 1964), pp. 15–19. The author had occasion in 1966 to discuss this question with General Talensky, and sought to persuade him of the destabilizing effects of ABM deployment.

4 In particular, for statements from the early 1970s, see Leon Goure, Foy D. Kohler and Mose L. Harvey, *The Role of Nuclear Forces in Current Soviet Strategy* (Coral Gables, Fla: Center for Advanced International Studies, University of Miami, 1974), *passim*; Lawrence T. Caldwell, *Soviet Attitudes to SALT*, Adelphi Paper No. 75, Institute for Strategic Studies, London (1971), esp. pp. 6–19; Thomas W. Wolfe, 'Soviet interests in SALT', in William R. Kintner and Robert L. Pfaltzgraff, Jr (eds), *SALT: Implications for Arms Control in the 1970s* (Pittsburgh, Pa: University of Pittsburgh, 1973), pp. 21–54; Thomas W. Wolfe, 'Soviet approaches to SALT', *Problems of Communism*, Vol. XIX, no. 5 (September–October 1970), pp. 1–10; C. G. Jacobsen, *Soviet Strategy – Soviet Foreign Policy* (Glasgow: MacLehose, 1972), pp. 71–121; Thomas W. Wolfe, 'Soviet interests in SALT: institutional and bureaucratic considerations', in Frank B. Horton, III, Anthony C. Rogerson and Edward L. Warner, III (eds), *Comparative Defense Policy* (Baltimore, Md: Johns Hopkins University Press, 1974), pp. 113–20; Thomas W. Wolfe, *Soviet Power and Europe, 1945–1970* (Baltimore, Md: Johns Hopkins University Press, 1970), pp. 273–7, 437–41, 499–510; and Samuel B. Payne, Jr, 'The Soviet debate on strategic arms limitation: 1968–72', *Soviet Studies*, Vol. XXVII, no. 1 (January 1975), pp. 27–45. There have been even more numerous statements since the late 1970s.

5 Yuriy N. Listvinov, *Pervyi Udar* (*First Strike*) (Moscow: IMO, 1971), p. 183.

6 As quoted in 'In the interest of strengthening peace: joint session of the foreign affairs commissions of the Council of the Union and the Council of Nationalities of the USSR Supreme Soviet', *Izvestiia*, 24 August 1972.

7 As quoted in 'Important contribution to strengthening peace and security: session of the presidium of the USSR Supreme Soviet', *Pravda*, 30 September 1972.

8 In addition to the writings cited in note 4, above, see in particular the excellent discussion by Marshall D. Shulman, 'SALT and the Soviet Union', in Mason Willrich and John B. Rhinelander (eds), *SALT: The Moscow Agreements and Beyond* (New York: The Free Press/Macmillan, 1974), pp. 101–21; and see David Holloway, 'Strategic concepts and Soviet policy', *Survival*, Vol. XIII, no. 11 (November 1971).

9 See *Documents on Disarmament, 1972* (Washington, DC: United States Arms Control and Disarmament Agency, 1974), pp. 207–325, for the texts and other official documents relating to the SALT I agreements. Of greatest significance was the ABM Treaty, limiting the US and the USSR each to no more than two antiballistic missile defense sites with no more than 100 ABM launchers and interceptors at each, and further limiting development and deployment of ABM systems. (A Protocol signed at the third summit in June 1974 reduced the allowed ABM sites to one on each side.) The SALT I Interim Agreement limiting the numbers of ICBM and SLBM launchers each side could have for a five-year period, during which negotiations would continue for a more comprehensive offensive strategic arms limitation, expired in October 1977, but both sides declared their intention to continue to abide by its terms while the SALT II negotiations continued.

10 See, in particular, Wolfe, *Problems of Communism*, Vol. XIX, no. 5 (September–October 1970), and Wolfe, in *SALT: Implications for Arms Control in the 1970s*, op. cit., pp. 24–8.

11 In addition to the writings of Thomas Wolfe and Samuel Payne cited in note 4, above, see Matthew P. Gallagher and Karl F. Spielman, Jr, *Soviet Decision-Making for Defense: A*

Critique of US Perspectives on the Arms Race (New York: Praeger, 1972); and Douglas Garthoff, 'The Soviet Military and Arms Control', *Survival*, Vol. XIX, no. 6 (November–December 1977), pp. 242–50.

12   Advisors during SALT I were: Vice-Admiral Peter V. Sinetsky, a submariner serving on the General Staff, probably as the senior naval officer in the Arms Control Section, who served throughout SALT I; Rear Admiral Mikhail A. Kovalevsky, who served in 1970; Major General Igor A. Afonsky, once the youngest general officer in the Soviet armed forces, representing the strategic missile forces command, who attended all SALT I sessions (and appeared again at meetings on SALT at the third summit in June 1974); Major General of Aviation Aleksei M. Gorbunov, an air defense specialist, 1969 and 1970; Colonel Aleksandr A. Fedenko, a World War II heavy bomber officer, presumably representing the interests of the Soviet long-range airforce, who served during 1969–end-1971, when discussion of bombers was suspended; Engineer Colonel Boris T. Surikov, an air defense forces specialist and author of articles on air defense and ballistic missile defense, who served in late 1971–early 1972; Engineer Colonel (later Major General) Vasiliy N. Anyutin, author of a book on ABM defense and serving in the air defense forces, in 1971 and 1972; and as we have noted Colonel Viktor P. Starodubov of the strategic missile forces served first as an advisor in the final SALT I session in 1972. During the seven years of SALT II an additional fourteen field-grade Soviet officers from all services were assigned as advisors to the Soviet delegation (and yet others have served in SALT I and II as 'experts' or interpreters).

13   In striking contrast to the rising careers of the Soviet 'SALT generals', as indicated earlier, General Allison was summarily dismissed in a 'purge' of the SALT I delegation in January 1973, and permitted to retire. General Rowny chose to resign and retire from the service on the eve of the signing of SALT II in June 1979 and to oppose its ratification.

14   See Michael Getler, 'Soviets reported stepping up flight testing of new missiles', *Washington Post*, 27 July 1974.

15   The 'news backgrounder' was given on 3 December 1974; after requests for its release, the transcript was released on 5 March 1975, except for two excerpts which were said to be security classified. After long-contested court proceedings, on 15 April 1981, the Department of State released the two excerpts, the key part of one of which is given here. The other was an admission by Kissinger that the negotiating record would 'exclude' the Backfire bomber from the category of heavy bombers in the forces to be limited under the agreed levels.

16   Secretary Henry A. Kissinger, 'News conference at Moscow, July 3', *Department of State Bulletin*, Vol. LXXI, no. 1831 (29 July 1974), p. 210.

17   In addition to Newhouse, *Cold Dawn*, op. cit., for extensive accounts of the SALT I negotiations, see Gerard C. Smith, *Doubletalk: The Story of SALT I* (New York: Doubleday, 1980); and for SALT II, Strobe Talbott, *Endgame: The Inside Story of SALT II* (New York: Harper & Row, 1979).

18   See Raymond Garthoff, 'Mutual deterrence and strategic arms limitation in Soviet policy', *International Security*, Vol. 3, no. 1 (Summer 1978), pp. 112–47; and Stanley Sienkiewicz, 'SALT and Soviet doctrine', *International Security*, Vol. 2, no. 4 (Spring 1978), pp. 84–100.

19   See 'Kosygin is cool to missile curb', *New York Times*, 10 February 1967, and 'Transcript of Kosygin news conference at the UN', *New York Times*, 26 June 1967.

20   In *Pravda*, 30 September 1972.

21   See Newhouse, *Cold Dawn*, op. cit., pp. 55–6, 192. This author was present at the discussions, excepting the one between Generals Ogarkov and Allison; he confirmed General Allison's account at the time with the American military interpreter, and also discussed it with a member of the Soviet delegation. Newhouse had been informed third-hand orally, and understandably the account became slightly garbled.

22   See R. Garthoff, 'Mutual deterrence, parity, and strategic arms limitation in Soviet policy', in D. Leebaert (ed.), *Soviet Military Thinking* (London: Allen & Unwin, 1981).

23   This account is based on interviews with Harold Brown and other participants.

24   Two useful studies which review the role of the Soviet military in SALT, expressions of military views on SALT related issues, and political-military relations in the SALT context, are Thomas W. Wolfe, *The SALT Experience* (Cambridge, Mass: Ballinger, 1979), esp. pp. 49–77; and Lt Colonel, USAF, Edward L. Warner, *The Military in Contemporary Soviet Politics: An Institutional Analysis* (New York: Praeger, 1977), pp. 220–67.

25 These details and others appear in the Agreed Common Understandings and Memoranda of Understanding; see *SALT II Agreement*, US Department of State, Washington, DC: Selected Documents 12A (1979), pp. 29–30, 36 and 49, for the examples cited, *et passim*.

26 Details of this presentation have not been disclosed, and my account is based on interviews with participants. One published account does refer to the presentation and elaborates on the American reaction; see Joseph Kraft, 'Letter from Moscow', *New Yorker*, 29 July 1974, p. 70.

27 Talbott, *Endgame*, op. cit., provides fairly detailed accounts of the negotiations over encryption of telemetry (pp. 194–202, 221–5, 237–44 and 256–65) and the Backfire bomber (pp. 33–7 and 213–14).

28 See Garthoff, *World Politics*, Vol. XXX, no. 1 (October 1978), pp. 1–25.

Part Three

Soviet Foreign Policy Decisionmaking

7 Soviet Decisionmaking on Czechoslovakia, 1968

JIRI VALENTA

On 3 August 1968, at the peak of the Czechoslovak crisis, Leonid Brezhnev and other members of the Soviet delegation to the Bratislava conference, together with the leaders of several Warsaw Pact countries – East Germany, Poland, Hungary and Bulgaria – appeared to have reached a *modus vivendi* with Alexander Dubcek's leadership. Simultaneously Warsaw Pact forces were ordered to cease their maneuvers on Czechoslovak territory. Many observers of Soviet politics interpreted these events as a victory for the Czechoslovak reformers. Yet only seventeen days later the agreement was broken by the sudden military invasion of Czechoslovakia by these same countries – all partners of Czechoslovakia in the Bratislava agreement.

Among observers of Soviet politics, there were some skeptics who doubted that the Bratislava rapprochement would last for long, but few expected a military move so soon. Indeed, as former commander-in-chief of the US army in Europe General James H. Polk recently noted, both US government and NATO officials considered a Soviet invasion to be highly unlikely.[1] Even Charles Bohlen, one of the most pessimistic US officials, frankly admitted that he underestimated Soviet timing on the use of military force.[2]

Why did so many policymakers and analysts fail to predict the Soviet decision to intervene? Recent literature on American foreign policy suggests that such failures often arise from a tendency to treat the state as a unitary actor, rather than analyzing bureaucratic conflict and consensus building within that state. Thus, some analysts tend to see Soviet foreign policymaking in the post-Stalin era through the conceptual 'lenses' of what Graham Allison has christened the 'rational policy paradigm'.[3] Many explanations of why the Soviets intervened in Czechoslovakia seem to fit this characterization. For example, some observers such as Hans Morgenthau and Herman Kahn conclude that the invasion was aimed at preventing Czechoslovakia from shifting its orbit closer to West Germany.[4] Others, like Boris Meissner, emphasize the importance of the so-called Brezhnev Doctrine, which stresses the 'limited sovereignty' of socialist states in Soviet decisionmaking.[5]

Can a better explanation of the Soviet decision to invade Czechoslovakia be found by applying the bureaucratic politics paradigm? Who were the central figures in Soviet decisionmaking? What were the interests of these decisionmakers and how did these interests affect their stands on the Czechoslovak issue? Who were the advocates of military intervention? Who were the skeptics? Did coalition politics evolve and how did various factors (for example, sources of information and external pressures) affect this evolution and the shaping of the final decision to invade Czechoslovakia? This chapter seeks to test the validity of the bureaucratic politics paradigm by placing these inquiries in perspective and applying the paradigm to Soviet management of the Czechoslovak crisis in 1968.

THE BUREAUCRATIC POLITICS PARADIGM

The general argument of the bureaucratic politics paradigm can be summarized as follows: Soviet foreign policy actions do not result from a single actor, the Politburo, rationally maximizing national security. Instead, these actions result from a process of political interaction ('pulling and hauling') among senior decisionmakers in the Politburo and the heads of several bureaucratic elites at the Central Committee level. The methodology of the bureaucratic politics approach used here does not suggest that purely abstract institutional and organizational interests motivate Soviet foreign policy actions. Bureaucratic politics is seen instead as based upon and reflecting the division of labor and responsibilities among Politburo members in various policy areas. This division arises from two conditions: a highly bureaucratic political system, and a collective leadership in which no single decisionmaker possesses either sufficient power, or sufficient wisdom, to decide all important policy matters.

It is reasonable to assume that Soviet leaders, like their American counterparts, share a certain set of images of national security.[6] This set of images conditions the answers to questions asked by key bureaucracies: Who are our friends and who are our enemies? With whom shall we ally, and with whom shall we struggle? Undoubtedly, the shared images of national security interests affect the attitudes and arguments of Soviet decisionmakers in internal debates. Despite these shared images, senior Soviet decisionmakers may differ as to how to approach and resolve various issues.

Organizational Actors

Foreign policy formulation among Soviet leaders proceeds within a conglomerate of organizations controlled and coordinated by the Politburo. The main organizational participants in the decisionmaking process are the various departments of the Central Committee of the Communist Party of the Soviet Union (CPSU) and the national security ministerial bureaucracies: the Ministry of Foreign Affairs, the Soviet Committee for State Security (KGB) and the Ministry of Defense and its various branches.[7] Under circumstances that will be discussed further, departments dealing with internal affairs and regional party bureaucracies in the non-Russian national republics (particularly the more important ones, such as the Ukraine) may also become involved in the decisionmaking.

The pursuit of various bureaucratic responsibilities with respect to constituencies leads to organizational conflict – disagreements over budgetary allocations, organizational values, scope of authority, organizational sense of mission and self-image. Organizations less concerned with the budgetary implications of their organizational missions, such as the Central Committee's International Department and Department of Liaison with the communist and workers' parties, and the Ministry of Foreign Affairs, are interested mainly in their self-image and influence in the Soviet decision-making process. For example, the International Department tends to assess foreign policy decisions on the basis of their effect on its mission abroad, notably in the maintenance of ties with such constituencies as the communist parties and the procommunist trade unions in the West and the 'progressive forces' in the Third World. In contrast, the subdivisions of the Soviet military establishment – groundforces, strategic rocket forces, air-defense forces, naval forces, airforces and rear services – themselves organizations with expensive proclivities, are greatly concerned with the budgetary implications of policy decisions.[8]

Some Soviet bureaucracies are assigned missions that can be accomplished mainly at home. Examples of such bureaucracies are the Central Committee's Department for Propaganda, the Party Control Commission, the Department of Science and Higher Education, and party bureaucracies in the Soviet national republics; all are charged with domestic and ideological supervision, indoctrination and 'party discipline'. International developments and Soviet foreign policy actions are generally viewed by these departments in terms of the effect on their stated missions. As one source has observed, segments of the foreign policy establishment, such as the International Department and the divisions of the Ministry of Foreign Affairs responsible for relations with the Western countries, are likely to be more interested in good relations with Western countries than the bureaucracies charged with ideological supervision or with political stability in the various Soviet national republics, such as the Ukraine and the Baltic republics. The latter departments tend to view détente with suspicion, for it makes their organizational mission of ideological supervision and indoctrination more difficult.[9]

Uncommitted Thinking

Most Soviet decisionmakers do not head organizations with homogeneous constituencies. Some run organizations that do not have clearly defined missions or formal organizational goals. Many have broad responsibilities and sometimes overlapping foreign and domestic interests. Although there are Soviet bureaucrats who seek organizational independence, the pattern of overlap somewhat invalidates Allison's notion: 'Where you stand depends on where you sit.' The decisions of some senior decisionmakers who are less influenced by organizational parochialism are characterized by *uncommitted thinking*. Personal interests, varying backgrounds and previous political career experience provide additional clues to a given Soviet decisionmaker's position on a given political issue. For example, those Soviet decisionmakers who, as leaders of party bureaucracies in non-Russian republics, had to deal with the volatile 'nationalism' issue share a background experience that can affect their political stand. Finally, each participant's position on an important issue is undoubtedly influenced by other personal factors – prestige within the Politburo, personal idiosyncrasies and the power struggle.

Domestic interests of Soviet decisionmakers likewise affect their stand on issues. In Soviet decisionmaking the challenges of internal politics are much more real and forceful than alleged threats of 'US imperialism', 'German revanchism', 'Czechoslovak revisionism', or 'Chinese adventurism'. Domestic political constraints on Soviet foreign policymakers have grown in importance in the past two decades. Particularly under the relatively more stable leadership of Brezhnev, Soviet decisionmakers were more susceptible than ever to domestic pressures.

THE NATURE OF THE CZECHOSLOVAK CRISIS

The political crisis in Czechoslovakia, which initially appeared to be only a power struggle, shaped up in several months as a struggle for a more pluralistic concept of socialism.[10] Subsequent events in Prague – the resignation of Antonin Novotny's Moscow-oriented supporters, the reformist orientation of Dubcek's leadership, the revival of freedom of the press – created from the Soviet point of view a dangerous political situation in one of the most important Warsaw Treaty Organization countries with a potential impact on neighbouring East European countries and the Soviet Union itself. 'Prague Spring', however, differed significantly from the kind of revolt that the Soviet leaders had experienced in Budapest in 1956. Dubcek's leadership did not challenge the basic elements of Soviet national security interests; it did not, for example, recommend revising Czechoslovakia's foreign policy orientation. Czechoslovakia would retain its membership in the Warsaw Pact and COMECON. Nor did Dubcek proclaim that a limited pluralism would signify loss of overall control by the Communist Party; power, although somewhat diffused, would remain in the hands of the reformist party leadership. Nevertheless, from the Soviet point of view, the developments in Czechoslovakia were problematic and potentially dangerous.

Still, any threat to the Soviet Union's dominant influence in Eastern Europe was only potential and not imminent, and would have been incremental at that. For a long time Soviet decisionmakers were unsure of their policy options with respect to Czechoslovakia. Should they reverse or merely limit the post-January changes in Czechoslovakia? What means should they use to contain Czechoslovakia's influence?

Parochial Priorities, Perceptions and Stands

All senior Soviet decisionmakers must have been disturbed by Czechoslovak reformism. They evidently agreed that the political situation in Czechoslovakia had to be stabilized and they seem to have recognized that the situation might require the use of military force. Thus, covert preparations for military action and possible intervention probably began in the early stages of the crisis – February–March 1968. This military buildup during the crisis served not only as a logistic preparation for the invasion, but also as an instrument of psychological pressure against Czechoslovakia. In fact, the military buildup had been accomplished by late June or early July; but the political decision to invade Czechoslovakia was taken only in August after a long process of pulling and hauling among the senior decisionmakers. Each player, depending on his bureaucratic position, domestic interests, personal background and idiosyncrasies, gave a somewhat different reading (or several readings) of the Czechoslovak issue. Consequently, the players took contrasting stands on the issue and disagreed on the means that should be used in its stabilization.[11]

The decisionmakers responsible for domestic affairs were especially concerned about the effect Prague reformism might have on the Soviet Union. In the perception of the Ukrainian party bureaucracy and its head P. E. Shelest,[12] as well as of other party bureaucrats in the Soviet Union's non-Russian republics (Belorussian leader P. M. Masherov and Lithuanian leader A. Iv. Snechkus, among others), 'deviant' ideas of reformism and federalism could spill over from Czechoslovakia to encourage nationalism in their own republics.[13]

To the party bureaucrats charged with ideological supervision and indoctrination, such as A. Ya. Pelshe of the Department of Party Control Committee, S. N. Trapenznikov of the Department of Science and Education and officials from the major cities (including Moscow's City First Secretary V. V. Grishin),[14] the Czechoslovak 'disease' posed a threat to the containment of domestic affairs. This was especially true among the intellectual, scientific and literary communities where Prague reformism was seen as reinforcing ideas among the members of the Soviet establishment (such as academician A. D. Sakharov), who hoped to see in their own society the same conditions then materializing in Czechoslovakia.

Another group of decisionmakers with strong organizational ties feared that Czechoslovak reformism would galvanize Soviet dissidents and reformists. For KGB officials assigned to the Warsaw Treaty Organization (WTO) as well as those responsible for domestic affairs[15] and for the WTO generals, Czechoslovak reformism was a threat to their organizational mission and authority. On the one hand, the first group of KGB officials, responsible for intelligence operations in the West, feared that an invasion would be detrimental to joint Soviet–Czechoslovak operations, and thus their organizational interests. Though little is known about the actual stand of former KGB chief and now Secretary-General Andropov on the Czechoslovak issue, he was probably deeply disturbed by the purge of KGB officials in Czechoslovakia and by the public revelations about past KGB activities, again because these were detrimental to the KGB's organizational image. To General A. A. Epishev's Department of Political Administration of the Soviet Army and Navy (concerned with ideological and political supervision of the Soviet armed forces), Prague reformism and the weakening of morale observed in the Czechoslovak military posed serious threats to discipline in the Warsaw Pact. Thus, it is not surprising that early in April 1968 General Epishev expressed the willingness of the Soviet military to respond to an appeal from 'healthy forces' (that is, antireformists) in Czechoslovakia 'to safeguard socialism'.[16] Chairman of the Supreme Soviet N. V. Podgorny, who was probably among the uncommitted players, signaled a hardline stand on the Czechoslovak issue.[17] His position was probably influenced by his own experience with 'nationalism' as the head of the Ukrainian party apparatus, where he was Shelest's predecessor.

Decisionmakers with responsibilities for foreign affairs appear to have taken a somewhat different reading of the Czechoslovak issue, concluding that intervention would be too costly. What was primarily a domestic issue to officials responsible for domestic affairs was primarily an issue of external relations and ties with constituencies in the West to officials responsible for foreign affairs. M. A. Suslov, chief coordinator of Soviet policies in the international communist movement, and B. N. Ponomarev and his deputy V. V. Zagladin, leading bureaucrats in the International Department, were concerned with the impact of the events in Czechoslovakia. A military intervention would undermine their organizational mission, their personal prestige and the maintenance of good ties with their constituencies – the communist parties and trade organizations in the West and the 'progressive' forces in the Third World. Moreover, it would threaten the coming World Communist Conference scheduled for November 1968.[18] And, they warned, the intervention would push the Chinese into the American camp.[19]

Premier A. N. Kosygin, who at that time was responsible for governmental diplomacy and was an advocate of the Nonproliferation Treaty (NPT) and an early start to SALT talks with the United States, probably also feared the harmful effects of intervention.[20] Bureaucrats at the International Department and the Ministry of Foreign Affairs seemed to feel that intervention would be detrimental to ongoing foreign policy strategies, would strengthen American opposition to SALT and would enhance the electoral prospects of Richard M. Nixon – the presidential candidate who at the time was perceived as a staunch anticommunist and an advocate of US strategic 'superiority'.[21]

The Secretary-General

In contrast to an American president's capacity to accept or reject the views of the National Security Council and to alter the composition of the government, the secretary-general of the CPSU must have the support of most of his colleagues in the ruling elite. Even though the events surrounding Nixon's resignation have shown that an American president can be removed from office by the threat of impeachment, the chief executive cannot be deposed by a mere coalition of National Security Council or Cabinet members. In Soviet politics this outcome is quite possible, as Khruschev's fall in October 1964 demonstrated. Whereas the American president has come to exercise 'the power to persuade', the secretary-general in the Soviet Union acts as first among equals and thus is required not only to persuade, but also to identify himself with, or better, to create, a winning coalition in the Politburo. (This was even more true in the late 1960s, when Brezhnev's personal influence as secretary-general was relatively minor compared with that of the 1970s.) These constraints of the office could be observed in Secretary-General Brezhnev's behavior during the Czechoslovak crisis. In trying to play the game according to the rules of first among equals Brezhnev vacillated between the interventionist and noninterventionist coalitions during the several stages of the crisis in an attempt to identify himself with the prevailing one.[22] Brezhnev's indecisiveness became obvious when he apologized in June 1968 to one of the most outspoken Czechoslovak reformers, J. Smrkovsky, for attacks of Soviet 'propaganda' against him, explaining that this had happened because of a lack of information.[23] Also, some shifting of stands by other players, particularly those with no organizational commitments, obviously took place during the protracted crisis. The continual changes in Soviet decisions, especially during the last strenuous phase of the crisis, indicate that some of the decisionmakers, including Brezhnev, altered their stands several times.

East European Players

As in the Soviet Union, there appear to have been two schools of thought among the East European elites regarding the Czechoslovak situation. One was represented by East German leader Walter Ulbricht and the Polish leader Wladyslaw Gomulka; the other by Hungarian leader Janos Kadar. Gomulka hated Dubcek and envied his popularity in Czechoslovakia. This animosity was fueled by the March 1968 student demonstration in Warsaw and the ongoing factional struggle in Poland, presumably influenced by Prague reformism.[24] Ulbricht feared the effects of the 'cancer' of Dubcekism in his own country.[25] Whereas Ulbricht and Gomulka considered Czechoslovak reformism a threat to their bureaucratic positions and saw intervention as an opportunity to improve their domestic as well as interbloc postures, Czechoslovak reformism was a boon to Kadar's cautious pursuit of greater domestic flexibility in Hungary. Kadar's tolerance and benign neutrality toward Czechoslovakia[26] were probably motivated, in his perception, by the chance of a nonmilitary resolution, which would allow the continuation of Hungary's moderate domestic policy; for example, the experiment with economic reform begun early in 1968 known as the New Economic Mechanism (NEM).

Contrary to most reports of the situation, during the 1968 crisis the Czechoslovak leadership was divided into two competing coalitions – reformists and antireformists. The antireformist coalition was composed of heterogeneous elements, including those who in the early stages of the crisis supported Dubcek (D. Kolder and V. Bilak) but later, for a variety of reasons, began to fear loss of their power at the forthcoming congress of the Czechoslovak party. After its defeat at the regional and district party conferences in June and July, the antireformist coalition intensified its effort to discredit the reformists in Dubcek's leadership and to secure Soviet 'fraternal assistance'[27] by providing 'proofs' to the Soviet Politburo of the presence of 'counterrevolution' in Czechoslovakia.

PLAYING COALITION POLITICS

Politics in the Soviet Union, as in Western countries, makes strange bedfellows. As suggested by a survey of several cases, most notably Robert

Tucker's and Stephen Cohen's analyses of Soviet politics in the 1920s, and Michael Tatu's study of Soviet politics in the 1960s,[28] coalitions in Soviet politics are loose, temporary, issue-oriented, heterogeneous alliances of convenience among different subgroups powerful enough to carry out their policies. Moreover, in the Soviet Union, the prime motivating factors in the formation of coalitions are not necessarily ideological considerations, but rather calculations of expected payoffs (including that of being on the winning side), or calculations of compatibility and conflicts of interest.[29] Although a winning coalition in Soviet politics at minimum is composed of a majority of senior Politburo members, it must also have the support of influential Central Committee bureaucrats.

The composition of such coalitions can change unexpectedly and dramatically. As stressed earlier, there was a diversity of opinion among senior decisionmakers on *how* to cope with the 'Czechoslovak threat'. The decisionmakers favoring Soviet intervention, in building up an interventionist coalition, conceptualized the Czechoslovak situation as a *zero-sum* game – one side's gain was the other side's loss. Although some differences of opinion about the implementation of military intervention probably existed among members of this coalition, they probably perceived it as the only option available. Their aim was the removal of Dubcek and his supporters by military force. The payoff of such a policy, as seen by the various segments of this coalition, rested in excising the 'cancer' of Czechoslovak reformism. Some members appear to have joined the interventionist coalition to obtain other kinds of payoffs, mainly bargaining leverage on other issues. Ideological bureaucrats like Trapeznikov may have hoped that the crush of Czechoslovak reformism would strengthen their positions in dealing with dissidents and reformers at home.

On the other side, members of the noninterventionist coalition, citing the high risks of military intervention, conceptualized the Czechoslovak crisis as a *nonzero-sum* game and thus recommended resolution of the crisis by political or economic means. Undoubtedly, a range of opinion existed among those Soviet officials who questioned the wisdom of military intervention, some advocating political bargaining, others perhaps political or economic coercion, or even actions aimed at 'the destabilization' of Dubcek's regime. For example, in April 1968 Zagladin, one of the skeptics of the intervention, was reported by D. Voslensky, an eyewitness and advisor to the Central Committee of the CPSU, to have stated that the situation in Czechoslovakia 'should not be dramatized' since 'it cannot be compared with Hungary' (in 1956). Zagladin agreed with Voslensky that the USSR's policy should be politically supportive of Dubcek against both extremes in Czechoslovak politics: the discredited supporters of Novotny as well as the anti-Soviet forces.[30] What united these policymakers were perceptions of the high risks of military intervention; but they apparently differed among themselves as to the means for dealing with the 'Czechoslovak threat'. Thus, they recommended resolving the crisis by a variety of means *short of invasion, and at considerably less political cost.*

These differences between coalitions were highlighted several times during the crisis. Whereas a Soviet military delegation (which included the interventionist Epishev) used pressure and coercion during its May visit to

Czechoslovakia, Premier Kosygin used persuasion.[31] Whereas Kadar displayed a moderate stand toward Czechoslovakia at the Warsaw Conference in July, Ulbricht pressed for intervention.[32] Shelest tried to break up the bargaining during the negotiations between the Czechoslovak and Soviet leaderships at Cierna-on-Tisa by insulting the Czechoslovak reformists and accusing them of actively supporting separatist tendencies in the Transcarpathian Ukraine; Suslov, under pressure from several influential communist parties (Italian, Spanish, Yugoslav and Romanian), and perhaps fearing for the forthcoming world communist conference, argued in favor of a political resolution of the crisis.[33]

The Decisionmaking Deadline and Consensus-building

During the crisis a *deadline* imposed by circumstances, together with the requirements of consensus-building, had an impact on coalition formation. The deadline, as projected by the interventionist coalition, was 9 September 1968, the date of the 14th Extraordinary Party Congress in Czechoslovakia, during which most of the pro-Soviet Central Committee members would be expelled and a new pro-Dubcek state would be elected, thus legitimizing his program. The interventionists argued that a decision must be made before the congress took place. According to one interventionist, Ulbricht, the date of the Czechoslovak congress set a deadline for the Warsaw Treaty Organization (WTO) countries, because afterward 'they would be faced with a completely new situation . . . All the good Communists would lose their posts'. Thus, the WTO must react 'before this Party Congress can take place'.[34] In short, the Congress of the Czechoslovak Communist Party provided the occasion for resolving the issue.

Various maneuvers took place in an effort to create a consensus on policy. The interventionist coalition evidently tried to enlarge the decisionmaking circle by bringing in new participants. For example, in April 1968 K. F. Katushev, a regional party official with no previous experience in foreign affairs, replaced an experienced, but not 'hard enough', foreign policy bureaucrat, K. V. Rusakov, in the important post of party secretary in charge of the Department of Liaison with Ruling Communist Parties. Another regional bureaucrat, Y. V. Ilnitskii, who as party secretary from Transcarpathia was even more obscure than Katushev, participated with Katushev in postintervention diplomacy. Ilnitskii[35] also spoke at the important July session of the Central Committee of the CPSU, which dealt exclusively with the Czechoslovak issue. The very fact that the rules of the game were probably being readjusted and tuned to the interests of the interventionist coalition (both Ilnitskii and Voss,[36] thought to be nonmembers of the Central Committee of the CPSU, spoke in this forum) suggests that the interventionists succeeded in expanding the circle to include participants who could dramatize the danger of Czechoslovakia's influence upon the non-Russian republics in the Soviet West. In general, bureaucrats from this part of the Soviet Union belonged to the interventionist coalition and constituted one of its most important factions. At the July session almost half of the speakers were representatives of these republics. These officials, because of geographic proximity and cultural and social peculiarities of their republics, seem to have been much concerned about 'contamination' from the Czechoslovak 'disease'.

Maneuvers in Influencing the Decision

The maneuvering among Soviet decisionmakers during the Czechoslovak crisis took place within an organizational context. An illustration is the performance of the WTO and its Commander-in-Chief, Marshal I. I. Iakubovskii, during the June–July military exercises on Czechoslovak territory. According to a Kosygin–Dubcek understanding, the regular Warsaw Pact units originally were not scheduled to participate in these exercises. But Iakubovskii reportedly insisted on deploying Warsaw Pact troops in Czechoslovakia until 20 September – the closing day of the party congress – and he was reluctant to order their withdrawal despite earlier assurances from Kosygin to Dubcek.[37]

The resignation of the Chief of Staff of Soviet Decision Making of the WTO, General M. I. Kazakhov, signaled that even at the top of the WTO Command there were fears that military intervention against the only 'natural ally' of the Soviet Union might have a detrimental effect on the Soviet Union's defense system in Eastern Europe. Moreover, for the Soviet military services, resolution of the Czechoslovak crisis probably had important budgetary implications. Perhaps it was not accidental that long-time advocates of the Soviet version of flexible response and groundforces lobbyists, Generals Iakubovskii and S. M. Shtemenko[38] (who replaced the reluctant General Kazakhov shortly before the invasion),[39] were numbered among the interventionists, and that General I. G. Pavlovskii, the new commander-in-chief of the Groundforces Command reestablished in December 1967, was in charge of the invasion. Perhaps the groundforces lobbyists within the armed forces saw in the crisis an opportunity to improve their organizational mission. There were also signs, however, that other branches of the armed forces, in particular Marshal N. I. Krylov's strategic forces, whose organizational mission was hardly affected by developments in Czechoslovakia, may have had doubts about the wisdom of military intervention.[40]

The Soviet Committee for State Security (KGB), particularly officials responsible for East European and domestic affairs, aligned itself with those bureaucracies whose organizational mission was adversely affected by Prague reformism. KGB men in Prague had been dismissed, their security surveillance system dismantled and past KGB activities revealed. It is therefore not surprising that the KGB engaged in various maneuvers to influence the Soviet decision, including producing such 'proofs of counterrevolution' and 'Western subversion' in Czechoslovakia as fabricated leaflets threatening the people's militia, and the discovery of a 'secret cache' of American-made weapons (packed in Soviet-made bags) near the Czechoslovak-West German border.[41] Moreover, the KGB conducted covert actions against reformists (which entailed distributing anti-Dubcek leaflets) and probably produced resolutions, letters and articles threatening and discrediting Czechoslovak Minister of the Interior J. Pavel and other Czechoslovak reformists. Andropov was reported by at least one Czechoslovak source to have displayed a relatively moderate attitude during negotiations with the Czechoslovak leaders.[42] Yet he must have been appalled by the Czechoslovak leadership's inability to prevent the dismissal of KGB agents in Prague and the impending publication of a government report implicating the KGB in the terror of the 1950s. Given these factors, it would be most unusual if he had not known and personally approved the KGB actions aimed at destabilizing Czechoslovakia. All of these actions, which dramatized the situation in Czechoslovakia, served to build support among Soviet bureaucracies and the public for intervention.

The Role of Information

The collection and processing of information is an important function of several Soviet foreign policy bureaucracies. The fiercely competitive atmosphere of the bureaucracies could conceivably compel an agency to 'manage' its information in the hope of enhancing its organizational or ideological mission or scoring an advantage over a rival agency.[43]

Soviet decisionmakers, like their Western counterparts, receive incomplete and distorted information from their agencies abroad. A case study relating to Czechoslovakia shows how information sent to Soviet decisionmakers can be manipulated. During the Novotny era Soviet leaders received more or less accurate information from Czechoslovakia through established organizational channels of the information and communication systems. With the personnel changes made under Dubcek's leadership, they lost control over these channels and many times appeared not to have adequate or accurate information. Thus, Soviet decisionmakers were forced to seek alternative East German, Polish and Czechoslovak antireformist sources of information on the critical Czechoslovak issue. Furthermore, they relied heavily on information and intelligence estimates of the KGB, which were affected by that organization's self-serving interests. Similarly, the reports of the Soviet ambassador to Czechoslovakia, Chervonenko, appear to have been influenced by his background experience as Soviet ambassador to China, by his relationship with Czechoslovak reformists and by his possible fear of becoming the man who 'lost Czechoslovakia'. The reports may also have been influenced by Chervonenko's fear that if the intervention did not occur, Czechoslovak reformists would succeed in convincing the Soviet leadership (as Smrkovsky had attempted to do during negotiations with Brezhnev in June 1968) to recall him from Prague.[44]

The KGB and Ambassador Chervonenko were ill-prepared to assess correctly the configuration of the non-communist forces in Czechoslovakia, the balance of forces between reformist and antireformist coalitions, and Dubcek's popularity; as a result, the picture they presented to the Soviet Politburo was a distorted one. Dubcek and other reformists were portrayed as a minority force in the Czechoslovak leadership who relied mainly on the support of 'radical' pressure groups and who were potential agents of the 'imperialist' powers. The antireformists in turn were characterized not as what they were – a small rival group fearing a loss of power – but as representatives of a widespread opposition among the healthy party cadres and as dedicated communists opposed to the right-wing coup in

Czechoslovakia.[45] The significance of certain developments during the Prague Spring – for example, the emergence of various political clubs, and radical pronouncements such as the famous 'Two Thousand Words Manifesto' – was vastly overrated and presented as proof of the counter-revolution in Czechoslovakia.

The Bureaucratic Tug-of-War

The negotiations at Cierna-on-Tisa between the Czechoslovak and Soviet leaderships (where nine of the eleven members of the Soviet Politburo were present) brought about an uncertain *modus vivendi*. Although no written agreement materialized and only verbal promises were made by both sides, selected teams from the Soviet and Czechoslovak contingents pledged to defuse the crisis. Shortly afterward, on 3 August, the conference of WTO members (minus Romania) took place in Bratislava. Here, despite the objections of Ulbricht and Gomulka, the ambiguous promises of the Cierna negotiations were incorporated in the loose ideological language of the Bratislava declaration. The provisional and ambiguous nature of the agreement was underscored by the fact that the Soviet leadership ordered the withdrawal of WTO units *from* Czechoslovakia, but *not* those units *concentrated around* the Czechoslovak borders. The latter units did not return to home stations, but remained in encampments along the Czechoslovak frontier.[46] The divided Politburo decided against intervention; but at the same time it did not order the dismantling of the military buildup. The outcome of the negotiations was perceived only as a provisional settlement that did not exclude intervention if the Czechoslovak reformists failed to implement the agreement.

The bureaucratic tug-of-war within the Soviet Politburo intensified after the negotiations. The Soviet leaders must have returned to the Soviet Union with differing expectations of the compromise – the noninterventionists hopeful that it would work, the interventionists convinced that it would not. Some elements of the noninterventionist coalition were satisfied with the results, particularly the removal of the direct threat to the World Communist Conference[47] and of a possible indirect threat to the SALT negotiations. The interventionists, on the other hand, were disappointed because their strongly felt bureaucratic demands were not included in the Bratislava declaration. As before the Bratislava accord, the interventionists sought to build a consensus for ending the temporary truce with Czechoslovakia.

At this crucial stage elements of the interventionist coalition – the party establishment in the Soviet Union's Western non-Russian republics, the departments of the Central Committee of the CPSU concerned with ideological supervision and indoctrination, the interventionists in the KGB and the interventionists in the armed forces – communicated to the Politburo their dissatisfaction with the sudden moderation of Soviet policy and intensified their efforts to reverse the trend. The bureaucrats responsible for ideological supervision and indoctrination used cryptic language to express their disapproval of the agreement, which did not call for reimposition of censorship in Czechoslovakia.[48] The interventionists in the non-Russian republics, particularly in the Ukraine, similarly communicated their disapproval of the policy of nonintervention.[49] Ukrainian party boss Shelest redoubled his efforts to mobilize the bureaucracies to undo the Cierna–Bratislava compromise, reportedly by supplying the Politburo with accounts of the alarming situation in Czechoslovakia and the stimulation of nationalist sentiment in the Ukraine.[50]

In not criticizing Czechoslovakia's dismissal of KGB agents from Prague (in whose behalf a high KGB official, Vinokurov, intervened unsuccessfully with the Czechoslovak Minister of Interior Pavel),[51] the Cierna–Bratislava agreement did not reinstate to its former prominence the KGB organizational mission in Czechoslovakia. This further angered the KGB leadership. Some Soviet generals who believed that during the Prague Spring Czechoslovakia's defense capabilities were seriously shaken and weakened considered the Bratislava declaration provisions too ambiguous and were probably displeased with the Politburo's decision to withdraw WTO troops from Czechoslovak territory.[52]

Pressure from East European Interventionists

Polish leader Gomulka, fearing that appeasement of the Czechoslovaks would intensify factional tension at home and possibly weaken his position at the November 1968 Congress of the Polish Communist Party, probably signaled to the Soviet leadership that he could give no guarantee of political stability in his country unless the Soviet Union used military force to restore order in Czechoslovakia.[53] East German leader Ulbricht, who in June had tried to create a political crisis with West Germany over Berlin, in August (shortly after the conference at Bratislava) unexpectedly proposed an exchange of missions of economic cooperation with West Germany's 'revanchists'. He also undertook a visit to Karlovy Vary in Czechoslovakia for negotiations with Dubcek shortly before the invasion on 12 August. Ulbricht's actions were aimed at convincing the coalition-ridden Soviet Politburo that the 'soft' nature of the Cierna–Bratislava understanding might have unfavorable consequences for East Germany and that Dubcek's regime was not complying with the Cierna–Bratislava agreement and should be removed.[54] To the Czechoslovak antireformist coalition, the Cierna–Bratislava compromise was seen as contributing to a defeat at the forthcoming Extraordinary Party Congress in Czechoslovakia on 9 September. Accordingly, shortly after Bratislava they apparently transmitted urgent reports to the Soviet Politburo, depicting the congress as leading to disintegration of the Czechoslovak leadership and to the generally unstable political conditions in Czechoslovakia.

THE FINAL DEBATE: LOGISTIC AND RATIONAL ARGUMENTS, SHARED IMAGES, COSTS AND DETERRENCE

The scattered evidence suggests that the Politburo's final decision was based on information and estimates provided by the KGB and Ambassador Chervonenko, and on 'urgent' reports from Ulbricht, Gomulka and the Czechoslovak antireformists, D. Kolder, A. Indra and V. Bilak, who forecasted a 'right-wing' takeover at the Extraordinary Party Congress.[55] All these signals and pressures probably made it easier for interventionists in the Soviet Politburo to argue that a military invasion after the congress would be much more difficult and costly, and that dealing with the impact of Czechoslovak reformism on the Soviet Union and Eastern Europe, should it be validated at the congress, would be much more problematic. The argument that invasion could not be delayed any longer was apparently reinforced by logistic considerations of the Soviet armed forces, particularly the rear service. Their commander-in-chief, General S. S. Mariakhin, in evaluating the so-called rear service exercise that took place in July (actually a preparation for a military buildup on the Czechoslovak borders), implied that if the Politburo were to decide to withdraw these troops, he could not guarantee the success of an invasion in the future without disruption of the Soviet economy and its transportation system.[56] As it was, the rear service exercise, in which thousands of reservists were called up and thousands of motor transport vehicles were mobilized from civilian resources, was probably already detrimental to the collective harvest in the Soviet Union. Continuation of the exercise would be even more costly, and the command of the rear services apparently did not consider an indefinite military presence around Czechoslovakia to be a viable organizational option. In short, the 'logistics' argument held that after Bratislava only two options were available: either dismantle the military buildup, or intervene.

Meanwhile, the United States – caught up in Vietnam, racial disturbances and presidential politics – was either unable or unwilling to do anything on behalf of embattled Czechoslovakia. This posture was implied by the public statements of Secretary of State Dean Rusk in July 1968, by the Johnson administration's continued interest in the SALT negotiations and by the behavior of the US armed forces in West Germany. (In July strict orders were given to the US command in West Germany forbidding all activity, including an increase of air or ground patrols, on Czechoslovak borders that might be interpreted by the Soviets as supportive of Dubcek's regime.) This state of affairs probably strengthened the case of the interventionist coalition.

Furthermore, Dubcek's dismissal of General V. Prchlik under pressure from the antireformist coalition shortly before the negotiations at Cierna and Bratislava signaled the possibility that Czechoslovakia would not use its military forces to resist an intervention. Prchlik, head of the Security Department of the Central Committee of the Czechoslovak Communist Party, was perhaps the only military man in an important position who suggested military defense as a possible government option in case of a Soviet invasion.[57] Dubcek's naïveté, indecisiveness and his inexperience in foreign affairs (which contrasted with his expertise in internal politics) were seen in his performance during the Cierna negotiations, when he apparently gave Brezhnev some awkward assurance about the composition of the Czechoslovak leadership.[58] His focus on intergovernmental games, while ignoring the mounting pressures on Czechoslovakia and the implications of intensified debate in the Soviet Politburo, hardly prepared him to expect or to deal with intervention.

Soviet decisionmakers increasingly came to share ideas propagated by certain bureaucracies that disposed them toward invasion. The view that the Soviet Union should prevent the spread of anticommunism and 'the unnecessary shedding of the blood of Czechoslovak Communists',[59] along with the analogy of Czechoslovakia as a 'second' Yugoslavia or Romania,[60] apparently struck a chord among uncommitted senior decisionmakers. Also, the one-sided characterization given in Czechoslovakia, in Eastern Europe (particularly Romania and Albania) and in the West, which portrayed the Cierna–Bratislava agreement as a Czechoslovak triumph and a Soviet defeat, while noting other signs of Soviet 'weakness', probably moved Soviet decisionmakers in the direction of invasion.[61]

It is unlikely that in their arguments the interventionists invoked the threat of Western intervention in the near or foreseeable future in Czechoslovakia, for such an argument would not have been taken seriously by Soviet officials. It was clear to them, particularly after Bratislava, that the Dubcek government would not 'deviate' in its foreign policy orientation,[62] and that NATO intervention in Czechoslovakia was highly unlikely. This is not to say that the argument of the 'threat from the West' was not employed in the debate preceding the invasion in order to 'move the bureaucracies' and create public support. However, for the most part, the interventionists probably based their arguments on the need for the Soviet Union to be in a position to cope with the unpredictability of internal developments in Czechoslovakia after the Czechoslovak party congress and to control the impact of these developments on the Soviet non-Russian republics (primarily in the Ukraine), on Soviet dissidents and reformers and on the unstable conditions in Poland and East Germany.

ANATOMY OF A DECISION

In the face of the growing consensus emerging from Soviet bureaucratic politics and the pressures from Eastern Europe, the arguments of skeptics of the wisdom of the invasion grew less persuasive. Secretary-General Brezhnev, in particular, was concerned with the domestic political effects of a policy of nonintervention. In the post-Bratislava period he apparently decided to join the interventionist coalition because of the various bureaucratic pressures that may have threatened to undermine his position in the Politburo. It seems that he assessed the Czechoslovak issue not only according to its national security implications, but also according to the increasingly powerful influence of the interventionist coalition. The desire to be on the winning side might also explain how Brezhnev and other uncommitted players made their final decision.

Brezhnev's final stand on Czechoslovakia may also have been affected by his disappointment with Dubcek. Brezhnev in particular seems to have trusted Dubcek at the beginning of the crisis, but may have believed himself cheated by Dubcek during the negotiations at Cierna. Brezhnev could not afford to be seen as weak and indecisive, or 'soft' on revisionism and anticommunism.[63] He was acutely aware that something had to be done about Czechoslovakia, and in the final bureaucratic conflict he was a member of the coalition that argued in favor of invasion. While Hungarian leader Kadar was engaged in secret negotiations with Dubcek to find a political solution to the crisis, a new consensus with the Soviet leadership materialized on 17–18 August, culminating in the reluctant decision to use military force. Still some noninterventionists such as Kosygin may have felt that the effects of the intervention could be minimized in the realm of foreign policy, as implied by diplomatic notes to the Western powers regarding Czechoslovakia and by Kosygin's message of 19 August to President Johnson agreeing to a summit meeting and an early October start to the SALT negotiations in Leningrad. His message was an attempt to moderate the probable US reactions to the invasion and a reassurance that arms control negotiations were expected to continue.

According to intelligence reports prior to the invasion from the KGB and Ambassador Chervonenko on 20 August, at the last session of the Czechoslovak presidium prior to the convening of the Slovak Party Congress (which was to take place on 26 August), the reformist coalition would be defeated and the antireformists would stage a coup. They would then create a new 'revolutionary' government and petition the Soviet Union for 'fraternal assistance'.[64] However, although they tried, the Czechoslovak antireformists succeeded neither in carrying out the coup, nor in proclaiming a new government. This failure suggests that the Politburo was not properly aware of the enormous popularity of Dubcek's 'right-wing opportunist' minority or of the weaknesses of the antireformists. This erroneous intelligence appears to have been the main cause of the initial political mismanagement of a militarily perfect intervention.

CONCLUSIONS

It is beyond the scope of this chapter to provide a general analysis of Soviet decisionmaking in foreign policy. The bureaucratic politics paradigm is only one of several means of approaching the subject. The conclusions of this chapter must be tentative, for, although some data are available, the study depends greatly on the author's interpretation of cryptic and incompletely known communications among the Soviet decisionmakers. Nevertheless, application of the bureaucratic politics paradigm to the Czechoslovak case demonstrates that the early Soviet 'soft' policy toward the Dubcek regime was not a ruse calculated to lull that regime into a false sense of security while plans for invasion were being perfected. The findings of the chapter generally support the arguments of writers who hold that the rational policy approach alone is inadequate in predicting Soviet foreign policy decisions. The Soviet decision to intervene militarily in Czechoslovakia was not based on a uniform set of perceptions of national security (such as fears of a 'West German threat'), but was shaped by many factors: the bureaucratic interests and perspectives of senior decisionmakers, manipulated information, East European political instability and pressures, intergovernmental games in Czechoslovakia, signals of US noninvolvement, logistic considerations and, finally, shaky compromises among various elements in the Politburo.

The prediction of Soviet actions is a venturesome exercise, and this chapter does not make the Soviet decisionmaking process any less mysterious.

It does make the point that the failure of Dubcek's advisors and of many Western observers to understand the significance of the internal dynamics of Soviet decisionmaking or of the signals among its members accounts in part for their being unable to anticipate the invasion of Czechoslovakia on 20 August 1968. Furthermore, Dubcek's advisors had not seriously researched Soviet politics; nor did they take seriously the signs of debate and the changing 'bureaucratic mood' in the Soviet Politburo. These deficiencies proved fatal. The bureaucratic politics paradigm does not guarantee foresight. The demand that an analyst be able to predict precisely an upcoming invasion is unrealistic. But the bureaucratic politics paradigm can improve the chances of detecting signals of serious debate in the Soviet Politburo. Perhaps the Soviet press is so boring that we sometimes ignore it. But as the Czechoslovak case demonstrates, signs of bureaucratic conflict as reflected in the Soviet press can shed light on the politics of invasion. Judicious application of the bureaucratic politics paradigm, then, focusing upon the dynamics of the role played by the bureaucracies involved, can be useful in the analysis of Soviet national security and foreign policy decisionmaking. The Czechoslovak case points to the possibility of usefully studying Soviet decisionmaking from this perspective.

NOTES: CHAPTER 7

1   General James H. Polk, 'Reflections on the Czechoslovakian invasion, 1968', *Strategic Review*, Vol. V, no. 5 (1977), pp. 36–7; the author arrived at the same conclusion while discussing the issue with several former high officials in the Johnson administration. See Jiri Valenta, 'The bureaucratic politics paradigm and the Soviet invasion of Czechoslovakia', *Political Science Quarterly*, Vol. 94, no. 1 (Spring 1979), pp. 55–76.

2   Bohlen's memorandum to Secretary of State Dean Rusk, 13 August 1968, as quoted in Charles E. Bohlen, *Witness to History, 1929–1969* (New York: Norton, 1973), pp. 530–1.

3   Graham T. Allison, *Essence of Decision: Explaining the Cuban Missile Crisis* (Boston, Mass.: Little, Brown, 1971); see also Morton H. Halperin, *Bureaucratic Politics and Foreign Policy* (Washington, DC: Brookings Institution, 1974).

4   See, for example, Hans Morgenthau, 'Inquisition in Czechoslovakia', *New York Review of Books*, 4 December 1969, pp. 20–1; and Herman Kahn, 'How to think about the Russians', *Fortune*, Vol. 78, no. 6 (November 1968), pp. 231–2.

5   The document usually referred to as the locus of the Brezhnev doctrine is an article by S. Kovalev, 'Sovereignty and the international obligations of socialist countries', *Pravda*, 26 September 1968. For a discussion, see Boris Meissner, *The Brezhnev Doctrine*, East Europe Monograph 21, Park College Governmental Research Bureau, Kansas City, USA (1970). Most published studies of the Czechoslovak crisis depend more or less upon a rational policy model.

6   On the 'shared images' of national security interests held by American leaders, see Halperin, op. cit., pp. 11–12.

7   For an examination of institutions involved in Soviet foreign policy decisionmaking, see Vernon V. Aspaturian, 'Soviet foreign policy', in Roy L. Macridis (ed.), *Foreign Policy in World Politics* (Englewood Cliffs, NJ: Prentice-Hall, 1962); Jan F. Triska and David D. Finley, *Soviet Foreign Policy* (New York: Macmillan, 1968); and Vladimir Petrov, 'Soviet foreign policymaking', *Orbis*, Vol. 17, no. 3 (Fall 1973), pp. 819–50.

8   For a discussion, see Roman Kolkowicz, 'The military', in Gordon Skilling and Franklyn Griffiths (eds), *Interest Groups in Soviet Politics* (Princeton, NJ: Princeton University Press, 1971), pp. 160–4; and Andrew W. Marshall, *Bureaucratic Behavior and the Strategic Arms Competition*, Southern California Arms Control and Foreign Policy Seminar, Santa Monica, California, USA (October 1971).

9   Dimitri Simes and Gordon Rocca, 'Soviet decisionmaking and national security affairs', Memorandum 20-KM-11-1, Georgetown University Center for Strategic and International Studies, Washington, DC, USA (November 1974), pp. 25–6.

10 For a detailed treatment of the origins of the Prague Spring, see, in particular, H. Gordon Skilling, *Czechoslovakia's Interrupted Revolution* (Princeton, NJ: Princeton University Press, 1976); and Galia Golan, *The Czechoslovak Reform Movement: Communism in Crisis, 1962–1968* (Cambridge: Cambridge University Press, 1971).

11 The differing perceptions of Soviet officials regarding the Czechoslovak crisis can be deciphered by an analysis of the contents of their speeches and public statements. Some officials consistently attacked the 'nationalist' and 'right-wing revisionist' elements, 'various demagogues and renegades' and 'degenerates' and their 'models of democratic socialism' and policies of 'limitless decentralism'. They called for 'revolutionary vigilance' in the USSR, and some of them began to hint at offers of 'fraternal assistance' to the 'healthy forces' of Czechoslovakia in their struggle 'against imperialist intrigues'. Meanwhile, other officials, who consistently refrained from cryptic assaults on the Czechoslovak leadership, pledged respect for 'each other's views', the 'right of autonomy' and 'noninterference in the internal affairs' of other communist parties, some of them occasionally expressing publicly their 'confidence in the Czechoslovak party'. During the crisis this group, instead of attacking the 'right-wing revisionists', consistently assaulted the 'left revisionism' or 'left adventurist perversion of Marxism' in the Chinese leadership as the main danger to the USSR. The former group of officials, on the other hand, probably because of their preoccupation with the Czechoslovak issue, did not express any concern regarding the policies of the Chinese leadership.
        Hereafter, in keeping with the purpose of this chapter, the public speeches and pronouncements of Soviet leaders will be referred to without going into lengthy analyses. For a detailed analysis, see Jiri Valenta, 'Soviet decisionmaking and the 1968 Czechoslovak crisis', *Studies in Comparative Communism*, Vol. VIII, nos. 1 and 2 (Spring–Summer 1975), pp. 147–73.

12 For Shelest's views of the Czechoslovak crisis, see his speeches in *Pravda Ukrainy*, 17 February 1968, and *Pravda*, 5 July 1968; see also an analysis by Grey Hodnett and Peter J. Potichny, *The Ukraines and the Czechoslovak Crisis* (Canberra: Australian National University, 1970).

13 For Masherov's views, see *Sovetskaia Belorussiia*, 11 May 1968. For Snechkus's views, see his article, 'The April session and some of our tasks', *Kommunist* (Journal of the Central Committee of Lithuania), no. 6 (June 1968), pp. 3–7; and *Kommunist*, no. 10 (October 1968), pp. 9–10.

14 For Pelshe's stand, see *Neues Deutschland*, 4 May 1968, and *Tribuna* (Prague), 26 March 1969. Trapeznikov's militant view on the Czechoslovak issue is developed in his book, *At the Turning Points of History* (Moscow: Progress 1972), pp. 73–8. For Grishin's stand, see *Pravda*, 23 April 1968.

15 For KGB position on Czechoslovak reformism, see Ladislav Bittman, *The Deception Game: Czechoslovak Intelligence in Soviet Warfare* (Syracuse, NY: Syracuse University Press, 1972), pp. 167–215; see also Josef Frolik, *The Frolik Defection* (London: Cooper, 1975), pp. 130–79.

16 As reported in *Le Monde*, 5–6 May 1968.

17 For Podgorny's views, see Radio Moscow, 6 May 1968; and *Pravda*, 20 July 1968.

18 For Suslov's views, see *Pravda*, 28 February and 6 May 1968; for Zagladin's views, see *Pravda*, 29 April 1968, and Radio Moscow, 21 March 1968.

19 Dimitri Simes, 'The Soviet invasion of Czechoslovakia and the limits of Kremlinology', *Studies in Comparative Communism*, Vol. VIII, nos 1 and 2 (Spring–Summer 1975), p. 178; see also hints in the 'The political course of Mao Tse-tung on the international scene', *Kommunist* (May 1968), pp. 95–108.

20 For Kosygin's views, see his speeches in *Sovetskaia Belorussiia*, 15 February 1968; and *Izvestiia*, 2 July 1968. As late as July, Kosygin expressed 'confidence in Czechoslovak communists', *Pravda*, 15 July 1968. For Kosygin's stand on SALT, see Lyndon B. Johnson, *The Vantage Point* (New York: Holt, Rinehart & Winston, 1971), pp. 484–5; John Newhouse, *Cold Dawn: The Story of SALT* (New York: Holt, Rinehart & Winston, 1973), pp. 91–4; and an interview with Dr Walt W. Rostow, 26 July 1974, Austin, Texas, USA.

21 Simes, 'The Soviet invasion', op. cit., p. 178; see also A. Grigorysants and V. Rogov,

'Leninist ideas are invincible: the policy of anticommunism meets with failure, Richard Nixon again', *Trud*, 13 August 1968.

22 For Brezhnev's views, see Radio Leningrad, 16 February 1968, and *Pravda*, 23 February, 30 March and 4 July 1968; and E. Weit, *At the Red Summit: Interpreter behind the Iron Curtain* (New York: Macmillan, 1973), pp. 209–10.

23 An interview with Josef Smrkovsky published posthumously in *Listy* (Rome), Vol. 5, no. 2 (March 1975), pp. 11–12.

24 Weit, op. cit., p. 205; Alexander Dubcek's letter to the Federal Assembly of Czechoslovakia and the Slovak National Council, October 1974 (hereafter referred to as Dubcek's letter), in *Listy*, Vol. 5, no. 3 (April 1975), p. 14.

25 Dubcek's letter, p. 14.

26 For Kadar's views on Czechoslovakia, see his interview in C. L. Sulzberger, *An Age of Mediocrity: Memoirs and Diaries, 1963–1972* (New York: Macmillan, 1973), pp. 476–7.

27 Dubcek's letter to Comrade K. Smrkovsky, *Listy*, Vol. 4, no. 2 (May 1974), p. 5; and an interview with Smrkovsky, *Listy*, Vol. 4, no. 2 (May 1974), p. 15; and Zdenek Mlynar, *Ceskoslovensky pokus o reformu 1968* (Koln: Index-Listy, 1975), p. 233.

28 Robert Tucker, *Stalin as Revolutionary* (New York: Norton, 1973); Stephen F. Cohen, *Bukharin and the Bolshevik Revolution: A Political Biography, 1888–1938* (New York: Knopf, 1973); and Michel Tatu, *Power in the Kremlin: From Khrushchev to Kosygin* (New York: Viking, 1969).

29 The concept of calculations of expected payoffs is developed in William H. Riker, *The Theory of Political Coalitions* (New Haven, Conn.: Yale University Press, 1962). For an important modification of Riker's theory, see Robert Axelrod, *Conflict of Interest: A Theory of Divergent Goals with Application to Politics* (Chicago, Ill.: Markham, 1970), esp. pp. 165–85.

30 See excerpts from the diary of a Soviet eyewitness Professor M. Voslensky, a former arms-control expert of the Central Committee of the CPSU, now living in Munich. 'This will only help Americans', *Der Spiegel*, 21 August 1978, p. 126.

31 Kosygin's moderate behavior was reported on Prague television, 22 May 1968; and in *Zemedelske noviny*, 22 May 1968. Here I benefited from an interview with a former deputy prime minister of the Czechoslovak government, Ota Sik, 5 June 1974, St Gallen.

32 Weit, op. cit., pp. 201–2.

33 Pavel Tigrid, *Why Dubcek Fell* (London: Macdonald, 1971), pp. 86–7; and interview with Smrkovsky, *Listy*, op. cit., p. 13.

34 Ulbricht quoted in Weit, op. cit., pp. 202–3.

35 Ilnitskii wrote several articles at the time expressing his concern about the Czechoslovak influence on the inhabitants of his region; see *Pravda Ukrainy*, 29 July 1968; 'Our light: internationalism', *Kommunist Ukrainy*, no. 1 (1969), pp. 85–93; and an analysis of Hodnett and Potichny, op. cit., pp. 144–5.

36 For Voss's view, see 'Some questions of ideological work of the party organization', *Kommunist Sovetskoi Latvii*, no. 10 (30 September 1968), pp. 7–15.

37 Tigrid, op. cit., p. 68.

38 For Shtemenko's and Iakubovski's views, see General Shtemenko, *Nedelia*, no. 6 (31 January–6 February 1965); and General Iakubovski, 'Ground forces', *Krasnaia zvezda*, 31 July 1967, and his articles 'Friendship born in battle', *Krasnaia zvezda*, 23 July 1968, and 'The battle-ready community of armies of the socialist countries', *Kommunist*, no. 5 (1970), pp. 90–100.

39 John Thomas, *Soviet Foreign Policy and Conflict within the Political and Military Leadership* (McLean, Va: Research Analysis Corporation, September 1970), p. 9.

40 John Erickson, 'Towards a new Soviet high command: "Rejuvenation" reviewed', *Royal United Service Institute Journal* (UK), Vol. 144, no. 655, no. 9 (September 1969), pp. 37–44.

41 An official Czechoslovak investigation of the 'secret cache' of weapons concluded that this allegation was 'a provocation'; see an interview with Smrkovsky, *Listy*, op. cit., p. 15.

42 For the activities of the KGB, see Bittman, op. cit., p. 214; and Frolik, op. cit., p. 148. For Andropov's role in the negotiations with the Czechoslovak leaders, see Zdenek Hejzlar, *Reform Kommunismus* (Cologne: Europaische Verlagsanstalt, 1976, p. 222).

43 See *The Penkovsky Papers* (New York: Doubleday, 1965), pp. 255–77; and a report in *Die Welt*, 1 November 1975.

44 Smrkovsky told Brezhnev that Chervonenko did not inform the Soviet leadership

'accurately', and indicated that Czechoslovak reformists hoped that he would be recalled; see an interview with Smrkovsky, *Listy*, op. cit., p. 15.

45 Tigrid, op. cit., p. 98; Soviet leader Ponomarev reportedly complained about the incompetence of Chervonenko after the invasion, in ibid., p. 227.

46 Polk, op. cit., p. 37.

47 See hints of this in the authoritative article, 'Strength in unity', *Pravda*, 5 August 1968.

48 For example, see hints in 'The political milk of *Literarni listy*', *Literaturnaia gazeta*, 14 August 1968; and G. Kibets and A. Stepanov, 'Dictatorship of the proletariat: its content and forms', *Sovetskaia Rossia*, 9 August 1968.

49 *Pravda Ukrainy*, 1 August 1968; 'Fidelity to Marxism-Leninism: source of the strength of socialist cooperation', *Kommunist Ukrainy*, no. 8 (August 1968), pp. 3–13; and *Sovetskaia Estoniia*, 4–7 August 1968.

50 See 'The removal of Shelest', *Listy*, Vol. 2, no. 4 (July 1972), p. 33; and 'The unexpected Soviet initiative-thaw in Prague', *Le Monde*, 17–18 June 1973.

51 Robert Little (ed.), *The Czechoslovak Black Book* (New York: Praeger, 1969), pp. 80–1; and Frolik, op. cit., p. 150.

52 Czechoslovak Prime Minister Cernik reported that this had been concluded by the Soviet general prior to the intervention; see Tigrid, op. cit., p. 95. For hints of military dissatisfaction with the Bratislava agreement, see *Krasnaia zvezda*, 18 August 1968.

53 Jan B. Weydenthal, 'Polish politics and the Czechoslovak crisis', *Canadian Slavonic Papers*, Vol. 14, no. 1 (January 1972), p. 46; and Weit, op. cit., p. 205.

54 For an analysis, see Melvin Croan, 'Czechoslovakia, Ulbricht, and the German problem', *Problems of Communism*, Vol. VIII, no. 1 (January–February 1969), pp. 1–5.

55 Dubcek, *Listy*, op. cit., p. 5; and Mlynar, op. cit., p. 233; and Tigrid, op. cit., p. 98. Also see hints in 'The letter of warning of the Soviet politburo', 17 August 1968, reported on Radio Prague, 20 August 1969.

56 An interview with General S. S. Mariakhin, *Krasnaia zvezda*, 14 August 1968; and Polk, op. cit., p. 32.

57 Jiri Pelikan, 'The struggle for socialism in Czechoslovakia', *New Left Review*, No. 71 (January–February 1972), p. 27 (Pelikan was the former chairman of the Czechoslovak Assembly's Foreign Affairs Committee). For an argument stressing the importance of the deterrence of East European countries facing Soviet intervention, see Christopher D. Jones, 'Soviet hegemony in Eastern Europe: the dynamics of political autonomy and military intervention', *World Politics*, Vol. 29, no. 2 (January 1977), pp. 216–41.

58 Tad Szulc, *Czechoslovakia since World War II* (New York: Viking, 1971), p. 374; and Dubcek's speech, 26 September 1969, as reported in *Svedectvi* (Paris), Vol. 9, no. 38 (1970), pp. 275–6.

59 Interview with Czechoslovak leader J. Piller, Prague Radio, 17 September 1969.

60 Brezhnev reportedly said that Czechoslovakia was not Romania or Yugoslavia and that the Soviets would not let Czechoslovakia go; reported by M. Vaculik in J. Pelikan (ed.), *The Secret Vysocany Congress* (London: Allen Lane, 1971), pp. 26–7.

61 See hints in 'The letter of warning of the Soviet politburo', reported by Radio Prague, 20 August 1969.

62 A. Snejdarek (a former foreign policy advisor to Dubcek's leadership), in Golan, op. cit., p. 51. Even Soviet Ambassador Chervonenko never complained about Dubcek's foreign policy. See the interview with Czechoslovak Foreign Minister J. Hajek, *Reporter* (Prague), no. 3 (16–23 October 1968), p. 45.

63 At the crucial Politburo session on 17 August 1968 several Politburo members reportedly were critical of the 'hesitation and weakness in dealing with the Czech question': Tigrid, op. cit., p. 97.

64 An interview with Smrkovsky, *Listy*, op. cit., pp. 16–19; and Havlicek, in Little, op. cit., pp. 23–9.

8 Soviet Decisionmaking in the Yom Kippur War, 1973

GALIA GOLAN

The purpose of this chapter is not to examine Soviet behavior during the Yom Kippur War; this has already been amply covered in a number of studies.[1] Rather, the present chapter will focus upon Soviet decisionmaking in connection with, and particularly during, the war. Nine key decisions will be analyzed with regard to the following factors:[2]

(1) global considerations, primarily the superpower relationship and détente, but also ideological and economic considerations;
(2) regional considerations, that is, Soviet strategic, economic, political and ideological interests in the Middle East;
(3) local considerations, that is, the Soviet relationship with the participants in the war, and the battle situation;
(4) domestic considerations, that is, political, ideological, economic, military and public constraints, which include differing institutional interests or policy preferences as well as personal differences of opinion;
(5) lines of command, that is, participants in decisionmaking and the degree and nature of their participation;
(6) information collection and dissemination.

Analysis by means of these categories should provide a picture of the policy options available, the priorities and the cost–benefit analyses to which these options and priorities were subjected. When dealing with any system, the researcher's conclusions can be speculative at best, but when dealing with the Soviet system, one is all the more limited. While internal political disputes or émigré revelations have occasionally produced some evidence regarding the Soviet decisionmaking process – for example, in the case of the invasion of Czechoslovakia in 1968 – no such evidence has become available in connection with the Yom Kippur War, with the exception of materials from the Arab and American sides. These materials are invaluable and will indeed be employed, but they relate to only a limited part of the decision-making process. Thus, for example, it must be said from the outset that there is no clear evidence as to when and by whom the essential decisions were taken. We merely assume that the Politburo was the main actor and that an inner core – likely to be the regular members of the Defense Council and consisting usually of Brezhnev, Podgorny, Kosygin, Grechko and Gromyko – were the major decisionmakers. The participation of others and the varying types of participation even of this inner core will be speculated upon in view of available information, but this speculation will perforce be based on a 'rationality' approach, that is, that the participants acted rationally and in accord with the logic of their positions and the situation. This assumption, however, is far from provable, and may well be the major flaw in an attempt to reconstruct the decisionmaking process of a closed system.[3]

The following decisions are to be examined:

	Decision or stimulus to decision	*approximate date of decision or stimulus*
(i)	resumption of arms deliveries to Egypt (decision)	January–February 1973
(ii)	knowledge of imminence of hostilities (stimulus)	mid-September– 4 October 1973
(iii)	outbreak of hostilities (stimulus)	6 October 1973
(iv)	bid for pan-Arab involvement (decision)	8 October 1973
(v)	airlift to Arabs (decision)	9 October 1973
(vi)	warning to Israel (decision)	12 October 1973
(vii)	Kosygin mission to Egypt (decision)	15 October 1973
(viii)	invitation to Kissinger (decision)	19 October 1973
(ix)	ceasefire violations and US alert (stimuli)	24–5 October 1973

THE SETTING: FACTORS INFLUENCING SOVIET DECISIONMAKING IN THE MIDDLE EAST PRIOR TO THE 1973 CRISIS

Global Considerations

The overriding policy objective of the Soviet Union in the global sphere was détente, mainly with the USA, but also with Western Europe and in Asia. The major impetus for Soviet interest in détente was probably economic, that is, Soviet interest in trade and Western technology, but the policy also had its strategic-political basis in the effort to limit the arms race (to levels desirable to the Soviet Union) and prevent the outbreak of superpower military confrontation, as well as to minimize the risks of US-Chinese or Chinese-Japanese rapprochement. This policy dictated a certain degree of superpower and interbloc cooperation, including crisis management, in the interests not only of preventing a superpower clash, but also of preventing hostile polarization which would impede the economic exchange sought by Moscow. Indeed, much progress had been made prior to the 1973 Middle East crisis; but the new relationships had yet to be tested in a crisis situation and détente was by no means a fully accepted, stable pattern of international relations. Moreover, détente in the Soviet view did not rule out military or any other type of competition with the West for influence in the world. Rather, détente was intended to provide a less volatile international atmosphere in which to pursue this competition. This thinking was not entirely accepted by many of Moscow's allies, and China, for example, never failed to point out to them that détente would be at their expense. Nor did the fall of Salvador Allende just prior to the 1973 war make matters easier for the prodétentists in Moscow.

Regional Considerations

Soviet interests in the Middle East as a region were intimately connected with Soviet global interests, particularly on a strategic level but also on economic and political levels. Beyond Moscow's traditional interest in this region beyond its southern borders, there were new motivations such as obtaining facilities for the expanding Soviet navy (both air and naval bases to cover the new Mediterranean and Indian Ocean contingents) and strategic positions to check the American naval presence or, in the case of the Indian Ocean, to defend against the eventual deployment of US long-range sea-launched nuclear missiles.[4] The Indian Ocean area was of increasing importance as the Western world entered a nascent oil crisis, augmenting the economic potential of the oil-producing states and increasing their strategic value to the superpowers. While Moscow's own future need for Middle Eastern oil is still the subject of debate, the Soviet Union had begun efforts both to improve relations with Arab states providing the West's and Japan's vital oil needs, and to reap the benefits of the oil revenues in the form of trade and sales of Soviet arms.[5] Thus, sometime in 1973 the Soviet Union began selling weapons to the Arab states for hard currency, demanding such payments even from Egypt (and later Syria), who were funded by the oil states. Soviet efforts showed a preference for the Red Sea–Persian Gulf–Indian Ocean area over the region of the Arab-Israeli confrontation.[6]

While the (Arab-Israeli) confrontation states maintained their importance in the eastern Mediterranean, and Egypt continued to be of prime importance within the region, both because of the Suez Canal and Egypt's influence in the Arab and nonaligned world, the Soviets did not attempt to recreate their military presence – or commitment – in Egypt or Syria anywhere near the scale it had been prior to the 1972 expulsion. In light of this, and particularly of the emerging Soviet preference for the Persian Gulf–Indian Ocean area, it is difficult to determine exactly what the Soviet attitude toward the Arab-Israeli conflict had been prior to the 1973 war. It is almost axiomatic that the Soviet Union did not favor hostilities because of the possibility of confrontation with the United States and this was, indeed, manifested by the Sadat–Brezhnev dispute. The question is, however, whether the Soviets favored a continuation of the no-war/no-peace status quo or whether they actually wanted a political settlement of the conflict. Soviet behavior in the two-power and four-power talks of 1968–9, and Soviet arguments with their Arab clients during 1970–3 as well as their stated position to Nixon seemed to indicate a Soviet desire to reach a settlement – perhaps engendered by the shift in their own regional priorities.[7] Therefore, although the Soviets appeared to be committed to the satisfaction of the Arab demands, they had already raised the ire of a faction of Syrian communists, as well as members of the PLO, Iraq and Libya, because of their preference for a political rather than a military solution, and their opposition to the destruction of Israel or to demands beyond the 1967 lines.[8]

Thus, in the 1968–73 period, there were signs that Moscow did not perceive any greater territorial demands, or for that matter the Palestinians' objectives, as feasible or even desirable.[9]

Local Considerations

Locally, the Soviets had already begun to improve economic relations with Libya and the Gulf States, including Iran. With the exception of Iraq, relations with the oil-producing states were no more than correct and less than cordial with some such as Libya and, of course, Saudi Arabia. Soviet-Iraqi relations had been on an upward swing since their friendship pact in 1972, followed in Iraq by the inclusion of the local communists in a national front in 1973, nationalization of the oil companies and the curtailment of oil sales to the West. Yet Iraq was still reluctant to grant Soviet naval rights in Um Qasr and the two countries were not in agreement about the best way to deal with the Arab-Israeli conflict. Thus, prior to the 1973 crisis, Moscow could not be said to have gained sufficient influence in the oil-producing states to control – or even significantly influence – the potential oil weapon.

With Egypt and Syria, Soviet relations were somewhat precarious. Of the two, the Soviet-Syrian relationship was the more stable, Moscow having signed a large arms agreement with Damascus in July 1972[10] and making a display of friendship in order to counter the negative effects of the expulsion from Egypt. Relations with Syria, however, had truly improved. Damascus had apparently agreed to expand the port of Latakia, thereby compensating partially for the losses in Egypt, and Assad had even acted as a mediator in an effort to patch up Soviet-Egyptian relations. But Assad jealously guarded his independence, refusing Soviet efforts to conclude a friendship treaty similar to the Egyptian and Iraqi treaties. Moreover, there was discord over the idea of renewed Arab-Israeli hostilities and tension following the Israeli downing of thirteen Syrian MIGs on 13 September.

Yet, however strained Soviet-Syrian relations, they were not nearly so bad as those with Egypt. As his power matured, Sadat became increasingly distrustful of the Soviets and he saw himself as having been treated dishonorably, even contemptuously, by them. He expelled the Soviets because they refused to supply Egypt with certain offensive weapons which were necessary for regaining the territories lost in 1967. The Soviets apparently preferred détente with the United States to an Arab military effort. Moscow responded to the expulsion order by (1) withdrawing all of its military men and equipment – which was more than what Sadat had demanded; (2) refusing to cooperate in a joint communiqué or to sell Egypt equipment which had been ordered; (3) recalling its ambassador; (4) suspending arms deliveries; and (5) stepping up relations with Syria, Iraq and the Palestinians. The ice was melted somewhat in October 1972, when the Soviets consented to return some of the equipment (mainly SAM 6s) with their advisors (a few hundred), but no other changes ensued in their relationship until the Soviet decision to reverse its policy. This will be the first decision to be analyzed, as it is the turning-point which marks the precrisis period for the Soviet Union.[11]

Domestic and Bureaucratic Considerations

Although the overriding foreign policy objective on the eve of the 1973 crisis was détente, there is evidence that a variety of opinions on the subject, and even opposition, existed among the Soviet political elite.[12] Brezhnev was the champion of détente, together with Kosygin and Podgorny, apparently, but in as much as Brezhnev was at this time consolidating his position as the dominant power in the party leadership, it is conceivable that Podgorny and Kosygin took special pains not to differ publicly from Brezhnev on this subject. Gromyko too may be considered a staunch supporter of Brezhnev's policy of détente. Indeed, the promotion of Gromyko to Politburo status in April 1973 was presumably intended by Brezhnev as a means of strengthening support within the Politburo for this foreign policy. For all three officials, good bureaucratic-institutional reasons could be found for their prodétente position. Kosygin was identified with Soviet economic interests, hence his professional commitment toward the trade and technological benefits expected from détente and perhaps relief from some of the economic burden of the arms race, while Gromyko – and possibly Podgorny – advocated the relaxation of international tension and the smoother course of interstate relations promised by détente.

The same could not be said for Grechko, Suslov, Andropov, Shelepin, Katushev and Ponomarev, whose bureaucratic responsibilities (internal and external security, ideology and the international communist and national liberation movements) brought them into conflict with various aspects of détente. The public utterances at the time of all these leaders were at variance with those of Brezhnev, Podgorny, Kosygin and Gromyko, as they emphasized the aggressive nature of imperialism and the need for vigilance, expressing pessimism about the fruits of détente. While this may merely have reflected the specific responsibilities and audiences of each, the distinctions were so clear as to suggest actual differences of opinion, especially when examined together with remarks made by Brezhnev and others to the critics of détente – not always directed to adversaries in the West.[13] Other critics of détente, possibly for institutional reasons but more likely for reasons of personal preferences and politics, were Shelest, Shcherbitsky, Polyansky and Voronov. A breakdown along similar lines was apparent in the journals connected institutionally if not personally with the various leaders. For example, *Trud, Komunist, Komsomol'skaia Pravda, Sovetskaia Rosiia, Krasnaia zvezda* and the various military journals all exhibited the same signs of reticence regarding détente; while *Pravda, Izvestiia, SShA, Mezhdunarodnaia zhizn', Novaia vremya* and the various economic journals waxed effusive. But the published stand of these publications does not necessarily reflect the position of their sponsoring institutions or ideologues. *Novaia vremya*, for example, is published by *Trud* and might therefore be expected to echo *Trud*'s more militant line – but doesn't probably because it is a propaganda magazine produced in a number of languages and, like *Mezhdunarodnaia zhizn'*, intended for foreign as well as domestic consumption. Similarly, the *World Marxist Review* and some of the various journals on Third World subjects did not consistently reflect the concerns over the negative effects of détente which were apparently held by Katushev,

Ponomarev, or Suslov, the leaders most directly concerned with foreign communist parties and Third World movements. Moreover, although it seems logical that the view of the military would be divided, some branches of the armed forces being more or less interested in détente than others, there is no outward sign whatsoever of such divergencies. To complicate this picture further, it is far from clear just who the journals and some papers actually represent – the institutes producing them, the Politburo members associated with them, or the directives of the agitprop department of the Central Committee. Yet, for all the complexity of interpreting public and published utterances, one cannot ignore the differences in presentation, the inclusion or omission of identical material, the emphasis or lack of it, in order to elucidate the prevailing attitudes.[14]

Institutional and ideological corollaries had been apparent before the Middle East crisis and could logically be expected to have influenced decisions during the crisis. Those who supported détente spoke of extending it to the Middle East, publicly advocating a political settlement which would reduce tensions in that area as was being done on a world scale. This global cooperation was said to be of benefit to the peoples of the Third World, including the Middle East, for greater concessions could be obtained in a cooperative East–West atmosphere than in one of mutual hostility. If this was the prodétente position, one might expect that the antidétentists would not be concerned over the prospect of continued tension and even military conflict in the Middle East; they had no need to seek a settlement which would eliminate issues impeding East–West cooperation. By extrapolation, antidétentists might actively pursue an expanded Soviet military presence in the area in response to the aggressive designs of imperialism. Similarly, these ideologists would be more militant in encouraging radical groups as distinct from moderate state-to-state relations.

Table 8.1 *Attitudes of Leading Soviet Publications toward Détente*

	Détente	Political settlement	Support for Palestinians	Opposition to Zionism
Pravda – Brezhnev	for	for	medium	medium
Izvestiia – Kosygin	for	for	weak	weak
Krasnaia zvezda Grechko (military)	indifferent/ against	against	weak	weak
Komsomol'skaia Pravda (ideologues)	against	against	strong	strong
Sovetskaia Rosiia (nationalists)	indifferent	indifferent	strong	strong
Trud – Shelepin (ideologues)	against	against	strong	strong

A study on the domestic influences on Soviet foreign policy during the October War found the attitudes in the leading publications regarding détente, a political settlement in the Middle East, the Palestinians and Zionism to be as set out in Table 8.1.[15] Interpreting the views of the press *vis-à-vis* the Middle East is as complex as analyzing their positions concerning détente. Again there is the difficulty of assigning 'responsibility' for the specific positions. Heikal, for example, indicates that there had been disagreement within the Soviet ranks over responsibility for Egypt's air defenses.[16] Western research also indicates specific press opposition, if only implicit, on the pages of *Krasnaia zvezda*,[17] but there is no information on the attitude of the navy, for example, which might have been expected to welcome full-scale involvement in order to protect its own strategic interests in the region. Some nationalistically minded members of the Politburo, such as Polyansky, were in accord with those elements of the military seeking greater involvement, but there is also some evidence of conflict. Shelepin, and possibly Ponomarev, for example, opposed massive Soviet involvement in the Middle East on ideological grounds, advocating support for local communists and liberation movements, while Brezhnev, Kosygin and Podgorny concentrated on the pursuit of Soviet policy through the Arab governments themselves.[18] It has also been argued, however, that the ideologists were advocating greater Soviet involvement as a means of bolstering the 'progressive' regimes, such as Egypt and Syria.[19] At the same time there may have been pressures from economic experts who were concerned that arming the Arabs was unprofitable and being pursued at the expense of Soviet industry.[20] And opposition by some Soviet leaders may have come in support of the popular view which blamed shortages in consumer goods on the burden of foreign aid.

Lines of Command

If it is difficult to identify the policy positions of the Soviet leadership, it is no less difficult to determine who actually participated in the decisionmaking process regarding the Middle East, and the lines of command. Formally, of course, the Politburo was the unit of primary responsibility. Just what role was played by others is entirely speculative. In addition to Brezhnev, Kosygin and Gromyko, whose involvement was institutionally natural, Podgorny seems to have participated and was sent to Egypt several times. He won Sadat's animosity by promising and then reneging on a Soviet commitment to Egypt's air defenses; he was also sent to demand a friendship treaty from Egypt following Sadat's moves against the Ali Sabry group in 1971. Other visitors to Egypt in pursuit of military interests included Grechko (promoted to the Politburo in April 1973), Naval Commander Gorshkov and Airforce Commander Kutakhov; CP International Department chief Ponomarev and Politburo ideologist Suslov figured in contacts with the communist parties of the area, and Ponomarev in contacts with the PLO as well as Egypt's ruling party. According to Heikal, Ponomarev also joined Brezhnev, Podgorny, Kosygin and Grechko in talks with Sadat in 1971. Visitors to Syria included Mazurov and Kirilenko, who appear to have been charged with Syrian affairs, though Mazurov had also been to Egypt in 1968. Sadat had said that Andropov (promoted to the Politburo in April 1973) was a close friend of Ahmad Ismail and willing to intervene on Egypt's behalf in case of difficulties.[21] Although Andropov did participate in the October 1972 meeting with Egyptian Prime Minister Sidqi in Moscow,[22] there is no other evidence of any Middle Eastern role for the then KGB chief. Similarly, Rashidov was dispatched to Iraq in 1972, but apparently was not otherwise involved in the Middle East. Thus, in terms of participation in meetings, it seems that the inner group dealing with the Middle East was composed of Brezhnev, Podgorny, Kosygin, Grechko and perhaps, upon occasion, Ponomarev. Gromyko was added when diplomatic steps were of importance, and others, such as Suslov, Kirilenko, Mazurov and Andropov, figured only occasionally.

Beyond the Politburo level, deputy foreign ministers Kosyrev and Kuznetsov were connected with the Middle East while the Soviet ambassadors to Egypt, Syria and Lebanon (Vinogradov, Mukhitdinov and Azimov) played a very active role in Soviet-Arab contacts. Just what function these officials had in decisionmaking is highly questionable. The role of the research institutes is even more ambiguous. Only Primakov, then deputy chief of the Institute for International Relations and Economics, is believed to have been a major spokesman on the subject, but like Arbotov, his counterpart on American affairs, it is not clear if Primakov had any real influence on policy decisions.

Information Collection and Dissemination

Aside from clandestine sources of information, such as satellites, intelligence installations and agents, and Soviet military personnel, a major source of information for Moscow was provided by its ambassadors in the Middle East, who were in very frequent contact with the leaders of the countries in which they were stationed, as well as with the PLO (mainly through the ambassador to Lebanon). Firsthand observation was obtained by visitors at all levels – military, government, Afro-Asian Solidarity Committee officials, economic, trade, cultural and trade union officials, party officials (to the ruling parties as well as the local communist parties), journalists (including some stationed there) and others – while the mass media, particularly of Egypt, Lebanon and Kuwait, provided raw intelligence. It can be assumed that information was also provided by other communist parties who maintained contacts with the Arabs, primarily those of Eastern Europe but also those of Italy, Romania and possibly even Yugoslavia.

Almost all the above channels of communication could be reversed for dissemination of information, signaling, and the like. Additionally Soviet and East European broadcasts in Arabic were often used to convey a message different from that of diplomatic language or the more generalized media; just as the Arab communist parties convey a message different from that of government bodies or media.

THE DECISIONS

(1) Resumption of Arms Deliveries to Egypt

The Soviet Union entered the picture prior to the Yom Kippur War with its decision to renew arms deliveries to Egypt, to supply Sadat with at least part of his requests, and to thereby 'normalize' relations once again. In terms of future Soviet involvement this was clearly the key decision, and there is every reason to believe that the Soviets were well aware of its significance. Sadat had already taken the operative decision to initiate a war, with the equipment already available to him.

Although Sadat had been making his intentions clear to the Soviets for over a year, all sources indicate that the Soviets were not directly informed of the Egyptian moves. Nevertheless, Moscow was undoubtedly aware of the gist of the planning at least through its Egyptian intelligence sources, particularly the military. Regular exchanges at the economic, trade union and cultural levels continued more or less normally, but Soviet ambassador Vinogradov, who had returned to Cairo only on 4 October, no longer had his regular talks with Sadat: he was received by Sidqi and national security advisor Hafez Ismail on 18 December 1972 and saw Sadat only on 24 January 1973.[23] This last meeting occurred simultaneously with meetings held by Soviet ambassadors with Assad and Saddam Hussein. All these ambassadorial visits were ostensibly connected with the Arab League Defense Council meeting due to open on 27 January, but the tone of Soviet propaganda in connection with this meeting suggested that they were already aware of Egypt's military plans and had decided to support them.

Vinogradov's 18 December meeting with Sidqi and Hafez Ismail was followed the next day by a report from *Al-Ahram*'s Cairo correspondent that the Politburo had initiated a thorough review of Soviet-Egyptian relations, to be concluded in January. According to *Al-Ahram*, Voronov was charged with this task, although he had never before been publicly connected with the Middle East. The Soviet press did not mention such a review, but East European diplomats in the West, according to at least one newspaper, were speaking of negative conclusions by the Soviets.[24] Perhaps to influence the outcome of this review, Sadat informed the Soviet Embassy in December that he would renew the contract for Soviet port facilities in Egypt, due to expire in March but up for renegotiation. He also appeared conciliatory in his 28 December speech to the Egyptian People's Assembly when he said, regarding arms requests to the Soviets: 'We must appreciate the circumstances and limits of every friend', and in an 8 January interview: 'We must realize that Soviet aid has its limits and avoid making reproaches.'[25]

Whether or not there was a Soviet review of relations with Egypt, the decision to resume military supplies does appear to have been taken in January 1973, apparently at the Politburo level, as Vinogradov's 24 January meeting with Sadat came upon his return from talks in Moscow. It is very likely that Vinogradov brought to Sadat a proposal for a Soviet military delegation to visit Egypt within a week (going on to Syria and possibly Iraq – as perhaps reported by the Soviet ambassadors to those countries on the same day) and an Egyptian delegation to visit Moscow. (National Security advisor Hafez Ismail, followed by Ahmad Ismail, were subsequently sent by Sadat.) That these visits were to implement the change in Soviet policy was indicated by the more militant line expressed in Soviet propaganda, including three references to the possibility of war in 1973. Soviet statements combined support for the Arabs to regain their territories by 'any means' with support for a peaceful solution. Use of the oil weapon was not discounted as a method for pressuring Israel, but the new tone was clear and the exchange of military delegations was apparently only to confirm the decision taken in Moscow. That clarification at the highest level was requested or required by Sadat is suggested by the fact that he did not receive the visiting Soviet military delegation for ten days,[26] that is, until the Hafez Ismail trip was completed. It appears that the Soviet ambassador had provided Sadat with just enough information to persuade him to send a delegation, or it may be that the information brought by Vinogradov was not entirely acceptable to Sadat. In any case the necessity of the high-level talks was suggested by the fact that Hafez Ismail held two conversations with Brezhnev,[27] whereas Sidqi had not met with him in his October 1972 visit.

The participants in this meeting may merely have represented the various aspects of Soviet-Egyptian relations: Mazurov, from the party, Gromyko and his deputy Kuznetsov from the Foreign Ministry, army Chief-of-Staff Kulikov and Deputy Economics Minister Arkhipov (known for his interest in the oil issue). Considering the nature of the difficulties between Cairo and Moscow, however, the presence of Kulikov and Arkhipov indicated the clarification of military matters, probably arms supply and payments. In Brezhnev's own meetings with Hafez Ismail – Gromyko was present but with no representative of the military or Defense Ministry – it was presumably explained just what assistance Egypt could expect from the Soviet Union in the case of war. The absence of Kosygin, Podgorny and Grechko did not necessarily indicate their disagreement with the renewal of Soviet-Egyptian cooperation. A Yugoslav account of these talks suggested that the Egyptians were warned not to count on Soviet intervention in a war and expressed reservations about Sadat's intentions.[28] The Egyptians had been told before that Moscow's task was to deal with the 'imperialist' West, while Egypt would have to contend with Israel.[29] Sadat later implied that he had accepted this principle and had reassured the Russians that he would not drag them into a war with the United States, nor have Soviet soldiers die for Egypt.[30]

The talks with the Egyptian military delegation under Ahmad Ismail were apparently also of importance. Brezhnev himself participated in these talks, along with Grechko. Though not announced, Andropov may also have participated, for it was in connection with these talks that Sadat revealed Andropov's offer to be of future assistance. Why the then KGB chief should participate in talks about war and arms may perhaps be attributed to his friendship with Ahmad Ismail, Egypt's former intelligence chief. (Andropov apparently played no further role in Soviet-Egyptian affairs, putting off with feeble excuses an invitation from Sadat to go to Egypt.)[31] The talks themselves dealt with Soviet deliveries and a new arms agreement; Brezhnev's presence was presumably required by the weightiness of the issues, that is, the role, in case of war, of several hundred Soviet military advisors in Egypt, the delivery date of SCUD surface to surface missiles, and who should operate them. Sadat claimed that he had once turned down some MIG-23s when the Soviets demanded prior specific permission for use of the aircraft.[32] This earlier refusal notwithstanding, all evidence indicates that the SCUDs were to be under Soviet control.

The reasons for the Soviet decision to resume arms supplies to Egypt, thus apparently reversing its previous opposition to military action, can only be speculated upon. In view of subsequent Soviet efforts to restrain the Egyptians, as well as continued support for a peaceful settlement, it is most likely that the apparent Soviet concession at this time was merely tactical – in order to avoid any further deterioration of the Soviets' Middle East foothold, particularly in view of the growing influence of the basically anti-Soviet Libyans and Saudi Arabia, as well as the ever-present possibility of an Egyptian turn to the West, specifically to the United States. Probably aware of Sadat's decision to go to war even without further Soviet arms supplies, the Politburo may have decided that it stood to lose too much in the Middle East if it persisted in its uncooperative attitude. The withholding of arms had not only failed to deter Sadat from the military option, but had further jeopardized Soviet aspirations in the area. Thus, if Egypt's intent was war, the Soviets would probably be faced with a decision to help the Arab armies, risking superpower confrontation, whether it had renewed arms supplies or not. Being back in the picture might in fact provide the Soviets some measure of control. Presumably détente might be used for crisis management in order to reduce the risk of confrontation, but the damage to détente might make this impossible – and jeopardize the future of détente. Thus, the question may have been one of priorities – renewed influence in the Middle East over a setback for détente.

On the other hand, it is also possible that Moscow, like other capitals in the world, did not take Sadat's threats seriously. It would not have been the first time that Soviet leadership had misjudged the Egyptians (for instance, May–June 1967), and there had indeed been sufficient hollow threats from Sadat, in particular the 1971 'year of decision', to justify skepticism. The Soviets may have believed that a limited amount of new equipment, Soviet control over the SCUDs, and withholding the long-demanded MIG-23s, would bring Sadat to postpone his program again. Payment in hard currency presumably also enhanced the attractiveness of the decision, but it does not seem likely that this shift in Soviet policy, with all its implications and risks regarding war, was determined primarily by economic considerations.

Just who argued which position can only be guessed. Heikal claims that the military, particularly Grechko, argued for speedy rearming of the Arabs, in order to maintain Moscow's military position in the Middle East; at least one Western analyst has argued that Sadat's renewal of Soviet port facilities strengthened the case of those interested in retaining the strategic advantages provided by the use of Egyptian ports.[33] Heikal also implies that some elements in the Kremlin – presumably Ponomarev and the ideologues – opposed the move on the ground that the expulsion of the Soviet advisors had demonstrated the failure of the policy of relying on bourgeois regimes, favoring aid to local communists. Those associated with Soviet economic interests presumably supported the resumption of deliveries, despite their prodétente attitude. Indeed, the fact that prodétentists, including Brezhnev, supported the military position need not be contradictory in as much as renewed arms supplies needn't impair détente, especially when withholding arms might result in an Egyptian turn to the West. Furthermore, the Soviet decision was not necessarily one to support the war option or Sadat's war plans. This was misunderstood even by Sadat, who later noted:

'some of the deal began reaching us after the Field Marshal's [Ahmad Ismail's] return in February [sic]. We were happy that our relations would return to normal. But the USSR persisted in the view that a military battle must be ruled out and that the question must await a peaceful solution.[34]

Judging from comments by Sadat and the Egyptian press, and even by other Arab sources, including pro-Soviet Arab ones, both before and after the war, Moscow sought to dissuade both Sadat and Assad from their war plans. As Sadat noted on 1 May:

There are no differences between us and the Soviet Union today except over one thing . . . *Continuation of the cease-fire serves Israel and serves U.S. aims in the end. Regarding a peaceful solution, our friends in the Soviet Union must know the true feelings of our people*. From the first moment we believed that what was taken by force could only be regained by force [applause]. Our friends in the Soviet Union must know that the *peaceful solution*, which the United States has been talking about, is fictitious . . . *Our friends in the Soviet Union continue to believe in the forthcoming process of the peaceful solution* . . . We appreciate the attitude of our friends. We may differ from them, but we do so honestly.[35]

Both Sadat and Assad indicated dissatisfaction with Soviet arms deliveries, suggesting that Moscow combined its arguments with some foot-dragging in the actual preparation for war.[36] Thus, the Soviets were not directly informed of the Arab war plans, and an atmosphere of some distrust characterized Soviet-Egyptian and even Soviet-Syrian relations prior to the outbreak of hostilities.[37]

(2)   Knowledge of Imminence of Hostilities

It is difficult to pinpoint the first operative decision regarding the war itself. There were periods between February and September 1973, most notably in June, when the Soviets apparently thought hostilities were imminent. (The Soviet media, for example, reported Israeli troop concentrations, apparently in order to prepare the public.) The operative decisions could, therefore, have been taken at any one of those times.

The tension between Egypt and the Soviet Union apparently during the summer need not have been in response to the awareness of Arab war plans, but rather implementation of the various elements of the January decision. Presumably the Soviets had contingency plans for the outbreak of war, having already outlined to Sadat the broad lines of what he could expect. Moscow, however, may have been weighing its options more concretely by the end of the summer, as well as showing numerous signs of uncertainty. It has been noted that in four out of five speeches from July to the outbreak of war Brezhnev failed to even mention the Middle East, and that aside from Gromyko's 25 September speech to the UN, no Soviet leader publicly mentioned the area during the last week of September and up to 4 October.[38] Similarly Soviet media had stopped speaking of the Arabs' right to use 'any means', continuously advocating a 'political' solution, while, none the less, Soviet arms deliveries continued. Further information – which could have preceded *or* followed the taking of a decision – was apparently sought with the launching of a Cosmos satellite on 21 September (the USA launched theirs a week later) and Vinogradov's visits to Sadat on 22 and 24 September.[39] In the same vein the trip to the Carpathian (Hungarian border) military districts by Grechko and Soviet military commanders on 26 September could have been, as suggested by one analyst, to oversee preparations for wartime resupplying of the Arabs on the basis of a decision already taken; it could also have been merely a contingency trip, in case such a decision should be taken; and of course the trip may have had nothing whatsoever to do with the impending war. The absence from Moscow in late September of Grechko, Kosygin (in Yugoslavia, 24 September–1 October) and Gromyko (at the UN), strongly suggest that the decision was taken after 1 October. If it had been taken prior to Kosygin's departure, one would not expect Brezhnev to have ignored the issue altogether in his 24 September speech. Thus, it may be that no decision was taken until 3 October, when Sadat informed the Soviet leaders of the imminence of hostilities.[40] Indeed, one analyst has argued that the dilemmas were so acute in the Politburo, that a decision was purposely postponed, ambiguity and dualism proving more practical for those involved.[41]

The major issue at stake was détente, so that the battleline may have been drawn between those who placed détente above Soviet Middle East interests, and those who placed the Arabs above détente considerations. According to one source, the 30–31 July Warsaw Pact conference (which, in what was an isolated lapse, failed to mention a 'political solution' for the Middle East), was followed by a Politburo meeting which took a hard line on détente in calling for 'vigilance' with regard to the imperialists.[42] There is no sign of such a meeting or statement in the Soviet press, but Brezhnev did refer to critics of détente in his Tashkent speech on 24 September. The antidétentists may in fact have been gaining ground, their case strengthened by the overthrow of Allende in early September. But if references to the Arabs' right to use 'any means' or to a 'political solution' are criteria (combined with the private and public arguments between the Soviets and the Arabs), there is no evidence of an operative commitment to the Arabs regarding the war.

On 3 October the Soviets were informed through Vinogradov that hostilities were imminent and were asked what they were willing to do. Brezhnev's answer, delivered by the ambassador on the following day, contained nothing operative with regard to wartime assistance, and may not have required prolonged discussions in Moscow. In any case the following steps were taken: (*a*) Brezhnev's answer that Sadat was sovereign to make his own decision and could count on Soviet support; (*b*) evacuation of Soviet civilian personnel from Egypt and Syria on 4 and 5 October; (*c*) the launching of a Cosmos satellite over the area and the return of the satellite launched in September; (*d*) movement of ships out of Alexandria and other Egyptian and Syrian ports, the fleet taking positions off Crete, plus diversion of two minesweepers to cover Soviet intelligence ships on regular duty off the coast of Syria; and (*e*) TASS commentary on Soviet intentions to continue 'moral and political support and material aid to the Arab peoples fighting for their freedom, national liberation and social progress'. The question is: when were these steps decided upon? Steps *b–d* may well have been part of Soviet contingency planning, activated without further discussion upon receipt of Sadat's 3 October notification (step *d* with receipt of Assad's more specific notification). But steps *a* and *e*, the private and public answers, as it were, to Sadat's news and query may have been the result of a decision taken on 3 October and early 4 October – which probably included the activization of the contingency plans. In as much as the Brezhnev reply was couched in general terms – Sadat said he was still trying on 6 October to clarify just what aid could be expected and was angry that the planes sent to evacuate Soviet personnel were arriving empty – Moscow may not yet have decided upon the final course of action. Removing Soviet personnel (except those attached to the Egyptian and Syrian armies) from direct involvement was a policy carried over from earlier Middle East wars. Although this airlift-out of personnel jeopardized Arab plans for surprise attack and angered Sadat, the desire to avoid direct involvement – and confrontation with the United States – outweighed the desire to maintain good relations with the Arabs. Good relations were sought, none the less, as evidenced by Brezhnev's reply to Sadat. Support, however vague, was preferred in order to secure Soviet interests with the Arabs.

Just who participated in the 3–4 October decision is difficult to determine; the known whereabouts of the Politburo members would not *ipso facto* exclude anyone except Kirilenko, who was in Georgia. Subsequent events indicate the dominance of the more cautious, prodétente elements, that is, those concerned about the risk of confrontation and unwilling to make a direct commitment to the Arabs. The military may have even shared this interest, at least at this stage, reluctant to risk direct involvement of and danger to the Soviet fleet. Even those more willing to see Soviet military involvement were presumably compensated by the augmentation of the Mediterranean squadron and the idea of neutralizing the US fleet off the coast of Crete. The antidétentist ideologues, who apparently favored greater Soviet commitment, had to make do with Moscow's general expression of support, hoping that the war itself would involve the Soviets more deeply. Brezhnev and the prodétentists, for their part, may have judged that lack of Soviet collusion with the Arab war scheme would pave the way for superpower cooperation in bringing a swift end to the battle, in keeping with the crisis management aspect of détente. Indeed, a decision to seek an immediate ceasefire may even have been part of the 3–4 October decision, as examined below, thus explaining Soviet agreement to what has been claimed as a request by Syria, on 4 October, that Moscow propose a ceasefire in the UN after forty-eight hours.

(3) Outbreak of Hostilities – Ceasefire Bid, Soviet Statement

With the outbreak of hostilities, the Soviet Union had three primary objectives: (*a*) to prevent escalation of the war which might precipitate superpower confrontation; (*b*) to limit those effects (the natural polarization of the international scene) detrimental to détente; and (*c*) to derive all possible benefit from the action for Soviet interests in the region. To appear as champions of the Arabs, without intervening directly and jeopardizing vital

Soviet interests *vis-à-vis* the United States, would be a difficult if not impossible task. It called for Soviet efforts to restrain the Arabs while in fact providing them the wherewithal – and apparent encouragement – to pursue the very goals opposed by Moscow.

On the basis of the first two objectives, Moscow's first act after the outbreak of hostilities was to send Vinogradov to Sadat with a request for a ceasefire, six hours after the Arab attack. An early ceasefire was consistent with Moscow's concern over escalation of the war. It is a moot-point whether the Russians were surprised by the Arabs' early victories (for instance, the taking of the Bar-Lev Line within a few hours), although Soviet estimates, like those of the West and Israel, probably considered the Israeli forces better prepared to repel even a surprise attack than they actually were. Even if the Cosmos surveillance satellite, returned on 4 October, had revealed to Moscow the lack of forward deployment of Israeli tanks in Sinai, these tanks could have been moved up on 5 October. Moreover, Moscow may have estimated that the Israeli airforce would be able to act more effectively in the first hours than it actually had. The assumption here is that Moscow was not certain either of the ability of the Egyptians to handle the sophisticated antiaircraft equipment, or of the effectiveness of the relatively untried SAM-6 missiles. Whatever the Soviet expectations, another rout of the Arab armies, this time with greater threat to their capital cities than in 1967, would pressure the Soviets to intervene as well as damage their prestige (as an arms supplier and trainer or as a world power). Thus, in Soviet eyes, prolongation of the battle ran the risk of reversing the Arabs' early victories, with all the attendant dangers to Moscow. The Soviets probably never believed that the Arabs could defeat Israel, nor would such an objective have been supported for fear of US intervention.

Whether there was any opposition among Soviet decisionmakers to the ceasefire proposal is not known. The media were uniformly sparse in their coverage of the war itself on 6–7 October while Vinogradov, on both days, was trying to gain Sadat's agreement to a ceasefire. (Vinogradov claimed Assad's interest in a ceasefire.) All the media gave priority to other foreign policy subjects, *Pravda* in particular emphasizing détente and, alone among the newspapers of 6–7 October, expressing concern lest the new conflict be escalated. An official Soviet statement on the outbreak of war – issued only on the evening of 7 October, after Vinogradov's second failure to achieve Sadat's agreement to a ceasefire – praised détente and placed the entire weight of responsibility for the war on Israel, without any reference to the West. Notably absent was any reference to reasons for Soviet involvement (such as proximity to Soviet borders). This emphasis on détente and its invocation as the means for limiting the conflict became the major line of *Pravda* and Brezhnev both during and after the conflict. Brezhnev did add the element of Soviet interests, because of proximity, in his speech on 8 October, but neither he nor *Pravda* was eager to discuss motivations for Soviet involvement in the conflict. Indeed, one analyst has argued that this may have indicated Brezhnev's ambivalence regarding major Soviet involvement in the Middle East.[43]

The antidétentists apparently persisted in their own line. Grechko, for example, emphasized the aggressiveness of the imperialists which had led directly to the war. This view was also apparent during and after the conflict on the pages of *Krasnaia zvezda*, *Komsomol'skaia Pravda*, *Trud* and, to a lesser degree, *Sovetskaia Rosiia*.[44] Those for whom the preservation of détente was not regarded as a restraining factor on Soviet behavior – the military, ideologues, nationalists and others – were not opposed to greater Soviet involvement on behalf of the Arabs. There is some sign of this in the newspapers associated with these groups, which indeed exhibited concern with ensuring the credibility of Soviet might, determination and value as an ally and leader.[45] The greater interest in Soviet involvement on the part of these groups would indicate not only reduced interest in détente, but also less concern over confrontation with the United States. Here even pro-détente *Izvestiia* joined the major dailies, *Pravda* alone demonstrating concern over escalation. This seems to reflect different estimates as to America's willingness to intervene, that is, the degree of risk; and, according to one theory, *Izvestiia* (presumably Kosygin) had more faith in the durability of détente than did *Pravda* (Brezhnev).[46] Nevertheless, even the Soviet military was cautious on the whole, generally signaling noninterventionist intentions until the crisis of 24 October.[47] Even Grechko, in his criticism of imperialism, did not mention the USA as such. The question is whether the less cautious public position indicated a controversy at the highest levels, particularly when the Arab situation deteriorated (to be examined below). The Soviet public itself was also considered, with the prodétente position dominating here too. The first protest meeting in a Soviet factory was reported only on 8 October, that is, after the official Soviet statement, and additional such meetings were reported only several days later. The absence of an organized internal propaganda campaign, together with undramatic press coverage, indicated a decision to minimize the crisis domestically. Presumably this was due to the unpopularity of the issue within the Soviet Union as well as a desire not to alarm the public or raise doubts regarding détente. It also indicated, as did Soviet military activity in the early part of the conflict, that direct Soviet involvement, for which some preparation of the public would be desirable, had not yet been decided upon.

(4)   Bid for Pan-Arab Aid

While Soviet Arabic broadcasts had already urged Arab solidarity and support for the Syrian and Egyptian war efforts, on 8 October Moscow implemented what appeared to be a decision to broaden the conflict by directly appealing to various Arab governments to help their allies. In reply to a letter sent by Boumedienne to each of the permanent members of the Security Council, Brezhnev wrote the Algerian leader (and, reportedly, other Arab leaders including Arafat), that 'Syria and Egypt must not remain alone in their battle with a treacherous enemy. There is an urgent necessity for the granting of aid and the greatest support for the progressive regimes'[48]. On the face of it this would seem to be an appeal designed to broaden the conflict and thus prolong it, implying a victory of those forces less concerned about détente, including the ideologues who were presumably worried about Moscow's image among its 'progressive' allies. Another interpretation, however, would view this appeal as prodétentist. It may well have come as a substitute and a cover for Moscow's lack of direct involvement, calling for Arab aid so as to prevent a Syrian-Egyptian defeat, and implying that Moscow cannot be expected to act unless those most closely attached to the combatants do so. Moreover, the letter to Algerian leader Boumedienne (the only one published) referred to Algeria's 'understanding' of the 'complexity' of the situation, possibly a hint at Soviet inability to act. If this were the case, the Soviet military might be satisfied that the Arab war effort was to be helped (transfer of tanks from Iraq was also reportedly arranged), the ideologues and nationalists could be satisfied that Moscow was explaining its position to its allies (Ponomarev and Suslov did so with the Syrian communists when they met with a delegation in Moscow on the same day), and the détentists could rest assured that the Soviet Union would still not be directly involved and even free to pursue a ceasefire. An appeal for expansion of the war would not, of course, enhance détente, but whatever the reasons for the letters to the Arab leaders, it was Algeria and not Moscow which published the communication. The Soviet media were never to make such a direct appeal, which suggests that Brezhnev's notes had come in response to direct queries, and were intended to maintain Soviet prestige in the Arab world without appearing or even intending to expand the conflict.

Boumedienne's letter was sent on 7 October; the Soviet reply, on the evening of 8 October; that same day, a group of Arab ambassadors had asked to see Gromyko probably with the same request for Soviet aid made by Boumedienne. Gromyko reportedly put them off for three days, receiving them only on 11 October, which suggests a number of things.[49] First, the Soviet leadership must have decided that an answer must be delivered at the highest level from Brezhnev as a personal note to the leaders in question. Secondly, that this reply must be conveyed without intermediaries such as foreign ambassadors, a practice which was relatively standard in dealing with the Arab states (messages from Brezhnev at least were conveyed through Soviet ambassadors on the spot rather than handed to the Arab ambassadors in Moscow). Direct personal contact was agreed to for Iraq, which sent its Foreign Minister Baqi on 9 October, but he was received by Podgorny or Grechko, not Brezhnev, even though the dispatch of Iraqi soldiers was reportedly discussed.

(5) Airlift to Syria and Egypt

A critical point seems to have been reached in Moscow, around midday on 9 October, when Brezhnev failed to begin scheduled talks with the visiting Japanese premier or to attend a luncheon with him.[50] Brezhnev's absence may have been due to first reports of the Israeli bombing of Damascus that morning which hit the Soviet cultural center, killing some Soviet personnel. The nature of this attack may have reassured the Russians that there was no immediate threat to Damascus, but a Soviet response may have been deemed necessary for the benefit of the Arabs – rather than the Israelis. There was in fact no Soviet warning to Israel on this occasion – that was to come only on 12 October when a Soviet merchant vessel was sunk.

An ostensible response to the bombing may have been the Soviet airlift to

Egypt, Iraq and particularly Syria. This airlift (and sealift) was one of the most controversial Soviet actions during the war, a direct intervention which, the Soviet leadership must have calculated, would invite similar American action, prolong the war, endanger détente and raise the risks of superpower confrontation. Even the date of the beginning of the airlift is unclear. Most accounts and official versions of the war refer to 10 October, in which case the bombing of Damascus on the morning of 9 October may have affected the timing of the airlift, if not the actual decision itself. However, a *New York Times* article datelined 10 October reported that some thirty Soviet planes had landed at Syrian airfields since the afternoon of 9 October. The same article attributed a report to Washington 'officials' that 'in the last day or so an unusually large number of Soviet transports have been observed landing at Egyptian and Syrian airports'.[51] If the airlift did in fact begin on 9 October, it would seem unlikely that it was in reaction to the bombing of Damascus just a few hours earlier. Indeed, most accounts claim that the decision for the airlift came in response to the early Arab victories, that is, prior to 8 or 9 October, so that the Russians could claim a role in the Arab victory, or, as Boumedienne would have us believe, to supply the wherewithal for a total Arab victory now that the Arabs had proved their worth in battle. It seems more likely, however, that the Soviet leadership decided on the airlift after the first signs of retreat on the Syrian front on 8 October, in order to prevent a serious Arab defeat and to bolster the Soviet position in the eyes of the Arabs. Thus the bombing of Damascus, if it did play a role, may have been the type of sign of Arab need for which Brezhnev had been waiting, in order to give the green-light for an airlift presumably already prepared – at least since the 8 October Israeli victories on the Golan, if not from the Soviets' first knowledge of the war.

On 9 October the first Soviet naval action connected with the war occurred (aside from the movement away from the area of conflict)[52] when naval surveillance of the US Sixth Fleet tightened, possibly to prevent interference in the resupply operation, and on 9 October the Cosmos satellite was returned to earth, six to eight days earlier than usual, perhaps revealing the extent of Israeli action on the Golan. No propaganda preparation was initiated, however, such as references to the USA or outside assistance to Israel, in order to justify the Soviet aid. Since such a campaign did develop later, its absence on 8 and 9 October may indicate that although plans existed for a Soviet airlift, the decision to implement them came only after midday 9 October. The stepped-up alert in Soviet airborne divisions on 10 October supports the interpretation that Moscow was responding to Syrian reverses. The alert may have been intended as preparation for, and therefore a deterrent against, serious Israeli interference in the resupply operation. It is more likely, however, that it was a precaution against Israeli moves into Syria now that the Golan had been recaptured.[53] But one cannot in fact pinpoint the time of the Soviet decision to undertake the resupply effort. They may have prepared this option in late September (for instance, the Grechko visit to the Carpathian district) or 3 October when notified that war was imminent, or on the first day or two of the war when Sadat refused an early ceasefire, or even on 8 October after the first Syrian reversals, the decision to go ahead coming somewhere between the 8 and 9 October.

The resupply decision was apparently the first Soviet decision during the war which placed Soviet interests in the Arab world over those of détente, reflecting in a sense a victory of the antidétentists. While Brezhnev was anxious to forestall an Arab defeat, he did not abandon détente or a political solution. In addition to censoring from the domestic media any antidétente comments or references to US involvement in the war, Moscow – more significantly – cooperated with a US ceasefire bid which began on 10 October (Vinogradov ceasefire bid again to Sadat), and culminated on 13 October with Israeli agreement and Sadat's renewed refusal. Indeed, a tug-of-war may well have been occurring in the Soviet Politburo over the issue of Soviet involvement in the ceasefire, for on 11 October *Pravda* was the only Soviet paper to carry a TASS report of the Israeli Communist Party calling for a ceasefire, and the Moscow domestic radio service broadcast another TASS report, carried again on 12 October by *Pravda* alone, quoting the French paper *Figaro* as saying that 'the success achieved by the Arab countries in the first days of the war is *quite sufficient* to make Israel understand that the times have changed'.[54] The same Soviet broadcast also revealed for the first time that Israeli forces had broken through some Syrian positions on the Golan. At the same time, however, Grechko, in a speech in Warsaw on the anniversary of the Polish army, again referred to the Middle East war as 'proof' of the continued power of reactionary and aggressive forces in the world. While he did not name the USA, his opposition to the ceasefire which Brezhnev was pursuing with the USA could be discerned by the failure of *Pravda* to report this speech, leaving it to *Krasnaia zvezda*. Similarly *Pravda* and *Izvestiia* failed to report Israeli chief-of-staff Elazar's threat to carry the war into the enemy's territory – a comment which *was* published in *Krasnaia zvezda* and *Trud*. Similarly *Krasnaia zvezda* on 11 October published a map showing the 1947 partition lines as one of Israel's three borders arousing speculation of support for the Arab attempt to reduce Israel to the partition plan lines.[55]

(6)   Soviet Warning to Israel

On 12 October the Soviet merchant ship *Ilya Mechnikov* was sunk in the Syrian port of Tartus, culminating a series of raids in which Soviet sealift vessels had been hit by Israeli forces. On the same day a Cosmos satellite which had been over the area during 7–11 October was returned with information regarding Israeli ground advances toward Damascus. These new data, the threat to the resupply operation and the Israeli bombing of strategic targets all over Syria, all contributed to what may have been a new Soviet decision. It is from late 12 October that a duality began to appear in the Soviet position, the military Arab-first alliance gaining greater expression if not actually a policy reversal. Even as the ceasefire was being pursued, several events in the military, political and propaganda realms reflected this change. In the military sphere a Soviet destroyer appeared north and east of Cyprus on 13 October; its mission, according to US naval specialists, was providing protection for Soviet merchant vessels as they approached the Syrian combat area.[56] At the same time the advance staff of a Soviet airborne division is said to have settled into Syrian military headquarters at Katana, near Damascus.[57]

On the political front the Soviets allegedly informed the USA of their airborne alert for the defense of Damascus, and TASS issued an official warning to Israel, referring specifically to the freedom of navigation. In the realm of propaganda Moscow resumed public protest meetings and Soviet media began to criticize the USA directly for its aid to Israel. *Pravda*, although critical, did not, however, concentrate on the USA with Israel seen as a mere puppet, as other papers did.[58] *Krasnaia zvezda*, apparently encouraged by these events, speculated on 13 October that the war would be long and therefore more difficult for Israel than for the Arabs. At the same time a Soviet radio and television commentary referred to the lands 'seized' by Israel in 1948 beyond the territory allotted by the 1947 partition plan.

All the above changes can be explained by Soviet concern that Damascus was in danger. Presumably even Brezhnev and the prodétentists shared this concern and, therefore, agreed to these measures as a deterrent.[59] They need not, however, imply a Soviet decision favoring protracted war and/or Soviet intervention. Although the Soviet military believed that Israel would be at a disadvantage in a war of attrition,[60] they must have calculated that their airlift to the Arabs would spark a US resupply of Israel (the discussion of which in Washington may well have been known to the Russians). Even with the entry of troops from Iraq and Jordan, it does not seem likely that Moscow would underestimate Israeli capabilities – especially after the breakthrough on the Golan and the threat to Damascus. And this very threat, alone, would mitigate Soviet desire for a protracted battle, while Soviet intervention to protect Damascus risked confrontation with the United States. This apparently was the thinking of the political leadership, at least of Brezhnev, for the Soviet efforts for a speedy ceasefire did not cease, and no other operational changes, such as augmentation of the Mediterranean squadron, occurred at this time.[61] But it is possible, as indicated in *Krasnaia zvezda*, that some elements of the military maintained their estimate regarding a protracted war and assessed differently the US response if Soviet troops would rescue Damascus.

(7)   Kosygin's Trip to Cairo

On 15 October the Soviets informed the USA (Dobrynin to Kissinger) that Kosygin would go to Cairo the following day in still another effort to gain a ceasefire.[62] The decision for the trip must have come late on the fifteenth, for in the morning of 16 October Kosygin personally canceled a meeting with the visiting Danish Prime Minister Jorgensen. Thus, the decision must have come after talks in Moscow with Boumedienne, although it was probably not connected with these talks. Boumedienne, who had initiated his visit, had urged protraction of the war through greater Soviet military assistance to Egypt and Syria ($200 million to pay the costs), but by his own account the Soviets had been most reluctant to comply.[63] The Soviet airlift did increase significantly after Boumedienne's visit, but the reason for this was most likely the deterioration of the Egyptian front after the failure of the Egyptian offensive on 14 October, rather than Boumedienne's demands, or even his money. There was nothing in Boumedienne's arguments to induce the Soviets to change their mind about the ceasefire, although they may have postponed the decision to send someone to Cairo until after hearing him out. Factors contributing to the decision itself were the deterioration of the Egyptian front, the failure of the Soviet-American ceasefire bid of 13 October and the beginning of the US airlift to Israel on the same day, and the USA informing the Soviet Union of their resupply decision.[64]

Why Kosygin was chosen for the job is not clear. Brezhnev, Podgorny, Gromyko, Grechko and Kosygin had all participated in the talks with Boumedienne, indicating that this was the inner group – perhaps the Defense Council – making the decisions during the crisis, with the exception of Grechko during his two or more day trip to Warsaw. Others previously involved in Middle East contacts, such as Kirilenko, Mazurov, or even Andropov, do not seem to have participated; Ponomarev operated only in contacts with communists, that is, the meeting with the Syrian communist delegation on 8 October, for which he was joined by Suslov. Thus, if the Soviets intended to make high-powered the ceasefire bid to Sadat, and if negotiating might be necessary, they preferred to send one of this inner circle who was directly involved in the decisionmaking. To send Brezhnev in the middle of a war, was of course out of the question. Sending the Defense Minister at such a delicate time might be misinterpreted by the USA as well as the Arabs. Of the remaining choices, Gromyko may have been considered not sufficiently high-level to persuade Sadat, while Podgorny, despite the appropriate rank, may have been unacceptable because of Sadat's personal dislike for him following the unfulfilled promises made by the Soviet President during visits to Egypt. Kosygin, then, would have been the best choice. Willingness to dispatch the Soviet prime minister in the middle of a visit by the Danish prime minister suggests that the Soviets viewed the mission with the utmost urgency.

The decision to send Kosygin presumably also included the following message: a proposal for a ceasefire in place as part of a peace proposal calling for Israeli withdrawal (with small 'corrections') to the pre-June 1967 borders; and international guarantees, by the superpowers, of both the ceasefire and the peace treaty, the latter to be reached at an international conference.[65] There is some evidence, albeit scanty, that there was not full agreement on these decisions. On 14 October, the eve of the decision, there was a reference in *Pravda* to the failure of hawks in the West to destroy détente. It described the encouragement of stepped-up support for Israel as an effort to disrupt détente, implying that increased superpower involvement would endanger détente. Had this been intended as a warning to the USA, it probably would have been spelled out. It is possible, therefore, that this was aimed at those within the Soviet hierarchy urging greater support for the Arabs. Kosygin, too, was to refer to efforts (in the West) to use the war to disrupt détente. Somewhat more directly, a Moscow Arabic broadcast late on 15 October noted that Egypt and Syria had 'no choice but to continue the fierce battle' (though the implication of the whole broadcast was that the Arabs, not Moscow, would have to defeat the Israelis). And Shelepin, in his extremely militant 16 October speech to a World Federation of Trade Unions (WFTU) congress in Bulgaria took up the line expressed by Grechko, linking the Middle East war to the aggressiveness of imperialism. Although this phrase was omitted from TASS, it was carried by *Trud* and, surprisingly, by *Pravda*. Moreover, *Trud* and *Krasnaia zvezda* took a near hysterical tone in describing Israeli atrocities, the latter even referring to an alleged Israeli order to take Damascus.

There may have been opposition to the peace proposals sent with Kosygin. *Pravda* and to a slightly lesser degree *Ivzestiia*, were the only papers consistently to advocate a peace settlement at all, while only *Pravda* wrote consistently of the Soviet role in such a settlement.[66] Similarly Brezhnev, Kosygin and Gromyko were the only spokesmen for this cause including that of a Soviet role in guaranteeing an agreement. Grechko, Ponomarev and Suslov (in the communiqué with the Syrian Communist Party delegation) and Shelepin all ignored the idea of a settlement in their speeches during the war. It is not surprising, therefore, that their newspapers, *Krasnaia zvezda*, *Komsomol'skaia Pravda* and *Trud*, showed none of the same willingness as *Pravda* and *Izvestiia* (or Brezhnev and Kosygin) to make concessions to Israel on the border issue or to respect Israel's right to a secure existence. On this last point, *Sovetskaia Rosiia*, which appeared relatively indifferent on the issue of a peace settlement, was not, however, willing to concede Israel's security. This, it has been suggested, is because of the clear anti-Zionist line of this nationalist organ, a position it shared with the military and the ideologues.[67] In addition to the idea of a settlement and Soviet guarantees, there may also have been opposition by some to the exclusion of the Palestinian subject from the proposal brought to Sadat. Statements, by Brezhnev, Grechko, Kosygin and even Malik at the UN, as well as others from the Soviet and East bloc, had almost entirely refrained from referring to the Palestinians during the first days of the war. Indeed, the October anniversary slogans published during the war even omitted the brief reference to the 'Palestinian people's rights' made in the previous year's slogans. This neglect of the Palestinians presumably resulted from Soviet reluctance to complicate the task of obtaining a ceasefire. This also accounts for the absence of even a resolution 242 type of reference to the Palestinians from the peace proposals taken to Cairo. This omission may have been opposed by the ideologues, for Shelepin, at least, was to champion the Palestinian cause in his 16 October speech. Even *Pravda* and *Izvestiia* differed here from the leaders they supposedly represented, Brezhnev and Kosygin, and joined *Trud* and *Komsomol'skaia Pravda* (for ideological reasons) in referring often to the Palestinians' cause, even 'national rights' and their role in the war. One possible explanation for these papers' interest has been the realization that a peace settlement was unobtainable without solution of the Palestinian problem. Thus, it is not surprising that Grechko, *Krasnaia zvezda* and *Sovetskaia Rosiia* did not give the Palestinians much coverage (given their lack of enthusiasm for a settlement), but this does not explain why the Palestinians were essentially ignored by Brezhnev, Kosygin, the official statements of 12 and 23 October and others in the Eastern bloc. A plausible explanation may be, however, that no one (except the ideologues) was particularly interested in the Palestinians: the military because they preferred to deal with governments which could satisfy their strategic interests and Brezhnev and Kosygin because they preferred not to complicate the ceasefire issue. But *because* the Palestinians were being neglected officially, *Pravda* and *Izvestiia* were to supply compensation, indicating what was to become the tone after the war – that any genuine effort to achieve a peace treaty would have to come to grips with the Palestinian problem.

(8) Invitation to Kissinger

At 1 a.m. on 19 October the Soviets were informed of Sadat's agreement to a ceasefire. The evidence is conflicting as to whether or not this notification preceded or followed Kosygin's departure from Cairo, though Sadat has explicitly stated that he made up his mind only after Kosygin's departure, notifying Vinogradov then, and that Kosygin had left because of Sadat's continued refusal.[68] One might speculate as to Soviet willingness to go ahead with an official ceasefire proposal with the Americans even without Sadat's agreement, but the Soviet invitation to Kissinger apparently came after Egyptian compliance was conveyed to Moscow. The reason for the urgency in calling for Kissinger (Moscow offered to send Gromyko to Washington if the Americans preferred) presumably was not only the sharp reversal of Egyptian fortunes after the 14 October defeat, but the successful Canal crossing by Israeli forces on 16 October, steadily augmented to significant numbers. The Soviets had a Cosmos over the battle area during 17–20 October,[69] capable of sending pictures back at least on 18 October, so information regarding the crossing (and the forces waiting to cross) was available to the Soviets if not to the Egyptians. (A further demonstration of Soviet concern for Egypt's fate may have been the dispatch of two Soviet destroyers through the Dardanelles on 19 October.)

While opposition to the ceasefire may have continued among some even after the growing threat to Cairo with the entrenchment of Israeli forces on the west bank of the Canal, the military daily appeared to adjust itself to the new reality. *Krasnaia zvezda* appeared to change its line, perhaps preparing its own public for a ceasefire, and spoke of the possibility of a 'sudden change' in the war in Israel's favor and 'all kinds of turns of events', as well as the necessity for Israel to cease fighting without victory if peace were to be achieved in the area. The earlier line of a protracted conflict to the detriment of Israel was absent, though the same item did seem to encourage Egypt to fight 'to the end'. There was no change regarding any of the other issues such as a peace treaty or Israel's existence and borders, nor was a change apparent in any other paper.

Although one can assume that the decision of what to tell Kissinger was decided on before his arrival on the evening of 20 October, it is still surprising that only Brezhnev and Gromyko, of the Soviet leadership, participated in these talks. Also present were Brezhnev's assistant Alexandrov, foreign official Korniyenko and the Soviet ambassador to the USA, Dobrynin, but no other decisionmaker was present, not even Kosygin, whose first-hand, up-to-date knowledge of Sadat's wishes should have made his presence desirable. While one might deduce from the few Soviet 'negotiators' that Brezhnev was empowered to make decisions without the other leaders, it is more likely that this indicated that the final Soviet decision had already been taken, any further changes being only apparent or tactical. (The details of the diplomatic side of the joint Soviet-American ceasefire proposal were left to Gromyko to discuss with Kissinger after the Brezhnev talks on 21 October.)

The major change in these talks was the sudden Soviet agreement, after hours of arguing, to the American formulation of a ceasefire in place linked to resolution 242, rather than a demand for total Israeli withdrawal. The Soviets preferred not to have any reference to resolution 242, since Syria had not officially accepted the resolution and there was much opposition to it in the Arab world. (Indeed, Iraq, Libya and the PLO all later criticized this aspect of the agreement.) The Soviets would have preferred a call for total Israeli withdrawal, but they were so convinced of the urgency of a ceasefire, they agreed to accept the American position (long-since known) if necessary. Despite earlier opposition through diplomatic channels, Brezhnev then agreed to negotiations between the parties involved (which Sadat had proposed in his 16 October speech), and that the USA and USSR would jointly chair such a peace conference.

The Soviets had probably hoped to convince the Americans to accept some part of their proposed ceasefire agreement, at least phased Israeli withdrawal and, therefore, had gone through all the motions of higher-level talks, rather than the Dobrynin–Kissinger channel in Washington used throughout the war. Consenting only after long argument to a US proposal (which the Soviet leadership had probably already agreed among themselves to accept if there were no alternative), had the advantage of repairing some of the damage done to détente during the hostilities. By this political concession, Moscow demonstrated its willingness to cooperate with the USA in the full spirit of détente, agreeing even to halt the airlift operation. Though this would appear to have been a clear case of Soviet preference for détente over Arab interests, as many in the Arab world and perhaps even inside the Soviet policy elite were to later claim, Brezhnev had at least tried to give priority to the Arab cause,[70] compromising only when faced with the alternative of total Arab defeat, a possible call to save Cairo (or Sadat's regime), and subsequent confrontation with America. To placate this opposition, Soviet media began to emphasize Soviet aid to the Arab cause and Moscow's own interpretation of resolution 242, which – as Soviet leaders reportedly assured Sadat and Assad – included Israeli withdrawal to the 4 June 1967 lines.[71]

It is worth noting that the failure of the Soviets to maintain consultation with Syria on the ceasefire issue, as they did with Sadat, says something about their almost contemptuous behavior toward Third World allies on some occasions. While Soviet leaders may have thought they had Syrian agreement to a ceasefire from the early days of the war, Assad, for one, was angry that he learned of the ceasefire proposal from news reports of the opening of the Security Council.[72]

(9)   Ceasefire Violations

The ceasefire went into effect the evening of 22 October, but not before an ominous event had transpired. On that day a Soviet ship emitting signals which indicated the presence of nuclear material, passed through the Bosporus. Washington received this information three days later, at which time it became part of the crisis that had developed between the USA and the USSR on 24 October. Why the Soviets dispatched nuclear material to the war area at this time remains, however, unclear. There has been speculation that the ship contained nuclear warheads for the SCUDs supplied to the Egyptian army, but it is difficult to believe that Moscow was willing to supply a nonbloc, erstwhile ally with nuclear warheads.[73] And if they had intended to provide nuclear warheads for the present emergency, they probably would not have done so via a three- to four-day sea passage through the heavily monitored Turkish Straits.[74] It is most likely that the nuclear material was intended for the Soviet fleet in the Mediterranean, but even so, the dispatch of such materials through the straits at this time could not but provoke alarm. Thus, it is difficult to rule out the possibility that this was part of a deliberate Soviet decision. In as much as the Soviets appeared to believe, like Kissinger, that the war would be winding down (Soviet media also reflected this attitude), this may have been intended as a signal of Soviet commitment to ensure implementation of the ceasefire, lest Israel try to exploit it. This would be an extremely strong and risky signal in the circumstances, but undeniably convincing, particularly when linked to the further alert in Soviet airborne divisions initiated the next day. On 22 October, the same day the ship passed the Bosporus, the Soviets flew two MIG-25s at high altitude over the Sinai, presumably also to demonstrate the commitment they had given Sadat to guarantee the ceasefire.

On 23 October there were in fact violations of the ceasefire, and concern grew over the developing Israeli thrust toward the town of Suez and the Egyptian 3rd army stranded on the east bank of the Canal. The Soviet response was both military and political. In the military sphere the Soviets raised the alert in the airborne divisions and two of the amphibious ships which had been anchored off the coast of Syria, were now sent steaming toward Egypt.[75] Also flights of Soviet transport aircraft to Egypt were almost totally halted, meaning that these aircraft were now free for the dispatch of airborne divisions. In the political sphere there were complaints to Washington (Dobrynin to Kissinger) over Israel's violation of the ceasefire, a joint request with the USA to the Security Council for UN observers and a return to the 22 October ceasefire lines, and an official Soviet statement of warning to Israel. Domestically, however, there was no propaganda in preparation for intervention; the media, on 24 October, optimistically claimed that the second ceasefire had taken hold. On the day of this announcement, however, when Israeli forces did reach the outskirts of Suez, cutting off the Egyptian 3rd army, the Soviets established an inflight airborne command post in southern Russia and, according to some reports, initiated special military orders associated with intervention. (Twelve Soviet transport planes were also en route to Egypt, despite the cessation of such flights the previous day, but it later became clear that these planes did not carry troops.) Late 24 October a Soviet helicopter carrier and two destroyers left their positions off Crete and relieved the anticarrier group covering the USS *Independence* – the group nearest the war zone. While this could have been routine, the timing – almost coincident with Brezhnev's note to Nixon – suggested an effort to counter movement of the US 6th fleet toward Egypt, and thus protect Soviet sea and air lines in time of airborne intervention.[76]

On the political front Dobrynin met again with Kissinger to discuss the Geneva Peace Conference, informing him that Moscow rejected Sadat's appeal for US-Soviet troops to enforce the ceasefire (publicly turned down by Washington an hour earlier). Later, however, at 7.05 p.m. Washington time, Dobrynin called to say that the Soviet Union would support the appeal at that evening's Security Council session. A few hours later, when no US response had been forthcoming, Dobrynin delivered (by telephone) a message from Brezhnev to Nixon 'inviting' the USA to join the Soviet Union 'to compel observance of the ceasefire without delay', adding the threat (our emphasis): *'I will say it straight, that if you find it impossible to act with us in this matter, we should be faced with the necessity urgently to consider the question of taking appropriate steps unilaterally. Israel cannot be permitted to get away with the violations.'* [77] The US response was a Defcon 3 alert and successful pressure on Israel to permit the passage of vital supplies to the 3rd army.

Was there a Soviet decision to intervene militarily? Reportedly even Kissinger did not anticipate massive Soviet intervention to battle the Israelis. His concern was over a symbolic display of Soviet force, such as the landing of a contingent to 'protect' Cairo airport or a small 'peace-keeping' force to bring supplies to the 3rd army. [78] The assessment of some in Washington was of 'high probability' [79] that the Soviets would dispatch airborne troops, which alone would be a potentially explosive measure. The Soviet capability of joining battle was also questionable. [80]

It seems more likely that the Soviets did not intend actual battlefield intervention, [81] but rather the threat of intervention – using the above as signals or, if that proved unsuccessful, the landing of some forces to be limited to Cairo, though this seems unlikely unless Cairo itself was threatened. The actual dispatch of even a small contingent ran the risk of battle with the Israelis and confrontation with the United States. While there may have been some in the Kremlin willing to risk this, it seems most likely that the Soviet estimate was that a threat (made credible by various alerts, fleet movements, airborne command and perhaps even the passage of nuclear material) would be sufficient to persuade the Americans – and assist them [82] – to pressure Israel.

The Soviet moves, however, jeopardized Soviet-American relations and détente, and even risked a US-Soviet confrontation. Indeed, this was what Moscow had been trying to avoid throughout the war. One explanation may be that the Soviets simply misjudged the Americans' likely response. Soviet naval action, it has been suggested, may have been based upon the expectation that the USA would respond merely by moving its fleet (and pressuring Israel) rather than by declaring a Defcon 3 alert (and pressuring Israel). Even so, the Soviet leadership cannot have been unaware of the risks, at the very least to détente. Brezhnev, Kosygin and Gromyko may have thought that détente could be renewed after the war, in view of Kissinger's position regarding superpower cooperation and a Middle East settlement (for which he did not think total Israeli victory would be helpful). But whatever the estimate of détente, their willingness to run the risks of threatened intervention indicated the seriousness with which they regarded Sadat's call for help. There was the danger that the 20,000 strong 3rd army would be destroyed or captured, Cairo placed in jeopardy, and with this the likelihood of Sadat falling from power. While under certain circumstances Brezhnev might not have regretted the fall of Sadat, a new leader would probably be more anti-Russian than Sadat if the change were to come under these conditions of military defeat.

There was also the damage to Soviet credibility and authority, particularly in the Arab world, for Brezhnev had negotiated the ceasefire and Moscow was partially responsible to ensure that it aided – not further endangered – the Arabs. Breakdown of the ceasefire and subsequent failure to act would not only strengthen those (including the Chinese) who had argued throughout for greater Soviet action and against a ceasefire, but it would fortify the arguments of those within the Kremlin who opposed détente. Thus, almost paradoxically, Brezhnev had to risk a blow to détente in order to save the policy. Postwar comments clearly reflected this dilemma. Brezhnev and Kosygin emphasized the role of détente in superpower cooperation which prevented world catastrophe, while Grechko and other military figures referring to the war as the work of the imperialists behind Israel and the need for vigilance. Suslov supported both views in part.[83]

One can only assume that the lines of argument were similarly drawn among the Soviet leadership during the 23 and 24 October deliberations. The only Soviet leader whose whereabouts on 24 October were mentioned in the press was Kosygin, who, when the inner core of leaders was presumably in almost continuous meetings, took time out to meet the Swedish and later the British ambassadors. Coupled with his absence from the talks with Kissinger, this might suggest that following his unsuccessful trip to Cairo, Kosygin was no longer an active member of the Middle East crisis decision-making team, but there is no other evidence of this. Détentists and anti-détentists alike apparently agreed as to the necessity of these decisions. The combination of military measures (alerts, naval deployments) and political measures (direct communication with Washington, warning to Israel, only peripheral use of the UN) was essentially the same type as those taken in the earlier critical period of the war, on 12 October. One can only speculate whether some argued for actual military intervention, and how persuasive they would have been had the United States not succeeded in its pressures on Israel.

The Soviet threat and the US alert in response did indeed accomplish what the Soviet Union had sought, bringing the war to a close. While the Soviets brought more ships into the Mediterranean on 26 October to cover the augmented US fleet,[84] it behaved cautiously, informing the US a day in advance of its intention to send a seventy-man peacekeeping contingent. Although he postponed his speech by one day to the World Peace Congress in Moscow, Brezhnev and almost the entire Soviet leadership attended the congress opening on 25 October. On 26 October the US alert began to be lowered.

CONCLUSIONS

Working from the six categories of factors affecting Soviet decisionmaking outlined at the beginning of this chapter, the following conclusions may be drawn about the decisions taken in connection with the October War. Moscow sought to accommodate both its global and regional interests, giving priority, none the less, to the global interests, particularly détente. This precedence appeared to dissolve when Moscow was faced with an almost total threat to its regional position (to some degree, the expulsion from Egypt; the threat to Damascus; the 24 October ceasefire breakdown). Even, however, in the decisions (1) to resupply Egypt (January–February 1973); (2) to airlift arms and, later, issue a warning to Israel; and (3) to threaten intervention (24 October 1973), it was believed that this pursuit of regional interests would not irrevocably impair détente. In the case of resupplying Egypt, Moscow had nothing to lose by being back in Egypt and might even be able to prevent or forestall the war planned by Sadat. In the second case the simultaneous efforts for a ceasefire and cooperation with the United States to this end would minimize the negative effects on détente. And in the third case the threat to intervene was designed not as a signal of genuine intention, but as a means of halting Israel and finally bringing the war to the end which was negotiated jointly with the United States. Especially in the third case the Soviets appeared to have severely miscalculated the potential damage to détente and Soviet-US relations; but even those who wished to pursue détente had to bear in mind the effect that nonaction on the Arabs' behalf would have had in strengthening antidétentists at home and abroad, or simply the damage to Moscow's world position if it failed to act. Thus, the Soviet response had to have the *appearance* of action, but be designed to eliminate the necessity of action – actual intervention – which would have destroyed détente and led to superpower military confrontation.

In view of the above it is difficult to determine if the various military steps (airlift, augmentation of the fleet, alerts of the airborne divisions, and so on) were taken by an overanxious military seeking to force Brezhnev's hand, or if they were the necessary operative moves to give credence to Moscow's political moves, in pursuit of its global and regional objectives. The movement of ships and the alerts would fall into this category, acting as signals while providing credibility. None the less, there is evidence, particularly in the media but also in leadership statements, of disagreement among the decisionmakers, some interpreting Soviet global interests as better served by aid to the Arab war effort, others viewing détente as crucial though perhaps differing in their estimates of how far it could be stretched or in what ways. Thus, the military steps, while strengthening Soviet credibility and acting as signals, may have also served to placate the antidétente, Arab-first faction. To what extent pressure from such a group, if it did in fact exist, acted as a restraint on the Soviet decisions may never be known. The effort by Brezhnev and other prodétentists, in their speeches and in the media (including radio) to minimize the culpability of the United States and even the seriousness of the crisis may indicate the concern over the image of détente and demonstrate, on the other hand, the unpopularity domestically of Soviet involvement in the Arab world.

The primary decisionmakers, or at least major participants in the decisionmaking process were apparently an inner core of Politburo members: Brezhnev, Gromyko, Podgorny and Grechko. Kosygin was also involved, but his absence from the talks with Kissinger (and thereafter during the crisis) suggests his exclusion from at least some of the significant decisions. Direct communications were carried out by means of Soviet ambassadors, particularly Dobrynin in Washington and Vinogradov in Cairo. Only when matters became critical on the battlefield from the Soviet point of view was a higher level used: the invitation to Kissinger (or dispatch of Gromyko) and the Kosygin mission to Cairo. The ambassadorial channel was maintained in the most critical crisis, 24–25 October, presumably because of the time pressure involved, though it is significant that this channel, that is, contact with Kissinger, was preferred over the red-line which would have put Brezhnev in direct touch with Nixon as had been maintained with Johnson during the Six-Day War. All of the major Soviet leaders did meet personally with Boumedienne in Moscow, but this meeting was at Algeria's initiative and, most likely, given such status in order to give the impression that Moscow was doing its utmost for the Arab cause, so as to appease the Soviets' 'progressive' allies and, possibly, enlist them in the effort to bring the war to a close. Such attention was not, however, granted the visiting Iraqi Foreign Minister, nor was Syria accorded the position of Egypt in Moscow's consultations regarding a ceasefire or a settlement, both demonstrating Moscow's preferences. Even more so, the Palestinians were almost totally ignored, although there were nuances in the Soviet media that some parties were interested in keeping their cause alive if not central.

If diplomatic channels were used for communications outwards, electronic surveillance was central to information collection, at least with regard to the situation in the battlefield. This was the first major crisis (or second if the Indo-Pakistani war at the end of 1971 is considered a major crisis) in which satellites were used for a large part of Soviet intelligence collection. Presumably the naval intelligence ships were also used, along with whatever clandestine sources were available, but the launching of the Cosmos satellites at critical times suggests a new input channel for Soviet decisionmakers. There is no evidence that Moscow shared this information with its Arab allies.

The Yom Kippur War itself and the decisions taken in connection with it clearly reflected the dilemmas facing Soviet decisionmakers, in particular the reconciliation of the global interest in détente with the globally connected but regional interest of influence in the Third World. Just as prior to the war Moscow sought to restrain as well as arm the Arabs, preparing them for the war Moscow sought to avoid; so, too, during the war, saving the Arabs from defeat by rearming them coincided with the contradictory effort to persuade them to agree to a ceasefire. This latter effort all but destroyed the good-will sought by the Soviets by rearming them. If Moscow miscalculated the elasticity of détente, it also miscalculated the Arabs' credulity. The results were a blow to détente *and* to Moscow's position in the Arab world, as many Western leaders accused the Kremlin of violating détente and many Arab leaders accused them of knuckling under to it. The antidétentists in the Kremlin must have been strengthened at least temporarily, as even the prodétentists ultimately had to concede to strong measures. The fact that Brezhnev did not directly intervene may have been of no comfort to the more cautious decisionmakers; the more aggressive faction – if there was one – could later point to the decline of Moscow's position in the Arab world as proof of the inherent error in Moscow's decision. On the other hand, Brezhnev and the other prodétentists could point to Soviet-US cooperation in the disengagement agreements and in other spheres after the war (SALT II talks, the European Security Conference) as proof of the advisability of giving priority to détente, crediting it with having prevented global disaster in the Yom Kippur War rather than admitting its failure in avoiding superpower confrontation.

NOTES: CHAPTER 8

1 Galia Golan, *Yom Kippur and After: The Soviet Union and the Middle East Crisis* (Cambridge: Cambridge University Press, 1977); William Quandt, *Soviet Policy in the October 1973 War*, R-1864, Rand Corporation, Santa Monica, California, USA, 1976. The following books include chapters of varying depth and accuracy on the Soviet role in the war: Jon Glassman, *Arms for the Arabs: The Soviet Union and War in the Middle East* (Baltimore, Md: Johns Hopkins University Press, 1975); Alvin Rubinstein, *Red Star on the Nile* (Princeton, NJ: Princeton University Press, 1977); Lawrence Whetten, *The Canal War* (Cambridge, Mass.: MIT Press, 1974); and Robert Freedman, *Soviet Policy toward the Middle East* (New York: Praeger, 1975). Any unfootnoted material in this study is based upon my book on the war in which all the original sources can be found.

2 For factors to be studied in connection with Soviet foreign policy decisionmaking, see Vernon Aspaturian, 'Internal politics and foreign policy in the Soviet system', in R. Barry Farell (ed.), *Approaches to Comparative and International Politics* (Evanston, Ill.: Northwestern University Press, 1966), pp. 491–551; Alexander Dallin, 'Soviet foreign policy and domestic politics: a framework for analysis', *Journal of International Affairs*, Vol. 23, no. 2 (1969), pp. 250–65; W. Zimmerman, 'Elite perspectives and the explanation of Soviet foreign policy', *Journal of International Affairs*, Vol. 24, no. 2 (1970), pp. 84–98; Jan Triska and David Finlay, *Soviet Foreign Policy* (London: Macmillan, 1968); see also Michael Breecher (ed.), *Studies in Crisis Behavior* (New Brunswick, NJ: Transaction, 1978) for a more universal model.

3 See Janice Stein, 'Can decision-makers be rational and should they?', op. cit., pp. 316–39 in Michael Breecher, ibid.

4 Michael McGuire (ed.), *Soviet Naval Policy: Objectives and Constraints* (New York: Praeger, 1975); Geoffry Jukes, *The Indian Ocean in Soviet Naval Policy*, Adelphi Paper No. 87 (1972); Bradford Dismukes and James McConnell, *Soviet Naval Diplomacy* (New York: Pergamon Press, 1979); and Bradford Dismukes, 'Roles and missions of Soviet naval general purpose forces in wartime: pro-SSBN operations?', Center for Naval Analyses, Virginia, USA (August 1974).

5 Martin Spechler and Dina Spechler, 'The Soviet Union and the oil weapon', in Yaacov Roi, *The Limits to Power* (London: Croom Helm, 1979), pp. 96–123; Marshall Goldman, *Détente and Dollars* (New York: Basic, 1975); and Gur Ofer, 'Economic aspects of Soviet involvement in the Middle East', in Roi, loc. cit., pp. 67–95.

6 Naval facilities were retained, but the six or seven airfields were lost.

7 See Whetten, *The Canal War*, op. cit., *passim*; Yaacov Roi, *From Encroachment to Penetration: A Documentary Study of Soviet Policy in the Middle East, 1945–1973* (New York: Wiley, 1974); and Golan, *Yom Kippur and After*, op. cit., ch. 2.

8 Galia Golan, *The Soviet Union and the Palestine Liberation Organization* (New York: Praeger, 1980).

9 ibid.

10 These deliveries included SAM-6s, at least temporarily manned by Soviet personnel. Soviet military advisors with the Syrian army, down to battalion level, numbered roughly 1,500.

11 One could begin in the periodization with the July 1972 expulsion or various other events marking the beginning of Sadat's preparations for war, but the January–February 1973 decision was chosen because it was the crucial decision which placed Moscow in the picture prior to the war.

12 Galia Golan, 'Internal pressures and Soviet foreign policy decisions: a study of leadership opinion on détente, China and the Middle East', unpublished paper, Hebrew University of Jerusalem, 1973; and Dina Spechler, *Domestic Influences on Soviet Foreign Policy* (New York: University Press of America, 1978). There are a number of studies on differences of opinion, group pressures and conflict politics during the Khrushchev era or on specific cases (particularly Czechoslovakia) in the Brezhnev period, but aside from studies on domestic issues there is nothing on the détente issue as such.

13 Grechko and Andropov were promoted to the Politburo in April 1973, possibly as a gesture by Brezhnev to reassure the antidétente camp that its legitimate interests would be represented there. It is equally possible, however, that these promotions, like that of Gromyko, were intended by Brezhnev to bring into the Politburo men personally loyal to him, regardless of their positions on specific issues.

14 See Spechler, *Domestic Influences*, op. cit., *passim*; Ilana Dimant-Kass, '*Pravda* and *Trud* – divergent attitudes toward the Middle East', *Soviet Union*, Vol. 1, pt 1 (Winter 1974), pp. 1–36; Ilana Dimant-Kass, 'The Soviet military and Soviet policy in the Middle East, 1970–3', *Soviet Studies*, Vol. XXVI, no. 4 (October 1974), pp. 502–21; and Uri Ra'anan, 'The USSR and the Middle East: some reflections on the Soviet decision-making process', *Orbis*, Vol. XVII, no. 3 (1973), pp. 946–77.

15 Extrapolated from the findings of Spechler, *Domestic Influences*, op. cit., pp. 17–62. These findings are generally consistent with those of Kass's study of an earlier period. Specific war-related subjects such as ceasefire, aid and involvement, and the oil weapon, will be treated below.

16 Mohammed Heikal, *The Road to Ramadan* (London: Fontana/Collins, 1976), pp. 85–6; and *Al-Nahar* (Lebanon), 1 March 1974 (from Bassam Frika, *Secrets of the October War*).

17 Dimant-Kass, *Soviet Studies*, op. cit., pp. 502–21; and Uri Ra'anan, 'Soviet policy in the Middle East', *Midstream*, Vol. XIX, no. 10 (1973), pp. 23–45.

18 Dimant-Kass, *Soviet Studies*, op. cit., pp. 1–5.

19 Glassman, *Arms for the Arabs*, op. cit., p. 119; and Spechler, *Domestic Influences*, op. cit., pp. 45–50.

20 Gur Ofer, 'The economic burden of Soviet involvement in the Middle East', *Soviet Studies*, Vol. XXIV, no. 3 (1973), pp. 329–48.

21 Cairo radio, 28 September 1975 (Sadat speech).

22 Rubinstein, *Red Star on the Nile*, op. cit., p. 213.

23 ibid., p. 225.

24 *New York Times*, 20 December 1972.

25 *The Times*, 9 January 1973; Cairo radio, 8 January 1973.

26 Rubinstein, *Red Star*, op. cit., p. 227.

27 ibid.: two meetings with Brezhnev; Sadat spoke of two long meetings, one with Hafez Ismail and one with Ahmad Ismail (Cairo radio, 26 March 1973).

28 *Politika*, 26 February 1973.

29 TASS, 29 October 1972 (interview in *Rose al-Yusuf* with Egyptian ambassador to the USSR Yahia Abdul-Qadir); and Cairo radio, 26 July 1972.

30 *Newsweek*, 9 April 1973 (Sadat interview).

31 Cairo radio, 28 September 1975.

32 *Al-Hawadess*, 26 April 1974, Sadat interview, in Rafi Israeli (ed.), *The Public Diary of President Sadat*, Vol. I (Leiden: Brill, 1979), p. 509 (referring to 1971 talks).

33 Mohammed Heikal, *Sphinx and Commissar* (London: Collins, 1978), p. 253; and Rubinstein, *Red Star*, op. cit., p. 235.

34 Cairo radio, 3 April 1974.

35 Cairo radio, 1 April 1973; emphasis added.

36 According to Sadat, in his 23 July 1973 speech and comments after the war, there was a cooling of relations again because of failure to deliver all, or speedily enough, the material requested (the SCUDs may have been delayed – reports of their arrival vary from April to the summer, even to September – and Sadat later claimed that his helicopter force was nearly nonoperational because of lack of spare parts; he had insufficient tanks; he had antiquated bridges for the Canal crossing; and he hadn't even known the Soviets had such large transport planes until the Antonovs flew in to evacuate Soviet personnel on 4–5 October.

37 Sadat and the Egyptian press made their dissatisfaction known to the Soviets throughout the summer. No communiqué was issued following Hafez Ismail's July visit to Brezhnev to

clarify the effect that détente, manifested by Brezhnev's June trip to the USA, would have on Soviet-Egyptian relations. Cairo commentaries on the visit referred to 'the right to differ' as the most prominent characteristic of Soviet-Egyptian relations (Cairo radio, 14 July 1973). The Syrians, too, had complaints, presumably put to Kirilenko during his visit to Damascus in early July, while Kirilenko, for his part, reportedly tried to dissuade Assad from going to war (*Al-Jadid* (Lebanon), 9 November 1973, cited in Moshe Maoz, *Syria Under Hafiz al-Assad*, Jerusalem, 1976.)

38   Rubinstein, *Red Star*, op. cit., Glassman, *Arms for the Arabs*, op. cit., though Kosygin's communiqué with Yugoslavia did refer to the Arab-Israeli conflict.

39   On 20 September Vinogradov met Hafez Ismail to ask for the meeting. The Egyptian ambassador to Moscow was reported by *Le Monde* (22 September) to be vacationing in the Crimea, but in any case communications were generally made through Vinogradov rather than the Egyptian envoy.

40   Assad informed them on 4 October of the actual date of attack.

41   Rubinstein, *Red Star*, op. cit., p. 262.

42   Glassman, *Arms for the Arabs*, op. cit., p. 101, but this source is not always accurate regarding Soviet press reports.

43   Spechler, *Domestic Influences*, op. cit., p. 21.

44   ibid., *passim*.

45   ibid., *passim*.

46   ibid., pp. 25–9.

47   See Dismukes and McConnell, *Soviet Naval Diplomacy*, op. cit., pp. 192–210 and 271–6.

48   Algiers radio, 9 October 1973.

49   Gromyko *was* busy on 7–10 October with the visiting Japanese premier, but at this critical time one might think that Gromyko or some other Soviet leader would have seen fit to receive the Arab ambassadors.

50   KYODO (Japan), 9 October 1973.

51   Heikal, *Road to Ramadan*, op. cit., pp. 212–13.

52   And the attachment of minesweepers to the intelligence ships. The fleet was not, however, otherwise augmented at this time (Dismukes and McConnell, *Soviet Naval Diplomacy*, op. cit., p. 197.)

53   ibid.; and Quandt, *Decade of Decisions*, op. cit., p. 179.

54   Emphasis added.

55   For differences of opinion on this issue see Victor Zorza, Radio Liberty, 'The Kremlin power struggle', FL 32/74, February 1974, pp. 13–17; John Dornberg, *Brezhnev* (London: Deutsch, 1974), p. 214; and *The Times* (London), 16 October 1973.

56   Two more appeared, on 15 and 20 October, also to deter Israeli attacks on the sea and airlifts; see Dismukes and McConnell, *Soviet Naval Diplomacy*, op. cit., p. 201.

57   ibid., pp. 202, 272.

58   ibid., though not in sources on Kissinger such as Marvin Kalb and Bernard Kalb, *Kissinger* (Boston, Mass.: Little, Brown, 1974).

59   Spechler, *Domestic Influences*, op. cit., p. 25.

60   A Soviet document, predating the war, which fell into Israeli hands during the hostilities, provides a military appraisal that the Israeli army strategy was based on a rapid massive strike into Arab territory, with strong reliance on the airforce and tanks; Israel would, therefore, be at a disadvantage in a war of attrition, also because of the economic difficulties of prolonged mobilization (*Yediot Ahronot*, 15 August 1974).

61   Indeed, on 13 October, Sadat refused still another ceasefire bid, this one produced by joint Soviet-US efforts through the intermediary of Britain. It has even been argued that the 12 October Soviet warning to Israel was an attempt to apply pressure to accept the ceasefire, which Israel did, despite its poor position on the Egyptian front.

62   Quandt, *Soviet Policy*, op. cit., p. 186.

63   Moscow may have suggested that Boumedienne request Yugoslav permission for Soviet overflights. Yugoslavian law provided that such permission be granted only if a third country, friendly to Yugoslavia, made the request (Dismukes and McConnell, *Soviet Naval Diplomacy*, op. cit., p. 309). Boumedienne stopped in Yugoslavia on his way home.

64   The Israeli crossing of the Canal came only after the decision was taken (the night of 15–16 October), though this development was reportedly used by Kosygin in his arguments with Sadat. Heikal even claims that reconnaissance photos were sent to Kosygin from Moscow to help make his case to Sadat (Heikal, *Ramadan*, op. cit., p. 245).

65 TANJUG, 19 October 1973; and Kalb and Kalb, *Kissinger*, op. cit., p. 480.
66 Spechler, *Domestic Influences*, op. cit., *passim*.
67 ibid., *passim*.
68 Cairo radio, 15 September 1975.
69 Launched on 16 October, possibly in response to the Israeli crossing on the night of 15 October.
70 On 18 October Dobrynin gave Kissinger a draft Soviet proposal, which was much more extreme, calling for Israeli withdrawal from all occupied Arab lands, including the old city of Jerusalem. This was categorically rejected by Kissinger on the spot (Kalb and Kalb, *Kissinger*, op. cit., p. 481).
71 Cairo radio, 22 October 1973; *Al-Anwar* (Lebanon), 30 October 1973; and Damascus radio, 29 October 1973.
72 Damascus radio, 29 October 1973.
73 Even in the case of Cuba, the nuclear warheads were sent to, and intended for use only by, Soviet forces in Cuba, in bases that were offlimits to the Cubans.
74 Quandt, *Soviet Policy*, op. cit., p. 198.
75 The enhanced alert in the airborne divisions had occurred on 10 October; three divisions reportedly were involved. On 23 October the remaining four divisions were put on enhanced alert.
76 Dismukes and McConnell, *Soviet Naval Diplomacy*, op. cit., p. 203.
77 The above reconstruction is based on Kalb and Kalb, *Kissinger*, op. cit., pp. 188–90; Quandt, *Soviet Policy*, op. cit., pp. 196–7; Dismukes and McConnell, *Soviet Naval Diplomacy*, op. cit., pp. 202–3, 273–4; see also Golan, *Yom Kippur*, op. cit., pp. 118–26.
78 Quandt, *Soviet Policy*, op. cit., p. 197.
79 Kalb and Kalb, *Kissinger*, op. cit., p. 491. State Department INR director at the time, Ray Cline, said later that his office had not been asked for any appraisal as to possible Soviet intervention; he expressed skepticism that the Soviets did intend to intervene (*New York Times*, 8 December 1974).
80 Dismukes and McConnell, *Soviet Naval Diplomacy*, op. cit., p. 274; J. L. Moulton, 'Seaborne and airborne mobility in Europe', *US Naval Institute Proceedings*, Vol. 100, no. 5(855) (1974), pp. 127–30; Graham Turbiville, 'Soviet airborne troops', op. cit., p. 283 in Michael McGuire and John McDonnell (eds), *Soviet Naval Influence* (New York: Praeger, 1977).
81 If such had been their intention, it would be surprising that Chief-of-Staff Kulikov should have taken time out in the morning to receive, with a full honor guard, a visiting Finnish military delegation.
82 The idea of assistance has been expressed by Dismukes and McConnell, *Soviet Naval Diplomacy*, op. cit., p. 274; amd Coral Bell, 'The October Middle East war: a case-study in crisis management during détente', *International Affairs*, Vol. 50, no. 4 (October 1974), pp. 531–43.
83 See Golan, *Yom Kippur*, op. cit., pp. 145–7 for postwar juxtaposition on détente and the war.
84 For naval activities of the two superpowers after the 24–25 October alert, see Dismukes and McConnell, *Soviet Naval Diplomacy*, op. cit., pp. 204–6.

9 Soviet Decisionmaking on Afghanistan, 1979

JIRI VALENTA

The Soviet invasion of Afghanistan in 1979 and of Czechoslovakia in 1968 are both examples of the Soviet determination to intervene militarily in neighboring countries when their governments become, in the Soviet view, untrustworthy and unable to maintain control. Whereas Czechoslovakia, a member of the Warsaw Treaty Organization (WTO), belongs inside the traditional Soviet security belt of Eastern Europe and had been a communist country for more than two decades before the invasion, Afghanistan, an Asian Muslim country, is not a member of the WTO and has had a ruling Leninist party only since 1978.

There are striking similarities between the official Soviet rationales for these invasions. The arguments advanced in both cases were rather confused and contradictory, ranging from a claim that the USSR responded to a call to 'assist healthy forces' to claims that military action was needed to put down an imminent 'counterrevolution' and prevent the countries' potential defection to the imperialist camp. In Czechoslovakia this threat was supposedly posed by the imperialist bloc, primarily the CIA in the United States, neighboring West German 'revanchists', and 'Zionists'. In Afghanistan the United States was again implicated, as were Egypt and neighboring Pakistan and China. After both invasions, the Soviet leadership concluded treaties providing for the 'temporary' stationing of Soviet troops in the occupied countries which, at least in the case of Czechoslovakia, has been permanent.

This chapter seeks to assess the similarities and differences, primarily on the political level of Soviet decisionmaking, but also on a military level, between the two invasions. What were the motives? How did domestic interests and foreign policy and strategic considerations affect the final decisions? What influence, if any, was exercised by an altered military balance? What other factors shaped the decisions? What was the nature of the deployments? What have been the consequences of the invasions?

SOVIET PERCEPTIONS OF INSTABILITIES AND FAILING RELIABILITIES

The decisions to intervene in Czechoslovakia and Afghanistan had several motivations, the most important being Soviet perceptions of both regimes' instability and unreliability. Domestic and strategic considerations followed. In the Soviets' view Alexander Dubcek and Hafizullah Amin were charting independent courses in domestic politics in disregard of Soviet counsel, and future developments in both countries were as unpredictable as they were dangerous.

However, the situations at the time of the respective invasions differed considerably. Under Dubcek the Czechoslovak Communist Party had pursued for several months a pluralistic concept of socialism in a developed, central European country with predominantly democratic traditions. On the other hand, under the leadership of Noor Mohammed Taraki and later Amin (after the coup of September 1979), the Khalq (People's) Marxist Party had pursued for more than a year a radical and at the same time oppressive and brutal program of socialization in an underdeveloped, Muslim country having no experience or history of democracy. Both Taraki, and to an even greater extent Amin, disregarded Soviet counsel to broaden their bases of support. In Czechoslovakia, in 1968, revolutionary changes had taken place peacefully and with the support of the masses. In Afghanistan civil war and a series of bloody coups were the prelude to change. In both Czechoslovakia and Afghanistan political developments were characterized by factional struggle. In Czechoslovakia pro-Soviet, antireform-oriented leaders, led by A. Indra and V. Bilak struggled against Dubcek and his reformist supporters. In Afghanistan Khalq Party leaders Taraki and Amin struggled against the more pro-Moscow Parcham (Banner) faction led by Babrak Karmal. As shown below, factional struggles and Soviet attempts to exploit them by organizing pro-Soviet coups were synchronized with the military interventions.

In Czechoslovakia the Soviets faced, using Soviet terminology, a serious 'right-wing deviation'. In Afghanistan, by contrast, they were challenged by a radical, even Maoist 'left-wing deviation'. Despite significant differences, both developments were viewed by the Soviets as having unpredictable and dangerous consequences. In Czechoslovakia the Soviets feared that Dubcek's consolidation of power at the forthcoming 14th Party Congress in September 1968 would be followed by a more independent foreign policy – with Czechoslovakia becoming, in effect, a 'second Yugoslavia'.[1] In Afghanistan, however, the chief worry was that Amin would turn traitor. Given their difficult experience with other fervent though independent communist leaders such as Josip Broz Tito and Mao Zedong, the Soviets were eager to oust the radical and unreliable Amin.[2]

The situation in Afghanistan was viewed as being even more perilous than the situation in Czechoslovakia. Amin's regime, despite increasing Soviet military assistance (including, since the spring of 1979, T-62 tanks, MI-24 assault helicopters and MIG-23 fighter planes) and the presence of 3,000–4,000 Soviet advisors, was unable to suppress the growing resistance of the Muslim rebels. This was in spite of the advisors' assumption of command and control responsibilities down to company-level posts and operation of jet fighters and helicopter gunships. In the fall of 1979 the rebels, with some covert assistance coming from Pakistan and China, had succeeded in repelling Amin's offensive and were effectively in control of most of the countryside. The Afghan army, having suffered mutinies and massive desertions to the rebels, was slowly deteriorating. Meanwhile the Soviet advisors themselves bore heavy casualties. In this situation Amin's greatest liability in Soviet eyes was that he not only was likely to become a 'counterrevolutionary' traitor, but also a loser, one who might decide in a desperate moment to seek rapprochement with the West or China. Indeed, Amin refused to visit Moscow in November and reportedly sent frantic requests in November and early December for an immediate meeting with Pakistan's General Zia ul Haq.[3]

The immediate challenge to Soviet interests in Afghanistan was the overall political-military situation, particularly the instability in late November 1979. Soviet inaction at this time could have led to growing chaos and the eventual overthrow of the Khalq regime in Kabul or a no-recourse shift by Amin to a more pro-Western or pro-Chinese foreign policy alignment. Moreover, Soviet inaction could have had repercussions in Eastern Europe, in the Third World and, perhaps, in the Soviet Union itself. As explained by two prominent Soviet writers: 'At the end of 1979, the situation became critical . . . We could not and did not want to betray our sense of responsibility. The USSR could not have acted otherwise. It could not allow a victory by religious fanatics', nor tolerate the 'counterrevolutionary ignominy' of Amin's group.[4]

SECURITY CONSIDERATIONS: SPILLOVER EFFECTS

The invasions of Czechoslovakia and Afghanistan were also motivated by more direct security considerations. Propaganda that intervention was in response to Western military threats (in the case of Czechoslovakia) or military threats from the West and China (in the case of Afghanistan) was used largely to create bureaucratic and public support justifying the Soviet action. More genuine were the Soviets' fears about instability on their own borders.

In Czechoslovakia the Soviets were concerned with the possible effects of Prague reformism – a kind of proto-Eurocommunism – on the intellectual, scientific and literary communities and liberal-minded members of the Soviet establishment. Such liberal-minded members had begun, albeit in limited numbers, to advocate that the Prague Spring should serve as 'an example' for the Soviet Union to follow. This point was made most persuasively by academician A. Sakharov in a manifesto urging the Soviet leadership to adopt some portions of the Czechoslovak reformist programs. More ominous for the Soviets were the possible effects on the non-Russian republics. Soviet leaders have always been extremely sensitive about nationalist trends. Thus, in 1968 they feared that 'deviate' ideas of reformism and, more importantly, Dubcek's experiments with federalization, would spill over from Czechoslovakia to encourage nationalism not only in the Ukraine, but perhaps also in Lithuania, Latvia and Estonia. The threat seemed to be particularly serious in the Ukraine, especially in the western portion, part of which had belonged to the Czechoslovak province of Ruthenia during the interwar period. Prior to the invasion there were indications that the Czechoslovak experiment with federalization, the restoration of national rights to the Ukrainian minority living in Slovakia, and the revival of the forbidden Greek Catholic Church, were also encouraging Ukrainian national sentiment. The Czechoslovak media, including Ukrainian language broadcasts and newspapers, publicized these ideas and even occasionally criticized the situation in the Soviet Union.

In spite of Soviet denials, similar fears probably contributed to the decision for the invasion of Afghanistan, though there is no solid evidence of this. The Soviets are naturally concerned about the loyalty of ethnic groups in the non-Russian republics of Central Asia and the Caucasus, all the more so because of growing militancy among Islamic fundamentalists in Iran in 1978–9 (and to a lesser degree in Turkey and Pakistan) and Muslim insurgency in Afghanistan in 1979 – countries of close proximity to the Soviet southern borders.

Muslim fundamentalism in Iran and Afghanistan, however, did not have concrete repercussions upon the Soviet republics in Central Asia and the Caucasus as had Dubcek's federalization on the Ukraine. Moreover, we do not have any solid evidence of significant Muslim dissidence in Soviet Central Asia or of the impact of Muslim fundamentalism on the Soviet Muslims. Yet, as James Critchlow has noted, the Soviet Muslims in Central Asia, mainly the Turkic and Iranian peoples, 'share proximity and historical experience' with respect to the bordering Muslim countries. Turkmenistan, Uzbekistan and Tadjikistan share over 800 miles of borders with Afghanistan. The Soviet Muslims 'have had extensive opportunities to interact with conationals in the Afghan population, which consists of four million Uzbeks and three million Tajiks, plus smaller but significant numbers of Turkmens'. Some of these are descendants of anti-Soviet Basmachi guerrillas who escaped from the USSR in the 1920s after having lost their ten-year struggle against Soviet hegemony in Central Asia.[5] This is particularly true of the Uzbeks, who constitute a majority of the population of northern Afghanistan. But while the Soviets are worried about the effects of Muslim fundamentalism among the Uzbeks and other Central Asians, they have also used their Uzbeks and other Turkish nationalities as a wedge in the Muslim Third World countries. Uzbekistan and other Soviet republics often serve as showcases for Third World Muslims. To be sure, there was no evidence of widespread sympathy among the Muslims in Soviet Central Asia for either the rebels, or for Amin's regime in Afghanistan. Yet it is intriguing to note, as Critchlow discovered, that the September 1979 account of the Afghan revolution – written by the Uzbek editor of the widely circulated literary journal *Sharq yulduzi*, who visited Afghanistan in March – pictured the pro-Soviet leader of Parcham, Babrak Karmal, as an untrustworthy villain, and Hafizullah Amin as a hero.[6]

On balance, however, any impact of Muslim insurgency or Amin's nationalism and search for independence upon the USSR was not immediate but rather very remote. One must consider long-term demographic, economic, religious and cultural trends to understand the Soviet leadership's concern about the potential spillover effects of the Muslim religious movement.[7]

STRATEGIC CONSIDERATIONS: THE BREZHNEV DOCTRINE?

The Soviet moves into Afghanistan and Czechoslovakia must be seen in the light of global strategic considerations. In the aftermath of both invasions, analysts tried to explain events in terms of the so-called Brezhnev Doctrine, which was presumably inaugurated with the 1968 invasion. According to this 'doctrine', the Soviet Union has the right to intervene in any communist country in order to safeguard established socialism. Although some of the ideological pronouncements after both invasions were similar, this explanation gives too much credit to Brezhnev's contributions to Soviet foreign policy. Russian tsars and Soviet leaders alike have traditionally been sensitive about the security of nearby countries. They have used force to restore 'stability' and maintain or bring into power friendly, pro-Russian or pro-Soviet regimes. Since World War II, these have been the reasons for three interventions in Eastern Europe: East Germany in 1953, Hungary in 1956 and Czechoslovakia in 1968. On one level Afghanistan is just another example of an old habit. However, Soviet interventions in dissenting communist countries are neither automatic, nor foreclosed. Although coming very close, the Soviets did not intervene in Yugoslavia after the break with Tito in 1948, nor in Poland during the upheavals in 1956 and 1970. Nor did they intervene on a large scale in 1969 during and after the conflict with the PRC on the Ussuri River. As the Czechoslovak and Afghan cases illustrate, Soviet decisions to use force in neighboring countries are motivated by a number of factors besides the doctrinal statements of Soviet writers and communist theoreticians, which serve more as *ex post facto* justifications than as real motives.

There were, however, some striking differences between the two invasions. Whereas in Czechoslovakia the Soviet intervention was limited strictly to the defense of the status quo, the invasion of Afghanistan seems to have contained both defensive and offensive elements. Afghanistan is the first country outside the East European security zone and Warsaw Treaty Organization in which the Soviets have intervened since World War II. It upsets the unwritten rules of the superpower game. At the same time, however, Russian tsars and Soviet commissars alike have traditionally considered the northern tier of Afghanistan to be within their sphere of influence. Also from Russian tradition is the difficulty in knowing where to draw the line with regard to expansion.[8] The Russians intervened in Afghanistan on a limited scale in 1885, 1928 and 1930. (In the nineteenth century British fear of and desire to halt Russian expansionism were the motives behind two costly Anglo-Afghan wars.) Yet the Russians never attempted a full-scale invasion of Afghanistan until 1979.

Although the initial reason for the invasion of Afghanistan was almost certainly not to secure a base for further interventions in Iran or Baluchistan, one cannot easily isolate the defensive from the offensive motivations. We do not know what ultimately triggered the Soviet decision to invade Afghanistan – whether internal conditions of that country, concerns of spillover effects on the USSR, or strategic designs beyond Afghanistan. In my judgement, however, the invasion was neither an exclusively defensive move (as believed by George Kennan), nor a solely offensive move (as viewed by Richard Pipes), but rather a combination of both.[9] Soviet concerns must be viewed in light of the strategic position of the Persian Gulf, particularly in the wake of the US naval deployment off the coast of Iran in November 1979. The Soviets feared that the fall of a pro-Soviet regime in

Afghanistan might have been manipulated by the United States and China,[10] and maintained that the United States was attempting to 'drive' Afghanistan into the 'notorious strategic arc' which the United States 'has been building for decades close to the USSR's southern borders'.[11]

In addition to any defensive motives was the Soviet desire to be in a better position to exploit future opportunities in unstable Iran. The Soviet deployment in Afghanistan would halve the distance from their own borders to the Straits of Hormuz. Soviet land-deployed aircraft in Afghanistan would be in a more advantageous position should they be needed to neutralize US air superiority provided by aircraft carriers in the area. The Soviets would in effect be able to cope with all likely contingencies in Iran, including US military intervention and/or civil war and greater chaos. Furthermore, forward deployment in Afghanistan would enable the Soviets to improve their strategic position *vis-à-vis* neighboring Pakistan and China, creating a more effective buffer and, if necessary, a source of pressure.

DECISIONMAKING: CONCEPTUALIZATION

Studies of Soviet decisionmaking are necessarily tentative, since they depend heavily on personal interpretations of cryptic communications within the Soviet bureaucracies. It is impossible to capture all the complexities of the Soviet decisionmaking process.

Soviet decisionmakers can be at once tough and flexible, and they share a similar Leninist *weltanschauung*. Yet the Politburo is a collective body which rules without the supreme authority of a dictator. It is composed of a group of men with divergent values, bureaucratic affiliations, constituencies and responsibilities. Decisions made by the Soviet collective leadership do not always reflect united sets of national security interests. They appear to be taken also in relation to a variety of inconsistent goals for internal and external policies, arising from participants with many differing personal and organizational interests.

The hypotheses of bureaucratic politics can offer a tentative, if partial explanation of how Soviet decisions are made. Under the conditions of collective leadership in the post-Stalin era, the major Soviet decisions have been made following debates at Politburo sessions where senior decisionmakers often express, in the Soviet idiom, 'different points of view'. The Politburo debate is aimed at reaching a consensus – in Soviet political terminology, a 'unanimous point of view'. Although most Soviet decisions are compromises, they are taken unanimously in order to preserve the unity and cohesion of the Politburo.

Unfortunately, analysts have little information about the decisionmaking process preceding the invasion of Afghanistan. Whereas with Czechoslovakia it was possible to demonstrate that the Soviet decision was influenced by coalition politics, in the Afghan case we have only very limited evidence of the existence of any preinvasion debate. Available evidence suggests it did occur, although it was certainly not as arduous and prolonged as the debate preceding the Soviet invasion of Czechoslovakia. The Soviet leaders had been concerned with the deteriorating situation in Afghanistan at least since the spring of 1979 when, according to Soviet sources, the late president Taraki began to ask them repeatedly for military aid.[12] Amin, who came to power in September, also reportedly asked for help. However, the Soviet Union did not respond to calls for military aid until December because 'moving troops into the territory of another state is always a difficult matter'. The Soviet leadership must 'carefully' view 'all aspects and inter-relationships' of such a move.[13] As Secretary-General Brezhnev himself pointed out, the decision to intervene 'was no simple decision'.[14]

The Soviet decisionmaking style has been affected by many changes in domestic and international politics since Czechoslovakia. During Brezhnev's tenure the most important change was the considerable strengthening of Brezhnev's power and his ability to outmaneuver, dismiss, demote, or retire several of his colleagues (P. Shelest, G. I. Voronov, D. S. Polianskii, A. N. Shelepin, K. T. Mazurov and N. E. Podgorny being good examples in the 1970s). The basic mode of Soviet decisionmaking probably has not altered drastically, however. As an astute observer of politics in communist countries V. Kusin pointed out, the bureaucratic politics paradigm probably still applies in the early 1980s, except that 'the inputs in terms of the specific weights of the various political actors and political considerations have changed'.[15] At the time of Brezhnev's death (November 1982) it is too early to speculate how the Soviet decisionmaking style will evolve under Andropov and his successors.

Brezhnev, unlike Stalin, was not the final arbiter in Soviet decision-making. Still, he was *primus inter pares* in the ruling oligarchy – what the Soviets call collective leadership. However, in the last few years before his death, during which his health had deteriorated remarkably, Brezhnev sometimes did not participate in the work of the Politburo, a factor which probably led to an increasing number of debates and policy conflicts.

Falin, first deputy chief of the International Information Department of the Central Committee, stated 'all our foreign policy and national security questions must be discussed and decided in the Politburo'.[16] Clashes over different policy positions occur in the various bureaucracies before the issues are submitted to the highest decisionmaking body. The senior decisionmakers try to avoid disagreements, 'often aggravated by poor con-tact', as Falin notes, and most of these are overcome by the time the issues reach the Politburo. Yet debate and disagreements still do occur while the Politburo carefully examines the pros and cons of the various policy options and tries to smooth over the existing differences by consensus-building. This ultimately led to unanimous approval of a course of action, and was very likely the process adhered to in Soviet decisionmaking on Afghanistan.

THE SOVIET DEBATE

The Soviet debate regarding Afghanistan and neighbouring Iran reached a peak in late November. It was not as intense as the one preceeding the Soviet invasion of Czechoslovakia. Unlike 1968, there was neither an intense media debate nor reports about a serious division in the leadership. While previously one could detect the pressures on the Politburo in favor of invasion by the leaders of the Soviet non-Russian republics in the West, such pressures did not exist or were well hidden in 1979. Two meetings of the Central Committee of the CPSU during which Czechoslovakia was debated occurred before the 1968 invasion. Such meetings probably did not take place prior to the invasion of Afghanistan.[17]

As in the decisionmaking process on Czechoslovakia, however, one can speculate on the influence of information and policy recommendations provided by high-ranking Soviet military officials and diplomats. Army General A. N. Epishev, head of the Main Political Administration of the Soviet armed forces (MPA), who is concerned mainly with ideological and political supervision of the Soviet military, had toured Czechoslovakia before the 1968 invasion and was concerned about the weakening morale in the Czechoslovak armed forces. He subsequently became one of the most outspoken advocates of the military intervention.[18] Epishev also toured Afghanistan in April 1979 with a half-dozen other Soviet generals. Later, on 23 November, Epishev called upon Soviet servicemen to be 'on the alert' and to approve and support 'our state's new foreign policy initiative', made necessary because 'aggressive imperialist circles and the Beijing leaders who form an alliance with them' oppose the USSR and strive to ensure their 'military superiority'.[19] After the invasion, Epishev would defend it as a just, defensive action, declaring that 'All the wars our state and its armed forces have been constrained to wage have been just wars'.[20]

During October and November the Soviet generals and the Soviet ambassador to Afghanistan came to view developments in that country as extremely volatile and unstable. Unlike in Czechoslovakia, where both senior Soviet policymakers and key military figures alike were intensively engaged in management of the crisis, in Afghanistan the main role was played by representatives of the military, though diplomatic sources undoubtedly played some role in the crises as well. Key Soviet military personnel who arrived in Afghanistan a few months prior to the invasion very likely concurred in a generally pessimistic assessment of the situation.[21] Besides Epishev, Deputy Minister of Defense and commander-in-chief of the Soviet groundforces, General I. Pavlovskii (who, incidentally, was commander-in-chief of the invading Soviet forces in Czechoslovakia in 1968), paid a two-month visit to Kabul, from late August until October. His reports very probably concluded that the regime was slowly disintegrating and that a few thousand Soviet advisors would not be able to stabilize the situation. It is probable that Pavlovskii, Epishev and other Soviet generals, mainly those in charge of the military districts adjacent to Afghanistan, urged a massive intervention to assist pro-Soviet elements to stabilize the restive southern borders and put an end as quickly as possible to the killing of Soviet advisors. As explained after the invasion by the commander of the Turkestan military district, Colonel-General Yu. Maksimov, and other Soviet generals of military districts in Central Asia, there was 'a real seat of war danger on the USSR's southern border'. In the view of Maksimov, 'the presence of our troops will permit the stabilization of the situation in Afghanistan, will allow the democratic forces to consolidate themselves and the gains of the revolution to be secured, and will permit the cooling of the ardor of those who initiated military adventures'.[22]

The Soviet leaders also rely on information from diplomatic sources about political developments in other countries. The importance of the activities and reports of S. V. Chervonenko, Soviet ambassador to Czechoslovakia during the Czechoslovak crisis, indicates that the notion prevailing among analysts that Soviet diplomats are merely 'messenger boys of the Kremlin' may not be entirely true. Chervonenko's opinion that Czechoslovakia could become a 'second Hungary', his exaggerated reports about 'counterrevolution', and his intimate relations and support for the nascent anti-Dubcek faction were important factors in the final decision to intervene in Czechoslovakia. Such Dubcek supporters as the Czechoslovak leader Josef Smrkovsky asked (to no avail) that Brezhnev recall Chervonenko because they were aware of his role and knew that he had provided inaccurate information to the Soviet Politburo.[23] There is less information available about the role of the Soviet ambassador to Afghanistan A. Puzanov during the 1979 crisis. Nevertheless, circumstantial evidence suggests some similarities. Amin, like the Czechoslovak reformers, requested that the Soviet leadership recall Puzanov. Like Chervonenko, Puzanov got involved in factional struggles, plotting against Amin. He also provided sanctuaries for anti-Amin forces at the Soviet embassy after the coup against Taraki in September 1979. Unlike Chervonenko, Puzanov was recalled on 8 November and replaced by F. Tabaiev, a Tartar Muslim by nationality and formerly the first secretary of the Tatar *obkom*. (Incidentally Tabaiev's appointment is an illustration of the skillful use of Soviet Muslim nationals to further Soviet interests.) According to some reports, Puzanov, who by now must have felt rather bitter about Amin, was one of the reliable consultants the Soviet leaders 'listened' to before they made the final decision to intervene.[24]

One can reasonably assume that the Soviet leadership, at the apparent suggestion of key military figures and Ambassador Puzanov, was considering two alternatives: allow events to develop on their own and be faced with the unpredictable, whereupon the Soviets could lose strategic gains in Afghanistan (as they had in Egypt and Somalia); or take drastic measures to stabilize the course of events in Afghanistan on both a military and political level.

Soviet leaders responsible for foreign diplomacy might have feared the adverse impact of a full-scale military response in Afghanistan on their relations with the West, the Third World and the international communist movement. Possibly Kosygin and even Brezhnev questioned for a time the wisdom of a military invasion. It cannot be excluded that, because of their failing health, they might not even have been present at the crucial Politburo deliberations. Kosygin was hospitalized, presumably for a heart attack, in mid-November. And in view of Brezhnev's failing health, which permitted him to work only two or three hours a day, and his bad bout with a cold in early December 1979, a select group was reportedly formed within the Politburo – including representatives from each of the most important bureaucratic elites (the KGB, the armed forces, the International Department and the Ministry of Foreign Affairs) – to deal with the emergency in Afghanistan on a day-to-day basis.[25] Yet it is very unlikely that the decision to invade was taken without Brezhnev's and Kosygin's consent, or that they were overruled. From what we know about Soviet decisionmaking, it is unthinkable that the secretary-general might be overruled without this having significant repercussions on his position. As Brezhnev explained in 1968 to one Czechoslovak reformist leader, 'If I had not cast my vote in the Politburo in favor of military intervention, what do you suppose would have happened? Certainly you would not be sitting here. And perhaps even I would not be sitting here either!'[26] As during the debate on Czechoslovakia in 1968, both probably joined in the final Politburo consensus that argued in favor of the invasion.

As occurred following the invasion of Czechoslovakia, Brezhnev was the first Politburo member who, after a period of official silence, attempted to justify the invasion in a major public speech. Former Politburo member and present Soviet ambassador to Japan, D. S. Polianskii, described the final decisionmaking on Afghanistan in the following manner:

> Decisions are made collectively, and in no case is a decision made individually. Questions are carefully discussed, but final decisions are made with unanimity. The decision on the dispatch of Soviet troops to Afghanistan was made in accordance with this practice . . . The debate on this question was not easy. But the final decision was adopted with unanimous approval.[27]

SOVIET RISK ASSESSMENT: THE PERCEIVED US RESPONSE

The shift of the Politburo in favor of the invasion most likely came in late November in response to the pessimistic reports from Afghanistan, new developments in Iran and assessments of consequences for the Soviet Union of events in these two countries. As in 1968 one of the most important points in the debate was the assessment of the risks involved, particularly the US response to the invasion and the general nature of US-Soviet relations.

By the time the decision was made to invade the Soviet leaders had reached very pessimistic conclusions about their relations with the United States and China. In late November it became clear that the political and propaganda efforts of the Soviet Ministry of Foreign Affairs and the International Department were going to be unsuccessful in deterring the United States and other NATO countries from their decision to modernize Europe's theater nuclear forces (TNF). In addition, the Carter administration's decision to deploy the new MX ICBMs and Trident SLBMs, to increase defense spending significantly and to create a rapid deployment force (RDF) were viewed by the Soviets as indicative of a new and dangerous course. The SALT II agreement was in trouble, either heading for indefinite postponement or doomed altogether. The Soviets concluded by the fall of 1979 that there were hardly enough votes in the US Senate for its ratification and that the 'hardliners' in the Carter administration were willfully opposing it. Even President Carter, according to Falin, had 'done everything to sabotage the agreement'.[28] In Brezhnev's view the Carter administration's actions had proved the United States to be 'an absolutely unreliable partner'.[29]

Similarly Soviet relations with China had deteriorated further as a result of the punitive Chinese invasion of Vietnam in early 1979 which infuriated and embarrassed the Soviets. Moscow's hoped-for rapprochement with the post-Mao leadership had become even more unlikely as Chinese aid to the Afghan rebels actually increased slightly following Vice-Premier Deng Xiao-ping's visit to Washington in January 1979. Moreover, in October the Carter administration had indicated it would do away with its even-handed policy for dealing with Peking and Moscow and proposed granting most-favored-nation trade status to China. The visit by US Secretary of Defense Harold Brown (essentially intended to signal US displeasure with the presence of a Soviet brigade in Cuba), announced in late October and planned for January 1980, was viewed by authoritative Soviet analysts as a step toward 'quasi-allied relations' with China.[30]

More important were developments in the area of the Persian Gulf and the Arabian Sea. The attack on the US Embassy in Tehran and the seizure of American hostages on 4 November was followed by US deployment of twenty-one ships, including two aircraft carriers – the strongest American presence in the area since World War II. For the Soviets, the events in Iran, accompanied as they were by reports about the US quest for military facilities in the region, were a deliberate pretext for an American military buildup.[31] Hints by President Carter and other American officials in late November and early December compounded the threat of a possible US military intervention in Iran. The unpredictability of developments in Iran posed a serious dilemma for the Soviet Union. The view that probably prevailed in the Kremlin, however, was that the USSR would not risk too much by intervening in Afghanistan, since US policymakers were too preoccupied with Iran to be able to formulate an effective response to a Soviet invasion of Afghanistan. In short, there was nothing significant to fear and nothing significant to be gained from the United States. Because of the November heart attack of Georgi Arbatov, head of the prestigious Institute for USA and Canada, a crucial role in estimating the American reaction was probably played by Soviet embassy personnel in the United States, particularly Ambassador Anatoliy Dobrynin, who was recalled unexpectedly to Moscow on 10 December when final preparations were being made for the invasion. American hesitancy and preoccupation with Iran, as well as previous US vacillation during the Cuban 'minicrisis' in September 1979 – when an 'unacceptable' Soviet combat brigade suddenly became acceptable – probably served as another powerful argument to the Soviet decisionmakers who argued in favor of the invasion.

The intervention could not be further delayed. 'The Soviet leaders', as Andrei Sakharov put it, 'chose this moment to act because, with the United States preoccupied with Iran and other problems, they judged the correlation of military and political forces to be in their favor'. All factors considered, particularly the developments in Afghanistan itself, the Soviet leaders decided to act. As Sakharov pointed out, 'the Soviet policymakers may have decided it was now or never'.[32]

PLANNING THE INVASION AND THE COUP

As in Czechoslovakia, contingency planning for the invasion of Afghanistan by the Soviet General Staff began at least several months prior to the invasion. In fact, the airlift to Kabul was perhaps even practiced in late August, when reportedly 10,000 troops plus military supplies were transported from the USSR to South Yemen and Ethiopia and back to the USSR. In September the Soviets undertook the first attempt to influence developments in Afghanistan by military force. When Taraki visited Moscow in that month, *Pravda* reported on 13 September that he was assured that he could 'rely on the all-round' assistance of the Soviet Union, which, in Soviet language, includes military support. Taraki was also reportedly warned about Amin and, as some former Afghan government officials have reported, the Soviets arranged a meeting between Taraki and Parcham's Karmal during Taraki's visit to Moscow. Upon Taraki's return to Kabul, the Soviets appear to have organized and supported an anti-Amin coup on 14–15 September, their objective being to establish a Khalq–Parcham coalition government led by Taraki and Karmal. At this time there was a reported attempt, with the involvement of Ambassador Puzanov, to assassinate Amin. Concurrently the Soviets deployed some airborne units on the Soviet-Afghan borders and a 400-man airborne unit to the important Bagram air base forty miles from Kabul. The coup was a failure and instead of Amin, Taraki was removed from power and subsequently murdered by Amin's officers, who used pillows to smother him.[33] The Soviets decided to accept this as a *fait accompli*, at least for the time being, since they had no other alternative. The Soviet decision to intervene on a massive scale as a means to overthrow Amin, however, seems to have been reached only in late November. This speculation can be supported by circumstantial evidence.

In early December Soviet diplomats began to implement a new policy, promising Iranian officials unspecified 'support' in the case of US military intervention. At the same time the Soviets also began to warn the Carter administration that any military action in Iran would carry grave consequences.[34] By offering their support to Tehran, the Soviets appeared to be trying to induce the Khomeini regime not to release the hostages, thereby assuring the United States' continued distraction with Iran. By issuing a warning the Soviets also appeared to be trying to manipulate the United States into a drawn-out deployment that would stop short of the actual use of force.

But Amin, who was rumored to have complained in the fall of 1979 about Taraki's warning to 'sell out the country to the Russians', apparently declined to follow the Soviets' new pro-Khomeini tactical line. That the Soviet leadership had decided or was deciding to get rid of him at this time, at least politically, is suggested by various references to 'left-wing extremists' in Afghanistan and omissions of any reference to Amin in some reports in the Soviet media.[35] At the same time Radio Moscow significantly changed its broadcasts to Afghanistan, where Amin was resented by the Muslim clergy; the broadcasts now ended with the invocation 'God protect us'.[36] Another bit of evidence that the Soviets had decided to dispose of Amin was the decision of 28 November to send First Deputy Minister of the Interior Lt General Victor Paputin to Kabul. His official mission was to help Amin with police affairs and counterinsurgency, perhaps even to protect him; yet in reality he was to prepare the coup by mobilizing Amin's opponents among Taraki's and Karmal's supporters.

As in Czechoslovakia in 1968, prior to the invasion, Soviet security officials and diplomats tried to exploit factional struggle to their advantage and to prepare the way for a new pro-Soviet government. In Czechoslovakia, as in Afghanistan, the Soviet strategy was to establish a government which would make an orderly call for Soviet assistance, thereby legitimizing the Soviet invasion. In Czechoslovakia they had tried to rally antireformist elements – mainly those leaders who had objected to Dubcek's reforms and were gradually being dismissed or feared dismissal at the forthcoming party congress. In Afghanistan, under the direction of Puzanov in September and Paputin in December, they tried to rally members of Parcham and some Khalq members (Taraki's supporters) in an effort to overthrow Amin. Karmal was living in Czechoslovakia. He and other exiles in Eastern Europe or underground in Afghanistan were activated already in November–December, if not earlier, while Soviet secret service men, under the direction of General Paputin, apparently made final preparations for the coup. This may explain the shooting in Kabul on 19 December in which an unidentified assailant shot and wounded Hafizullah Amin's nephew Assadullah and slightly wounded the president. Replacement of Amin, which, according to a Soviet source, was supposed to be carried out in the middle of December, was subsequently postponed until 27 December.[37]

Other evidence that the decision to intervene was made in late November is provided by changes in Soviet military deployment along the Afghan and Iranian borders. US intelligence was not surprised by the Afghan invasion, as it was by the invasion of Czechoslovakia. In late November US intelligence detected the mobilization of Soviet troops in Turkmenistan and in other areas along the Afghan borders. Local reserves were being called up. In early December analysts noticed a military buildup on the Afghan borders when some Soviet forces and tactical aircraft were shifted from the Iranian frontier. On 8–9 December airborne units of over 1,000 men, equipped with tanks and artillery, were airlifted to the Bagram airfield, where they were able to reinforce the Soviet units deployed there in September. The mission of this unit became clear during the invasion when it began handling incoming flights and clearing the Russian-built highway between the Soviet border and Kabul. Concurrently, the Soviets airlifted a number of small units into the Kabul municipal airport. Also, in early December a number of high-level consultations occurred, involving the Soviet and other WTO officials along with the commanders of the military districts bordering Iran and Afghanistan. At the same time, several Western embassy attachés in Moscow were denied permission to visit Soviet Central Asia.

MILITARY DOCTRINE AND CAPABILITIES

The invasion of Afghanistan was planned to be a smooth, effective operation based on surprise. This had also been the case in Czechoslovakia. Soviet military doctrine has long emphasized the surprise attack in military operations, aimed at preventing any effective counteraction by the opponent. After Khrushchev's fall, some Soviet generals also began to emphasize the concept of *gibkoe reagirovanie* (flexible response). Those who believed that Soviet military doctrine does not exclude limited, non-nuclear warfare and who at the same time advocated this concept were generals with backgrounds in the Soviet groundforces, such as Generals I. Iakubovskii and S. Shtemenko and commander-in-chief of the groundforces, General Pavlovskii. All three, incidentally, were among the most outspoken advocates of the Soviet invasion of Czechoslovakia.

The Soviets had learned an unforgettable lesson from the German attack on the USSR in 1941 and from other World War II German military operations. The Soviet generals probably also learned a lesson from their experience in Hungary in 1956 – when two armored divisions used in the first military intervention were not sufficient, and the second intervention required the deployment of ten divisions – and perhaps from the US experience with gradual escalation in Vietnam. They knew that a military intervention must be an efficient, rapid and overwhelming action to be successful. It was, in fact, shortly before the invasion of Czechoslovakia that studies began to appear in such Soviet military journals as the authoritative *Voennaia mysl' (Military Thought)* of the Soviet General Staff, which addressed the issue of 'surprise attack' in modern warfare as 'one of the main factors which insures victory in a battle or operation'.[38] This greater emphasis on flexible response and surprise reflected, in part, the growing Soviet military capabilities, particularly air- and sea-lift.

A very illustrative example of a Soviet operation based on flexible response and surprise was the Soviet invasion of Czechoslovakia. Here the Soviet blitzkrieg operation succeeded in capturing the capital of Prague and other vital centers on 20–21 August 1968 while at the same time Soviet groundforce units, along with a few Polish, East German and Hungarian divisions, and a brigade of Bulgarians, were moving from the borders along strategic highways and railroads toward vital centers: the capital, the big cities and important communications centers. The story of Czechoslovakia in 1968 repeated itself in 1979 on a lesser scale, but in an even more daring and bold fashion.

DECEPTION, SURPRISE AND COUP

The actual invasion of Afghanistan was scheduled for 25–26 December, during the Christmas holidays when most Western officials would not be available. As in Czechoslovakia, the plan was to surprise and replace the existing regime in a short time and thereby prevent any strong, organized defense. There were operational deceptions a few days before both invasions. In 1968 the Soviet generals succeeded in lowering fuel and ammunitions stocks of the Czechoslovak army by transferring these to East Germany, supposedly for an 'exercise'. They also secured the consent of the Czechoslovak Ministry of Defense for an unexpected military exercise of the Czechoslovak armed forces, with the participation of Warsaw Treaty observers.

The exercises were to take place on 2 August, the second day of the invasion, a maneuver to divert the attention of the Czechoslovak generals from the forthcoming invasion. In Afghanistan the Soviet advisors disarmed two Afghan armored divisions (one of them garrisoned in Kabul) by convincing their commanders to hand over their ammunition and antitank weapons for inventory and their tank batteries for wintering, while retiring some tanks to repair depots for the correction of a supposed defect.[39] The Afghan leaders, like the leadership in Czechoslovakia, apparently failed to anticipate the invasion. In both cases, the invasion came as a surprise.

As many as 200 flights of An-12s, An-22s and IL-76s landed in Kabul on 24–26 December, deploying 10,000 Soviet airborne troops of the 105th airborne guards division. Two mechanized divisions drove down from the north, advancing toward the capital and other vital centers. In both invasions the Soviets at first did not try to seal the borders with adjacent Western countries, fearing an enlargement of the conflict. Control of the borders was left to a later stage. In several days the Soviets had deployed at least 80,000 combat troops to Afghanistan in a surprising, bold and speedy invasion. (In Czechoslovakia the invading forces were estimated to number 200,000–500,000.) The 1968 invasion was hampered when the logistical system broke down at several points and the invading forces were handicapped for several days by a lack of food, water and fuel, sufficient supplies of which had not been brought in with the troops. By 1979, in contrast, the Soviets displayed more efficiency and even more self-confidence in the operational abilities of their troops.

A political coup d'état accompanied both invasions. Amin, like Dubcek, refused to give his official approval. We do not know if the Soviets asked him to legitimize the invasion or whether Amin was supposed to be only demoted and not killed. Whether, as the Soviets profess, Amin's death was not their doing, but the work of Afghans, or whether it was a 'coincidence' or error is unclear.[40] Thus far it is also not possible to establish whether Babrak Karmal returned secretly to Afghanistan several weeks prior to the coup, as the Soviets say.[41] It is much more likely that he returned with the invading forces in a well-planned and well-executed coup.

In both cases the invasions were legitimized only *ex post facto* and superficially. However, there were some significant differences. In Czechoslovakia the political coup began with the arrest of Dubcek and his faction and ended when the Soviets were unable to establish a new 'revolutionary government of workers and peasants' led by Dubcek's rival, the antireformist Indra. In a short-lived compromise, the Soviets had to let Dubcek and his supporters return to power after their brief abduction. He was forced to resign in April 1969 under the threat of yet a second Soviet invasion. In Afghanistan Soviet actions were more expedient and more brutal due to Amin's decision to resist forcefully Soviet arrest.[42] He reportedly gave instructions to his officers to fight the Russians should they try to take his palace on the outskirts of Kabul. On 27 December a special Soviet assault unit, probably led by General Paputin and perhaps some Afghans, attacked Amin and his supporters who, unlike Dubcek, refused to surrender. Amin died after a few hours of fierce battle. In turn, General Paputin himself mysteriously died during or after the assault amid rumors that he committed suicide in Moscow after the invasion.[43] Whereas in Czechoslovakia the antireformists Indra and Bilak – isolated, fearful and without political support – were hesitant to establish a new revolutionary government, in Afghanistan, where the Soviets appeared to act more boldly and brutally, the transition was much smoother. On 27 December Karmal took over, declaring that the 'healthy forces' in Afghanistan had asked for 'fraternal aid'.

IMPACT AND LESSONS

It is impossible as yet to estimate the long-term impact of the Soviet invasion of Afghanistan. But it seems already to have had a more profound effect than the invasion of Czechoslovakia. The 1968 invasion had its most lasting effects not on East–West relations, but on the communist movement as a whole, contributing to a deepening of the split with China and encouraging the emergence of 'Eurocommunism'. It did not significantly alter the general pattern of the East–West relationship because the West correctly interpreted the 1968 invasion as a purely defensive and reactive move (like the invasion of Hungary in 1956), aimed primarily at preserving political stability in Czechoslovakia, Eastern Europe and the Soviet Union.

The invasion of Afghanistan was a different story. Although it was not an integral part of an offensive to control the Persian Gulf, the Soviets were by no means pulled involuntarily into Afghanistan solely for reasons of defense. While the most significant Soviet motivations for the invasion were related to internal events in Afghanistan, there were also other important concerns of a strategic nature, related particularly to the situation in Iran and to the changing US–Soviet global context. Though less important and less pronounced, another factor in the Soviet decisionmaking on Afghanistan was concern over potential spillover effects from developments in Afghanistan, as well as from Iran, on the Central Asian Muslims. The 1979 invasion was probably seen in Moscow as a defensive move, but unlike the invasion of Czechoslovakia, it had at least some offensive elements with serious implications for the United States. The invasion of Afghanistan challenged the perceptions of American policymakers regarding Soviet intentions. It called into question the Soviet perception of détente and Soviet intentions in the vital areas surrounding the Persian Gulf and the Arabian Sea.

The lesson to be drawn is that Soviet military invasions are responses to what the Soviets believe are dangerous developments and/or attractive opportunities in countries located in geographic proximity to the USSR as well as in strategic areas of the Third World. Yet Soviet military interventions in such situations are not automatic or foreclosed. They occur after a deliberate process of weighing the pros and cons of such actions. As studies of both the Czechoslovak and Afghan invasions (as well as the military interventions in Hungary in 1956, Angola in 1975 and Ethiopia in 1977) illustrate, factional struggles and divisions in the leadership, political instability and calls for assistance by pro-Soviet groups within a country are factors that encourage Soviet leaders to decide in favor of military assistance.

Soviet perceptions of possible US responses are central to calculations of risks involved in the use of military force. The Czechoslovak and Afghan examples, together with many others, suggest that US policymakers should be aware that their sometimes unconscious signals are influences in the Kremlin's deliberations. Heavy US involvement in Vietnam, accompanied by the well-advertised noninvolvement policy regarding Czechoslovakia very likely helped the interventionists prevail in the Soviet debate in 1968. True, US intelligence was not as surprised by the invasion of Afghanistan as it was in 1968, when US intelligence lost track of Soviet combat troops that were conducting maneuvers around the Czechoslovak borders and found them again when their tanks rolled through the streets of Prague, and even then only by way of Czech radio news broadcasts.[44] During the Afghan crisis US intelligence monitored the movement of combat troops before the invasion and the US expressed concern to Moscow in March, in early August, and in early December.[45] Yet US preoccupation with the hostage crisis since early November was so intense that it prohibited any strong response. Vacillation in previous crises in the late 1970s (the Soviet-Cuban use of force in Africa in 1975–6 and in 1977–8, as well as the Soviet combat brigade question in September–October 1979) may have assisted the interventionists in the Soviet debate on Afghanistan. The crucial turning-point during the Afghan crisis was the seizure of the American hostages in early November. US failure to respond promptly with firm measures, including the use of military force, and the subsequent agonizing over the crisis were likely additional factors in the Politburo assessment of the cost and benefits of the invasion.

There is little, however, that the United States can do to directly influence any particular Soviet decision on the use of force. The outcome of the Soviet decisionmaking process is mainly determined by events beyond the control of US policymakers. Yet if any lesson can be drawn from the Czechoslovak and Afghan military interventions, it is that US policymakers should try to avoid the well-advertised noninvolvement of 1968 or any tendency to vacillate as happened before the Afghan invasion. Indecision, weakness and division of opinion are signs readily interpreted and skillfully exploited by the Soviets. The contradictory signals and policies, improvization and lack of coordination coming from Washington in 1976–9 were harmful to US interests. Confrontation should be sought only in extreme cases and when American leaders are prepared, as during the Cuban missile crisis in 1962, to back words with deeds. Both invasions suggest that it is better to say as little as possible, and to even let the Soviet leadership guess about possible US responses, than to be inconsistent. Incoherent policies leave the Soviets with the impression that the United States is neither a formidable rival, nor a reliable partner. Whether or not the USSR under the leadership of Brezhnev's successors will repeat an Afghanistan-like invasion elsewhere will depend, at least to some degree, on the determination of US decisionmakers, drawing appropriate lessons from past cases of Soviet interventions, to discourage and, if necessary, obstruct the influences that favor such undertakings.

NOTES: CHAPTER 9

1 Jiri Valenta, *Soviet Intervention in Czechoslovakia, 1968: Anatomy of a Decision* (Baltimore, Md: Johns Hopkins University Press, 1979), pp. 134–9. Also Jiri Valenta, 'From Prague to Kabul: the Soviet style of invasion', *International Security*, Vol. 5, no. 2 (Fall 1980), pp. 114–41.

2 One Soviet observer even suggested that Amin would follow the same path as Egyptian President Sadat. V. Sidenko, 'Undeclared war on Afghanistan', *Pravda* (Moscow), 5 February 1980. Also see V. Sidenko, 'Two years of the Afghan revolution', *New York Times*, 25 April 1980, pp. 18–25, and a letter of the Director of Oriental Studies Ye. Primakov and *Izvestiia*'s political observer A. Bovin, *L'Unita*, 25 April 1980, and interviews with Soviet analysts.

3 'Amin reportedly appealed to Zia', *Washington Post*, 14 February 1980, and interviews with former Afghan officials.

4 Primakov and Bowin, *L'Unita*, 25 April 1980, op. cit.

5 James Critchlow, 'Minarets and Marx', *Washington Quarterly*, Vol. 3, no. 2 (Spring 1980), pp. 47–57. In my discussion of the Central Asian Muslim factor I benefited from consultations with Critchlow. I also consulted essays by S. Enders Wimbush, Alexander Bennigsen and Steven L. Burg in *Survey*, Vol. 24, no. 3 (Summer 1979), pp. 36–82; Alfred J. DiMaio, 'The Soviet Union and population: theory, problems and population policy', *Comparative Political Studies*, Vol. 13, no. 1 (April 1980), pp. 97–136; and Helen Carrere d'Encausse, *Decline of the Soviet Empire: Soviet Republics in Revolt* (New York: Newsweek, 1979). I also benefited from my discussion of this issue with Alexander Dallin, whose view that there is not solid evidence about the ferment in Soviet Central Asia as a contributing factor in the decision by Afghanistan I fully share.

6 Mirmuhsin (Mirsaidov), 'Chodrali ayal (Woman with Veil)', *Sharq yulduz*, no. 10 (1979), p. 67. Here I am indebted to Critchlow, ibid., pp. 54–7.

7 See the analysis of a leading Soviet demographer V. Perevedentsev, *Literaturnaia gazeta*, 3 October 1979, and the analysis 'Training cadres from the local population in the Central Asian republics', *Voprosy ekonomiki* (May 1979). For preliminary results of the population census, see *Pravda*, 22 April 1979.

8 See my discussions, 'Soviet invasion of Afghanistan: the difficulty of knowing where to stop', *Orbis* (Summer 1980), and *Baltimore Sun*, 19–22 February 1980.

9 See an interesting debate between Richard Pipes and George Kennan in 'How real is the Soviet threat?', *US News and World Report*, 10 March 1980, p. 33.

10 For this point, see an interview with Primakov, *Literaturnaia gazeta*, 13 March 1980.

11 Ye. Shaskov, 'Milestone in the struggle for peace', *Sovetskaia Rossiia*, 4 January 1980.

12 An interview with V. Falin, first deputy chief of the International Information Department, and V. Zagladin, first deputy chief of the International Department of the Central Committee of the CPSU, *Stern*, 31 January 1980.

13 ibid.; see also a speech of a secretary of the Central Committee of the CPSU, V. Dolgikh, *Akahata* (Tokyo), 1 March 1980.

14 Brezhnev's statement, *New York Times*, 3 January 1980.

15 See V. Kusin's essay review of my book, 'How Moscow decides to invade', *Inquiry*, 5 May 1980, pp. 25–6.

16 An interview with Falin by H. Branden, 'How decisions are made in the highest Soviet circles', *Washington Star*, 15 July 1979.

17 There was a meeting of the Central Committee of the CPSU on 27 November 1979 at which some of the spokesmen who delivered talks were from Central Asia and Transcaucasia – first secretary of the Uzbekistan Communist Party S. Rashidov and first secretary of the Azerbaidjan Communist Party G. Aliyev. According to a Soviet source the meeting was devoted exclusively to economic problems and, indeed, there is no evidence it was otherwise: Moscow Radio, 27 November 1979.

18 According to reliable sources, Epishev reportedly made the first interventionist appeal in April 1968, when he suggested that if the 'healthy forces' in Czechoslovakia (pro-Soviet elements in the Soviet lexicon) called for 'fraternal assistance' against 'counterrevolution', the Soviet Army would do its duty: see Valenta, *Soviet Intervention in Czechoslovakia*, op. cit., p. 22.

19 *Komsomol' skaia pravda* (Moscow), 23 November 1979.

20 A. A. Epishev, 'Loyalty to Lenin's banner', *Krasnaia zvezda*, 22 February 1980.
21 See the explanation of a high Soviet official, 'Wegen Afghanistan gibt es keinen Krieg', *Der Spiegel*, 28 January 1980, pp. 88–9.
22 Col. General Yu. Maksimov, 'Mighty guard of socialist achievements', *Pravda vostoka* (Tashkent), 21 February 1980. For similar views, see Lt General V. Rodin, chief of the Political Directorate of Turkestan military district, 'Guarding socialist achievements', *Turkmenskaia iskra* (Ashkhabad), 23 February 1980; and Lt General V. Gorchakov, first deputy commander of the Central Asian military district, 'Always with the people', *Sovitskaia Kirgiziia* (Frunze), 23 February 1980. Although most of the speeches by politicians on the invasion were also tough, they lacked the emphasis given by some military leaders to such ideas as 'noble mission', 'just wars' and 'stabilization of the situation'. See, for example, the speech of the head of the International Department and a secretary of the Central Committee of the CPSU, B. Ponomarev, *Pravda*, 5 February 1980. A main thrust of his speech seemed to be to convince the United States that the invasion of Afghanistan 'in absolutely no way affects US state interests'.
23 For a detailed treatment, see Valenta, *Soviet Intervention in Czechoslovakia*, op. cit., pp. 123–8.
24 Radio Madrid, 10 January 1980. Puzanov's role was also discussed on Radio Beijing, 7 November 1979. Here I also benefited from interviews with former officials of the Afghan government.
25 An interview with Soviet historian R. Medvedev, *Corriere della Sera*, 4 February 1980.
26 Valenta, *Soviet Intervention in Czechoslovakia*, op. cit., p. 144; emphasis added.
27 An interview with Polianskii, *Asahi Shinbun* (Tokyo), 8 March 1980.
28 An interview with Falin, in *Stern*, op. cit.
29 *New York Times*, 13 January 1980.
30 V. B. Lukin, 'Washington-Beijing: quasi-allies?', *Ekonomika, politika, ideologiia*, 12 November 1979, pp. 50–5.
31 *Krasnaia zvezda*, 2 December 1979; and *Pravda*, 5 December 1979.
32 *New York Times*, 3 January 1980.
33 *Al Watan, Al-Arabi* (Paris) in Near East–North Africa Report, 11 June 1980, and interviews with Afghan refugees.
34 *Pravda*, 10 December 1979.
35 L. Mironov's reports in *Pravda*, 11 and 13 December 1979. In contrast, other Soviet reports were favorably quoting Amin at that time; see, for example, *Turkmenskaia iskra*, 9 December 1979, but also *Pravda*, 8 December 1979.
36 *Toronto Globe and Mail*, 13 December 1979.
37 P. Demchenko, 'Afghanistan: guarding the people's gains', *Kommunist*, 5 November, and 5 March 1980, pp. 71–8.
38 Major General N. Vasendin and Colonel N. Kuznetsov, 'Modern warfare and surprise attack', *Voennaia mysl'*, 6 November 1968, pp. 42–8.
39 *The Times* (London), 9 January 1980; and *Newsweek*, 21 January 1980, p. 115.
40 V. Sidenko, 'Two years of the Afghan revolution', op. cit., p. 23; and *Christian Science Monitor*, 31 March 1980.
41 V. Sidenko, ibid., pp. 22–3.
42 An interview with a commander of the 5th tank brigade of the Afghan army, Lt Colonel Alawoddin, Radio Moscow, 16 January 1980, and interviews with Afghan refugees.
43 The only certain knowledge is that Paputin is dead, since there was an obituary marking his death in *Pravda*, 3 January 1980.
44 Valenta, *Soviet Intervention in Czechoslovakia*, op. cit., pp. 2–3.
45 *Washington Star*, 13 December 1979.

10 Risk Aversion in Soviet Decisionmaking

DENNIS ROSS

In the past several years increasing Soviet military power has worried many in the West that traditional Soviet caution was bound to wane and their risktaking propensities certain to grow. The Soviet invasion of Afghanistan – a country outside the 'socialist commonwealth' – has tended to heighten and (for some) validate these concerns. While the Soviet invasion of Afghanistan and its relationship to the Soviet willingness to run risks should concern us, we should be careful not to draw open-ended conclusions about changing Soviet risktaking propensities too quickly. Indeed, though we might draw these conclusions anyway, one would have more confidence in them if they reflected more systematic analysis and more of a feel for Soviet history and the Soviet system.[1]

With this in mind, I propose in this chapter to look at a number of specifically Soviet factors that affect the willingness of the Soviet leadership to run risks. Here I refer to the character of the Soviet decisionmaking process and the sociology or general attitudes of Soviet leaders. As we will see, both the character of the decisionmaking system and the sociology of at least the current leaders are likely to produce a high degree of caution in Soviet leaders – and, given leadership perceptions of certain lessons of the past, also a strong sensitivity to the high costs of failure. Neither the built in caution nor, more importantly, the fear of failure rule out decisive action internally or externally. Indeed, the Soviets have proven their ability to act decisively – especially in the direct use of their military forces – on several occasions. What is noteworthy, however, is that in each case – Hungary, 1956; Czechoslovakia, 1968; and Afghanistan, December 1979 – Soviet action (that is, invasions) seem to have been driven by the perceived high costs of inaction; that is, the consequences of not acting were seen by the Soviet elite as quite severe, and thus, amounted to what would have been a failure. In a sense, therefore, decisive Soviet action may result more from the need to pre-empt or avert failure than the desire to create big successes.*

If this is so, the main implication for us is to keep the costs of Soviet action high; in the concluding section of the chapter I will briefly discuss what this might mean. I will also take note of two factors – the broadening of Soviet international interests and the upcoming generational changes of the leadership – which could significantly reshape or alter future Soviet behavior. At

---

* This would be consistent with a principle of human behavior that some psychologists believe exists; that being, that individuals are risk-averse when the problem is seen as one of possibly making gains, but are 'risk-acceptant' when the problem is seen as one of avoiding losses.[2]

this point, let us turn to a discussion of a number of related factors that have come to characterize the system and influence the risktaking impulses of the Soviet leadership.

THE EMERGENCE OF COALITION MAINTENANCE AND ITS IMPACT ON THE SYSTEM AND ITS LEADERS

The Soviet Union has evolved over time from a system where one interest (namely, Stalin's) largely governed behavior, to a system where the country's major interests (as embodied in the central institutional actors) meet at the apex of the regime, and have their interests mediated and minimally satisfied.[3] That totalitarian dictatorship would gradually give way to a pluralism of elites and related oligarchal rule flowed logically from the elite decision to abandon terror and to forsake revolutionary change engineered from above. In deciding to dismantle Stalin's terror apparatus and, somewhat later, agreeing that they should, in Richard Lowenthal's words, administer the results of the revolution rather than carry one out,[4] the Soviet leadership responded to the abiding desire for personal and bureaucratic security of the vast majority of elite members. In so recognizing and responding to the elite's deep yearning to secure their individual and institutional position the post-Stalin, and much more directly the post-Khrushchev, leadership ensured that the institutional pillars of the regime (which had been little more than the instrumentalities of Stalin's rule*) – would increasingly be able to press as well as defend their interests.

In a real sense the advent of oligarchy, its durability in the face of Khrushchev's onslaughts, and its consolidation in the current period, have over time made the Soviet decisionmaking process one that is characterized by a kind of political incrementalism. By this I refer to the emergence of a decisionmaking process that has increasingly come to be based on elite consensus and mutual adjustment and, as a result, is characterized by very limited – indeed marginal – change in policies.[5]

Why should the emergence of oligarchal rule have had this effect on the Soviet Union? Perhaps the main reason is to be found in the key ideological myth of the system which denies the possibility of conflict among an infallible, monolithic party and, therefore, has provided no fully authoritative provisions for resolving conflict. That created no special problems so long as Stalin's personal dictatorship prevailed, but with the advent of oligarchy and the emergence of competing power centers conflict was likely and needed to be contained. Indeed, while it should be noted that a struggle for power among a very narrow circle of leaders was inevitable in a system that provided no institutional means for the transfer of power, the fact that different leaders have come to represent competing interests, and not just themselves,† has increased the potential for conflict and made it especially

* The party apparat, state-administrative organs, economic-industrial managers, military establishment and security organs.

† Lacking constitutional or more traditional grounding for their positions, Soviet leaders derive much of their personal security from their institutional bases of support. Not surprisingly, therefore, their interests are often defined in terms of the well-being of their institutions.

dangerous, thereby necessitating the creation and acceptance of certain unwritten norms that control and limit the conflict or change that can occur.

More than anything else, it is the emergence of these uncodified norms as a means to control conflict that reflects (and indeed probably requires) the operation of what might be termed coalition maintenance in the Soviet setting.[6] Here one sees that there seems to be a very strong correlation – at least theoretically – between the components of coalition maintenance and the characteristics of the current Soviet political environment. For example, the factor considered most crucial to the survival or maintenance of coalitions is the actors' fear of the alternative – that is, the fear that the breakup of the coalition may trigger potentially devastating results provides the members with perhaps their strongest incentive to maintain the coalition.[7] In the Soviet Union the 'fear of the alternative' factor seems especially relevant; after all, if, as we have noted, the key legitimizing myth of the system rules out elite conflict, then the breakup of the leadership coalition and elite equilibrium must undermine the legitimacy of the leadership's claim to power, erode (at least psychologically) the individual security of elite members, and perhaps even threaten to convulse the whole system. Hence, the risk associated with a disruption or breakup of the leadership coalition is high and Soviet leaders seek to avert or minimize it.*

However, merely having a strong incentive to avert coalition disruption may not be enough to preserve a coalition intact. Here coalition maintenance theorists have noted that while a fear of the alternative makes actors very willing to compromise, it does not necessarily reduce basic conflicts of interest or propensities for dissatisfaction that can still destroy a coalition over time.[8] Consequently, in addition to the fear of the alternative, certain mechanisms that reduce internal conflict and increase the coalition's capacity to handle the remaining conflict must exist if a coalition is to endure – and once again we see a natural fit with the more current operation of the Soviet political system.

Note, for example, that three mechanisms have been identified as critical for minimizing and controlling coalition conflict: (1) the operation of a unanamity rule in decisionmaking (all members must give their consent or agree before a decision on any significant question is made); (2) the existence of a real power broker (an actor that is able to offer incentives or impose sanctions sufficient to induce the other members to compromise – so

---

* Even during the Khrushchev period when the politics of oligarchy, consensus and collective decisionmaking were a good deal less entrenched than they have become, the importance of simply *maintaining appearances* and minimizing leadership turnover were clearly believed to be important. For example, despite their support of the antiparty group, in June 1957, Bulganin, Voroshilov, Pervukhin and Saburov were not identified as being members or supporters of the group until much later and Bulganin and Voroshilov retained their membership in the Presidium, while Pervukhin was only demoted to candidate member status. Similarly, when Malenkov was demoted in February 1955, he did not lose his Presidium membership. In both instances Khrushchev could not have liked the fact that obvious opponents of his retained their membership in the leading decisionmaking body. The importance of maintaining an air of normality, minimizing the appearance of elite turmoil and turnover, and limiting Khrushchev's power (and therein ability to shake up the leadership on his own), all favored retention of Khrushchev's opponents in the Presidium – and, in a sense, reflected the operation of coalition maintenance in these cases.

necessary for achieving consent); and (3) the partial exclusion of issues (the avoidance of decisions on issues that are so inherently polarizing as to make compromise very difficult).[9] Each has its Soviet analogue in both abstract and more concrete and current political terms.

In the first place, as indicated above, ideological demands and legitimacy requirements have always dictated a general rule of unanimity in the conduct of Soviet political decisionmaking. Secondly, what tends to give the unananimity rule substance as well as form is the existence of the Soviet power broker – the Secretary-General. His power of patronage, ability to monitor and intervene in the work and activities of other institutions, capacity to play off the differences of other institutional and party leaders – together with a career pattern that socializes him to assume such a brokering role – facilitates and enhances both the adherence to and operation of the unanimity or consensus rule in the Soviet political context. Finally, a mechanism for partial exclusion of divisive issues has emerged. For example, in especially the post-Khrushchev period, discussion of contentious issues has increasingly been delayed and their content defused by the Politburo's deliberate use of *ad hoc* committees.[10] Brezhnev, himself, in an interview with foreign journalists referred to the use of small subgroups or committees of Politburo members to resolve disputed issues so as to facilitate consensus rule in the Politburo.[11]

A point to note here is that the use of 'exclusion', 'unanimity' and the 'power-broker' mechanisms to ensure leadership stability and continuity (that is, coalition maintenance) has been most pronounced in the Brezhnev period. In part this is a function of the further hardening of oligarchal rule during this period. In part also it resulted from Brezhnev's personal style and commitment to rule by consensus. But in noting the latter, one should not forget that (as the Soviets might say) Brezhnev's commitment to consensus rule was probably no accident; by this I mean the lessons of Khrushchev's demise most certainly were not lost on Brezhnev and as a result he was careful not to violate the norms or trappings of collective decisionmaking. In behaving in this manner Brezhnev was able to keep his colleagues happy and also to ensure that any mistakes or failures were collective ones and could not be pinned easily on him. Having once begun a consensual or collective process of decisionmaking, however, it may prove difficult for Brezhnev's successors to reverse or alter it.

What emerges from the preceding discussion is basically this: as oligarchal rule developed in the Soviet Union, the Soviet decisionmaking process took on characteristics associated with that of coalition maintenance. Necessarily, as the form and methods of coalition maintenance have come more and more to describe high politics in the Soviet system, the Soviet decisionmaking process has taken on a rule by committee or lowest-common-denominator character. Under these circumstances the major interests in the system are taken into account and at least minimally satisfied before policy choices or decisions are made. As a result, precipitous decisions and major or fundamental policy changes are eschewed and only more calculated and painstaking decisions and limited policy changes are tolerated. In effect, the need to accommodate all the strategic elites ensure that a kind of 'muddling-through' approach to policy obtains.

In saying this I do not mean to suggest that all the interests represented at the apex of the system are equal or that there is a wide gulf that separates them. On the contrary, one set of interests that favors the continued militarization of the system (most clearly embodied in some parts of the party apparat-military-defense-heavy industries) clearly has enjoyed a predominant position in the system and is 'more equal' than others; moreover, even if some may favor a limited or even marginal shift in allocation priorities, all in the leadership share an ethos that emphasizes security above all else, that fears any demonstration of weakness or disunity, that highlights ongoing struggle and competition with the United States and that offers a common view of Soviet destiny and purpose. Where there is a difference, it is perhaps best described conceptually as one between those who tend to favor the building of communism internally to make it an attractive model for export and those who see the expansion of Soviet power as the best basis on which communism can be spread and built internationally – each obviously has differing implications for resource allocation, economic development, relaxation of external tensions, and so on.

In reality, the distinction is neither that sharp nor likely to fall so neatly into two broad groupings. Rather, elements of both attitudes are probably found in different proportions throughout the strategic elites who make up the central leadership; the relative mix of these attitudes is likely to vary depending upon the international environment (perceived threats and opportunities), the urgency of domestic or internal problems (for example, in agriculture, energy, and so on), and the differing parochial concerns related to the institutional well-being and perceived needs of the leading bureaucratic actors (that is, their relative standing, the continued pursuit of favored programs, and so on).

It is against this backdrop that the mediation of competing concerns and the minimal satisfaction of the leading actors and their interests take place.* Hence, though we should be mindful that the differing interests are neither equal in weight nor all that diverse, they do exist, they are implicitly recognized and the process of minimally satisfying them guarantees a muddling-through style of decisionmaking.

In relating this decisionmaking style and process to our theme of Soviet risktaking, two points seem worthy of note. First, a muddling-through style – that depends on consensus being achieved before decisions are made – must have a leavening effect on behavior. At the very least, rash decisions are unlikely. More than this, however, a willingness (and perhaps a need) to muddle through reflects a basic cautiousness in style and approach, and this

---

* Here it should be noted that while the masses are not one of these actors or directly represented in the regime, their interests, none the less, may be one of those that must be minimally satisfied; that is, to the extent that ideological dynamism has declined, it has been replaced by a new legitimating requirement – namely, the need to satisfy popular welfare desires. Because the masses have become accustomed to the gradual increase in the availability of consumer goods, improvements in housing and diet, and general income increments accompanied by stable prices, and because the central leadership has demonstrated some concern about not frustrating mass expectations, it may well be that the regime considers it essential to satisfy at least minimally the expectations of the masses. In this sense the masses may represent one of the competing, if unequal, interests in the regime.

really raises the second and more important point; that is, a system like the Soviet system that emphasizes the need to assuage at least minimally all elite interests and a system that more and more demonstrates an aversion to assaulting any vested interests in society, is a political system that appears determined to avoid running risks. A legitimate question to pose, therefore, is whether such a political system, which seems increasingly structured to avoid risks internally, is prepared to run them externally.

Here the answer should probably be a qualified yes; by this I mean that the clear and abiding commitment that Soviet leaders have to preserving their own security – and *the political order that guarantees it* – suggests that they would be quite prepared to run significant external risks if their internal position depended on it. Barring this, however, their inclination to run risks would seem low – especially since the structure of the system, its need for unanimity and its incremental approach to policy, place such a premium on caution and risk avoidance. This is really the critical point of this part of our discussion – that being, that the character and dynamics of the Soviet decisionmaking process, as it has evolved, dictate a kind of general caution and relatively low risktaking propensity.

Another factor, or perhaps a subset of the above factor, that contributes to the muddling through/cautious character of the Soviet political process is something that might be termed the sociology of Soviet leaders. In this connection Soviet leaders are socialized from an early point in their careers about the need to avoid failure on issues that have high political currency. Failing to meet certain norms can be very costly to one's career, given the prevailing political ethos. Note, for example, that at the local level 'stealing' from available resources committed to light industries to meet heavy industrial goals – a time-honored practice for regional party secretaries – may result precisely because local officials understand that they can not afford to *fail* in this area.

In addition, because Soviet leaders tend to value the maintenance of their personal positions above all else, they are very sensitive to anything that can jeopardize their standing or position; as a result, because the surest, safest, and most legitimate way to challenge a leader is to be able to pin a failure on him, one would expect that Soviet leaders at the Politburo level are especially aware of the very high costs of failure.

In this regard it is quite possible that Soviet leaders have come to believe that the potential costs of failure outweigh the possible benefits of success – something that would result from their view that while success can bolster their authority and position, failure can erode and kill it. For leaders who are totally politicized, who have no alternatives outside the party/the state, and who understand that losing their position may make them into nonpeople with no status or stature, pursuing objectives that risk failure may simply be considered too costly, even if these objectives also hold the promise of success. If true, this suggests that Soviet leaders will avoid taking high risks, will be reluctant to launch bold initiatives and will be content to muddle along.

In a survey I have done of the elite struggles during the 1953–64 period the high costs of failure come through very clearly. Indeed, whether the result of an inability to preclude or a bold initiative that creates new dangers or embarrassments or simply reflects incompetence, one can see that 'failures' provided the key basis on which dominant leaders in the party Presidium were challenged and/or put on the defensive during this period. Going through and discussing a number of these cases of leadership challenges is useful at this point not only to illustrate the 'high cost' of failure, but also – and this is especially important – because of what it is likely to tell us about current leadership attitudes. Here it should be remembered that the current leadership assumed their *high-level* party and government positions at this time, were very much a part of the leadership struggles, and most significantly, have drawn their own approach to leadership and decisionmaking style from the lessons of this period.

SURVEYING LEADERSHIP CHALLENGES, 1953–64

In surveying a number of the leadership challenges in this period there is no need in this chapter either to be exhaustive in our treatment of each case, or in the number of the cases we cover. Rather, it is sufficient for our purposes to select and summarize briefly a limited number of cases that highlight how a failure eroded the authority of a dominant (or potentially dominant) leader in the Presidium and/or made a challenge likely.

Starting with the Beria ouster, it is worth noting that the riots in East Berlin in June 1953 provided the pretext and the trigger for a move against Beria. What is interesting to note here is that Beria's attempt to use the nationalities issue to purge others and to build a base of support outside the police organs had been in evidence for several months and clearly presaged a bid for power by him. Notwithstanding this, and the fact that everyone feared Beria, it apparently took the riots in East Europe, especially in East Germany – an area for which Beria was clearly responsible* – to congeal the leadership and make it think his ouster was possible.

On a less grand scale Khrushchev was able to make his initial move against Malenkov in September 1953 by casting doubts on Malenkov's competence in the agricultural area. Contrasting the true state of affairs with Malenkov's claims in 1952 (at the 19th Party Congress) and in August 1953 (to the Supreme Soviet) that the country's grain problems had been solved, Khrushchev was able to erode Malenkov's standing and build his own.

Subsequent to this in December 1954 Khrushchev was able to use the Leningrad affair to actually demote Malenkov. Here, Malenkov's responsibility for the 1948 Leningrad affair – the purging of Zhdanov, Voznesensky, and the others – was considered heinous enough even six years later to help force his resignation as Prime Minister.

Khrushchev, however, was to commit his own blunders which put him very much on the defensive and nearly led to his removal as first secretary in 1957. While he was fortunate that the Virgin Lands program was a relative

---

* Beria, as part of an overall policy of relaxation internally and externally favored reducing controls in Eastern Europe and was slow to react to the initial riots. He could thus be blamed for what had happened and charged with presiding over policies that posed great dangers for the Soviet Union.

success in its first few years (or else Molotov and Kaganovich might well have been able to zero-in on him on this issue), Khrushchev's leading position on de-Stalinization and the linkage between de-Stalinization and the subsequent turmoil in Eastern Europe in the fall of 1956 clearly was a major blow to Khrushchev. Not only was he put on the defensive on all the major issues he was identified with and forced to retreat, but his major rivals made remarkable comebacks. In particular, Molotov who had been humiliated in private at the July 1955 plenum and in public with his September 1955 recantation of an ideological error, not only accompanied Khrushchev to Poland during the crisis but also became Minister of State Control. Even more impressively, Malenkov, who had been forced to resign as prime minister with a public admission of what amounted to incompetency and had been relegated to political backwaters also made a strong comeback. He and Khrushchev, alone, journeyed secretly to meet with Yugoslav leaders during the height of the Hungarian crisis – testimony to this new-found importance as well as to the importance the Soviets attached to portraying the unity of the leadership.[12]

While it is true that Khrushchev survived the subsequent challenge to his leadership, it is clear that his authority had been eroded to the point where his challengers thought they could be successful. In the end what saved Khrushchev was his ability to maintain the full backing of his institutional base (something that was facilitated by the party vs state nature of this conflict) and his success in cultivating the military's support.

Khrushchev's ultimate fall in 1964 came in no small part because of his responsibility for two major and humiliating failures. The first was the Cuban missile crisis and the second was the horrendous 1963 harvest and the decision to buy wheat from the United States and Canada.

In the Cuban case Khrushchev's 'risky' adventuristic behavior in putting the missiles into Cuba led to a nuclear confrontation. While Khrushchev saw the potential to achieve a great success – and thereby significantly build his domestic and international stature – he miscalculated the US response, was forced to retreat and as a result he and the Soviet Union suffered a humiliating loss. It was difficult to put any sort of positive face on what was an unmistakable defeat for the Soviet Union and one that was witnessed by the whole world. Although the Soviet Union seemed to have little alternative but to yield (though the military and other elements of the leadership apparently favored driving a harder bargain),[13] the consequences of retreating were severe – especially to a leadership ever-driven by the twin needs of cultivating an image of growing strength and equality with its rival and avoiding the appearance or manifestation of weakness. Khrushchev's authority was never the same after Cuba. Here again he retreated on every major issue (de-Stalinization, emphasizing investment in chemicals rather than metals, and so on) he had vigorously supported; of even greater significance, he even referred to his own possible retirement – something that is rarely exercised voluntarily by Presidium members. Only Kozlov's heart attack seems to have saved Khrushchev from being ousted in the spring of 1963.

Though Kozlov's illness stemmed the tide against Khrushchev and he was able to recoup his position in part, he was again put on the defensive as a result of the disastrous 1963 harvest. Since Khrushchev prided himself on his agricultural expertise and since his decision to cultivate lands that normally lay fallow was blamed by many in the elite for the disaster,[14] he was bound to have this failure pinned on him. What compounded this failing was the decision to buy wheat from the USA to cope with the grain shortfall. Having to admit what at this time seemed to be a kind of dependence on the USA and the outside world to feed itself was a further humiliation that was very difficult for the leading socialist state to make and it was clearly opposed by some in the leadership.[15] While the decision to buy the grain wasn't Khrushchev's alone, he no doubt was blamed for putting the Soviet Union in this position.

The harvest failure and grain purchase didn't directly lead to the Khrushchev ouster, but like the other failures we have noted it put the blamed leader on the defensive, forced him to retreat on key issues, made him appear vulnerable (and therefore assailable), and made the subsequent challenge possible and thinkable.

If nothing else, the experience of these leadership challenges must have given the members of the current leadership a very powerful stake in not putting themselves in a position where a mistake, blunder, or obvious failure can be pinned on them – the potential costs are simply too high. This, alone, could give them an incentive in emphasizing collective decisionmaking and therefore collective responsibility. Similarly, as suggested above, it must also make them prone toward caution and not eager to pursue paths that carry high risks and potential failure. (Indeed, as Khrushchev demonstrated, bold initiatives often produce embarrassing and costly failures.)

This does not mean that Soviet leaders cannot take advantage of opportunities or be decisive in especially foreign and defense policy. Indeed, the Soviets will be quick to exploit opportunities that appear to involve *low risks or costs* – especially because they have also been habituated to take advantage of opportunities.* In effect, not seizing opportunities that involve low risk may itself constitute a kind of failure for which a Soviet leader could be held accountable.

Moreover, in a related way the Soviets can act decisively; that is, they can be very decisive if they face a severe problem. Put another way, to pre-empt a potential failure – and its high costs – the Soviet leaders are quite likely to act decisively. They have, after all, a tradition of 'storming' their problems when they become acute. More importantly, they have demonstrated their ability to be decisive in the national security area with three overt military invasions in the post-Stalin era.

The point to reemphasize here is that the Soviets – given leadership perceptions of the high costs of failure – are most likely to take action when

* What should be noted here is that the Soviets believe they must continually further the historical process, taking advantage or creating opportunities where they can so long as the risks are low. This means that in the Third World – the real target of opportunity – the Soviets will use indirect means to foster their goals of spreading their influence and presence and undermining ours. These will include military aid (advisors, arms, logistic support), covert action, proxies, and so on, to support 'liberation struggles' and local actors involved in civil or regional conflicts. In using these indirect means in places like Angola and Ethiopia the Soviets are able to advance their goals, without running serious risks.

they see that the consequences of inaction are severe – indeed when not acting creates a failure. At the same time the coalition maintenance style of decisionmaking (that is, the consensual constraints) suggests that any such action is likely to follow a period of some hesitancy.

It is within this general context that one can perhaps best understand the Hungarian, Czechoslovak and Afghan invasions.* As demonstrated by Valenta's studies of two later invasions,[16] not only does one see some hesitancy prior to each invasion, but more importantly, Soviet action seems to result from a Soviet sense that the cost of inaction is too high.

In Hungary and Czechoslovakia the Soviet hold over Eastern Europe was in question. The Hungarian leadership, after fits and starts, had declared its intention to drop out of the Warsaw Pact, become neutral, and inaugurate a multiparty system. Aside from forging a critical breach in the Soviet Western defense, the Hungarian moves – especially in light of the announced US policy of rollback – promised to set a very dangerous precedent that the rest of Eastern Europe would follow unless they were decisively checked. Similarly, in 1968, the Czech Spring posed a more subtle but unmistakable threat to party rule that potentially could spread and infect not only the rest of Eastern Europe, but also the Soviet Union as well.

In both cases a fundamental threat to a basic and legitimizing Soviet achievement – that is, the creation and security of the socialist commonwealth – was involved and if unanswered posed a major catastrophe for the Soviet Union and its leadership. Herein it should be noted that the Soviets will do whatever it takes and will be prepared to run very high risks in responding to threats to the Soviet Union or its fundamental achievements. This very sentiment may well trigger Soviet intervention in Poland today – even though the Soviets know the costs in terms of Polish resistance and Western reaction are likely to be high. Significantly the Polish case may highlight what appears to be conflicting Soviet impulses – basic cautiousness (reflected in Soviet hesitancy in going into Poland) and decisiveness (reflected in what may be the eventual willingness to intervene with massive military force). The point is that when the stakes – as they define them – are high the Soviets will act very decisively as they have in Hungary and Czechoslovakia and as they may yet in Poland. In reality, however, it should not be forgotten that though Soviet stakes were very high in Hungary and Czechoslovakia, their risks were not necessarily great – what with local Soviet military superiority, the West preoccupied with the Suez crisis in 1956, the USA tied down in Vietnam in 1968 (and seemingly having recognized the Soviet sphere twelve years earlier),† and so on.

---

* Hungary has been included here – though it occurred during the Khrushchev period – because Soviet decisionmaking following the Polish riots in the summer of 1956 took on a collective decisionmaking flavor – note the 'delegations' of Soviet officials who visited Poland and Hungary during the crisis.

† In both cases we also sent immediate signals that we would not intervene. This is not to say that the Soviets believed that these were cost-free ventures. There must have been some uncertainty about our reaction and clearly the Soviet 'peace-loving' and progressive image – something that is important to the Soviets for internal reasons and for attracting Third World states to the socialist bloc – was bound to suffer. However, these were obviously seen as acceptable costs given the stakes involved.

In cases where Soviet stakes are lower they may still act decisively and accept certain risks if the costs of inaction are deemed to be high. Afghanistan is a good case in point. In Soviet eyes, if they did not act, a pro-Soviet, Marxist regime along its border would be toppled and replaced not by neutralist elements, but rather by Islamic fundamentalist forces that were positively hostile to the Soviet Union. Aside from seeing any hostile presence along their border as threatening (partly because it might be the launching-point for attacks or intrigues and partly because it could be used to contain Soviet movement and influence), the Soviets were probably concerned about the impact that another radical-proselytizing Islamic regime along its border might have – and the conclusions their own Muslims, more independently minded East Europeans, and their clients and their foes in the Third World might draw about the Soviet willingness to allow this to happen. Indeed, allowing what would clearly be a defeat and reversal of the revolutionary process to occur in their own backyard, at a time when the correlation of forces looked increasingly favorable and the costs of the Soviet action looked relatively low,* was something no Soviet leadership could do without being charged with a serious lack of will and the responsibility for a significant failure.

If, as these cases show, the Soviets will intervene directly with their own military forces – but will essentially do so only to avert the consequences of inaction or perceived failures – then the conclusions we draw about Soviet risktaking should not be particularly alarmist. In this regard it might be said that the character of the Soviet system and the sociology of the Soviet leaders will continue to render a general caution that is unlikely to change in the near future, and that permits the use of decisive and perhaps risky action far more readily for *defending* as opposed to *extending* Soviet gains.

Before deriving too much comfort from this general conclusion, however, several points need to be mentioned. To begin with, Soviet perception of what constitutes a risk may have changed over the last decade. The buildup of Soviet military power; Soviet perceptions of US 'paralysis'; divisions between the USA and its allies and the Soviet ability to play on and exploit these divisions; as well as the number of successful interventions that the Soviets have engineered in Angola, Ethiopia and perhaps also the People's Democratic Republic of Yemen, may have changed the Soviet calculus of what constitutes a risk. Though Soviet problems in Afghanistan and the new signs of US assertiveness could reverse the trends in this regard, the political-military changes and precedents of the past decade may have succeeded in altering the baseline of Soviet risk assessment.

Beyond this, there are two other factors that could affect Soviet risktaking behavior in the future, regardless of whether the Soviets have come to define

---

* After all, international attention was riveted on the US-Iranian embroglio; the USA was preoccupied with the hostage situation and was unlikely to respond militarily (directly or indirectly) in any event; Iran itself was in chaos and unlikely or unable to support the Afghan rebels in a meaningful way (something that made a costly war of attrition against the Afghanis unlikely). SALT appeared dead, Brezhnev's initiative had not pre-empted the NATO decision to deploy Pershings and GLCMs, and the USA was embarked in an election year which in Soviet eyes tended to rule out any useful cooperation. In short, the costs seemed manageable given the stakes involved.

risks differently. First, the continuing Soviet need for external success (as signposts of progress) in conjunction with the deeply felt Soviet desire to have the full trappings of global power and status are increasingly leading the Soviets to broaden the scope of their interests and 'internationalist' responsibilities. Combined with the Soviet perception of the retrenchment of US power and international trends that are yielding a more favorable correlation of forces,[17] the Soviet Union seems increasingly determined to emphasize its global role and rights.

In this connection Soviet officials and commentators seem to be going beyond their earlier recitation of the clear recognition of Soviet status as an international arbiter – for instance, 'no [international] question of any significance . . . can be decided without the Soviet Union or in opposition to it'[18] – and at least suggesting that Soviet standing and power give them the same rights of global intervention that the USA has had.* The significance of this is not that the basic Soviet caution that we have discussed is likely to change soon; rather, the significance is that as the Soviets define their interests and internationalist commitments more broadly, threats or losses to these more distant interests may be cast as failures – something that may impel the Soviet leadership to act more decisively and run greater risks in areas more distant from the Soviet Union.

The second emerging development or factor that should be noted is that of the ongoing succession in the Soviet leadership. As nature takes its course, and the current political elite dies off, it will be replaced by officials whose formative experiences – and therefore sociology – are different from the current group of leaders. Indeed, rather than having the purges, World War II, and 'Khrushchev's failures' as the crucibles that forged their outlook, the next generation's attitude-shaping experiences have been the anti-Stalin revelations and shocks, the Khrushchev campaigns waged against admitted shortcomings of the Soviet system and the muddling-through character of the Brezhnev period.

If nothing else, the formative experiences of the current generation help explain why they place such a premium on their personal security and are cautious by nature. Though it is difficult to measure the impact that the next generation's experiences will have on them, it seems safe to say that they may be more self-assured both about the security of their personal positions and the Soviet Union's place in the world. If so, and if they are quite frustrated by the lack of political and social movement in the current period as some observers have suggested,[21] then the next generation of leaders may be less cautious, less concerned about failure and more convinced of the need to act decisively.

On the one hand, this could mean that they will be more assertive in pressing Soviet interests and rights internationally – especially as they are more confident in the nature of Soviet power, achievements and the status

---

* Two especially blunt statements in this regard were made by an unnamed Soviet consular official in an interview with *Die Welt*[19] and also by the Soviet ambassador to France, S. V. Chervonenko, in a speech in Paris in April 1980.[20] Both the *Die Welt* interview and the Chervonenko speech offer stern warnings about Soviet international rights, what they're prepared to insist on and the meaning of equality.

that must be accorded the USSR. On the other hand, they may be less satisfied with seeking external success as substitutes for internal progress; as a result, they may want to focus much more heavily on solving internal problems – something that could make them less adventuresome and also more desirous of cooperation with the USA. Here again we should recognize that the distinctions are not likely to be so neat and in reality probably both sets of impulses will be found in different mixes within the future leadership.

In any case it is hard to know or predict how the next generation will behave; while it is important to take note of the potential changes and their impact on Soviet risktaking propensities, we should not forget that it is easy for Westerners to exaggerate just how extensive the changes in the Soviet system or leadership outlook may be.

Having identified the systemic conditions and leadership attitudes that foster caution and low risktaking among the current Soviet leaders, and having discussed the emerging factors that may affect and perhaps alter Soviet behavior in the future, we might usefully ask in concluding this chapter what are the implications for our behavior? Put simply, it would seem that we must keep the costs of Soviet military action high so that the risks of action come through clearly; that is, we must be able to ensure that the costs of action – measured in terms that matter most to the Soviets – outweigh the costs of inaction, even when the consequences of inaction look undesirable to the Soviets. This means in a case where the Soviets contemplate the direct use of military force that they must see by the character of our commitments and capabilities that the probability of escalation is high; that their ability to achieve a pre-emptive or rapid success is low; that we can frustrate their military objectives; and that the price in men and material as well as the potential for visible Soviet reverses is likely to be great.

In cases where the Soviet perceptions of the costs of inaction are high, only these kinds of costs which directly play upon Soviet fears are likely to be sufficient to deter them. (In effect, they pose the worst threats or failures for the leadership.) Even, then, if Soviet stakes are high enough as in Hungary and Czechoslovakia, even these costs may not prove sufficient. That should tell us – if we don't already know it – that we should be very careful about challenging basic Soviet achievements or its fundamental standing as a superpower. At the same time we should be very sensitive to the need to prevent the Soviets from expanding the areas that fall (or could fall) into these categories.

Doing this becomes especially critical now in light of the current trends and the need for us to be establishing precedents for the next generation of Soviet leaders. With regard to the latter, we once again see the importance of making it clear that the costs of military adventurism will be very high in military, political and economic terms. This, however, should not rule out conveying other impressions and establishing other precedents as well – that is, that we are prepared to do business with them, that cooperation offers significant payoffs and is possible and so on. Indeed, to the extent that the next generation of Soviet leaders is inclined to focus on internal developmental problems, we should try to provide incentives for them to do so –

both in terms of how our cooperation can be helpful and in terms of how our opposition or resistance can be very costly.

In other words, even as we strive to make the next generation of Soviet leaders aware of the high costs of adventurism, we should recognize the importance of not closing the door on cooperation. That, after all, may only succeed in increasing the likelihood of what we most want to prevent – increasing Soviet international activism.

NOTES: CHAPTER 10

1   One of the few attempts to be systematic about Soviet risktaking behavior was made by Hannes Adomeit; see Hannes Adomeit, 'Soviet risk taking and crises behavior: from confrontation to coexistence?', Adelphi Paper No. 101 (Autumn 1973).
2   See Amos Tversky and Daniel Kahneman, 'The framing of decisions and the psychology of choice', *Science*, Vol. 211, no. 4481 (30 January 1981). I am indebted to Robert Jervis for pointing this out to me.
3   For a discussion of the emergence of oligarchy in the USSR, see my 'Coalition maintenance in the Soviet Union', *World Politics*, Vol. XXXII, no. 2 (January 1980), pp. 262–9. The importance of coalition politics in Soviet foreign policy decisionmaking was first discussed by Jiri Valenta, *Soviet Intervention in Czechoslovakia: Anatomy of a Decision* (Baltimore, Md: Johns Hopkins University Press, 1979).
4   Richard Lowenthal, 'The revolution withers away', in Richard Cornel (ed.), *The Soviet Political System* (Englewood Cliffs, NJ: Prentice-Hall, 1970), p. 190.
5   Charles Lindblom has provided the best discussion of the underpinnings and implications of political decisionmaking characterized by incrementalism; see Lindblom, 'Policy analyses', *American Economic Review*, Vol. XLVIII, no. 3 (June 1958).
6   See Ross, 'Coalition maintenance in the Soviet Union', op. cit., pp. 259–62.
7   See , for example, William Riker, *The Theory of Political Coalitions* (New Haven, Conn.: Yale University Press, 1962), pp. 174–82; and John Schwartz, 'Maintaining coalitions: an analysis of the EEC with support evidence from the Austrian grand coalition', in Sven Groennings, E. V. Kelley and Michael Leiserson (eds), *The Study of Coalition Behavior* (New York: Holt, Rinehart & Winston), pp. 235–49.
8   ibid., p. 240.
9   ibid., pp. 245–6.
10   Dimitri Simes and Gordon Rocca, 'Soviet decision-making and national security affairs', Georgetown CSIS Memorandum 20-KA-12-4 (January 1974), p. 10.
11   Theodore Shabad, 'Brezhnev, who ought to know. Explains the Politburo', *New York Times*, 15 June 1973.
12   For a discussion of the Khrushchev–Malenkov secret trip to Yugoslavia during the Hungarian crisis, see Veljko Mičunović, *Moscow Diary* (New York: Doubleday, 1980), pp. 132–40.
13   Note, for example, the article that appeared in *Krasnaia zvezda* on 27 October that essentially called for trading the US missiles in Turkey for the Soviet missiles in Cuba; see A. Leont'ev, 'Ashes and a cold shower', *Krasnaia zvezda*, 27 October 1962. Note also the second letter sent to Kennedy.
14   See Roy and Zhores Medvedev, *Khrushchev: The Years in Power* (New York: Columbia University Press, 1976), pp. 165–75.
15   Khrushchev made a number of speeches during the fall of 1963 in which he justified the need to buy grain and referred to those who would turn the clock back and treat the Soviet people the way Stalin would have.
16   See Jiri Valenta, *Soviet Intervention in Czechoslovakia, 1968: Anatomy of a Decision* (Baltimore, Md: Johns Hopkins University Press, 1979) and 'From Prague to Kabul: the Soviet style of invasion', *International Security*, Vol. 5, no. 2 (Fall 1980), pp. 114–41.
17   For a very good recent discussion on Soviet views of the correlation of forces, see Vernon Aspaturian, 'Soviet global power and the correlation of forces', *Problems of Communism*, Vol. XXIX (May–June 1980), pp. 1–18.

18   From Andrei Gromyko's speech to the 24th Party Congress, *Pravda*, 4 April 1971.
19   Thomas Kielinger, 'A Soviet diplomat: we bridle slowly but do some fast riding', *Die Welt*,
     14 January 1980, trans., *FBIS*, Soviet Union, 15 January 1980, p. A-4-6.
20   Chervonenko speech is cited in Aspaturian, op. cit., p. 17.
21   See Seweryn Bialer, 'The politics of change in the Soviet Union', National Council for
     Soviet and East Europe Research, October 1979, esp. pp. 3–5.

Part Four

Summary and Outlook

11 Soviet National Security Decisionmaking: What Do We Know and What Do We Understand?

STEPHEN M. MEYER

With memories of US-Soviet détente rapidly fading, policymakers, defense analysts and scholars are showing renewed interest in Soviet defense decisionmaking, and well they should. Given that the Soviet Union is America's main political and military protagonist of the postwar world, understanding the motivations, processes, influences and constraints acting on Soviet defense decisionmaking and Soviet military behavior is of central importance to the formulation and implementation of US foreign, defense and domestic policies. It is from this perspective that this chapter undertakes a review of the 'open' literature on Soviet military policy. In particular, I am interested in what the literature offers in the way of a fundamental understanding of the Soviet defense decisionmaking process.

Of course, my use of the term 'defense decisionmaking' lumps together a number of different types of decisions. There is the overarching decision of how much of the Soviet economy's resources should be devoted to military preparedness – what price defense? There are decisions pertaining to weapons acquisitions – how should scientific, technical and industrial resources be distributed for research and development, production and procurement, and innovation and modernization? There are decisions concerning deployment – which forces should be positioned where (for example, Eastern Europe vs the Sino-Soviet border) and in what quantities? There are decisions related to employment – how, when and where should military forces be used in support of Soviet policies?

But isn't the suggestion that we can observe and understand the machinations of Soviet defense decisionmaking a bit naïve? After all, the Soviet Union is one of the most secretive societies in the world. Here two contradicting factors come into play. On the one hand, Soviet defense decisionmaking may be easier to study than US defense decisionmaking because it is more highly centralized, has fewer actors, is more bureaucratized and the longevity of key actors is considerably greater. Also relevant is the fact that, in contrast to the information overload we suffer with respect to US decisionmaking, we are clearly working with less than full information in the Soviet case. Here 'sampling' may provide a more accurate picture than 'full information'. Working to confound research on Soviet defense decisionmaking, on the other hand, is the fact that Soviet secrecy may consistently mask specific key pieces of information which serves to systematically bias our data. Moreover, the small-group structure of the decision setting in the Soviet Union has seen numerous periods of instability, where alignments have shifted rather suddenly. Thus, abrupt changes in Soviet policy are possible. The question remains: is it possible to know anything about Soviet defense decisionmaking?

When we turn to the open literature, it turns out that we actually 'know' quite a bit. That is to say, we possess a large quantity of facts, figures, descriptions and insights pertaining to the Soviet military establishment. There is, for example, a surprising amount of data on Soviet military strategy and doctrine, the organization of the defense establishment, and weapons programs and force deployments.

However, a simple catalogue of individual bits of data gives a misleading impression. A critical examination of the relevant literature reveals that we really *understand* very little about the nature of and relationships between defense-related policy inputs, policy process(es), policy outputs and result- ant outcomes. That is to say, there is little if any agreement regarding how motivations, processes, influences and constraints combine to produce Soviet military policy and behavior. Where do the impulses and require- ments for new weapons systems originate? How are these translated into specific programs? How are choices between and among different programs (and service needs) reconciled, and how do the resulting acquisition pro- grams correlate with program plans? What determines if and when Soviet leaders choose to employ Soviet military forces? What criteria are weighed and how are such decisions reached?

To facilitate the discussion, this chapter divides the study of Soviet defense decisionmaking into two broad issue areas: decisions related to weapons acquisition and force structuring, and decisions related to force deployments and the use of military forces. In discussing each issue area I begin by outlining the predominant models (that is, key schools of thought). These are presented as they appear in the literature – *as contending models* – so as to draw out the full range of relevant arguments.* The various models are described in terms of inputs, processes and outputs – where *inputs* include those goals, influences and constraints deemed most significant in affecting decision outcomes, and processes reflect the structure, organiza- tion, setting and algorithms by which inputs are transformed into outputs. Analytic methods and patterns of data usage are then discussed. In the final section concerned with research opportunities I illustrate how, when levels of analysis are considered, the various models and findings may fit together into an integrated composite model.

WEAPONS ACQUISITION AND FORCE STRUCTURING

In examining the Soviet weapons acquisition process interest focuses on the allocation and distribution of R&D (science and technology) resources, manpower and raw materials, and industrial plant capacity. What is the

---

* The works of a large number of authors are referenced in the context of describing specific models – not necessarily suggesting that these authors either subscribe to a particular model or hold similar views among themselves.

underlying impetus behind the selection of weapons systems for production? What criteria determine the size of production runs? Why are certain capabilities emphasized, and others ignored? In considering Soviet force structure issues we are interested in the determinants of organization, allocation and distribution of existing military assets: manpower and equipment. Why are the fundamental units of the Soviet groundforces (divisions and lesser formations) organized around significantly smaller numbers of personnel than their Western counterpart, while their equipment levels are about equal? What accounts for the 30 percent increase in the number of Soviet motorized rifle divisions during 1965–80, while the number of tank divisions declined slightly? Why have the Soviets placed so much of their strategic assets in land-based ICBMs?

As Soviet weapons procurement and force structuring are among the most observable traces of the outputs of Soviet defense decisionmaking, it is natural to expect studies of these activities to be used for inferring underlying Soviet intentions. At minimum, research on Soviet weapons acquisition and force structuring can be useful in investigating the kinds of conflicts the Soviets are preparing for – and/or their abilities to fight them.

SPECULATION, HUNCHES AND MODELS

Action–Reaction Model

In a setting where information is incomplete, a model serves to 'fill in the blanks' and provide a basis for predicting behavior. The most desirable model is one that can explain and predict the widest range of behavior with the fewest number of inputs. It is not surprising, then, to find that in the effort to try to explain and predict Soviet weapons procurement one of the most frequently encountered models is the *action–reaction model*. In essence, the Soviet decisionmaking process is viewed as *a reactive decision process that reflexively and systematically responds to external events (stimuli) in an effort to offset and neutralize increased threats to Soviet national security*. One can imagine reactions that are 'imitative' (that is, an increased Soviet ICBM deployment in response to an adversary's increased ICBM deployment) or 'offsetting' (that is, new Soviet antitank weapons in response to an adversary's tank modernization program). As Triska and Finley (1965, p. 38) postulate: 'unilateral initiation of a novel course of action which effectively unbalances the conflict between two antagonists, novel either in nature or in magnitude, must elicit a compensating response from the target.' Thus, Soviet decisions for force modernization, the design and acquisition of new weapons systems and the structuring of forces are each taken *in response to* the changing aspects of external threats – in particular, American defense-related activities.

The action–reaction model has received considerable attention in the literature dealing with strategic nuclear forces. Its most ardent proponents tend, quite logically, to be chroniclers of the arms race and arms control advocates; Ralph Lapp (1968), Herbert York (1970) and Edgar Bottome (1971) being among the better-known analysts who utilize this model. Bottome (1971, p. xvi) remarks:

the United States has led in the development of military technology and weapons production throughout the Cold War . . . The Soviet Union has been placed in a position where all it could do was react to American initiatives in bomber or missile building programs.

Accordingly, the initial Soviet ICBM program was a direct response to America's superiority in manned strategic bombers. Soviet ABM programs were an obvious reaction to US ICBM programs, and Soviet antisatellite programs were stimulated by early US efforts to militarize space. Indeed, an action–reaction model was widely presumed to underlie the Soviet strategic buildup of the 1960s and 1970s.

The action–reaction model requires little input formation. The goals and motivations underlying Soviet military policy revolve around trying to 'keep pace' with the USA. The driving influences are obviously the defense-related activities of the USA, though French, British and Chinese activities must be considered as well. Constraints, where they exist, involve the limits of Soviet industrial, economic and technological abilities as well as organizational inertia. Often, an analytic decision process is presumed – one in which the costs and benefits of alternative reaction options are weighed, and a utility-optimizing solution is chosen. Triska and Finley (1965, p. 38) offer: 'any stimulus inserted into the process by one of the opponents may be expected to bring about a *proportionate response in kind*.' This is, however, an unnecessarily restrictive interpretation, and Steinbruner (1974) offers an interesting alternative: a *cybernetic decision process*. Here the decision-makers' assessment of external stimuli is limited to a few 'critical' variables (for example, gross quantities of warheads, equivalent megatonage, number of tanks, and so on), the search for 'appropriate' responses is constrained and optimization gives way to satisficing. Correspondingly reactions need not be proportionate, nor equitable. A cybernetic process does not necessarily respond to every change it senses, but may wait until a particular threshold is crossed. Delayed responses involving either overreactions or underreactions are to be expected. Lastly, regardless of whether the decision process is analytic or cybernetic, outputs are expected to be decisions to procure weapons systems that are either imitative, and/or offsetting, with outcomes accurately reflecting those decision outputs. Thus, all the action–reaction model requires is that one knows which indicators of military activity are most important to the Soviet calculus, what the bounds of Soviet response capabilities are, and how 'reactive' their military-industrial planning is.

One major weakness of the action–reaction model, however, is that to a large extent, the evidence often cited in its support confuses the first appearance and deployment of Soviet weapons with weapons conceptualization and development. In fact, many of the postulated Soviet reactions actually began to take shape concurrent with, and sometimes prior to, their purported American stimuli. For example, Soviet research on atomic weapons began in early 1942 – as did the US Manhattan Project. Soviet efforts to develop an ABM system began years before the first successful American ICBM test. Many of the Soviet missiles that are commonly viewed as *reactions* to the US buildup in the 1960s were actually programmed in the late 1950s.

Technological Dynamic Model

To account for such anomalies, a variant of the action–reaction model is offered: *a technological dynamic model*. Simply stated, this model argues that, in the absence of overt constraints (for example, budgetary limits, or arms control agreements), *a technologically feasible weapons system will be built because it can be built*. Interpreted in a somewhat broader fashion, and placed in the context of an action–reaction decision setting, a technological dynamic model argues that the Soviets acquire additional and/or new weapons systems in response to technological options that *Soviet* scientists recognize as forthcoming, as well as to actual US weapons procurement activities. It reflects a kind of 'pre-emptive thinking' toward technological threats from an adversary. Thus, the Americans and the Russians (as well as the British, the Japanese and the Germans) began atomic bomb research projects within two years of each other. Daniloff (1972, p. 46) presents evidence that Soviet scientists' awareness of foreign interest in the possibility of an intercontinental bomber boosted by rocket engines was enough to stimulate a corresponding project in the Soviet Union. Glagolev (1978, pp. 772–3), a Soviet émigré, recounts how in the early 1960s the Soviet Academy of Science recommended that the Soviet Union halt bomber production in response to an observed end to US strategic bomber production and the dismantling of US air defenses. The General Staff responded with a definitive 'no', noting the potential of the US F-111 – then only in R&D. Today both the US and the USSR are actively engaged in high-energy beam weapons research.

As far as inputs are concerned, the goals and motivations consist of the desire to incorporate the latest state-of-the-art technologies into Soviet military hardware – to provide the armed forces with weapons with unsurpassed scientific-technical qualities. Relevant influences include discoveries in Soviet laboratories and developments in foreign military establishments. The constraints that come into play once again are the limits of Soviet industrial, economic and technological capabilities and organizational inertia. Little is said regarding the nature of the decision process under the technological dynamic model, precisely because the nature of 'decision' is not viewed as particularly relevant. Instead, the logic of new technology is seen as so compelling as to make the 'option' to build a new weapon a foregone conclusion.

For all their intuitive appeal, however, it is argued that neither of these models may really take us very far toward understanding Soviet weapons acquisition or force structuring. First, among those things they do appear to explain (for example, Soviet strategic nuclear weapons programs) fundamental similarities in technological options available to both the USA and the Soviet Union ensure that an overall action–reaction pattern will be observed, regardless of whether or not *reactive decisions* are being made. Though a nation's level of technological development may imply a large number of alternative weapons designs, the practical choices are indeed limited. Both the Soviet Union and the United States could be expected to produce missiles, submarines and bombers within some noticeable span of time – though at differing levels of sophistication. The point is that two completely independent and autonomous weapons development policies will exhibit 'reactivity' if their industries are technologically competitive and they produce new weapons systems on a fairly frequent basis.

The question becomes whether or not there is evidence for action–reaction-type behavior that is not confounded in this manner. Indeed, it seems there is. For instance, Wolfe (1970, pp. 32–42) suggests that the buildup of Soviet conventional forces facing Europe in the late 1940s, and the later Soviet buildup of MRBMs/IRBMs, were in direct response to a growing US nuclear threat to the USSR. However, by allowing aspecific reactions, a second problem arises, for these models then become incapable of accounting for (and predicting) the observed characteristics of decision outcomes. Almost any military buildup could then be described as a reaction to some prior military action by an adversary. At issue is whether an observed increase in Soviet defense procurement would have occurred in the absence of any prior US activity. At one time or another, for example, the Soviet response to the US Polaris SSBN has been tagged as its own SSBN, its ABM complex, its ASW forces and its ICBM buildup. Which is it – or is it all four?

A third and equally disturbing problem that has been raised is that some major Soviet strategic program decisions remain unexplained by either of these models. As aerospace technology advanced, why has no new Soviet strategic bomber appeared as the technological dynamic model implies?

Lastly, neither of these models offers any insights into Soviet force structuring. The distributive balance between Soviet ICBMs, SLBMs and bombers is not explained. Imitative reactions, for example, would result in a force structure that mirrors the US force. However, in this writer's view, the most serious problem is that neither of these models at all accounts for what is surely the greatest bulk of Soviet weapons procurement: conventional weapons systems. In particular, why were the Soviets investing so heavily in their navy at a time when the US navy had been steadily shrinking? Why are they building so many attack helicopters? What US actions stimulated the buildup of Soviet airpower, armor and artillery in the European theater in progress since the late 1960s – a time when the USA was seriously considering lessening its military presence in Europe? Why do the Soviets continue to produce some 200 tanks each month when they already possess a pool of more than 40,000 tanks?

Military Superiority Model

An equally popular model is what might best be called the *military superiority model*. As can be gleaned from the name, this model explains Soviet weapons acquisitions in terms of the *purposeful and self-directed pursuit of unequalled military power*. One can clearly find the influences of this model in the writings of analysts like Nitze (1976), Gray (1977a) and Lee (1969).

The inputs to this model are rather easy to surmise. The key goal is achieving military superiority over the Soviet Union's adversaries. This is usually presumed to be desirable for reasons of political leverage against Europe (see, for example, Finely, 1980; Vincent, 1975; and Wolfe, 1970), if not for real warfighting. To be sure, the Soviets themselves consistently write about the need to acquire military-technical superiority and the importance of the military component in assessing the correlation-of-forces, though for deterrence purposes only. Influences would logically include new technological opportunities and military developments among Soviet adversaries, Soviet ideology, and an expansion-oriented foreign policy. Constraints would consist of technological, economic and industrial limitations in the USSR, and offsetting military activities by the adversary nations. The postulated process is assumed almost always to be rational goal-seeking – selecting weapons systems and force structures that maximize the appearance and substance of Soviet military power.

With this model, the explanations for the Soviet buildup of countersilo nuclear forces (for example, SS-18 and SS-19); their incredible level of tank production, aircraft production and ship/submarine production; and the level of military burden they are willing to place on the Soviet economy are obvious. Similarly the structuring of the Soviet army – its divisions so highly weapons-intensive and its employment strategy so offense-oriented – is understandable in the context of trying to achieve the appearance (if not the substance) of military superiority.

Where this model gets into trouble is with the question: are the Soviets really doing their best to build up their military power? Couldn't they spend more and buy more? Some have argued that Soviet adherence to the SALT agreements belies this model – after all, they agreed to several kinds of constraints that implied parity with the USA. Others have pointed to their tremendous investment in a large groundforce that reputedly has neither the strategic mobility, the endurance, nor the logistics to project itself far beyond Soviet borders. Could not the Soviets have invested more wisely to maximize military power? Then, too, there is an implicit assumption of a monolithic actor that plods along on a singular course. Yet we know that there have been serious disagreements within the Soviet leadership on both 'guns vs butter' issues and 'guns vs guns' issues. And there have been rather radical shifts in Soviet weapons production and procurement.

Interest-Group Models

Experience with American governmental decisionmaking in general, and its defense decisionmaking in particular, has led some students of Soviet politics to look for comparable phenomena within the Soviet system. I will use the generic term *interest-group models* to refer to the collection of models that posit that *Soviet weapons acquisitions and force structuring are derived from the pulls, pushes, bargaining and compromises that occur as various individual and institutional actors within the Soviet Union compete for resources and power*. Kolkowicz (1971a, p. 450) argues: 'the [Soviet] political process is marked by frequent collisions of the several bureaucracies and institutions, whose spokesmen lay claim to political power and to the shaping of national priorities.' In this same vein Aspaturian (1973, p. 105) points out that:

it is conceded in the Soviet press that certain decisions affect the fortunes of various groups unevenly and support for or opposition to various courses of action can often be traced not only to a given policy's abstract merits, but also to the perceptions of different groups and individuals as to how that policy will affect their interests, power, and status.

Thus, unlike the action–reaction/technological dynamic models, interest-group models emphasize factors that are inherent within the Soviet system itself, rather than external to it.

The key inputs to interest-group models are the relevant interest groups' claims on resources and their relative power within the decision setting. Higher-level goals consist of trying to maintain if not enhance one's own career and decisionmaking influence – and/or that of one's organization. This often involves accumulating control over information and resource flows within the larger governmental system. Relevant influences and constraints include the pace and direction of science and technology, the relative political power of other individuals and interest groups, one's own previous performance record, adversary activities, and so on. The process is essentially one of striking some kind of internal bargain with respect to the allocation and distribution of national resources among a number of individual actors. However, because of the dominance of the Communist Party over all Soviet politics, competition between contending interest groups may not necessarily manifest itself in open conflict. Advancing what he calls 'tendency analysis' Griffiths (1971) argues that interest groups may attempt to influence the long-term policy directions of the system by emphasizing certain societal values over others. What he labels as 'value articulation' and what is known as 'nonantagonistic contradictions' in Soviet lexicon permits comradely disagreement over distributional decisions. In contrast to the popular notion of insatiable institutional aggrandizement here the accent is on the mere articulation of societal and, hence, policy priorities (values). None the less, such 'nonantagonistic contradictions' must still remain within the bounds set by CPSU guidance. The eventual decision output, then, is a result which may be some distance from ideal in terms of 'rational' defense planning and national security policy – but acceptable in terms of CPSU guidelines and internal political constraints.

At its highest level of aggregation an interest-group model postulates two contending groups: the military-industrial complex (that is, the armed services, the defense industrialists and sympathetic political leaders) and the consumer-industrial complex (that is, the light-industry sectors of the economy). Vernon Aspaturian (1973) formulates a very interesting case for a Soviet military-industrial complex, in which external threats serve merely as justifications for the continued growth of the Soviet defense sector. Lee (1972) expands the discussion to include explicit limits to the party; Agursky and Adomeit (1979, p. 107) draw on Agursky's tenure in the Soviet military industry to argue:

> the USSR is a military-industrial complex . . . In the USSR, military and civilian values overlap considerably, and . . . there is a high degree of consensus between those who set the priorities of foreign and defense policy (the Politburo), those who conduct military R&D and produce the weapons (the military-industrial ministries), and those who receive the weapons (the military).

And, of course, the 'consumer-industrial complex' has had its spokesmen. Malenkov, Khrushchev, Podgorny and Kosygin have each spoken out over concern that the military-related industries were being fattened at the expense of the light industries.

This notion of a military-industrial complex is certainly consistent with several observable characteristics of the Soviet weapons procurement process. The constant 4 percent growth in Soviet defense spending (which for almost two decades has been relatively insensitive to changes in the rest of the Soviet economy), and the continuous assembly line production of tanks, aircraft, ships and missiles are cases in point.

There are some, however, who find the notion of a unified military-industrial complex a bit too harmonious. The research of Alexander (1976), Caldwell (1971), Colton (1979), Deane (1977), Kolkowicz (1967), Warner (1977) and Wolfe (1965; 1980) point in the direction of interest-group competition between the political, military and industrial leadership as well as further down within the defense establishment itself. Colton (1979), Deane (1977) and Kolkowicz (1967) each chronicle the CPSU leadership's fundamental distrust of the military, and the efforts to impose party control through, among other organs, the Main Political Administration (MPA). In this respect (and in direct contradiction to Agursky and Adomeit, 1979), Kolkowicz (1971b, p. 133) remarks: 'the political leaders and the basic political values and the ideology are inherently anti-military . . . [which results in] a profound distrust of the professional military.' What is clear is that the history of relations among the party, the MPA and the professional military has been one of fluid alignments – what one would expect in an interest-group setting.

Moreover, it is not hard to find evidence of competition for resources and influence between the various branches of the armed services. Khrushchev (1977) notes how the airforce (that is, long-range aviation) lost out to the strategic rocket forces in the late 1950s when he pushed to scrap their intercontinental bomber program in favor of ICBMs. And also in the late 1950s the Soviet army was pushed aside (losing its independent command) in favor of the strategic rocket forces and the PVO-Strany (strategic air-defense forces); only to rebound in the late 1960s. Holst (1969, p. 152) posits that in the early 1960s the PVO-Strany's ABM program was gutted to free resources for the strategic rocket force's ICBM projects. And in a more general sense CIA (1980) estimates of changes in the armed services' *relative* percentages of the Soviet military budget seem to lend additional support.*

In the same vein Alexander (1970), Boyd (1977) and Simpson (1970) describe the project competition among the various Soviet aircraft design bureaus. Alexander (1976) discusses competition among the designers of Soviet tanks, and it has been suggested that the Soviet tendency to procure several ICBM models within a given generation is due to a peculiar form of technological risk aversion – with commensurate competition between missile design bureaus.

* Alexander (1976) discusses competition among weapons designers, while Spielmann (1976, p. 63) notes that defense industrialists tend to side with the particular service branches that are their lieutenants.

The defense industrialist, in turn, will tend to side with those particular service branches that are his clients. In a discussion of defense industrialists in the USSR Spielmann (1976, p. 63) conjectures: 'simply because of their different weapons development and production responsibilities, the top defense industrialists can be expected, from time to time, to have disagreements as to what weapons systems should be added to the Soviet arsenal.'

Because of their capability to delve into fine-structure, interest-group models (theoretically) can account for a wide range of Soviet defense decisionmaking activities. Why are three different ICBM designs procured? Why is tank and aircraft innovation incremental and conservative? The answers here again lie in interest-group politics. Perhaps three ICBM designs are accepted to permit the corresponding design teams and production units to remain viable entities (military-industrial complex). Spreading around the 'goods' helps to maintain institutional health. Incremental and conservative patterns of innovation may also be explained by interest-group politics. Organizational health within the Soviet system is based on two principles: (1) do not make large and attributable mistakes; and (2) maintain production output (quotas and goals). The particular characteristics of Soviet manufacturing systems make it very risky to attempt to incorporate radical innovations in designs and significantly alter production procedures. Central planning creates substantial 'pipeline' inertia in parts and other unassembled products. (Perhaps Western analysts have not taken Soviet five-year plans seriously enough.) Here, then, there is both confluence and contradiction between higher-level goals and the constraints imposed by Soviet industrial technologies. The best way to guarantee production – and, thereby, organizational health – is not to try to change too many things at once. Gregory (1970) and Alexander (1976) in their studies of Soviet tank development, Alexander (1970), Boyd (1977) and Simpson (1970) in their discussions of Soviet aircraft production, and MccGwire (1973) in his examination of Soviet naval procurement all make similar observations.

Interest-group models have also been advanced as offering some possible insights into Soviet force structuring – if one is willing to posit interest-group politics between the various arms of an individual service. Within the Soviet groundforces, one can imagine the existence of 'nonantagonistic contradiction' in emphasis between tank, infantry and artillery commands. The allocation and distribution of resources between these commands may be determined by bargaining and compromise which, in turn, results in a particular force structure. Hence, the significant increase in artillery witnessed over the past decade is a consequence of the increasing influence of the artillery command within the groundforces. Such shifts in relative influence may be the result of changes in the staffing of the High Command – the promotion of new personalities who personally favor the artillery perspective. They may be due to developing changes on the battlefield and in technology that allows the artillery command to argue for the increased significance of the missions and roles of artillery. In any case interest-group models posit that, in general, increased influence leads to increased resource flows – though some degree of interaction can be expected.

There are, however, many students of the Soviet military who find little evidence of interest-group politics where broad issues of policy are concerned. Holloway (1977a, p. 129) asserts: 'There is no evidence that the industrial or R&D side of the armaments complex has generated pressure for innovation or expansion.' Jacobsen (1979) and Odom (1975; 1976), in particular, deny that this phenomenon plays any significant role. On the contrary, they argue that Soviet political, military and industrial leaders are all quite in agreement on military policy and its attendant priorities. In this regard Odom (1976) suggests that notions of totalitarian rule were abandoned prematurely.

National Leadership Model

Consistent with this view, an alternative offered by Gallagher and Spielmann (1972) and enhanced by Spielmann (1978) is a *national leadership model*. Briefly, this model posits that abrupt changes, as well as broad trends and directions in Soviet weapons procurement, are determined by the particular interests and pet-notions of the Soviet leadership – the Stalins, the Khrushchevs, the Brezhnevs. Accordingly, the inputs to the national leadership model revolve around the capabilities of the leadership to move the system in the desired direction. Higher-level goals are basically the personal preferences of the dominant political leaders (usually a 'collectivity' of one) of the CPSU. Influences and constraints consist of the amount of leadership consensus required for major decisions (that is, relative political power within the leadership hierarchy), the extent to which the leadership wishes to get involved in the weapons acquisition process, scientific-technical-industrial constraints, and the degree of organizational inertia and resistance within the defense establishment. The process consists simply of the various armed services, the military industrialists being knocked into line. Boyd's (1977) study of the Soviet airforce clearly portrays this process under Stalin. Khrushchev's (1977) autobiography, Yakovlev's (1968) memoirs, Hudson's (1976) study of the evolution of the Soviet navy, Kolkowicz's (1967) examination of party-military relations and Wolfe's (1965) study of shifts in Soviet military strategy reinforce the notion that *leadership preferences have been a dominating influence in Soviet defense decisionmaking* – even at remarkably low levels of policy. Consequently the outcome is a direct response to the leadership impulse imparted to the system – the system moves toward what the leadership demands.

From this perspective, the Soviets built ICBMs instead of bombers because Khrushchev preferred missiles to bombers. The Soviet army was relegated to secondary status in 1960 because Khrushchev believed a large conventional army was unnecessary in the nuclear age. And as Gallagher and Spielmann (1972, p. 32) posit: 'a case can be made that the effort [to develop a fractional orbital bombardment system] stemmed originally from a desire by Khrushchev to find some dramatic instrument to support his missile-rattling diplomacy of the early 1960s.'

While the leadership model may help explain broad trends in Soviet military policy, its analytic power has been called into question. In particular, the national leadership model offers little in the way of predictive capability. Certainly, it provides an 'after-the-fact' explanation for the continued Soviet development of 'heavy' ICBMs (Brezhnev and company liked big rockets), the lack of large (Nimitz-class) Soviet aircraft carriers (the party leadership fears the loss of command and control of so many pilots and aircraft), and investment in chemical defense capabilities (since the 'doctors' plot', Soviet leaders have an inordinate fear of poisons). The problem is that leadership 'character' and 'preferences' can manifest themselves in many ways – and indeed Stalin and Khrushchev reversed their own weapons procurement courses several times. Would knowing that Brezhnev and Kosygin were going to succeed Krushchev have led one to predict the rebirth of the Soviet navy?

Even where leadership preferences could be shown to account for major weapons procurement decisions, what remains unaddressed is the stimulus for having to make any decision at all. Would Khrushchev have chosen to procure missiles instead of bombers if the Soviet Union had had no need for an intercontinental nuclear delivery system? Perhaps. The addition of a large number of motorized rifle divisions to Soviet groundforces may be attributable to a Brezhnev–Kosygin faith in manpower – but why expand the army at all? If the impulse for new weapons lies with the leadership's domestic political 'needs', then this is essentially an interest-group model. Here the works of Colton (1979), Kolkowicz (1967), Wolfe (1965) and Deane (1977) are particularly relevant for they refute the notion that Soviet political leaders, since Stalin, have been totally free to dictate strategy and force postures unilaterally. Both Khrushchev and Brezhnev depend to some extent on the support of sympathetic 'interest groups' to promote their policies. Yet the leadership model implicitly depends on the presence of a Stalin-like leader. For at least the last fifteen years, the necessary structural requirements of the national leadership model have probably not existed.

Military Mission Model

One final model that is encountered is what I shall call the *mission model*. The mission model posits that *decisions regarding Soviet weapons acquisition and force structuring logically follow from the designation of specific military missions devised by the Soviet military*.[1] These missions have their roots in Soviet military doctrine and strategy, institutional histories, organizational self-image and interpretations of the objective nature of the scientific-technical revolution in military affairs (that is, new threats). While at first the mission model might seem to be merely a new name for the 'organizational' model, there are some significant differences between the two. First, the organizational model explains present behavior in terms of standard operating procedures, routines and organizational habit. These are taken as given. The mission model begins several steps back, examining the institutional origins and premises of those 'standard operating procedures'.

Secondly, the organizational model does not really make allowance for rapid organizational change – either structural change, or behavioral change. If the potential for change is recognized, it is only through incremental learning and adaptation. The mission model, however, can accommodate radical organizational change because it allows for the redefinition of organizational roles and missions. In this way the post-Khrushchev growth of the Soviet (surface) navy can be linked to the recognition of new naval missions:

power projection, extension of the Soviet 'defense' perimeter, and the political role of creating a Soviet 'presence' around the world. In the end I think that an argument can be made to subsume the organizational model within the structure of the mission model. The latter is simply a more highly explicated model.

Elaborations of the missions model come primarily from studies of Soviet strategic and tactical nuclear programs, Soviet naval programs and, more generally, Soviet military writings. In the first category some of the research of Deane (1980), Meyer (forthcoming), and Berman and Baker (forthcoming) point to a Soviet orientation toward mission-procurement. In the second category the work of Dismukes and McConnell (1979), Murphy (1978a), MccGwire (1973), MccGwire and McDonnell (1977), McGruther (1978) and Connell (1980) lend support to this model. In the third category one could look at Douglass (1980), Goure *et al*. (1974) and Hudson (1976).

The mission model results in procurement behavior that is distinctly different from that expected by the other models. Here the acquisition of additional and/or new weapons systems is determined by the dictates of prescribed missions – those activities that the various branches of the Soviet armed forces must be able to carry out in order to implement Soviet military doctrine and strategy. From a mission perspective, the more assets one brings to bear, the more likely the chance of successfully fulfilling the mission. Thus, for example, new high-altitude strategic air defense systems (for example, MIG-25) may be purchased even though no new strategic air offense threat emerges. Silo-busting warheads are developed for Soviet ICBMs despite deliberate US decisions not to build such systems. Upgrades and improvements to the Moscow ABM system are pursued within the limits of the ABM Treaty. The production of new tanks continues unabated long after Soviet tank stocks eclipse those of the West. Ships capable of sea denial are funded. Moreover, the mission model also argues that weapons which the Soviets are technically capable of building, but for which no current missions exist, will not be built. Examples include long-range bombers, SSBN/SLBMs until the mid-1960s and large aircraft carriers.

With few exceptions, most key missions can be expected to persist for relatively long stretches of time (say, more than a decade). For any given mission, the quantity of resources dedicated to that mission will be roughly proportional to the priority of that mission in carrying out Soviet military doctrine and strategy. As old weapons systems (dedicated to a given mission) begin to age, or as new technologies or performance capabilities become available, new weapons are brought on line. However, as long as the old weapons systems are still capable of performing the basic mission, they are not removed and replaced, just augmented.[2] Thus, we would expect to see both old and new weapons systems deployed side by side and the slow and incremental introduction of new weapons systems into the Soviet arsenal. The inputs, then, consist of mission specifications and capability demands. Higher-level goals are tied by trying to ensure as favorable a *post-conflict* correlation-of-forces as is feasible. Both the relative priority of missions and their degree of success are seen as the bases for affecting that correlation of forces. Influences and constraints are many: Soviet and foreign military-technical developments, internal cognitive factors (for

instance, historical experience, tradition, institutional biases and operational codes) and external analytic factors (for instance, the deployment
changes in adversary weapons systems). (One way in which this model
differs from the action–reaction model is that changes in the characteristics
of the adversary threat have only a partial – and perhaps nonsubstantial –
impact on output.) The process involves transforming set mission requirements into an operational weapons system given fiscal, technological and
other resource constraints.

There are, of course, a number of problems with the mission model. The
research of scholars like Erickson (1979) and Holloway (forthcoming) point
to considerable two-way interaction between technology and strategy – and,
hence, mission. The Soviets in fact have always acknowledged this, as
Lomov (1973) and Savkin (1972) repeatedly note. New weapons technologies may create (or invalidate) certain military missions, while mission
requirements may 'push' specific weapons technologies and designs. Thus, a
'chicken vs egg' paradox emerges. This is, in fact, part of the dynamics of
what the Soviets refer to as the scientific-technical revolution in military
affairs. Moreover, the mission model fails to explain anomalies like the
concurrent procurement of the SS-17, SS-18 and SS-19 – or the simultaneous procurement of Sukhoi and MIG ground attack aircraft – unless separate missions exist for each. And how soon after the decrease of a particular
threat is the corresponding mission downgraded, if not eliminated.

Methods and Data Usage

The study of Soviet weapons procurement and force structure relies heavily
on the traditional case-study essay. For the most part the focus tends to be on
the individual service branches of the Soviet armed forces. The historical
evolution of the service is described, prominent individuals who played key
roles in the service's development are introduced, the growth of institutional
strategies, tactics and organization are detailed, combat experiences are
discussed and, of course, the relevant service hardware is described. These
studies bring together information collected from a variety of sources –
memoirs, biographies and autobiographies of Soviet military men, political
leaders and scientists, Soviet military journals, declassified Western military
studies and interviews with Soviet émigrés. For the most part, however, *there
is very little in the way of analysis* in these works and hence they should be
considered sources of data, albeit once removed, for analysis.

Among Soviet weapons systems, strategic nuclear weaponry has received
the greatest amount of attention. The return, however, has not been great.
The overwhelming bulk of the relevant writing is found in the arms control
literature – and the 'defense' literature that attempts to rebut it. Thus, data
and analyses tend to concentrate on information and issues relevant to the
current hardware-related problems and politics of US-Soviet arms control.
The result is an awesome 'ghost' literature that recounts with incredible
repetition the throw weight, yields, accuracies, ranges, and so on, of each
strategic nuclear system.

With the exception of work by Spielmann (1978), who attempts to explain
Soviet decisionmaking pertaining to its first ICBM; Warner (1974), who

explores alternative explanations of Soviet strategic force postures; Berman and Baker (forthcoming), who examine Soviet strategic force developments from a mission perspective; and Holloway (1977b), who looks at the historical change in the technical characteristics of Soviet ICBMs, there has been little effort to study Soviet strategic nuclear forces from an institutional perspective. The only bit of organizational information one finds is that the strategic rocket forces grew out of an artillery tradition, and *assumptions and assertions seem to be preferred to empirical analysis*.

There is a substantial body of literature that looks at Soviet strategic doctrine. Using Soviet writings, specialists like Goure *et al*. (1974), Dinerstein (1962), Douglass and Hoeber (1979), Garthoff (1962), Scott (1975), Lambeth (1974) and Wolfe (1965) attempt to tease out Soviet thinking on strategic nuclear matters, and, thereby, understand Soviet goals, if not intentions. The problem with this work is that the volume of relevant Soviet writings is quite large. Consequently, the various analysts are forced to construct their studies using bits, pieces and excerpts. A question thus arises as to whether their conclusions follow from the selections they find significant and important, or whether the selections they find significant and important follow from their own preconceptions. (Since Wolfe, 1965, actually examines Soviet doctrinal debates, he avoids this problem by explicitly incorporating conflicting writings into his analyses.) Curiously, no real effort has been made to systematically investigate the 'correlation' between Soviet strategic weapons procurement and Soviet strategic doctrine until a recent study by Berman and Baker (forthcoming), who claim to find a strong association between hypothetical mission requirements and weapons acquisition.

In studies of the Soviet groundforces, emphasis is divided between descriptions of service history, organizational structure, equipment and Soviet conventional force doctrine. The early history of the Soviet army is described by Liddell-Hart (1956), Gardner (1966) and MacKintosh (1967), to name just a few. Researchers like Erickson (1978) and Donnelly (1980) continue to provide up-to-date information on changes in tactics, strategy, equipment and organization. Record (1975) provides some descriptive analysis of Soviet groundforce capabilities, mobilization potential and employment practices. Translated Soviet materials on groundforce tactics and doctrine are available in the Soviet Military Thought series available from the US Government Printing Office. Douglass (1980) provides the most recent synopsis of current Soviet writings on ground warfare.

Some effort has been made to check for correspondence between weapons procurement and mission requirements, but this has involved largely anecdotal *post hoc* inferences and evidence. That is to say, it is rather easy to plug a single weapons system (for example, a BMP) into a groundforce strategy. The question is whether procurement across the Soviet division's table of organization and equipment fits a pattern. Considerable work needs to be done in this area. A difficulty arises, however, because the Soviet literature on groundforce doctrine is quite large; the same 'chicken vs egg' paradox exists here as in the case of strategic nuclear doctrine.

What are sorely missing are operational analyses of Soviet groundforce capabilities – not what they have, but what they can do. For example, those who most fear a Soviet tank thrust through Iran and decry US capabilities to halt it seem disinterested in Soviet failings in logistics, weaknesses in organization and command, control and communications outside the European theater, and problems of equipment maintenance and operations in 'alien' environments. Heiman's (1969) postmortem of the Soviet invasion of Czechoslovakia and Vigor's (1980) assessment of Soviet weaknesses and vulnerabilities, in general, seem to be practically the only works that have given these issues any attention at all. More systematic and operational studies are needed.

All that can be said about the Soviet strategic-defense forces is that they have not attracted much attention in the unclassified literature. True, there is a spattering of articles, but they are, by and large, unrevealing and repetitious. Most of these are centered around Soviet interests in ABM systems and implications for arms control. More noteworthy works include Holst (1969), who examines Soviet attitudes toward strategic defenses in the context of arms control; Davis *et al.* (1980), who updated Holst's analyses in the context of arms control in the 1980s; Deane (1980), who analyzes Soviet writings and force structure pertaining to strategic defenses; and McDonald, Ruina and Balaschak (1980), who examine Soviet strategic defense capabilities against US cruise missiles. Soviet civil defense activities have received some attention in recent years. ACDA (1978) and the CIA (1978) both released analyses of the organization and potential effectiveness of Soviet civil defense preparations against nuclear attacks. Their studies drew on Soviet civil defense documents and manuals and intelligence data on actual preparations and activities. Jones and Thompson (1978) report on the results of simulations of Soviet approaches to protecting industrial assets and explore the implications for Soviet 'postwar' recovery. Kaplan (1978) examines the sensitivities of Soviet civil defense activities, arguing that they are more image than substance. Unfortunately, little concerted effort has been devoted to pursuing the broader issues of Soviet strategic defense activities. What synergisms do the Soviets see between their active and passive defense activities? How do institutional relationships affect tradeoffs between the two?

Studies of the Soviet airforce are abundant and parallel those of the Soviet groundforces. Lee (1959) and Kilmarx (1962) are two of the earliest and best-known studies. The service history is outlined, key individuals and events in the development of the airforce are discussed, the development of Soviet aircraft and aircraft industries is covered, as is the evolution of air strategy and tactics. Boyd (1977), and Higham and Kipp (1977), update these studies. Berman (1978) and Petersen (1979) attempt some elementary operational analyses of contemporary Soviet air power, exploring its capabilities in the context of specific missions. Berman emphasizes a few basic parameters as measures of capability (for example, thrust-to-weight ratios), while Petersen pursues a more qualitative approach.

The only service studies that attempt to go beyond description or simple one-dimensional analysis are those concerned with the Soviet navy. Here Soviet naval strategy, Soviet shipbuilding programs and Soviet naval operations are brought together. Herrick (1968) provides the more traditional organizational history of the Soviet navy. The works of MccGwire (1973),

MccGwire, Booth and McDonnell (1975), MccGwire and McDonnell (1977), Murphy (1978a), Dismukes and McConnell (1979) and Hudson (1976) are particularly noteworthy.[3] It is interesting to note the analytic growth that has taken place in the field of Soviet naval studies. Early work (early 1970s) was simply descriptive – ship production rates, deployment statistics, employment strategies and writings on strategy and tactics. However, this work has moved on quite rapidly. Some studies, like Connell (1980), have tried to 'correlate' Soviet shipbuilding with postulated missions – missions derived from Soviet writings. Others have tried to 'correlate' ship deployment and movement with Soviet foreign policy interests. Finally, production and force structure patterns have been examined in the context of shifting Soviet naval strategy and changing mission priorities. McGruther (1978) offers a particularly interesting set of analyses examining the relative influence of internal factors (for example, the navy's self-image) and external factors on Soviet naval development. The literature on the Soviet navy also contains a substantial amount of comparative analysis, contrasting East and West approaches to naval building, doctrine and employment policies.

Some of the most detailed analyses in the literature are of individual weapons systems. To try to understand the Soviet approach to weapons innovation Alexander (1970; 1978) has examined Soviet fighter aircraft design and procurement. Campbell (1972) has done a case study of Soviet airship research. Moore, Flanigan and Helsel (1977) examine Soviet submarine development, while Stoiko (1972), Shelton (1968) and Riabchikov (1971) each chronicle the development of Soviet rocketry through its early ICBM programs. Alexander's studies clearly set the standard, bringing together data from memoirs, biographies and autobiographies, émigré interviews, technical analyses and studies of Soviet industry. He attempts to trace the source of innovation impulses, unmask the roles of various institutional actors (for example, research bureaus, design bureaus and the armed services) and chart the internal dynamics of the Soviet weapons acquisition process from conception to production. There are also a considerable number of studies that take a more general look at the development of service equipment. Simpson (1970) looks at Soviet aircraft, Gregory (1970) describes Soviet army procurement, MccGwire (1978b) illuminates developments in Soviet naval programs, while Murphy (1978b) discusses Soviet naval force structure. This latter group of studies does not have the level of detail one finds in the former group.

While case studies of specific Soviet weapons developments yield valuable insights into Soviet choices in military hardware, they may fail to illuminate alternative options not pursued. Analyzing those items not procured may reveal as much about Soviet defense decisionmaking as studying those things that are acquired. Technical, economic, military and political logics may not be the same for all nations. It is interesting to note that Western analysts most often assume 'technical difficulties' when the Soviets do not procure a weapons system which Western military logic dictates they should. A more explicit examination of 'paths not chosen' is clearly warranted.

Of course, this leads the researcher to consider explicit cross-national comparisons. Alexander (1974) contrasts aircraft production in the Soviet Union, the USA and France. Alexander (1976) compares the development of armor in the Soviet Union with that in the United States. These are essentially comparison case studies that concentrate on design philosophies, patterns of technological innovation and production-run trends. MccGwire (1977) tabulates ship production figures (by weight class) for the East and the West in a time series that runs during 1965–75. Kehoe (1977) compares US and Soviet warship design in terms of major qualitative parameters: hull, propulsion, payload, habitability, and so on. Brodeur (1975) compares Soviet and Western weapons systems across a range of performance parameters. Holloway (1977a) compares East and West tank developments and Soviet and US ICBM programs. Kehoe *et al*. (1980) compares frigate designs among the USSR, the USA and several other countries.

As useful as case studies of individual weapons systems or service systems are, they examine their subject outside the military context in which the weapons exist. That is to say, if tradeoffs and substitutions are in fact made between different types of weapon systems with related roles and tasks, segregated weapon-specific case studies may prove misleading. Economic and industrial bottlenecks may force Soviet military industrialists to alternate innovation product cycles, so what appears to be slow development of a particular system may actually represent a fraction of more substantive growth in a particular mission area. For example, case studies of the development of air defense interceptor aircraft might be merged with similar studies of other air defense systems such as surface-to-air missiles. This type of integrated case study of the air defense mission might reveal some interesting details of how the Soviet apportion R&D and production resources. For instance, during one five-year plan, new interceptor aircraft might be emphasized. During the following five-year plan, new SAMs might be emphasized. Perhaps this is how a weak economy systematically supports a strong weapons procurement program. Similar tradeoffs may take place between missions or branches of an armed service – if not between the services themselves. Can such patterns be found? CIA data on Soviet military budget trends suggest they do exist.

Another focus of empirical investigation is Soviet defense expenditures. CIA (1980; 1978b) has provided some interesting and provocative estimates of Soviet defense spending. Lee (1977) and Rosefield (1981), on the one hand, argue that the CIA estimates are too low. Holtzman (1980), on the other hand, protests that the estimates are far too high. Cockle (1978) reviews the various estimating procedures and describes their strengths and weaknesses. To a large extent these numbers have been used almost exclusively to compare US and Soviet military power. (This is perhaps their *least* appropriate application owing to methodological problems related to the way in which they are constructed.) And some have used this data for elementary model testing. Kugler and Organski (1980) have attempted to test the action–reaction model using US and Soviet strategic weapons expenditures. While in terms of the study of Soviet defense decisionmaking a more interesting use of the CIA figures might be for comparing the internal distribution of resources among the services, little effort has been made in this direction.

In sum, the set of methods employed in the study of Soviet weapons acquisition and force structuring by and large consists of essay analysis, descriptive enumeration and the tabular arrangement of quantitative data. The database, however, is broad and rich. We do know quite a bit about Soviet defense decisionmaking as it relates to weapons acquisition and force structuring. Diverse types of data are available, and in considerable quantity. However, as I will discuss in the last section of this chapter, the available data are significantly underused.

MILITARY DEPLOYMENTS AND THE USE OF SOVIET MILITARY FORCES

Since the mid-1970s, questions regarding Soviet thinking on the appropriate use of military force in foreign policy have lost their solely academic flavor. Soviet military 'adventures' in Angola, Somalia, Ethiopia; the Soviet invasion of Afghanistan; and the Soviet role in Poland's domestic crisis each have important security policy implications for the West.

The success or failure of Western efforts at deterrence, crisis management and conflict will, as George and Smoke (1974), Williams (1976) and George (1980) point out, heavily depend on abilities to accurately assess and evaluate Soviet capabilities, 'intentions' and likely behavior before the fact and as events unfold. As noted earlier, US policymakers resort to 'mental models' out of necessity. Marshalling facts *they* possess of past events, and using what information is available regarding current conditions, policymakers must generalize into the uncertain future. They must plan in the face of *expectations* as well as observations. Thus, as Zimmerman (1980) notes, the particular model of Soviet defense decisionmaking US policymakers subscribe to, can and will influence US policies and behavior.

Models: Why Do the Soviets Do What They Do?

Past reviews have examined the Soviet foreign policy literature in terms of predominant models and methods, theoretical development and empirical content. Most notable are the surveys by Welch and Triska (1971) and Horelick, Johnson and Steinbruner (1975). The latter is particularly comprehensive, and so I will just touch on those aspects of the literature that directly address Soviet decisionmaking with regard to the use of military force.

Strategic Actor Model

One model, again in vogue, for explaining and predicting Soviet military behavior is what I call the *strategic actor model*. The strategic actor model pictures the Soviet leadership as cold, calculating and in active pursuit of a master plan. The model inputs are largely internally derived drives and influences – cognitive factors – emanating from historical, cultural, social, geopolitical and ideological imperatives. The confluence of historical Russian expansionism and Soviet ideology form the basis of higher-level goals: extending the influence and power of the Soviet regime and creating a world socialist system. Adversary capabilities and behavior are relevant, too, but only to the extent they call into play specific cognitive factors or set limits and constraints on Soviet options. Geopolitical influences and constraints are specifically addressed by Gray (1977) and Gasteyger (1978). The decision process involves rational (that is, utility-directed) goalseeking. Pipes (1980a) and Jacobsen (1977; 1979) in their essays on Soviet global strategies, Haselkorn (1978) in his studies of Soviet alliance behavior, and Glagoler (1978) and Burt (1979) in their essays on Soviet arms-control policy employ this model. In this regard it is often assumed that the application of the strategic-actor model demands that the Soviet leadership consists of a unitary rational actor (for instance, Stalin or Khrushchev) with supreme power. Actually, as Jacobsen (1979), Odom (1975) and Pipes (1980a; 1980b) suggest, all one need assume is that the recruitment process for the Soviet leadership ensures that 'like-minded' individuals rise to the top. While they may have disagreements with respect to tactics, Soviet leaders may none the less possess highly convergent views of long-range foreign policy goals and the role of military force in the pursuit of those goals. Thus, there could be disagreements as to whether covert military aid to indigenous groups in target regions is preferable to the interventionary use of Cuban troops; or whether the use of Cuban troops is preferable to the use of Soviet forces. But there would be fundamental agreement among the leadership that specific countries in specific regions should be 'targeted' for destabilization in concert with Soviet 'strategic' interests. In other words, the 'why's, where's and who's' are given, and only the details regarding the 'how's' need be decided upon.

Pipes (1980a, p. 36) observes:

Soviet global strategy is implemented by means of pressures exerted at various points of the globe in a bewildering succession of shifts and causes [leading] some observers to interpret it as a mere exploitation of random opportunities . . . [and with regard to thrusts into the Third World]. The Soviet Union may be said to be laying siege to Western Europe and Japan in the same manner in which medieval castles were blockaded.

From this perspective, the geographical distribution of Soviet military aid, military alignments, arms transfers and interventions (for example, transporting Cuban troops) assumes a rather ominous pattern.

Many students of Soviet affairs, however, find the notion of a Soviet 'grand design' a bit hard to swallow. Perhaps, as Luttwak (1979, p. 62) suggests, it is because: 'Having no plan of concerted action ourselves, we imagine that others, too, are without plans.' Or, perhaps, it is because the observed correlation between Soviet military presence and 'trouble' in a given region is as much a function of a Soviet propensity to flock to political instabilities (fanning the flames *ex post facto*) as it is to their efforts to create instabilities – irrespective of geographical location. None the less, the fundamental motivation behind this opportunistic Soviet foreign policy is desire to reinforce favorable trends in the global correlation of forces. An elaboration by Aspaturian (1980) is particularly well argued.

Opportunist Model

This variant of the strategic actor model, which I will refer to as the *opportunist model*, and those who subscribe to it, accept the argument that the Soviet leaders have some overall notion of direction in their foreign policy. What they find hard to accept is that the Soviet Union systematically attempts to implement some precise master plan. Instead the opportunist model postulates that Soviet leaders, rather than magically creating instabilities and conflict, fan pre-existing flames until some specific opportunity presents itself. Thus, the strategic actor model and the opportunist model differ with regards to assumptions about constraints and processes. As Legvold (1977, p. 60) interprets: 'By and large, the Soviet Union is, as we are, the beneficiary or victim of the processes of change, not their source.'

Some of the basic premises of both these models, however, seem to be contradicted by the history of Soviet foreign policy and the politics of the leadership itself. In terms of the strategic actor model, many of the international 'crises' that some have attributed to Soviet witchcraft – Greece, 1946; Korea, 1950; and the Six-Day War, 1967 – are questioned by others who argue that the Soviets were acting as followers, not initiators. More recent events, like the Soviet 'flip-flops' from Somalia to Ethiopia, China to India and Iraq to Iran speak better for opportunism than grand design.

And in the larger context Sonnenfeldt and Hyland (1979) find a subtle but substantial transformation of Soviet objectives and goals – from core security (Stalin), to peripheral security by leapfrogging containment (Khrushchev), to attaining recognized global status and prestige (Brezhnev) – as they describe the evolution of postwar Soviet thinking on security and foreign policy. Thus, the overarching assumption of a relatively constant and singular Soviet foreign policy orientation comes into question.

To be sure, since the end of World War II, there have been a number of leadership conflicts that, at least on the surface, appear inconsistent with the basic assumption of attitudinal conformity among Soviet leaders. Raanan (1969), for example, describes the split between Khrushchev and Molotov over the wisdom of the Soviet plunge into the Third World. Mičunović (1980) reveals, in a diarylike outline, the fundamental schisms he observed among the Soviet leadership during his tenure as Yugoslavia's ambassador to Moscow in the 1950s. And, of course, the Khrushchev ouster has in part been attributed to major disagreements with the direction and style of his foreign policy. Indeed, there have been a number of identifiable lurches in Soviet foreign and defense policy, which, at least on the surface, imply changes in strategy if not goals.

Interest-Group Models

Students of Soviet politics who emphasize the epochal divisions in Soviet history have turned to what again may be generically termed *interest-group models* of Soviet decisionmaking. Whether one thinks in terms of institutional actors as interest groups, or in terms of individual actors, as bureaucratic actors (or both), the interest group approach views Soviet decisionmaking as a form of internal competition for resources, influence and power.[4] Valenta's (1979a, 1979b) analysis of the Soviet invasion of

Czechoslovakia is particularly noteworthy for its explicit and systematic application of the bureaucratic politics model. One might also note Dallin's (1980) review of the Soviet invasion of Afghanistan, and Caldwell's (1971), Payne's (1980) and Wolfe's (1980) interest-group studies of Soviet involvement in the SALT negotiations.

From the perspective of interest-group politics, the inputs revolve around the needs, values and goals of the individual and organizational actors. The process is bureaucratic bargaining. Kolkowicz (1967, pp. 291–2) argues, for example, that the Soviet military establishment has an institutional interest in maintaining some minimal level of international tension and 'threat'. In this regard might the Soviet adventures in Angola, Ethiopia, Afghanistan, and so on, have been at the urging of the military organs? Similarly Aspaturian (1973, p. 116) wonders out loud whether: 'Soviet defense industries may unwittingly be developing a vested interest in an expanding Soviet globalism.'

Alternately, Ulam (1980) suggests that both the succession struggles among the Soviet leadership and leadership desires to divert domestic attention away from social/economic ills at home have produced periodic impulses for expansion. Echoing this view Secretary of State Haig told the Senate Foreign Relations Committee (during his confirmation hearings) that increasingly evident 'failures' of the communist system will create pressures for 'external diversions'. 'Kremlinological' analyses, like those of Conquest (1961) or Tatu (1969), tend to focus more heavily on the interplay of the values, aspirations and personalities of the top leadership for clues to policy and action. Perhaps, then, the Soviet invasion of Afghanistan was as much a result of jockeying for position in the Kremlin's leadership succession contest, as it was of strategic reasoning.

Ross (1980) has proposed an interesting variant based on coalition theory. His *consensus model* argues that Soviet decisionmaking does involve reconciling 'conflicting' viewpoints. But the keys to institutional bargaining do not come from power-based *ad hoc* compromises but rather by resort to prior solutions: past behaviors, decisions and approaches. The highest political objective becomes preserving group consensus ('we must all hang together, or . . .') and institutionalized relationships. Thus, the Hungarian invasion is followed by the Czechoslovakian invasion which is followed by the Afghanistan invasion which, etc. The consensus model dictates resorting to solutions that have worked in the past.

One would expect, then, that this kind of decisionmaking gives rise to routinized behavior in the face of risk. 'What did we do the last time this kind of situation arose?' The research of Ulam (1974) and Vincent (1975) point to a rather consistent pattern of conservative risk avoidance in Soviet foreign policy. And it is interesting to re-examine the works of Adomeit (1973), Triska and Finley (1968) and Horelick and Rush (1966) on Soviet risk-taking behavior with this model in mind.

Paranoia Model

One last model that is frequently encountered is a *'paranoia' model*. Simply stated the paranoia model argues that both tsarist Russia and the Soviet

Union's rather discouraging experiences in international relations have indelibly etched distrust and paranoiac fear in the minds of Soviet leaders. Compounding this history is the fact that the Soviet Union has no ally with independent nuclear capabilities, nor an ally with significant industrial capabilities. Today, in fact, the Soviet Union is on adversary terms with all the world's nuclear weapons countries (and many potential nuclear proliferators). As a result Soviet leaders approach international relations, international treaties, obligations and agreements with a special cynicism. In particular, they have 'learned' that no other country or international body can or will guarantee Soviet security (that is, military alliances or treaties of friendship and peace are ephemeral). Only Soviet power can do that. Consequently the Soviet Union will continually try to avoid encirclement and expand its buffer system: the core (mother Russia) surrounded by Sovietized republics, which are surrounded by subserviant satellites, which are surrounded by 'friendly' and 'sympathetic' countries, etc. This model, highly regarded by revisionist Cold War historians like LaFeber (1976) and Kolko and Kolko (1972), has found great acceptance among those who subscribe to the action–reaction and technological-imperative models of Soviet weapons acquisition behavior. Essentially the Soviets seem doomed to a never-ending search for total security, as Simes (1981) describes it.

The inputs to this model consist both of external stimuli and (internal) cognitive factors. Political, military, or economic actions by the USA or its allies provide the initial impulse. However, *it is the perception and interpretation of those actions*, suitably warped and distorted by the various neuroses of the Soviet mindset, *that are the effective inputs upon which decisions are based*. Some inputs may be completely artificial (self-) stimuli. The higher-level goals are simple: increasing the objective security of the Soviet homeland. Influences and constraints, of course, include the actions and capabilities of adversary nations, and the political, economic and industrial capabilities (and limitations) of the Soviet Union itself. The decision process involves formulating an appropriate response not necessarily to the stimulating action, but to the perception and image of what the action (or threat) represents. Then, too, the paranoia model could produce preventative Soviet behavior – moving in the *expectation* of unfavorable developments. Zimmerman (1980) posits a cybernetic decision process in which a few key indicators of the external environment are monitored by Soviet leaders who respond to those particular cognitive triggers by adjusting policy accordingly. In this case the slightest warming of relations between China and the USA can result in a 'violent' series of Soviet diplomatic outbursts and provide substantial impetus for new Soviet weapons programs. The paranoia model may indeed explain why the Soviet Union began building up its forces on the Sino-Soviet border directly following the first Chinese nuclear test in 1964 and why it currently deploys some forty-six divisions along the Sino-Soviet border when, in fact, the Chinese military has rarely been less capable.

The problem with the paranoia model is that while it can explain Soviet military 'adventures' around the Soviet Union's extended periphery, it has a hard time accounting for past and present Soviet activities in Angola, Libya, Indonesia, Egypt, the Congo and Cuba. Moreover, the paranoia model offers little in the way of predictive utility since paranoia is a universal prescription for any kind of behavior. Almost anything that the Soviets do could conceivably be explained in terms of paranoid psychology. But how does the model account for things that the Soviets do not do? Why haven't the Soviets given more direct military assistance to Iraq during its war with Iran? Why cultivate relations with Somalia and then scrap everything in a jump to Ethiopia? Why get so involved in Southern African politics rather than investing more effort in the near periphery – Eastern Europe, the Middle East, the Persian Gulf and Asia. In this regard Raanan (1980, p. 44) argues that the notion of Soviet paranoia is absurd, for in fact the Soviet leadership 'prides itself, not without cause, upon its unemotional, pragmatic, realistic, cold-blooded, "scientific", Bolshevik approach toward policy.'

Methods and Data Usage

The primary mode of research in examining Soviet use of force in its foreign policy is the case-study essay. Historiographies of particular eras and events dissect Soviet policies and behavior in terms of cultural and sociological variables, national psychology, ideological drives, 'strategic imperatives' and leadership personalities. Examples include: Davidson's (1958) study of the Berlin crisis of 1948, an examination of Khrushchev's missile rattling in the late 1950s and early 1960s by Horelick and Rush (1966) and Schick's (1971) study of the Berlin crises of 1958–62. Drawing on speeches and writings, documents, historical chronologies, and events, researchers attempt to piece together likely explanations of Soviet policy and actions. That is to say, they try to construct models. The problem here is that these become highly idiosyncratic and case-specific models, with each study employing its own analytic framework and pursuing its own distinct set of questions. Unfortunately, while these works bring together a considerable quantity of data, provide important and useful insights and generate a number of interesting questions, they also expend great amounts of energy retreading old conceptual ground. There is a distinct lack of building on prior research – that is, little cumulation. Their *ad hoc* approach to analysis makes it difficult, if not impossible, to directly draw their results together as a single body of knowledge.

Resort to focused comparison case studies would be the first remedy. Asking the same questions over and over again from case to case would not only generate case-study material, but perhaps reveal cross-case consistencies and inconsistencies. Triska and Finley (1968) took an early step in this direction, but little else has been done. Kaplan's (1981) edited volume on the Soviet use of force could have moved far ahead in this direction had an analytic framework been devised *a priori* (as was done by George and Smoke, 1974). As might have been feared, Kaplan's authors each went off in their own direction, resulting in a volume that consists of an excellent set of historical case studies, but one that is strongly lacking in coherence, analysis and synthesis. What is still needed, then, is some effort to draw together the many disparate case studies that do exist and restructure them in the fashion of focused comparison case studies, in much the same way that George and Smoke (1974) produced their study. In this respect Valenta's (1980) examination of the Soviet invasion of Afghanistan deserves attention. As was noted earlier, Valenta is one of the few researchers who *began* his study by laying out the analytic framework – then scrupulously adhering to it. Thus, it is possible for Valenta, or any other researcher, to build directly on that study by producing new case studies that, likewise, apply the explicated model described in the original study. In this manner a cumulative set of comparative case studies could result.

In the way of contemporary social science techniques, some work has already been done using content analysis, a procedure that uses word counts from speeches and writings to analyze overall content, topical emphasis, and so on. Theoretically, content analysis is a rigorous and systematic method for determining the underlying attitudes of the authors of the material being analyzed. Unfortunately, the amount of time required to code and store the data has been prohibitive, resulting in somewhat haphazard coverage. As a result the issue of selection bias is raised – is what comes out of the data analysis truly representative of Soviet speeches and writings in general? At least to date, the traditional approach to content analysis – the lone reader, the document and a pot of coffee – appears superior. None the less, some interesting work has recently been done by Stewart (1980) and CACI (1979). Stewart used content analysis to dissect speeches and writings of the Soviet Politburo leadership. By tabulating patterns of content that emphasized defense and security issues he attempted to discern the constituents of the Defense Council. In an effort to try to derive an independent measure of Soviet perceptions of international tensions and crisis CACI (1979) performed content analyses of Soviet journals and newspapers to build annual indices of the Soviet leadership's *expressed* perceptions of relative crisis levels in the world. They found that Soviet perceptions of crisis did not correspond to US perceptions as closely as many believe. Perhaps, as data bases grow and as computer scanning techniques improve, the selection bias issue (and inter-coder-reliability issue) may vanish. This would permit a significant increase in the quantity of material that could be studied.

Though considerable behavioral data exist in raw form (for example, Kaplan, 1981; Murphy, 1978a), little work has been done to exploit such data beyond simple descriptive analysis. At issue is whether postwar Soviet behavior reveals any trends, patterns, or regularities. Do the Soviets do everything *ad hoc*? Do they exhibit learning behavior? Clearly, many of the models of Soviet defense decisionmaking imply some forms of recognizable (repetitive) behavior. Can any of those patterns be empirically verified? The behavioral data is plentiful – the analyses are nonexistent. As Horelick *et al*. (1975) point out, this is an area of methodology that has received rather haphazard attention.

AN AGENDA FOR RESEARCH

Below, in the section on modeling, I sketch out a way in which these contending models can be integrated when attention is explicitly paid to context and level of analysis. This leads directly to issues of empirical research. Specifically, it is argued that two fundamental sets of questions require attention: do the predominant inputs and processes of Soviet defense decisionmaking shift according to time and context? How? Do decision outcomes differ as inputs and processes change? How?

Modeling

The number of contending models for explaining and predicting Soviet defense decisionmaking is not terribly large. There may be four or five key models for each of the two major areas of interest I have discussed, and several distinguishable variants. While some of the underlying assumptions of these different models vary quite substantially, and their implications for US policies are significantly different – and in some cases directly contradictory – scant attention has been paid to testing assumptions and validating the various models.

It may, indeed, be naïve to believe that any single model can account for Soviet defense decisionmaking as a whole. But it may be equally foolish to hold that there are as many models operating as there are decisions made; that is, that every decision involves a unique and *ad hoc* set of procedures. A middle ground exists that is reasonable and intuitive.[5] The idea is that it is possible within the highly centralized but bureaucratically stratified decisionmaking setting of the Soviet system that a set of specific routines has evolved. The decisionmakers themselves do not have to be aware of the routines (models) of decisionmaking they employ in order for those routines to exist. Habit and convenience, as well as intention, can spawn routinized decision processes. Decisions of a certain type are handled by one set of procedures. Decisions of another type are dealt with by a second and different set. Thus, a small and discrete set of interlocking models in a composite structure could have quite a bit of explanatory power.

Consider decisionmaking pertinent to weapons acquisition and force structuring. Table 11.1 summarizes each of the models described in the first section of this chapter. A moment of inspection will reveal a curious set of relationships among the input components of the models. The goals and influences in some models reappear as influences and constraints in other models. This interlocking pattern among the models' input components reflects the fact that, in the end, many models recognize the relevance of the full range of factors that are believed to influence Soviet defense decisionmaking. None the less, the models do differ in terms of those input components they consider to be most decisive in determining decision outcomes.

This conflict of emphasis, however, is at least partially ameliorated when the level-of-analysis of the individual models is taken into account.[6] The action–reaction actor model, the military superiority model, and the technological dynamic model operate at the nation level-of-analysis. These models seem to be at their strongest when addressing the broad patterns and large perturbations in the allocation and distribution of Soviet defense resources. Their emphasis on the major military activities of Soviet adversaries and pivotal developments in military technology may be most appropriate for explaining this kind of macrolevel phenomena. Of course, within this level of analysis, there are inconsistencies among these three models – again in terms of the relative emphasis on inputs. Here, then, is where focused research (that is, testing assumptions, assessing empirical validity, and so on) could prove particularly useful.

Interest-group models and the mission model operate at the institutional level-of-analysis. What little systematic empirical research has been done suggests that these models may be particularly useful in understanding the more microlevel patterns in Soviet weapons acquisition and force structuring. Stressing the roles played by institutional actors (for example, the armed services, the defense industrialists, and so on) and the ways in which those actors conceptualize and define military issues and options, these models may well be 'at their best' when it comes to understanding the peculiarities and intricacies of the implementation of Soviet military policy. These models may be most appropriate for explaining the day-to-day aspects of Soviet military policy and behavior. All this, however, is bounded by the macrolevel issues of adversary military activities and technological developments.

The leadership model operates at the individual level-of-analysis. It addresses many of the same aspects of Soviet defense decisionmaking as do the action–reaction model and the technological dynamic model: broad patterns and large perturbations in the allocation and distribution of Soviet defense resources. Emphasis is placed on personal preferences and characteristics of the leadership and how they affect defense decisionmaking via critical interventions. This last qualification – critical interventions – suggests an important time dimension to this model that allows it to coexist with the others. Leadership intervention provides periodic jolts to the system, sometimes adding momentum, sometimes redirecting efforts, and sometimes restructuring the entire decisionmaking and implementation setting of Soviet defense policy. Thus, this model might be most useful for explaining deviations from established patterns of Soviet behavior, or the initiation of new patterns of behavior.

By again referring to levels-of-analysis, the various decision processes can simultaneously operate within the decision setting. Analytic or cybernetic processes as well as technological momentum define the bounds of reasonable options and alternatives. Bureaucratic bargaining and compromise and leadership direction may account for choice within such bounds. For example, the momentum of technology and the need to react to US military programs may push certain military options to the top of the Soviet list. Leadership direction may, in turn, constrain alternatives (or direct adoption of specific alternatives) – 'no long-range bombers will be considered'. Finally, bureaucratic bargaining is left to resolve the particulars. What I have suggested, then, is a composite model, a fairly simple amalgamation of the various models found in the literature. This is, of course, a hypothesis, and there may well be more appropriate models and composite models. Ross (1977), for example, suggests a number of ways that alternative inputs to Soviet defense decisionmaking may simultaneously combine in influence and constrain Soviet options and choices. In any case what is evident is that abilities to handle very complex decision structures and patterns of behavior can be significantly enhanced with little increase in the complexity of the model itself. The composite model remains fairly easy to detail and test.

Similarly decisions related to the deployment and use of Soviet military

Table 11.1 *Models of Soviet Defense Decisionmaking (Weapons Acquisition)*

Model	Goals	Inputs		Process
		Influences	*Constraints*	
Action–reaction	to 'keep up' with adversary military developments	military developments in adversary countries institutional and leadership bases	industrial, economic, technological capabilities of Soviet Union organizational inertia leadership preference/priority	analytic (measured) response to stimuli, or cybernetic response to stimuli
Technological dynamic	maximizing technological level of armed forces pre-emptive thinking toward technological threats	technological developments in Soviet Union and abroad	industrial, economic, technological capabilities of Soviet Union institutional inertia	self-induced momentum of state-of-the-art technology
Military superiority	attain military superiority over USA ultimate military-technical security	adversary military activity Soviet industrial, scientific and technical capabilities biases of military establishment leadership preferences	Soviet economic/industrial, scientific and technical capabilities adversary military activity leadership preferences organizational inertia	

Interest group	maintain/enhance decisionmaking influence, institutional health increase control over resources	pace and direction of military technology and industry relative political power, alignments and institutional structure adversary activities	pace and direction of military technology and industry relative political power, alignments and institutional structure adversary activities	conflict, bargaining compromise, or value articulation
National leadership	maximize leadership status, prestige, power enhance Soviet security and status	Soviet scientific, technological and industrial capabilities personal characteristics and preferences of leadership	leadership interest organizational inertia of military establishment extent of pluralism within leadership structure	leadership direction
Mission	ensure as high a favorable postconflict correlation-of-forces as feasible fulfill designated missions	military developments abroad Soviet industrial, scientific and technological capabilities institutional self-image historical experience, tradition, etc.	institutional/interest group biases in military establishment Soviet industrial, technological and scientific capabilities organizational inertia and institutional self-image	analytic decisionmaking, priority satisficing

Table 11.2 *Models of Soviet Defense Decisionmaking (Use of Force)*

Model	Goals	Inputs — Influences	Constraints	Process
Strategic actor	global expansion, ultimate security	cognitive factors, social, historical, ideological imperatives Soviet politicomilitary capabilities	adversary capabilities and intervention Soviet politicomilitary capabilities	rational goal seeking active pursuit
Opportunist model	global expansion, ultimate security	cognitive factors international instability Soviet politicomilitary capabilities	adversary capabilities and intervention Soviet politicomilitary capabilities	opportunistic goal seeking satisficing, passive pursuit
Interest group	individual/institutional power and control over resources	Soviet domestic political alignments Soviet domestic political stability	Soviet domestic economic/industrial capabilities	bureaucratic bargaining, conflict and compromise
Consensus	preserve unanimity of decisionmaking limit political responsibility (liability)	domestic and foreign events identifiable prior analogues	individual and institutional interests	consensus politics – lowest common denominator
Paranoia	protect integrity of Soviet homeland	cognitive factors adversary capabilities and activities	Soviet politicomilitary and economic capabilities adversary capabilities and interventions	mediated stimulus response cybernetic response to stimuli

forces may best be understood in terms of a composite model that links the various individual models. As Table 11.2 shows, noting the interlocking relationship between the input components of the models and the different levels-of-analysis allows 'rationalizing' the apparent contradictions between many of the models. Here, too, a number of alternative composite models can be devised.

We also need to give some thought to the nature of the 'switches' that link the models. That is to say, what factors combine to move decisionmaking from one model to another. For example, one switch affecting weapons acquisitions decisions may be budgetary ceilings. An armed service may have the authority to initiate and pursue any R&D project it wishes as long as expenditures remain below some number of rubles per year. Once that limit is crossed, however, decisionmaking is bumped up to the Ministry of Defense level. Or another switch might be nuclear technology vs non-nuclear technology. All nuclear weapons acquisition decisionmaking may be at the Politburo level – hence, the leadership model may dominate – while non-nuclear weapons decisionmaking may take place within the Main Military Council of the Ministry of Defense. Time, the level of international tensions and leadership stability – just to name a few – may all be important switches in determining which model – or composite model – is dominating Soviet defense decisionmaking. Further research in what I would call *contextual modeling* certainly seems warranted.

There may also be model linkages between the two issue areas – linkages between composite models. Interestingly enough, one finds that those students of Soviet defense decisionmaking who subscribe to the strategic actor model (regarding the Soviet use of military force) also tend to subscribe to the military superiority (of the Soviet weapons acquisition process). Similarly those who subscribe to the paranoia model to explain Soviet military activities around the globe, also believe that Soviet weapons procurement can be explained by action–reaction and technological-dynamic models. And, of course, faith in interest-group models at the higher levels of Soviet government and policymaking implies belief in interest-group politics further down in the decisionmaking establishment. So, to some degree, the conceptual basis for speculating on linkages between composite modeling has already been established.

Empirical Research

However, before we can hope to construct composite models or define 'contextual switches', a considerable amount of theoretical and empirical work needs to be done. First, the individual models discussed in this chapter (and probably several that weren't) remain little more than hunches about Soviet defense decisionmaking. They are based largely on anecdotal evidence which is merely illustrative and provides no basis for assessing validity. So, in the broader context of testing and evaluating the empirical validity of the various models, we could begin by explicitly elaborating the pivotal assumptions (including time-dependence and level-of-analysis) of each model, followed by a check to see whether they hold up in appropriate cases. For instance, the strategic actor model assumes that there is fundamental conformity in the thinking of Soviet leaders. What do the biographies and memoirs say? Are the known schisms within the Politburo more common, or less common, than *a priori* agreement? Are certain types of decision issues more likely to spawn disagreement than others? (Khrushchev, 1977, and Mičunović, 1980, seem to argue that disagreement is more the rule than the exception.)

Secondly, the expected outputs of individual models can be compared to known history. If the action–reaction model is correct, one should expect to see boom/bust cycles in aggregate Soviet weapons procurements – perhaps even synchronized to US boom/bust cycles. If the military-industrial complex model is correct, one would expect to see certain floors below which Soviet weapons acquisitions do not drop – independent of US defense activities. Are either or both of these expected patterns of behavior consistently observed? In the same vein the strategic actor model implies that one should observe a well-defined and predictable pattern to Soviet involvement around the world. The opportunist model, conversely, argues that this apparent 'pattern' will mimic the availability of appropriate opportunities. Which is it? Or is it neither? These questions can be addressed empirically.

Thirdly, a conscious effort must be made to engage in follow-on research. Several individual researchers have, as one would expect, systematically built on their own prior work. (Curiously, many have not.) However, my reference to follow-on research is in the context of researchers building on others' findings. Only in the area of Soviet civil-military relations has true follow-on research by different researchers been conducted, as Colton (1979) restudied the issues raised by Kolkowicz (1967). Colton's follow-up study actually supports many of Kolkowicz's hypotheses and assumptions (though in many instances Colton seems unaware of it). Though others have looked at party-military relations, in general, topics like cycles in party-military relations, political military-professional military relations, and leadership perceptions of international tensions have not received further direct attention.

What these three observations point to is the need to explicitly formulate and test hypotheses. Very little of the literature is framed in terms of the clear articulation of testable hypotheses. Finley (1980) is perhaps one of the best examples of what *could* be done in the way of postulating assumptions and testing hypotheses. Without testable hypotheses to use as benchmarks, it is doubtful that research can move very far in the direction of understanding Soviet defense decisionmaking.

Lastly, we should take advantage of opportunities to bring to bear 'multiple streams of evidence' on critical research issues. In the study of Soviet weapons acquisition and force structuring two types of data predominate: Soviet military writings (that is, thinking) and actual procurement and deployment behavior. As previously noted, only infrequently are the two brought together in a single analysis. A third type of data that is simply absent in the literature is Soviet work on analytic modeling.[7] Appearing in Soviet military policy journals like *Voennaia mysl'*, these simple mathematical models attempt several things: (1) to operationalize the concepts and principles that appear in their writings on strategy, operational art and tactics; (2) to investigate the dynamic aspects of their plans; (3) to empirically validate the concepts and principles that appear in their writings; and (4) to study the impact of new military-technical developments on those concepts and principles. In the words, the work on analytic modeling tries to link the soft side (that is, strategy, operational art and tactics) with the hard side (that is, military-technical capabilities) of military planning. I would argue that the value of these analytic models for understanding Soviet defense decisionmaking has been highly underrated. To the extent that they reflect how the Soviet military conceptualizes and operationalizes military problems – and the extent to which they differ from US views – studying these analytic models may help us to break away from simple mirror-imaging. Does this modeling work truly reflect the Soviet writings? Are observed Soviet weapons procurement patterns consistent with the 'optimization' of the analytic models? One should expect a strong correspondence here if Soviet military writings truly reflect what they would like to be able to do, and if their analytic models truly reflect their conceptual approach to attaining those goals. This third stream of evidence, *used in conjunction with the other two*, could prove extremely useful in helping to sort out the relative strength of postulated goals (for example, as contained in military writings) and influences (for example, technology) in Soviet defense decisionmaking.

Research Strategies

It is disappointing to note that what often passes for analysis in the literature is really description – the elaboration of data. This is probably due to the fact that the case-study essay remains the dominant method of the field. The problem with *singular* case studies is that they are not 'summable'. Because they are designed and researched independently (that is, conceptually disconnected from other works), they can only contribute to our understanding of Soviet defense decisionmaking in a scatter-gun fashion. Broad analytic essays have the same weakness. Because they contain little more than snapshots of the larger historical record, they are of little direct use in assessing the relative validity of models. Thus, *the literature often degenerates into a contest of 'flinging and dodging anecdotes'*. While these kinds of case studies are unsurpassed in providing data and context, and quite useful in testing assumptions in specific historical contexts (when the effort is made to do so), they, none the less, represent the weakest of all analytic approaches.

Where this obviously is leading is to an analytic framework based on focused-comparison case studies (*à la* George, 1979). Here fixed sets of questions are systematically applied across a number of individual case studies. In this way not only are important similarities, patterns and trends illuminated, but significant deviations from past behavior are noted as well. Often overlooked is the fact that a deviant case may be more revealing than a dozen consistent cases. But you cannot tell what is deviant until you know what is consistent. Focused-comparison case studies allow you to bring together, in a systematic and synergistic way, the truly large amounts of data that are currently floating among many disjointed studies. What would we find if Alexander's (1978) study of Soviet aircraft production was followed up by parallel studies (using Alexander's framework) of Soviet SAM production, submarine production, helicopter production, ICBM production, and so on? Or following Raanan's (1969) lead, what might identical analyses of contemporary Soviet military activities in Egypt, Libya, Somalia and Ethiopia reveal? Dallin (1964) argues, for example, that the Soviets have been responsive to shifts in US policies and military activities. Zimmerman (1980) concurs and calls attention to what he argues is a pattern of Soviet adaptation and learning behavior. Gati (1980), on the other hand, refutes both the notion of substantive change in Soviet foreign policy and indications of learning behavior. Obviously, they cannot all be correct. By asking and re-asking the same sets of questions across a series of cases, we might shed some light on the dynamics of Soviet behavior – something that could not (and has not) come out of individual *ad hoc* case studies.

From the same perspective, Simes (1981) notes that there is a strong bias in the literature reflecting the belief that a pluralistic Soviet decision system represents less of a threat to the West than does a totalitarian system and, hence, is preferable. This assumption is most likely the product of faith that in any pluralistic setting there must be moderating influences. But a pluralistic system might just as easily decay into a 'who is the best Bolshevik' contest with an increasingly hostile policy output. Given that the Soviet system has moved through several positions on the totalitarianism-pluralism scale, it would seem that these two contending assumptions could be explicitly tested by comparison case studies.

The findings from such studies could then be used to revise the sets of questions (hypotheses) and devise new questions. This interactive application of the focused comparison case study method could make possible some degree of theoretical, analytical and empirical convergence in the study of Soviet defense decisionmaking.

At this point we should begin constructing more complex composite models, models which presume the need to match individual decision models with distinct decision settings. This theoretical linkage of specific models would be sensitive to the peculiarities in the structure and context of Soviet defense decisionmaking. In particular, the work of Kolkowicz (1971a), Sonnenfeldt and Hyland (1979), Simes (1978) and Wolfe (1970) caution that Soviet decisionmaking styles can shift over time. As a consequence analysts must be sensitive to the possibility that time must be explicitly considered as a variable in any testing of hypotheses or attempts to construct models.

Arthur Alexander has suggested, for example, that the leadership model is most salient to understanding Soviet defense decisionmaking immediately following leadership change. The argument is that this is the period when the leadership can best expect to leave its 'mark' on defense policy, establish itself within the system and set the tone for the regime in general. Can such a pattern be discerned from historical examinations covering the last thirty years of Soviet defense policy?

The traditional case study approach, then, with its emphasis on fact-finding and detail can screen the raw data, serve as a basis for generating assumptions and hypotheses, and ensure that important contextual factors remain part of the analysis. These are the concrete case histories. Moving to a comparative framework – at the expense of some case detail – can provide additional information from the same data by accentuating contrasts and patterned behavior. In particular, time-dependent characteristics will be accentuated, and behavioral dynamics can be studied.

Lastly, statistical analysis – admittedly at the expense of more detail – can offer a check against the 'forest-for-the-trees' error. Details that are pursued far enough will always make it seem as though nothing is related to anything else. There will always be 'differences'. The question of how much analytic weight to assign to such differences is a highly subjective matter. Consequently it may be useful to step back from the detail of one's data and look at it in terms of highly visible (macroscopic) properties. Many analysts are already incorporating statistical data into their studies – MccGwire and McDonnell (1977) display substantial quantities of ship production data, Murphy (1978a), and Dismukes and McConnell (1979) tabulate Soviet ship deployment rates and geographic concentrations, and Colton (1979) and Dcane (1977) use percentage distributions of military officers in the CPSU and on the Central Committee. These analysts then go on to argue that they see patterns and trends in the data. More often than not, individuals have argued that they see patterns where in fact none exist. There are a large number of systematic techniques for determining whether a pattern really exists in the data, or whether it is random noise. If we are going to search for, and then infer patterns in, Soviet weapons procurement or Soviet military behavior, it should be done as rigorously as possible. Probability-based methods like Markov analysis seem particularly useful in analyzing trends that are now predicted – often incorrectly – by simple straight-line projections. Is there a correlation between changes in the size of US naval deployments in various bodies of water and shifts in Soviet naval deployments? Are the trends and cycles some analysts claim to recognize in Soviet weapons programs real, or random noise which the analyst's expectations lead him to see as patterns? Is it possible to distinguish between individual Soviet leaders by analyzing the contents of speeches? Are shifts we observe in military representation on the Central Committee truly related to specific policies or domestic events, or just due to chance occurrence? As long as we find this kind of data illuminating, we might as well analyze it correctly.

In this respect it is often argued that there is a terrible lack of information regarding Soviet defense decisionmaking and that this, in turn, limits the analytic (methodological) repertoire that can be brought to bear. The cry is 'we need more data'. While no one could argue with the desire for more data, the question must be raised as to whether we are getting all the information inherent in the data we already possess. First, I question whether we are using all the various types of data we have to the fullest advantage. As Moore *et al.* (1977, p. 160) notes: 'Apparent mismatches between technical parameters and operational employment, as well as seemingly inexplicable Soviet pronouncements, often cause Western analysts little concern, as long as there is possible a "mirror image" or "the-way-we-do-it" interpretation of the data.' We may, indeed, throw away a lot of useful data because it doesn't fit. Secondly, there may be more than one appropriate method for analyzing a given set of data. What I am suggesting here is that we can squeeze some additional and potentially useful information out of our data through the *combined* application of different methods together – symbiotically. On the one hand, a system-by-system case study of each new class of ship procured by the Soviet navy may provide useful information regarding the mission priorities and reactivity to US naval activities of Soviet naval procurement. On the other hand, a statistical analysis of Soviet and US ship production by mission would ask some of the same questions but use different aspects of the data. By resort to multiple streams of data, and by employing several different analytical techniques simultaneously, we can better protect our analyses from the biases, peculiarities and idiosyncrasies of any one type of data or methodology.

None of the various methods described are substitutes for any other. They each address different kinds of questions or some similar questions in different ways – they are complementary, not competing. It is precisely because there are important gaps in our data on Soviet defense decision-making that every valid and reliable approach to extracting information from the data should be applied. If we hope to advance our understanding of Soviet defense decisionmaking, then new detailed case studies are needed that will build on prior works, producing new data (and correcting old data) and generating new hypotheses. Focused-comparison case studies are necessary if we are to begin to bring together all the data we have in a coherent and revealing fashion. And a wide selection of analytic techniques should be employed to extract as much information from the data as is possible.

CHAPTER 11: NOTES

1   Illustrations of 'missions' include: the counter-ICBM mission, the air defense mission, the countercarrier mission, and so on.
2   This is distinguishable from task-oriented procurement in which new systems that can perform a given task better than old systems actually replace the old equipment.
3   Many of these studies are edited volumes. Consequently, my observations below refer to specific pieces found in these works.
4   Interestingly, one of the basic approaches to the study of Soviet politics, 'Kremlinology', is rooted in the bureaucratic politics paradigm – even though 'Kremlinology' long predates the recognition of the bureaucratic politics paradigm as such.
5   The author wishes to thank Arthur Alexander and Alexander George with whom several discussions greatly helped to clarify and extend my thoughts on this matter.
6   'Level-of-analysis' refers to the degree to which the model aggregates actors into an action unit. A national level-of-analysis posits a unitary national actor, ignoring actors at a lower level (for example, government, individual leaders, elites, and so on). An institutional level-of-analysis assumes the key action units are the organizations, elites and other identifiable subgroups that influence national policy. The individual level-of-analysis looks to the characteristics and actions of individual personalities (for instance, Stalin) to chart national behavior.
7   I am not referring to the highly detailed operations research models that are used for microlevel cost–benefit or efficiency studies. Rather, I am interested in a class of broad analytic models that are applicable to macrolevel assessment and force planning – for example, simple models for assessing the nuclear correlation of forces.

REFERENCES: CHAPTER 11

Adomeit, Hannes (1973), 'Soviet risk-taking and crisis behavior: from contribution to coexistence?', Adelphi Paper No. 101, International Institute for Strategic Studies, London.

Agursky, Mikhail and Hannes Adomeit (1979), 'The Soviet military-industrial complex', *Survey*, Vol. 24, no. 2 (Spring), pp. 106–32.

Alexander, Arthur (1970), *R&D in Soviet Aviation* (Santa Monica, Calif.: Rand).

Alexander, Arthur (1974), 'Weapons acquisition in the Soviet Union, the United States, and France', in Horton *et al*. (1974), pp. 426–43.

Alexander, Arthur (1976), *Armor Development in the Soviet Union and the United States* (Santa Monica, Calif.: Rand).

Alexander, Arthur (1978), 'Decisionmaking in Soviet weapons procurement', Adelphi Paper No. 148, International Institute for Strategic Studies, London.

Amann, Ronald, Julian Cooper and R. W. Davies (1977), *The Technological Level of Soviet Industry* (New Haven, Conn.: Yale University Press).

Aspaturian, Vernon (1973), 'The Afghan gamble: Soviet quagmire or springboard', in Aspaturian *et al*. (1980), pp. 23–5.

Aspaturian, Vernon (1980) 'Soviet global power and the corrclation of forces', *Problems of Communism*, Vol. 29, no. 3 (May–June), pp. 1–18.

Aspaturian, Vernon, A. Dallin and J. Valenta (1980), *The Soviet Invasion of Afghanistan: Three Perspectives*, ACIS Working Paper No. 27, UCLA, Los Angeles, USA.

Aspin, Les (1978), 'What are the Russians up to?', *International Security*, Vol. 3, no. 1 (Summer), pp. 30–54.

Berman, Robert (1978), *Soviet Airpower in Transition* (Washington, DC: Brookings Institution).

Berman, Robert and John Baker (forthcoming), *Soviet Strategic Forces: Requirements and Responses* (Washington, DC: Brookings Institution).

Bottome, Edgar (1971), *The Balance of Terror* (Boston, Mass.: Beacon Press).

Boyd, Alexander (1977), *The Soviet Air Force* (New York: Stein & Day).

Brodeur, Nigel (1975), 'Comparative capabilities of Soviet and Western weapons systems', in MccGwire *et al*. (1975), pp. 452–68.

Burt, Richard (1979), 'Arms control and Soviet strategic forces: the risks of asking SALT to do too much', in Erickson and Feuchtwanger (1979), pp. 157–82.

CACI, Inc. (1979), *Analysis of the Soviet Crisis Management Experience* (Arlington, Va: CACI).

Caldwell, Larry (1971), 'Soviet attitudes toward SALT', Adelphi Paper No. 75, International Institute for Strategic Studies, London.

Campbell, Heather (1972), *Controversy in Soviet R&D: The Airship Case Study*, Rand, R-1001-PR (Santa Monica, Calif.).

Cherednichenko, M. I. (1971), 'Modern war and economics', *Kommunist vooruzhennykh sil*, no. 18 (September), pp. 20–8.

Cockle, Paul (1978), 'Analyzing Soviet defense spending: the debate in perspective', *Survival*, Vol. 20, no. 5 (September–October), pp. 209–19.

Colton, Timothy (1979), *Commissars, Commanders, and Civilian Authority* (Cambridge, Mass.: Harvard University Press).

Connell, George M. (1980), 'The Soviet navy in theory and practice', *Comparative Strategy*, Vol. 2, no. 2, pp. 129–47.

Conquest, Robert (1961), *Power and Policy in the USSR* (London: Macmillan).

Dallin, Alexander (1964), *The Soviet Union and Disarmament* (New York: Praeger).

Dallin, Alexander (1980), 'The road to Kabul: Soviet perceptions of world affairs and the Afghan crisis', in Aspaturian *et al*. (1980).

Daniloff, Nicholas (1972), *The Kremlin and the Cosmos* (New York: Knopf).

Davidson, William (1958), *The Berlin Blockade* (Princeton, NJ: Princeton University Press).

Davis, Jacquelyn, Robert Pfaltzgraff Jr, Uri Raanan, Michael Deane and John M. Collins (1980), *The Soviet Union and Ballistic Missile Defense* (Cambridge: Institute for Foreign Policy Analysis).

Deane, Michael (1977) *Political Control of the Soviet Armed Forces* (New York: Crane, Russak).

Deane, Michael (1980), *Strategic Defense in Soviet Strategy* (Washington, DC: Advanced International Studies Institute).

Dinerstein, Herbert (1962), *War and the Soviet Union* (New York: Praeger).

Dismukes, Bradford and James McConnell (1979), *Soviet Naval Diplomacy* (New York: Pergamon Press).

Donnelly, C. N. (1980), 'Soviet mountain warfare operations', *International Defense Review*, Vol. 13, no. 6, pp. 823–34.

Douglass, Joseph (1980), *Soviet Military Strategy in Europe* (New York: Pergamon Press).

Douglass, Joseph and Amoretta Hoeber (1979), *Soviet Strategy for Nuclear War* (Stanford, Calif.: Hoover Institution Press).

Erickson, John (1962), *The Soviet High Command* (London: St Martin's Press).

Erickson, John (1978), 'The ground forces in Soviet military policy', *Strategic Review*, Vol. 6, no 1 (Winter), pp. 64–79.

Erickson, John (1979), 'The Soviet military system: doctrine, technology, and style', in Erickson and Feuchtwanger (eds) (1979), pp. 18–44.

Erickson, John and E. J. Feuchtwanger (eds) (1979), *Soviet Military Power and Performance* (London: Macmillan).

Finley, David (1980), 'Conventional arms in Soviet foreign policy', *World Politics*, Vol. 33, no. 1 (October), pp. 1–36.

Gallagher, Mathew and Karl Spielmann (1972), *Soviet Decision-Making for Defense* (New York: Praeger).

Gardner, Michael (1966), *A History of the Red Army* (New York: Praeger).

Garthoff, Raymond (1962), *Soviet Strategy in the Nuclear Age* (New York: Praeger).

Garthoff, Raymond (1966), *Soviet Military Policy* (New York: Praeger).

Gasteyger, Curt (1978), 'Soviet global strategy', *Survival*, Vol. 20, no. 4 (July–August), pp. 159–62.

Gati, Charles (1980), 'The Stalinist legacy in Soviet foreign policy', in Cohen (ed.) (1980), pp. 270–311.

George, Alexander (1979), 'Case studies and theory development: the method of structured, focused comparison', in Lauren (ed.) (1979).

George, Alexander (1980), *Towards a Soviet-American Crisis Prevention Regime: History and Prospects* (Los Angeles, Calif.: Center for International and Strategic Affairs, UCLA).

George, Alexander and Richard Smoke (1974), *Deterrence in American Foreign Policy* (New York: Columbia University Press).

Glagolev, Igor S. (1978), 'The Soviet decision-making process in arms-control negotiations', *Orbis*, Vol. 21, no. 4 (Winter), pp. 767–76.

Godson, Roy (ed.) (1980), *Intelligence Regiments for the 1980s: Analysis and Estimates* (Washington, DC: National Strategy Information Center).

Goure, Leon, Foy Kohler and Mose Harvey (1974), *The Role of Nuclear Forces in Current Soviet Strategy* (Miami, Fla.: University of Miami Press).

Gray, Colin S. (1977a), 'The future of land-based missile forces', Adelphi Paper no. 140 (London: IISS).

Gray, Colin S. (1977b), *The Geopolitics of the Nuclear Era* (New York: Crane, Russak).

Gregory, F. E. (1970), 'Soviet army procurement', in Royal United Services Institute (1970), pp. 95–9.

Griffiths, Franklyn (1971), 'A tendency analysis of Soviet policy making', in Gordon Skilling and Franklyn Griffiths (1971), pp. 335–78.

Haselkorn, Aigdor (1978), 'The expanding Soviet collective security network', *Strategic Review*, Vol. 6, no. 3 (Summer), pp. 62–73.

Heiman, Leo (1969), 'Soviet invasion weaknesses', *Military Review* (August), pp. 38–45.

Herrick, Robert (1968), *Soviet Naval Strategy* (Annapolis, NS: Naval Institute Press).

Higham, Robin and Jacob Kipp (1977), *Soviet Aviation and Air Power: A Historical View* (Boulder, Colo.: Westview Press).

Holloway, David (1977a), 'Technological change and military procurement', in MccGwire and McDonnell (1977), pp. 123–32.

Holloway, David (1977b), 'Military technology', in Amann *et al.* (1977), pp. 407–88.

Holloway, David (forthcoming), 'Doctrine and technology in Soviet armaments policy', in Leebaert (forthcoming), ch. 9.

Holst, Johan J. (1969), 'Missile defense, the Soviet Union, and the arms race', in Johan Holst and William Schneider Jr (eds) (1969) *Why ABM?* (New York: Pergamon Press), ch. 7.

Holst, Johan and William Schneider, Jr (eds) (1969), *Why ABM?* (New York: Pergamon Press).

Holtzman, Franklyn (1980), 'Are the Soviets really outspending the US on defense?', *International Security*, Vol. 4, no. 4 (Spring), pp. 86–104.

Horelick, Arnold, A. R. Johnson and John Steinbruner (1975), *The Study of Soviet Foreign Policy: Decision-Theory-Related Approaches* (Beverly Hills, Calif.: Sage).

Horelick, Arnold and Myron Rush (1966), *Strategic Power and Soviet Foreign Policy* (Chicago: University of Chicago Press).

Horton, Frank, Anthony Rogerson and Edward Warner (1974), *Comparative Defense Policy* (Baltimore, Md: Johns Hopkins University Press).

Hudson, George (1976), 'Soviet naval doctrine and Soviet politics, 1953–1975', *World Politics*, Vol. 29, no. 1 (October), pp. 90–113.

Hutchings, Raymond (1973), 'The economic burden of the Soviet navy', in MccGwire (1973), pp. 210–27.

Hyland, William (1980), Keynote Address, Conference on Soviet Decision-Making for National Security, Naval Postgraduate School, Monterey, California, USA, 14–16 August.

Jacobsen, C. G. (1979), *Soviet Strategic Initiatives* (New York: Praeger).

Jones, T. K. and Scott Thompson (1978), 'Central war and civil defense', *Orbis*, Vol. 22, no. 3 (Fall), pp. 681–712.

Joshua, Wynfred and Stephen Gilbert (1969), *Arms for the Third World* (Baltimore, Md: Johns Hopkins University Press).

Kaplan, Fred (1978), 'Soviet civil defense: some myths in the Western debate', *Survival*, Vol. 20, no. 3 (May–June), pp. 113–20.

Kaplan, Stephen (ed.) (1981), *Soviet Armed Forces as a Political Instrument* (Washington, DC: Brookings Institution).

Kehoe, James, Jr (1977), 'Warship design: ours and theirs', in MccGwire and McDonnell (1977), pp. 364–86.

Kehoe, J. W., G. Graham, K. S. Brower and H. A. Meier (1980), 'NATO and 1 Soviet naval design practice', *International Defense Review*, Vol. 13, no. 7, pp. 1003–32.

Khrushchev, Nikita (1977), *Khrushchev Remembers: The Last Testament*, 2 vols (Boston, Mass.: Little, Brown).

Kilmarx, Robert (1962), *History of Soviet Airpower* (New York: Praeger).

Kolko, G. and J. Kolko (1972), *The Limits of Power: The World of U.S. Foreign Policy 1945–1954* (New York: Harper & Row).

Kolkowicz, Roman (1967), *The Soviet Military and the Communist Party* (Princeton, NJ: Princeton University Press).

Kolkowicz, Roman (1971a), 'Strategic parity and beyond: Soviet perspectives', *World Politics*, Vol. 23, no. 3 (April), pp. 431–51.

Kolkowicz, Roman (1971b), 'The military', in Skilling and Griffiths (1971), pp. 131–70.

Kugler, Jacek and A. F. K. Organski (1980), 'Deterrence and the arms race', *International Security*, Vol. 4, no. 4 (Spring), pp. 105–38.

LaFeber, Walter (1976), *America, Russia and the Cold War* (New York: Wiley).

Lambeth, Benjamin (1974), 'Sources of Soviet military doctrine', in Frank Horton *et al.* (eds) (1974), *Comparative Defense Policy* (Baltimore, Md: Johns Hopkins University Press), pp. 216–32.

Lambeth, Benjamin (1979), 'The political potential of Soviet equivalence', *International Security* Vol. 4, no. 2 (Fall), pp. 22–39.

Lambeth, Benjamin (1980), 'Soviet strategic conduct and the prospects for stability', Adelphi Paper No. 161, International Institute for Strategic Studies, London.

Lapp, Ralph (1968), *The Weapons Culture* (Baltimore, Md: Penguin Books).

Lauren, Paul (ed.) (1979), *Diplomatic History: New Approaches* (New York: The Free Press).

Lee, Asher (ed.) (1959), *The Soviet Air and Rocket Forces* (New York: Praeger).

Lee, William T. (1969), 'The rationale underlying Soviet strategic forces', in William Kintner (ed.) (1969), *Safeguard: Why the ABM Makes Sense* (New York: Hawthorn), pp. 142–79.

Lee, William T. (1972), 'The politico-military-industrial complex', *Journal of International Affairs*, Vol. 26, no. 2, pp. 73–86.

Lee, William T. (1977), *Estimation of Soviet Defense Expenditures* (New York: Praeger).

Lee, William T. (1981), 'Soviet nuclear targeting strategy and SALT', in Rosefield (1981), pp. 55–88.

Leebaert, Derek (ed.) (forthcoming), *Soviet Military Thinking* (London: Allen & Unwin).

Legvold, Robert (1977), 'The nature of Soviet power', *Foreign Affairs*, Vol. 56, no. 1 (October), pp. 49–71.

Liddell-Hart, B. (1956), *The Red Army* (New York: Praeger).

Lomov, N. A. (1973), *The Revolution in Military Affairs* (Washington, DC: US GPO).

Luttwak, Edward (1979), 'Cubans in Arabia? Or, the meaning of strategy', *Commentary*, Vol. 66 no. 12 (December) pp. 62–6.

MccGwire, Michael (1970) 'Soviet naval procurement', in Royal United Services Institute (1970), pp. 74–87.

MccGwire, Michael (ed.) (1973), *Soviet Naval Developments: Capability and Context* (New York: Praeger).

MccGwire, Michael (1977), 'Comparative naval building programs: East and West', in MccGwire and McDonnell (1977), pp. 327–36.

MccGwire, Michael (1978a), 'Naval power and Soviet global strategy', *International Security*, Vol. 3, no. 4 (Spring), pp. 134–98.

MccGwire, Michael (1978b), 'Soviet naval programs', in Murphy (1978), pp. 77–108.

MccGwire, Michael, Kenneth Booth and John McDonnell (eds) (1975), *Soviet Naval Policy: Objectives and Constraints* (New York: Praeger).

MccGwire, Michael and John McDonnell (1977), *Soviet Naval Influence* (New York: Praeger).

McDonald, Gordon, Jack Ruina and Mark Balaschak (1980), 'Defense against cruise missiles: an analysis of Soviet air defenses', unpublished paper (Cambridge, Mass.: MIT).

McGruther, Kenneth (1978), *The Evolving Soviet Navy* (Newport, RI: Naval War College Press).

MacKintosh, Malcolm (1967), *Juggernaut: A History of the Soviet Armed Forces* (New York: Macmillan).

Meyer, Stephen (forthcoming), 'Innovation in Soviet weapons design: a time series analysis' (Cambridge, Mass.: MIT).

Meyer, Stephen (forthcoming), 'Patterns in Soviet weapons procurement: an analysis by mission' (Cambridge, Mass.: MIT).

Mičunović, Veljko (1980), *Moscow Diary* (Garden City, NY: Doubleday).

Moore, K. J., Mark Flanigan and Robert Helsel (1977), 'Developments in submarine systems, 1956–1976', in MccGwire and McDonnell (1977), pp. 151–84.

Moore, John (1975), *The Soviet Navy Today* (New York: Stein & Day).

Murphy, Paul (ed.) (1978a), *Naval Power in Soviet Policy* (Washington, DC: US GPO).

Murphy, Paul (1978b), 'Trends in Soviet naval force structure', in Murphy (1978), pp. 109–34.

Nitze, Paul (1976), 'Deterring our deterrent', *Foreign Policy*, no. 25 (Winter), pp. 195–210.

Odom, William (1975), 'Who controls whom in Moscow', *Foreign Policy*, no. 19 (Summer), pp. 109–23.

Odom, William (1976), 'A dissenting view on the group approach to Soviet politics', *World Politics*, Vol. 28, no. 4 (July), pp. 542–67.

Payne, Samuel B. (1980), *The Soviet Union and SALT* (Cambridge, Mass.: MIT).

Petersen, Phillip (1979), *Soviet Air Power and the Pursuit of New Military Options* (Washington, DC: US GPO).

Pipes, Richard (1977), 'Why the Soviet Union thinks it could fight and win a nuclear war', *Commentary*, Vol. 64 (July), pp. 21–34.

Pipes, Richard (1980a), 'Soviet global strategy', *Commentary*, Vol. 67, no. 4 (April), pp. 31–9.

Pipes, Richard (1980b), 'Militarism and the Soviet state', *Daedalus*, Vol. 109, no. 4 (Fall), pp. 1–12.

Raanan, Uri (1969), *The USSR Arms the Third World* (Cambridge, Mass.: MIT).

Raanan, Uri (1980), 'The USSR and the encirclement fear: Soviet logic or Western legend', *Strategic Review*, Vol. 8, no. 3 (Summer), pp. 44–50.

Record, Jeffry (1975), *Sizing up the Soviet Army* (Washington, DC: Brookings Institution).

Riabchikov, Eugeny (1971), *Russians in Space* (New York: Doubleday).

Rosefield, Steven (1981), *World Communism at the Crossroads* (Boston, Mass.: Martinus Nijhoff).

Rosen, Steven (1973), *Testing the Theory of the Military Industrial Complex* (Lexington, Mass.: Lexington).

Ross, Dennis (1977), 'Rethinking Soviet strategic policy: inputs and implications', ACIS Working Paper No. 5, Center for Arms Control and International Security, Los Angeles, California, USA.

Ross, Dennis (1980), 'Coalition maintenance in the Soviet Union', *World Politics*, Vol. 32, no. 2 (January), pp. 258–80.

Royal United Service Institution (1970), *The Soviet Union in Europe and the Near East: Her Capabilities and Intentions* (London).

Savkin, V. Ye. (1972), *Operational Art and Tactics* (Washington, DC: US GPO).

Schick, Jack (1971), *The Berlin Crisis, 1958–1962* (Philadelphia, Pa: University of Pennsylvania Press).

Scott, Harriet F. and William F. Scott (1979), *The Armed Forces of the USSR* (Boulder, Colo.: Westview Press).

Scott, William (1975), *Soviet Sources of Military Doctrine and Strategy* (New York: Crane, Russak).

Shelton, William (1968), *Soviet Space Exploration* (New York: Washington Square Press).

Shulman, Marshall (1974), 'SALT and the Soviet Union', in Willrich and Rhinelander (1974), pp. 101–24.

Simes, Dimitri (1978), 'The Soviet succession: domestic and international dimensions', *Journal of International Affairs*, Vol. 32, no. 2 (Fall–Winter), pp. 211–22.

Simes, Dimitri (1981), 'Deterrence and coercion in Soviet policy', *International Security*, Vol. 5, no. 3 (Winter), pp. 80–103.

Simpson, J. (1970), 'The military aircraft procurement process in the USSR, 1950–1970', in Royal United Service Institution (1970), pp. 88–94.

Skilling, Gordon and Franklyn Griffiths (1971), *Interest Groups in Soviet Politics* (Princeton, NJ: Princeton University Press).

Sonnenfeldt, Helmut and William Hyland (1979), 'Soviet perspectives on security', Adelphi Paper No. 150, International Institute of Strategic Studies, London.

Spielmann, Karl F. (1976), 'Defense industrialist in the USSR', *Problems of Communism*, Vol. 25, no. 5 (September–October), pp. 52–69.

Spielmann, Karl F. (1978), *Analyzing Soviet Strategic Weapons Decisions* (Boulder, Colo.: Westview Press).

Steinbruner, John (1974), *A Cybernetic Theory of Decision* (Princeton, NJ: Princeton University Press).

Stewart, Philip (1980), 'Elite perceptions and the study of Soviet decisionmaking', paper presented at the Conference on Soviet Decisionmaking for National Security, Naval Post-Graduate School, Monterey, California, USA.

Stoiko, M. (1972), *Soviet Rocketry* (New York: Holt, Rinehart & Winston).

Sullivan, David (1980), 'Evaluating US intelligence estimates', in Godson (1980), pp. 49–74.

Tatu, Michael (1969), *Power in the Kremlin* (New York: Viking Press).

Triska, Jan and David Finley (1965), 'Soviet-American relations: a multiple symmetry model', *Journal of Conflict Resolution*, Vol. 9, no. 1 (March), pp. 37–53.

Triska, Jan and David Finley (1968), *Soviet Foreign Policy* (New York: Macmillan).

Ulam, Adam (1974), *Expansion and Coexistence* (New York: Praeger).

Ulam, Adam (1980), 'How to restrain the Soviets', *Commentary*, Vol. 67, no. 12 (December), pp. 38–41.

US Arms Control and Disarmament Agency (1978), *An Analysis of Civil Defense in Nuclear War* (Washington, DC: US GPO).

US Central Intelligence Agency (1978a), *Arms Flows to LDCs: US-Soviet Comparisons, 1974–1977*, ER78-1049U (Washington, DC).

US Central Intelligence Agency (1978b), *Estimated Soviet Defense Spending* (Washington, DC.).

US Central Intelligence Agency (1978c), *Soviet Civil Defense* (Washington, DC).

US Central Intelligence Agency (1980), *Soviet and US Defense Activities, 1970–1979*, SR80-10005 (Washington, DC).

Valenta, Jiri (1979a), *Soviet Intervention in Czechoslovakia, 1968: Anatomy of a Decision* (Baltimore, Md: Johns Hopkins University Press).

Valenta, Jiri (1979b), 'The bureaucratic politics paradigm and the Soviet invasion of Czechoslovakia', *Political Science Quarterly*, Vol. 94, no. 1 (Spring 1979), pp. 55–76.

Valenta, Jiri (1980), 'From Prague to Kabul, the Soviet style of invasion', *International Security*, Vol. 5, no. 2 (Fall, 1980), pp. 114–46.

Vigor, P. H. (1980), 'Doubts and difficulties confronting the would-be attacker', *RUSI*, Vol. 125, no. 6 (June), pp. 32–8.

Vincent, R. J. (1975), 'Military power and political influence: the Soviet Union and

Western Europe', Adelphi Paper No. 117, International Institute of Strategic Studies, London.

Vladimirov, L. (1971), *Russian Space Bluff* (New York: Dial Press).

Warner, Edward (1974), 'Soviet strategic force posture', in Horton *et al*. (1974), pp. 310–25.

Warner, Edward (1977), *The Military in Contemporary Soviet Politics: An Institutional Analysis* (New York: Praeger).

Watson, Thomas (1981), 'View from Moscow', *US News and World Report*, Vol. 92, no. 3 (January), pp. 35–6.

Welch, William and Jan Triska (1971), 'Soviet foreign policy studies and foreign policy models', *World Politics*, Vol. 23, no. 4 (July), pp. 704–34.

Williams, Phil (1976), *Crisis Management* (New York: Wiley).

Willrich, Mason and John Rhinelander (eds) (1974), *SALT: The Moscow Agreements and Beyond* (New York: The Free Press).

Wolfe, Thomas (1965), *Soviet Strategy at the Cross-Roads* (Cambridge, Mass.: Harvard University Press).

Wolfe, Thomas (1970), *Soviet Power and Europe* (Baltimore, Md: Johns Hopkins University Press).

Wolfe, Thomas (1980), *The SALT Experience* (Cambridge, Mass.: Ballinger).

Yakovlev, A. (1968), *Target of Life* (Washington, DC: NTIS).

York, Herbert (1970), *Race to Oblivion* (New York: Simon & Schuster).

Zimmerman, William (1980), 'Rethinking Soviet foreign policy: changing American perspectives', *International Journal*, Vol. 35, no. 3 (Summer), pp. 548–68.

12 The Study of Soviet Decisionmaking for National Security: What Is To Be Done?

WILLIAM C. POTTER

A major survey of research on Soviet foreign policy decisionmaking, published in 1973, concluded that despite the large volume of literature on Soviet foreign policy, the making of policy was a virtually unexplored topic.[1] A more general review of the study of Soviet policymaking, completed in 1980, reached much the same conclusion and attributed the dearth of scholarship on Soviet policymaking to three factors: (1) the complexity of the subject of decisionmaking itself; (2) the inaccessibility of the Soviet political process in particular; and (3) the lack of adequate tools to conceptualize and analyze the information that is available.[2] The chapters in this volume represent significant progress in overcoming these methodological difficulties and contribute to a better understanding of the process and product of Soviet decisionmaking in one major policy arena – national security. The purpose of this chapter is to identify a number of important questions in the national security policymaking arena which remain inadequately addressed and to suggest what can be done to obtain satisfactory answers.

The preceding chapters by Arthur Alexander and Stephen Meyer are particularly rich in the questions they raise for future research. The research agendas they propose also are informed by sophisticated conceptual views of the Soviet decisionmaking environment. Insufficient differentiation of the policy process, however, results in their neglect of important questions pertaining to policy initiation and implementation. It also may account for the omission on their research agendas of questions about the relationship of issue area and policy process and the manner in which political elite and expert perceptions of the international milieu shape policy inputs and outcomes.

POLICYMAKING AS A SEQUENTIAL PROCESS

Contributors to this volume have been at the forefront of scholarly efforts, both in academia and government, to focus attention on the bureaucratic political/organizational processes dimension of Soviet policymaking. Neither they nor other analysts, however, have yet fashioned an extended case study of a particular Soviet foreign policy or defense decision in which the decision process is explicitly analyzed in terms of a sequence of stages from policy initiation to policy implementation.[3] This neglect may be due in part to the previously cited difficulty of data accessibility. It also may be the consequence of the analyst's preoccupation with the policy controversy stage of the decisionmaking process in which the articulation and aggregation of diverse interests occurs. The tendency of analysts to become wedded to a single analytic model appropriate for explaining only a limited range of decisionmaking behavior may further discourage a longer, more historical/ diachronic view of the policy process.[4]

One potentially useful method of conceptualizing Soviet national security decisionmaking is to view it as a sequential process involving four analytically distinct phases: policy initiation, policy controversy, the formal decision and policy implementation.[5] This is essentially the same conceptualization of the policymaking process recommended by Brzezinski and Huntington nearly two decades ago, but infrequently applied subsequently in the Soviet context.[6]

Policy Initiation

The policy initiation or agenda-setting phase of the decisionmaking process is rarely the focus of studies of Soviet foreign and defense policy. It is at this stage when 'problems come to be defined as political issues and make their way onto the political agenda'.[7]

Although temporally prior to the frequently studied stage of policy controversy, policy initiation is by no means an apolitical phase in the decisionmaking process and represents the period during which the 'other face of power' is exercised, that is, the power to determine which issues will be considered and which alternatives will be accepted as legitimate policy options.[8]

To the extent that one assumes that Soviet national security policy is susceptible to change and is interested in how, when and why major changes in policy take place, it is essential to study the process of policy initiation. A central question regarding policy initiation, but one rarely asked in the Soviet context, is 'who controls the agenda?' That is, who exercises the power to select issues and options for consideration and whose perceptions must change before there is a possibility for policy innovation.[9] Although there is a temptation to assume that one knows *a priori* the answer to this question, especially in the realm of foreign and defense policy, one should not discount altogether the specialist's role in agenda setting under circumstances in which the political leadership is severely fragmented or is receptive to new ideas because of the obvious failure of existing policies.[10] Even if one is correct in assuming a minimal role for the specialist, one would like to know the conditions under which that role is maximized. One would also wish to learn who among the political actors (both in terms of individuals and organizations) provides the original impetus for specific policy changes and the extent to which the role of policy initiator varies across issues and over time. For example, on what kinds of defense-related issues did the impetus for policy change come from the political leadership, other levels of the party apparatus, the military, the scientific community and other professional specialists? An excellent first effort to address this question with respect to Soviet weapons development is made by Jerry Hough in this volume and illustrates that the topic can be researched profitably. The need persists, however, to study the topic across a much broader range of foreign and defense policy issues. One might, for example, seek to test Thane Gustafson's hypothesis, developed in a nonsecurity area, that Soviet specialists do sometimes take part in agenda setting, but wait for a 'window to open' before vigorously promoting proposals for policy innovation.[11] Such an opening, it could be argued, occurred in the early 1970s for the 'scholar-publicists of détente'.[12] Although an accurate assessment of the impact of that opening on the agenda setting role played by these specialists (that is, Americanists such as Georgi Arbatov) may be impossible to make, it should prove feasible to at least map any changes in the scope and intensity of their policy advocacy in public pronouncements.[13] One might expect to find, for example, a change in the kind of arguments used – or not used – in urging official consideration of particular issues, as well as greater reference in public sources to the relevance of Western experience in dealing with certain problems and in adopting certain policy innovations.[14]

Arthur Alexander's useful discussion in this volume notwithstanding, the question 'what accounts for change in the policy agenda over time?' is almost as neglected in the study of Soviet policymaking as the question 'who controls the agenda?' This neglect may be due, in part, to the widespread assumption that the central features of Soviet national security policy are shaped by relatively constant domestic factors (that is, the nature of the political system and ideology) and that Soviet national security behavior is largely unresponsive to the actions of others.[15] It also reflects a general lack of awareness of the extensive organization theory literature on policy innovation and its possible relevance for the study of Soviet policy initiation.[16] Drawing upon this literature one may ask, for example, to what extent do Soviet foreign policy decisionmakers learn from their past mistakes and those of others?[17] What is the effect of crisis in bringing new approaches to old problems to the fore? What is the impact of change in elite attributes such as education, wartime experience, international background and organizational affiliations on receptivity to policy innovation?[18] What are the characteristics of the change agent (that is, the principal proponent of policy change) and how does he package and present the innovation?[19] What role is played by professionals outside of the political leadership in interpreting changes in reality which may have occurred? As Peter Solomon notes, it can be argued that even if the political leadership dominates agenda setting and can consider or ignore issues at will, they are still part of a broader process of social learning and one still wants to know how the leaders come to change their thinking.[20]

Policy Controversy

The second stage of the policymaking process, that of policy controversy, has received the most attention by students of Soviet foreign and defense policy, although the absolute number of studies remains small. It is at this stage when the process of bargaining and consensus building occurs. The merits and deficiencies of alternative proposals are debated (although the basic premises of the policy may or may not be questioned), different interests are articulated, and support is mobilized for a particular proposal or proposals.

Excellent studies of the policy controversy phase exist for such cases as the Soviet intervention in Czechoslovakia,[21] the Soviet atomic bomb program,[22] Soviet policy toward the 1963 Test Ban Treaty[23] and Soviet policy during the Cuban missile crisis.[24] These studies are particularly successful in identifying the major individual and institutional actors engaged in the policy controversy, the resources at their disposal and, to a lesser degree, the strategies they employed to gain support for their policy preferences. With several notable exceptions, however, case studies in the national security field continue to display the same disregard for explicit decisionmaking theoretical frameworks noted a decade ago by Horelick *et al.*[25] As Arthur Alexander and Stephen Meyer point out in this volume, most studies also lack a comparative perspective both with respect to time and place. In other words, they tend to ignore the questions: (1) have the principal actors and points of controversy shifted markedly over time?; and (2) how unique to the Soviet context are the observed patterns of inputs and processes?

The first question, admittedly, is a very difficult one to answer for many foreign and defense-related issues. Valenta's efforts to address the question with respect to Soviet intervention policy and Meyer's work on Soviet weapons procurements,[26] however, illustrate that the comparative approach is feasible and rewarding theoretically. Examples of other issues which would appear to lend themselves to similar comparative treatment are Soviet policymaking in the recurrent Berlin conflicts,[27] Soviet decisionmaking during the periodic crises in the Middle East, and Soviet policymaking for a series of treaties to retard proliferation (for example, the 1963 Partial Test Ban Treaty, the 1967 Treaty of Tlateloco, the 1968 Non-Proliferation Treaty, the 1974 Threshold Test Ban Treaty and the 1976 Treaty on Underground Explosions for Peaceful Purposes).

More attention also could profitably be devoted to the testing of the hypothesis – frequently examined in studies of Western foreign and defense policymaking – that organizational role is a good predictor of policy advocacy. Although this hypothesis may be borne out in the Soviet context, there is a tendency for studies which examine Soviet decisionmaking from an organizational perspective to take the assumption as a given and to derive plausible scenarios of interorganizational conflicts from that insight rather than first trying to demonstrate that the actors in question have regularly articulated views consistent with their apparent organizational interests.[28] An alternative model which emphasizes the importance of personality over role and individual over organizational interests and which allows for considerable variation of views within an organization may, in fact, better capture the nature of the decisionmaking process for certain issues at the policy controversy stage. It would be interesting, for example, to examine in the Soviet context the hypothesis, articulated by students of Western policymaking, that the principle 'where you sit determines where you stand' is less applicable in crisis situations when one might assume that parochial organizational interests would be subordinant to more overarching national concerns.[29] Testing of this hypothesis obviously requires the comparison of decisionmaking for different issues under crisis and noncrisis conditions and, preferably, for a broad range of policy issues.

Formal Decision

The policymaking phase during which an authoritative body or individual makes a commitment to undertake a course of policy action (broadly defined to include the policy option of 'doing nothing') may be thought of as the stage of formal decision. It is at this stage that the decision acquires legitimacy.

Brzezinski and Huntington suggest that 'the mechanisms of decision reflect the sources of legitimacy'.[30] In the Soviet Union, they maintain, the party leadership's monopoly of authority to confer legitimacy (that is, to decide whether policy is in accord with ideology) results in a formal decisional phase – 'the authoritative legitimization of a proposal' – which is brief and unitary. This is in contrast, they contend, to the drawn-out and segmented formal decisional phase in the United States which results from the diffusion of policy legitimacy among a number of governmental institutions reflecting a multitude of publics and interests.[31] Although not implausible, the Brzezinski and Huntington hypothesis takes no account of possible variations in the decision process across issue areas and remains largely untested for issues in the foreign policy and defense sectors.[32] A comparative study of Soviet and US decisionmaking for nuclear nonproliferation, conventional arms transfers and Berlin, for example, might lend support to William Zimmerman's alternative hypothesis – also untested with respect to the Soviet Union – that differences in policy process across issue areas within a state are as great as differences within an issue area between states.[33] The chapters in this volume by Dennis Ross and Dimitri Simes also suggest that in so far as the secretary-general's position rests upon his ability at coalition maintenance, policy legitimacy is not something that is bestowed casually or automatically by the *Vozhd'* (the leader), but is achieved by a process of consensus building among the other top power holders.[34] If this image of coalition maintenance is correct, the formal decisional phase in the Soviet Union for certain issues may be less brief and more segmented than Brzezinski and Huntington imply. If that is the case, we should also like to know: Who participates in making different kinds of 'formal decisions'? What are the rules governing participation by different actors? What 'decision rule' is followed in arriving at decisions (that is, unanimity, majority rule, decision by the secretary-general after consultation)? What rules, if any, exist to allow discontented members of the decisionmaking body to raise for reconsideration or evaluation policies they regard as ineffective or unfair?[35]

Implementation

The fourth stage of the policymaking process, like the first, has received little attention among Soviet specialists. This is the stage of policy implementation at which time those with the responsibility for executing policy may either further, or frustrate, the objectives of those who make the formal decision.

A considerable body of literature on policymaking, in the West, including studies of national security decisions, indicates that policy implementation often involves the modification and distortion of the policy objectives intended by the formal decisionmakers.[36] As such, policy implementation frequently may represent the continuation of policy controversy by other, less visible, means. Those who execute policy, moreover, may become in a very real sense policymakers.

The ability of the executors to become policymakers and to interpret selectively the formal decision is apt to depend on a number of factors including: the division of responsibilities among actors charged with formal decisional and implementation tasks; the workload, resources and efficiency of the organization; the existence of mechanisms for policy evaluation and review; the specificity of the formal decision and rules for its implementation; the degree of conflict among the objectives embodied in the policy at the formal decision stage; the extent to which the policy represents a modification of existing policy, the linkage of the policy in question to other policies and policy realms (that is, does it straddle issue areas?); the legitimacy of the body making the formal decision; and the development of conditions unanticipated by the original policy architects.

Although the phenomenon of policymaking by implementation is largely unexplored for Soviet foreign and defense issues, numerous anecdotal accounts of Soviet bureaucratic inefficiency, poor organization and over-planning suggest that the implementation stage of policymaking in the Soviet Union includes many unintended as well as intended policy outcomes. The few scholarly studies of policy implementation in the Soviet Union, however, also indicate that the groundrules for policy execution may differ considerably from those in effect in other states.[37] Formal and informal rules which restrict the specialist from fighting back after formal decisions have been taken and the monopoly of information by certain organizations (particularly acute in the areas of foreign and defense policy) may, for example, give rise to very different kinds of strategies for modifying or sabotaging policy at the implementation stage in the Soviet Union in contrast to other countries. What, we would like to know, are these different strategies, and what is the capacity of specific individual and organizational actors to sidetrack or defeat policy once a formal decision has been made? More generally, as Valerie Bruce and John Echols have recently argued, we need to analyze rigorously and in comparative fashion the gap between policy pronouncements and their implementation in the Soviet Union and other political systems and the responsiveness of bureaucracies in different systems to the political leadership.[38]

Graham Allison's bureaucratic politics and organizational processes models may be particularly relevant to the implementation phase of the policymaking process.[39] This is because these models emphasize nonrational determinants of policy outcomes and recognize that considerable slippage in terms of policy design may take place between the time of formal decision and the actual execution of policy. Models of Soviet decisionmaking, in other words, may vary not only in their applicability to different policy issues (for example, high politics, low politics), but also in their applicability to different stages of the policymaking process for the same issue.

THE QUESTION OF FEASIBILITY

It is, of course, much easier to call attention to questions that should be asked than to outline research strategies capable of producing satisfactory answers. It may be argued, for example, that regardless of the desirability of disaggregating the policymaking process, it may be impossible to provide much operational content to several of the decisional phases in the Soviet setting, at least for issues of foreign and defense policy. More generally, the argument also may be raised that in addition to insurmountable obstacles to data acquisition, many of the insights into organizational behavior drawn from studies of policymaking in the West are not applicable in the Soviet context.[40]

These notes of caution should not be hastily dismissed. The lack of consensus among Western analysts (including representatives of different US intelligence agencies) on such basic issues as the composition of the Soviet Defense Council, its place in the organizational hierarchy of Soviet national security decisionmaking and the existence of an independent staff for the Council serves to highlight this point. Nevertheless, Stephen Meyer is also correct in his assertion that a surprising amount of data does exist on the organization and operation of the Soviet military establishment, although much of that information exists in unassembled and underanalyzed bits and pieces scattered throughout the memoir literature, biographies, and as Jerry Hough demonstrates, even the obituaries in *Krasnaia zvezda*. To this list of underutilized sources one might add the increasing number of lower-level participant observers in the policymaking process who have left the Soviet Union as part of the recent third wave of emigration.[41]

A strong case also may be made that lack of progress in understanding Soviet decisionmaking for national security results as much from the failure to employ explicit decisionmaking models and to test hypotheses against the available evidence as from the absence of data or the abuse of Western decisionmaking models and concepts. Meyer's suggestions regarding the use of focused comparison, multiple streams of evidence, a combination of analytic techniques and the comparison of outputs predicted by individual models with observed behavior represent additional methods for maximizing the amount of useful information that can be gleaned from available data sources.

This is not to suggest that application of Meyer's recommended strategy of research to the questions raised in this chapter will yield remarkable breakthroughs in our understanding of Soviet decisionmaking for national security. No approach or formal method of analysis is a substitute for careful and time-consuming observation and the intelligent sorting of facts. The employment in tandem of multiple approaches, moreover, does not guarantee the accumulation of knowledge. The prudent combination of alternative methods of analysis, such as those represented in this volume, however, may enable us to exploit the strengths and avoid the more serious costs of the respective approaches. In the process, it should help us narrow the gap between informed speculation about Soviet decisionmaking for national security and reality.

NOTES: CHAPTER 12

1 Arnold Horelick, A. Ross Johnson and John D. Steinbruner, *The Study of Soviet Foreign Policy: A Review of Decision-Theory-Related Approaches*, Rand Corporation, R-1334, Santa Monica, California, USA (December 1973).

2 Gail Lapidus, 'The study of contemporary Soviet policy-making: a review and research agenda', paper prepared for the Workshop on Contemporary Soviet Policy-Making, Berkeley, California, USA (August 1980), pp. 1–3.

3 This deficiency is not peculiar to the national security area. The only published study organized in this manner with which I am familiar is James B. Bruce, *The Politics of Soviet Policy Formation: Khrushchev's Innovative Politics in Education and Agriculture*, University of Denver Monograph Series in World Affairs, Denver, Colorado, USA, Vol. 13, no. 4 (1976).

4 Alexander, of course, is correct in noting that the inherent limitations of Soviet models of defense decisionmaking have not prevented their frequent misapplication.

5 For a discussion of the utility of this framework for analysis, see Lapidus, op. cit., pp. 21–3.

6 See Zbigniew Brzezinski and Samuel Huntington, *Political Power: USA/USSR* (New York: Viking Press, 1963), pp. 202–23.

7 Lapidus, op cit., p. 21.

8 See Peter Bachrach and Morton Baratz, 'Two faces of power', *American Political Science Review*, Vol. 61, no. 4 (December 1962), pp. 947–52.

9 For a discussion of this point, see Peter H. Solomon, Jr, 'The study of Soviet policy-making: research agenda', paper prepared for the Workshop on Contemporary Soviet Policy-Making, Berkeley, California, USA, June 1980, p. 2. Among the few studies which address this issue for Soviet politics but not with respect to national security policy are Daniel Tarschys, *The Soviet Political Agenda: Problems and Priorities, 1950–1970* (New York: Macmillan, 1979); Thane Gustafson, *Reform and Power in Soviet Politics: Lessons of Brezhnev's Agriculture and Environmental Policies* (Cambridge: Cambridge University Press, 1981); and Peter H. Solomon, Jr, *Soviet Criminologists and Criminal Policy: Specialists in Policy-Making* (New York: Columbia University Press, 1977).

10 On the impact of specialists in the national security sector, see Franklyn Griffiths, 'Images, politics, and learning in Soviet behavior toward the United States', Ph.D. dissertation, Columbia University, New York, USA, 1972; Morton Schwartz, *Soviet Perceptions of the United States* (Berkeley, Calif.: University of California Press, 1978); William F. and Harriet Fast Scott, 'The social sciences institutes of the Soviet Academy of Sciences', *Air Force Magazine*, Vol. 63, no. 3 (March 1980), pp. 60–5; and Oded Eran, 'A comparative analysis of foreign and defense policy-oriented research establishments and their political function in the USA and USSR with lessons for Israel', Center for Strategic Studies Memorandum No. 1, Tel Aviv University, Israel, May 1979. The previously cited books by Solomon and Gustafson provide excellent interpretations of the role of specialists in other sectors.

11 Gustafson, op. cit., p. 88.

12 The phrase is Morton Schwartz's; see Schwartz, *Soviet Perceptions*, op. cit., p. 160.

13 A preliminary effort to do this with respect to arms control policy is reported in my study, *Soviet Perspectives on US Arms Control Policy*, report prepared for the US International Communication Agency, Washington, DC, June 1980; see also William D. Jackson, 'Soviet Images of the US as nuclear adversary, 1969–1979', *World Politics*, Vol. 33, no. 4 (July 1981), pp. 614–38.

14 A similar point is raised by Lapidus, op. cit., p. 22.

15 Alexander takes a very different perspective and emphasizes the importance of learned behavior based on experience (see Chapter 1 of this volume). For a discussion of different Western images of the determinants of Soviet foreign policy behavior, see William

Zimmerman, 'Soviet foreign policy in the 1970s', *Survey*, Vol. 67, no. 4 (Spring 1973), pp. 188–98.

16   For a review of some of this relevant literature, see William C. Potter, 'Innovation in East European foreign policies', in James A. Kuhlman (ed.), *The Foreign Policies of Eastern Europe: Domestic and International Determinants* (Leiden: Sijthoff, 1978), pp. 253–302; see also Zvi Y. Gitelman, *The Diffusion of Political Innovation: From Eastern Europe to the Soviet Union* (Beverly Hills, Calif.: Sage, 1972).

17   On this point, see William Zimmerman and Robert Axelrod, 'The "lessons" of Vietnam and Soviet foreign policy', paper prepared for delivery at the International Congress of Slavicists, Garmisch, 29 September–4 October 1980.

18   An excellent summary of interdisciplinary research findings relevant to this issue is provided in Everett Rogers and Floyd Shoemaker, *Communication of Innovations* (New York: The Free Press, 1971), pp.·346–87; see also William Potter, 'Continuity and change in the foreign relations of the Warsaw Pact states, 1948–1973: a study of national adaptation to internal and external demands', Ph.D. dissertation, University of Michigan, USA (1976), pp. 64–5.

19   One of the few studies to address this question is by Gitelman.

20   Solomon, 'The study of Soviet policy-making', op. cit., p. 5.

21   Jiri Valenta, *Soviet Intervention in Czechoslovakia, 1968: Anatomy of a Decision* (Baltimore, Md: Johns Hopkins University Press, 1979).

22   David Holloway, 'Entering the nuclear arms race: the Soviet decision to build the atomic bomb, 1939–1945', Working Paper No. 9, Wilson Center for International Security Studies Program, Washington, DC, USA (1979).

23   Christer Jonsson, *Soviet Bargaining Behavior: The Nuclear Test Ban Case* (New York: Columbia University Press, 1979).

24   Herbert S. Dinerstein, *The Making of a Missile Crisis* (Baltimore, Md: Johns Hopkins University Press, 1976); see also Graham T. Allison, *Essence of Decision: Explaining the Cuban Missile Crisis* (Boston, Mass.: Little, Brown, 1971).

25   Horelick, *et al.*, op. cit., p. 42. Valenta's study is an exception, as is the work of Karl Spielmann and Dennis Ross; see Karl F. Spielmann, *Analyzing Soviet Strategic Arms Decisions* (Boulder, Colo: Westview Press, 1978); and Dennis Ross, 'Rethinking Soviet strategic policy: inputs and implications', *ACIS Working Paper*, No. 5, UCLA Center for International and Strategic Affairs (June 1977).

26   See Stephen Meyer, *Patterns in Soviet Weapons Procurement: An Analysis by Mission* (Cambridge, Mass.: MIT, 1981); mimeo.

27   For an effort to test several hypotheses about Soviet behavior in the 1948–9 and 1961 Berlin crisis, see Raymond Tanter and William Potter, 'Modeling alliance behavior: East–West conflict over Berlin', *Papers of the Peace Science Society (International)*, Vol. 20 (1973), pp. 25–41.

28   One promising effort to examine the organization role-policy advocacy hypothesis for Politburo members is Philip Stewart's ambitious elite perceptions project. For a preliminary report of his research, see 'Elite perceptions and the study of Soviet decisionmaking', paper prepared for the Conference on Soviet Decisionmaking for National Security, Naval Postgraduate School, Monterey, California, USA (August 1980).

29   See, for example, Sidney Verba, 'Assumptions of rationality and non-rationality in models of the international system', in James N. Rosenau (ed.), *International Politics and Foreign Policy* (New York: The Free Press, 1969), pp. 217–31; and Arnold Wolfers, 'The actors in international politics', in Wolfers, *Discord and Collaboration* (Baltimore, Md: Johns Hopkins University Press, 1962), pp. 3–35.

30   Brzezinski and Huntington, op. cit., p. 216.

31   ibid., p. 217.

32   An exception is Arthur Alexander's comparison of 'Weapons acquisition in the Soviet Union, the United States, and France', in Frank Horton, Anthony Rogerson and Edward Warner (eds), *Comparative Defense Policy* (Baltimore, Md: Johns Hopkins University Press, 1974), pp. 426–43.

33   William Zimmerman, 'Issue area and foreign policy process: a research note in search of a general theory', *American Political Science Review*, Vol. 67, no. 4 (December 1973), pp. 1204–12; see also William Potter, 'Issue area and foreign policy analysis', *International Organization*, Vol. 34, no. 3 (Summer 1980), pp. 405–28.

34   For a useful discussion of the concept of policy legitimacy, see Alexander George,

'Domestic constraints on regime change in US foreign policy: the need for policy legitimacy', in O. Holsti, R. Siverson and A. George (eds), *Change in the International System* (Boulder, Colo: Westview Press, 1980).

35 This list of questions pertaining to the procedural dimension of policy legitimacy is derived from a longer set of questions raised by Alexander George in his comments at the Conference on Soviet Decisionmaking for National Security, Naval Postgraduate School, Monterey, California, USA (16 August 1980).

36 See, for example, Graham T. Allison, *Essence of Decision: Explaining the Cuban Missile Crisis* (Boston, Mass.: Little, Brown, 1971); and Morton H. Halperin, *Bureaucratic Politics and Foreign Policy* (Washington, DC: Brookings Institution, 1974).

37 See especially Thane Gustafson's excellent study.

38 Valerie Bruce and John Echols, 'From Soviet studies to comparative politics: the unfinished revolution', *Soviet Studies*, Vol. 31, no. 1 (January 1979), p. 48.

39 See Allison, op. cit., pp. 67–100, 144–84.

40 On this point see, for example, Mathew Gallagher and Karl Spielmann, *Soviet Decision-Making for Defense* (New York: Praeger, 1972); and William Odom, 'A dissenting view on the group approach to Soviet politics', *World Politics*, Vol. 28, no. 4 (July 1976), pp. 542–67.

41 This source, to date, has not been systematically exploited for information on foreign and defense policy decisionmaking. A major émigré interview project under the supervision of James Millav, William Zimmerman and Brian Silver, however, has recently been organized to explore this among other topics.

Publications

PUBLICATIONS OF THE PROGRAM OF SOVIET AND EAST EUROPEAN STUDIES, DEPARTMENT OF NATIONAL SECURITY AFFAIRS

Aspaturian, Vernon, Jiri Valenta and David Burke (eds), *Eurocommunism between East and West* (Bloomington, Ill.: Indiana University Press, hardcover and paperback, 1981).

Valenta, Jiri, *Soviet Intervention in Czechoslovakia, 1968: Anatomy of a Decision* (Baltimore, Md: Johns Hopkins University Press, 1979; paperback, 1981).

Valenta, Jiri, and William C. Potter (eds), *Soviet Decisionmaking for National Security* (London: Allen & Unwin, hardcover and paperback, 1983).

PUBLICATIONS OF THE CENTER FOR INTERNATIONAL AND STRATEGIC AFFAIRS, UCLA

Brito, Dagobert L., Michael D. Intriligator and Adele E. Wick (eds.), *Strategies for Managing Nuclear Proliferation: Economic and Political Issues* (Lexington: Lexington Books, 1983).

Jabber, Paul, *Not by War Alone: The Politics of Arms Control in the Middle East* (Berkeley, Calif.: University of California Press, 1981).

Kolkowicz, Roman , and Andrzej Korbonski (eds), *Soldiers, Peasants, and Bureaucrats: Civil-Military Relations in Communist and Modernizing Societies* (London: Allen & Unwin, 1982).

Potter, William C., *Nuclear Power and Nonproliferation: An Interdisciplinary Perspective* (Oelgeschlager, Gunn & Hain, 1982).

Potter, William C. (ed.), *Verification and SALT: The Challenge of Strategic Deception* (Boulder, Colo: Westview Press, 1980).

Ramberg, Bennett, *Destruction of Nuclear Energy Facilities in War: The Problem and Implications* (Lexington, Mass.: Lexington Books, 1980).

Spiegel, Steven L. (ed.), *The Middle East and the Western Alliance* (London: Allen & Unwin, 1982).

Thomas, Rajn G. C. (ed), *The Great Power Triangle and Asian Security* (Lexington: Lexington Books, 1983).

Tschirgi, R. D., *The Politics of Indecision: Origins and Implications of American Involvement with the Palestine Problem* (New York: Praeger, 1983).

Notes on Coeditors and Contributors

COEDITORS

JIRI VALENTA is a Woodrow Wilson Center Fellow and an Associate Professor, and the Coordinator of Soviet and East European Studies in the Department of National Security Affairs, the US Naval Postgraduate School, Monterey, California. While editing this volume he was an International Affairs Fellow at the Council on Foreign Relations and an International Relations Fellow at the Rockefeller Foundation. Dr Valenta is author of the book *Soviet Intervention in Czechoslovakia, 1968: Anatomy of a Decision*, coeditor of, and contributor to, *Eurocommunism between East and West* and coauthor of a forthcoming work, *Polish Crisis*.

WILLIAM C. POTTER is Associate Director of the Center for International and Strategic Affairs, University of California at Los Angeles. He is editor and contributor to *Verification and SALT: The Challenge of Strategic Deception* and author of *Nuclear Power and Nonproliferation: An Interdisciplinary Perspective*.

CONTRIBUTORS

ARTHUR J. ALEXANDER is a senior staff member and Associate Head of the Economics Department at the RAND Corporation. Mr Alexander is the author of *Decisionmaking in Soviet Weapons Procurement* and *Soviet Science and Weapons Acquisition*, among many other publications.

VERNON V. ASPATURIAN is an Evan Pugh Professor of Political Science and Director of the Slavic and Soviet Language and Area Center, Pennsylvania State University. He has been a Distinguished Visiting Professor at the US Naval Postgraduate School on several occasions. Dr Aspaturian is the author and coeditor of several books on Soviet foreign policy and comparative communism including, among others, *The Soviet Union in the World Communist System*, *Process and Power in Soviet Foreign Policy*, *Eurocommunism between East and West*, and *The Union Republics in Soviet Diplomacy*.

RAYMOND L. GARTHOFF is presently a Senior Fellow at the Brookings Institution. He has served as a member of the US SALT I delegation and as ambassador to Bulgaria as well as in other senior positions. Ambassador Garthoff has authored several books, including *Soviet Military Policy* and *Soviet Strategy in the Nuclear Age*.

GALIA GOLAN is a Professor in the Department of Political Science at the Hebrew University, Jerusalem. Dr Golan has written several books, among them *Yom Kippur and After: The Soviet Union and the Middle East Crisis* and *The Soviet Union and the Palestinian Liberation Organization*.

JERRY F. HOUGH is a Professor of Political Science at Duke University and a visiting Senior Fellow at the Brookings Institution. Dr Hough has written several books including *How the Soviet Union Is Governed* and *Generational Changes in the Soviet Union*.

WILLIAM G. HYLAND is a Senior Fellow at the Carnegie Endowment for International Peace. Ambassador Hyland is the author of many studies and articles on Soviet national security and foreign policy. He was director of the State Department's Bureau of Intelligence and has served in several other senior US government positions, among them Deputy Assistant for National Security to President Gerald Ford.

DR ELLEN JONES is a senior analyst with the Defense Intelligence Agency, Washington DC and the author of many studies and articles on Soviet national security and the Soviet military.

STEPHEN M. MEYER is an associate professor in the Department of Political Science and a Research Associate for the Center for International Studies of the Massachusetts Institute of Technology. Dr Meyer is the author of several studies and articles on Soviet national security.

DR DENNIS ROSS is Deputy Director of Net Assessment, US Department of Defense. He is the author of several articles on Soviet foreign policy. The views presented in his chapter are his own and do not represent the office of the Secretary or the Department of Defense.

DIMITRI K. SIMES is Executive Director of the Soviet and East European Research Program at the Johns Hopkins School for Advanced International Studies. Mr Simes was a staff member of the Institute of World Economy and International Relations (Moscow) and the Director of Soviet Studies at the Center for Strategic and International Studies of Georgetown University. He is the author of *Détente and Conflict: Soviet Foreign Policy 1972–1977* and of many articles on Soviet foreign policy.

Index